Dramatic Essays of the Neoclassic Age

Dramatic Essays of the Neoclassic Age

Edited by

HENRY HITCH ADAMS

AND

BAXTER HATHAWAY

BENJAMIN BLOM, INC.

New York

Printed in U.S.A. by
NOBLE OFFSET PRINTERS, INC.
NEW YORK 3, N. Y.

Preface

In this book we have attempted to assist a reader to arrive at an understanding of the drama of the so-called "neoclassic" period. Never in the history of the theatre has the practice of dramatic writing been so influenced by formal criticism as it was in the period included here. Practicing playwrights made sincere efforts to conform to the best critical ideas, to help to maintain drama in its preeminent position in literature. In spite of their best efforts they failed, and the eighteenth century became the age of the novel rather than the age of the drama, as the Elizabethan period had been in England and the times of Molière, Corneille, and Racine had been in France.

Since the dramatic practice of the neoclassic period was distinctly subservient to the Rules, the Rules themselves become highly important for an understanding of the plays of the time. To assemble and select the most important statements of dramatic theory and to make them easily accessible to students of the drama has been the aim of this book. We have selected from among the French and the German critics those whose influence seemed to be strongest internationally, particularly those who were known and read in England.

The beginning date for this collection needs, perhaps, a comment. The year 1660 marks the beginning of the Restoration period in England, and the serious impact of French neoclassic ideas on English writers. Therefore, since this volume is oriented largely to English literature, the starting point was clear, even though it is evident that beginning in 1660 is *in media res* in so far as the French critics are concerned. We regret this necessity, but in the space at our disposal, such an arbitrary practice is unavoidable. We have kept to a minimum the discussions of individual plays and of Shakespeare, because such essays are mostly applications of the principles stated more generally in the selections in this volume. For this reason, and because of considerations of space, we have reluctantly omitted Johnson's "Preface to Shakespeare."

Preface

We have used the most authoritative texts we have been able to find for the critics quoted. In many cases we have had to use the original editions, because they never have been reprinted. We used contemporary English translations of French critics if it seemed advisable to do so, and especially in the case of translations widely known in England. All other translations are new for this volume. In the interests of ease of reading we have modernized the spelling and punctuation. We have kept introductory material and notes to a minimum in order to have more room for the selections themselves.

We wish to thank the Oxford University Press for permission to quote from Ingram Bywater's *Aristotle and the Art of Poetry*.

We are indebted to Gordon M. Kirkwood and William F. Oechler for editorial assistance. The careful attention of Miss Matilda L. Berg has removed many errors and infelicities from this book. We wish also to express our gratitude to Catherine S. Adams and Sherry Hathaway, for assistance, encouragement, and counsel. To them this volume is gratefully dedicated.

HENRY HITCH ADAMS
BAXTER HATHAWAY

Ithaca, New York
November 1, 1949

Contents

Contents

Contents   ix

x   # Contents

Introduction

I

WITH THE RESTORATION of the monarchy and the return of Charles II to England in 1660, after his exile in France, interest in the theatre was quickly revived, and patents were issued to Sir William Davenant and Thomas Killigrew to open two playhouses. Though it is not true that the old tradition was completely broken, a new group of playwrights took over the dramatic writing, men whose interests had been conditioned partly by the French influence brought back by Charles. While French dramatic criticism had long been established and was influential in determining the practice of French dramatists, in Restoration England, for the first time in English literary history, practicing dramatists were aware of, were influenced by, and even wrote dramatic criticism. Among the Elizabethans, such men as Jonson and Chapman had been conscious of the ideas of the Ancients, but were little affected by the contemporary critics. But in the Restoration every man was his own critic, as the writers sometimes bitterly complained, and woe to the hapless playwright who offended against any of the Rules that sprang to life full-blown, like Minerva from Jove's head.

Much of the critical discussion resulted from an effort to reconcile the Rules with dramatic practice, with what would work in the theatres. The tradition of Renaissance criticism, particularly as it developed in Italy and France, was to codify, examine, and reinterpret the treatises of Aristotle and Horace to attempt to find the eternal keys to successful playwriting. All were agreed that the works of Aeschylus, Sophocles, Euripides, Plautus, Terence, and Seneca were as near perfection as mortal man could attain and that a modern author could never hope to surpass them. The best he could do was to examine the works of the Ancients, study the Rules that men like Vossius and Scaliger had formulated for him, and write according to these precepts. Such, briefly, was the position of the "Ancients." The "Moderns" opposed this view, saying that the Rules were all right for ancient times, but that a modern dramatist had other problems to face and could best imitate Shakespeare, Fletcher, and Jonson or, perhaps, follow their practice of not imitating anybody. Shakespeare and Fletcher had obviously violated the Rules, but their work was good, so the Rules must be questioned. Also, they were pleased to mock, with Saint-Évremond, that the Rules often resulted in a very dull play.

The first part of Dryden's *Essay of Dramatic Poesy* illustrates the Ancients-Moderns quarrel, and then the essay proceeds to consider another big problem of the period, the relative excellence of the French and the English. This problem is really an off-shoot of the Ancients-Moderns one, because it was considered that the French were the better classicists, and objection was often made to the comparative complexity of the incidents presented in English tragedy as contrasted with the bare, sometimes barren, simplicity of the French.

But the Moderns were not so very modern in our sense of the word. The heroic tragedy of the Restoration is for most of us cold and unmoving. Full as it is of violence and bloodshed, the eternal beat of the heroic couplet and the absence of reference to much that is significant in our own lives make it dull reading. The type of plot common in Restoration tragedy is based on an unhappy concern of dramatists for the fable, the story with a somewhat abstruse moral point. The artificial conflicts of love and honor, perhaps, owe their lack of interest to an oversimplification, for they are based on a simplicity of emotion that is incredible today, but which put into practice some of the ideas of the critics, that the fable should present us with a whole action which had a clear moral purpose. The basic concepts of the heroes in Restoration tragedy were far removed from the ideas of the nobles of that time, for they distrusted honor, and their idea of love, as was said of Charles, had little of the Seraphic part. Therefore, the heroic tragedy was something to be argued about from the point of view of art, but the art had little to do with normal life.

Restoration comedy better reflects the life of the time, but unfortunately comedy did not have the critical backing of authority. The critics had ideas on comedy, but the ideas were foreign to comedy as it was written between 1660 and 1700. As the idea of art for art's sake had not yet developed, so the idea of comedy for comedy's sake was not a part of the critical thinking of the time on this subject. Comedy, they said, had a moral purpose, which was to recommend virtue and to discountenance vice. It is obvious that Restoration comedy had another plan, to recommend good social usage and to laugh at the discomfiture of those who, however good at heart they may have been, did not know the social usages. Ignorance and innocence, far from being objects of sympathy, were objects of scorn and fair game for the unscrupulous rakes of the town. Within this atmosphere, a work such as Farquhar's *Discourse upon Comedy* makes more sense than does a blast such as Collier's *Short View*.

Collier is commonly credited with changing the taste of the age away from licentiousness and toward virtue, but there is considerable evidence that taste was already changing. In 1696 Colley Cibber's *Love's Last Shift* paved the way for sentimentalism, a view of human nature directly opposed to the Hobbeseanism of the Restoration. Collier probably did have some influence, and a long and bitter controversy raged over his book, but if the plays written after 1700 are less immoral than those written before, it cannot be justly said that Collier was solely responsible.

The years from 1660 to 1700 mark some extremely interesting critical writing, the two outstanding works of the period being Corneille's *Three Discourses* and Dryden's *Essay of Dramatic Poesy*. Corneille's discussions represent a kind of culmination of the textual exegesis of Aristotle's *Poetics*, for, in one or another of the Discourses, nearly every part of the work is examined with keen, continuous probing into the applicability of the ideas for the French theatre. Corneille would like to respect the authority of Aristotle, but finds him often difficult, vague, and opposed to theatrical suitability. It is almost with despair that he takes issue with him on occasion, admitting that he does not know how he is going to criticize Aristotle and still retain the veneration that he knows Aristotle should have; but the criticism must be made.

Dryden brings a different kind of inquiring mind to the argument. The *Essay of Dramatic Poesy* is in dialogue form, and presents fully and fairly four of the chief contemporary views on drama—the Ancients, the Moderns, the French, and the English, in that order. Dryden himself takes the last position and is thus able to counter the arguments that have been presented against him. The argumentation is brilliant, and the writing is in a style to make it delightful reading.

In this essay Dryden airs most of the important critical arguments of his time, and we could reconstruct a great deal about the period if no other piece of dramatic criticism remained.

In Saint-Évremond we find a man who was able to take an impartial view between the Ancients and the Moderns, who was, in a sense, a comparative critic. He brought not much that was new to the problems, but he sought to find what was worthy among the ideas of the authorities and among the modern practitioners. He was quite different from his compatriot Rapin and the latter's translator, Rymer, who both insisted with considerable vehemence on a strict application of the ancient methods of writing. Rymer's idea of decorum, that a character should be represented as a type, not as an individual, was important in Collier's argument and later in the eighteenth century. Rymer meant by "decorum" that the actions of a character should be true to his type, that a soldier should be bluff and hearty, not sly and insinuating like Shakespeare's Iago, that a clergyman should be grave and serious, and that it was a mistake in taste to show a clergyman as a rake or a wit. Rymer is also chiefly known for having given a name to the doctrine of poetic justice, thus furnishing critics with a term for the age-old moral purpose of drama.

With the beginning of the reign of Queen Anne, the new purpose of the theatre was pretty well established, and as theatrical customs changed, so, too, did the criticism. While eighteenth-century writers did not forget or ignore the critics of the seventeenth, they became chiefly concerned with newer ideas.

H. H. A.

II

IT GIVES THE APPEARANCE OF PARADOX to assert that the principal shift that took place between the preceding age and the eighteenth century —a century long considered the Age of Reason—was away from an absolute reliance on reason and in the direction of a considerable trust in emotionality. At least according to one possible set of definitions of terms, men of the eighteenth century were rarely as complete rationalists as were the men of the seventeenth. Their rationalism admitted to good standing instinctive or irrational thought processes that the philosopher of the seventeenth century sought to disown.

Prose in the so-called Age of Reason is, it is true, often abstract, highly Latinized, utilizing only a small amount of figurative speech, in other words, relatively uncluttered with poetic connotations and emotionality, while the prose of the seventeenth century is more distinctly poetic and involved with emotionality. To every age its paradox. The philosopher of the eighteenth century believed in emotion, probed the workings of man's mind and found that his loves and hates and pleasures and pains motivated most of his actions and could be expected to do so in an ideal, natural man. Reason, yes; but a reason the sole function of which was to guide the machine, not be it.

One of the distinct features of this so-called Age of Reason, in dramatic criticism as elsewhere, is its sentimentalism. But beware! Sentimentalisms are not all alike. Emotion disproportionate to meaning, emotion in excess of what is called for in a given situation, indulgence in emotion for its own sake—these are common meanings of sentimentalism. Unlike the men of most periods of time, writers, moralists, and philosophers of the eighteenth century created an elaborate thought structure that had sentimentalism as its base. Consequently, the sentimentalism of the eighteenth century was not naive and not unattached to meaning. We may quarrel with the thought structure, but not with its product. Although a sentimental tragedy of the period may still be unpalatable to us, constituted as we are, we cannot dispose of it historically by simply applying the tests of our own thought structures to it. Thought structure must contend with thought structure. Eighteenth-century drama may be condemned because it did not rise above its thought structure and become immediately communicable to us, as Shakespeare's theatre rose above the thought structure of its time, but Shakespeare is a lone example in four hundred years of English dramatic history.

Sentimentalism in the eighteenth century is usually identified with the followers of Anthony Ashley Cooper, the third Earl of Shaftesbury, an avowed deist, who in the early years of the century outlined a theory of morality that was founded upon universal benevolence and an instinctive implement for it implanted in us by God, called a "moral sense," which without the intervention of reason determined whether actions were or were not in accord with proper moral behavior. This in its time was a contradiction of the ideas of Thomas Hobbes and a host of other seventeenth-century writers, who were wont to explain our moral behavior in terms of self-interest and a social contract based upon self-interest. The eighteenth century became the battleground of the contending forces. "Egoism versus altruism" was one of the chief intellectual battles of the period, and though, in the concessions and compromises that eventuated, neither side won, in practice the day was carried by the Shaftesburians. Writers began to strive for pathetic effects, because, according to the system of Shaftesbury and of Hutcheson, his follower, the expression of pity was the sign of a properly constituted moral being, one whose natural propensities had not been warped or contaminated by the false ideas that often attended civilization and complex social structures. The expression of pity was also considered pleasant, because the exercise of any of our natural instincts, such as the moral sense, was accompanied by a delicious pleasure.

All in all, the drama of the eighteenth century did not present a radically different appearance from that of the seventeenth. The hands of Aristotle and of Horace were still heavy upon the dramatic poet. Once firmly established, the Rules were not to be lightly cast off; they were still in force far into the nineteenth century, however much the Romantic critics found them inadequate to explain the beauties of Shakespeare. Heroic drama was modified to meet the demands of the sentimentalists but with a few notable exceptions kept its external shape. Plays, especially tragedies, were still usually written in poetic form. Five acts were still standard. It was still common practice for the writer of tragedy to plunder the histories of Greece and Rome for plots and characters. When the playwright turned to exotic lands for material—to China, Peru, or Hindustan—he more often made his play carry a thesis applicable at home than did the writers of the love-and-honor tradition of the seventeenth century.

The argument that tragedy should come nearer home (comedy had always stayed near home) had been raised often in the seventeenth century without making notable headway. In the eighteenth century it became forceful. Republican sentiments were rising. It was more difficult to continue the pretense that only kings and princes should rule the tragic stage. Although it was on occasion argued that pity for the woes of a princess, whose road to happiness in love was long, could actually increase the ability of the spectator to be compassionate and charitable toward beggars and other sufferers that he might encounter in real life, common sense demanded a closer parallel. There were many real evils in the immediate neighborhood that called for treatment: widows left penniless as a result of dueling, gambling, or drinking; pure maidens seduced and destroyed by black-hearted villains whose motives were guided by "self-interest"; honest men reduced to penury because they refused to be opportunists or vile courtiers. The eighteenth century tragedy writer was still under obligation to provide a moral lesson, more so, perhaps, than the tragedy writer of any other period.

But a word of explanation is necessary here. The Horatian demand for a "moral lesson" had been strengthened by the critics of the seventeenth century—by D'Aubignac, Rapin, Le Bossu, Dacier, Collier, Rymer, Dennis, and Gildon, to mention only a few outstanding names. The seventeenth-century moral lesson was a teaching based upon fear. Its ally was poetic justice that punished the misbehaving characters and rewarded the good. The main moral concern was the punishment of guilt. The king is led by ambition or lust or jealousy into terrible wrongs and owes his downfall to his passion. The spectator sees his punishment and profits by it. Consider George Lillo's *The London Merchant* as the continuation of this same kind of moral lesson. A young apprentice commits the crime of robbing his employer's cashbox. His fortunes go from bad to worse, and in the end he is executed. The lesson is obvious, and the effect is fear. The critic of the eighteenth century, at least if he was a sentimentalist, was concerned with a different kind of lesson—with what in fact was scarcely a lesson at all. He wanted his virtuous characters to suffer so that the sight of virtue in distress could increase our ability to feel pity. In this way he reclaimed us and brought us back to virtue. The intent was still to give drama moral efficacy, but not to teach a direct lesson. Needless to say, there was much confusion in practice and criticism alike, but here is the crux of many a critical argument in the eighteenth century. The moral lesson through fear was a holdover from the seventeenth century. This distinction cuts across the lines of heroic drama, domestic tragedy, and sentimental comedy.

The problem of sentimental comedy provides one of the distinct features of eighteenth-century criticism. Beginning with Colley Cibber's *Love's Last Shift* (1696) and continuing in the eighteenth century with the plays of Sir Richard Steele, Marivaux, and soon a swarm of others, comedy found a new level. Tragi-comedy had been tried in the Renaissance and found wanting. The writers of sentimental comedy were not so much interested in a mixture of tragic and comic happenings as in presenting happenings that aroused pleasant and sad emotions at the same time. Ultimately the psychologists of the century worked out their theory of mixed sensations. The sentimental comedy was serious in that it put its characters into real, but scarcely tragic, troubles. It assumed their good nature throughout and asked us to sympathize with them. In the end it left them happy. Essential to sentimental comedy certainly was the doctrine of the inherent goodness of man. Strict neoclassic comedy, in theory at least, held up its characters to ridicule on account of their affectations or foibles. The writer was on the outside poking fun at his characters, laughing them down. The writer of sentimental comedy asked the spectator to move closer and look at the world through the eyes of his characters. In this way sentimental comedy allowed an expansion of the ego of the common man and was limited by the extent of the common man's ego. Even the common man's inadequacies—and here by "the common man" is meant the man of the middle classes—are glorified into norms, and he can reassure himself from the play that all of his opinions are right opinions. Much of the popular literature of the twentieth century is still in the framework of sentimental comedy.

An important feature of dramatic criticism in the eighteenth century is the rise of what may be called "psychological criticism." The critic goes less often to Aristotle to discover the principles upon which a play should be constructed. Instead, he makes an analysis of the workings of our minds. The psychological critic was primarily concerned with the question why some things are pleasant and some are unpleasant, and, consequently, out of psychological criticism grew what we know as aesthetics. Although Clarence DeWitt Thorpe has shown that psychological criticism goes back as far as Hobbes, the empirical spirit of the eighteenth century gave it its main form and content. Writers such as Addison, Du Bos, Hume, and Burke were as much concerned with psychological analysis as with the formulation of dramatic theory. Much of the important criticism of the century is hardly criticism at all. Lessing's *Hamburgische Dramaturgie* stands out among the critical undertakings of the period as one body of material that is chiefly concerned with what makes a play good or bad or even with the philosophy of drama as drama. The more typical eighteenth-century critic is either a repetitious Aristotelian or he is a prober into the workings of the human mind, and drama provides him with convenient material for analysis.

Throughout the century relations were close between England and France on all matters relating to plays. Each country kept its own traditions to some extent, but there was a steady flow of ideas back and forth across the channel. This was the period of the Enlightenment, and European society was straining to become one society. The chief difference between the French and the English stages was the difference between the great writers of the two traditions. Because they could not escape the influence of Shakespeare, the English playwrights did many things of which the French could not approve. Even though the English themselves found fault with Shakespeare, they put his plays on the stage almost as often as they put on plays of their own creation. They modified and altered him, they borrowed from him, but they could not avoid following him. The French, on the other hand, were forced to adjust themselves to seventeenth-century models, to Corneille and Racine, and the French critics throughout most of the eighteenth century were still spending much of their time debating which of their two models was to be preferred. The English playwright had a freer atmosphere to work in, even if he found serious fault with the model that he imitated. The weakness of both stages was, perhaps, the absence of new forms expressive of their own time, the weight upon them of the dead hand of tradition. Against this pressure the sentimentalists, with their new set of ideas, made only scanty headway.

B. H.

Pierre Corneille
1606-1684

Beyond question Pierre Corneille ranks as one of the three greatest dramatists of France. His plays are known to every serious student of the theatre. His critical works, however, have suffered a strange eclipse, particularly in English, for no complete English translation has been made of his three *Discourses,* and his *Examens* are available in only a few cases. This neglect is strange, for Corneille's criticism had a strong influence. Dryden knew the three discourses, as the notes to the *Essay of Dramatic Poesy* indicate, and such men as Rymer owe certain of their ideas to the Frenchman. The three discourses appeared in 1660 after Corneille had written his most significant plays, and they represent his considered defense against his attackers in the *Académie Française.*

The present selection is the first complete English translation of the second *Discourse, On Tragedy.* It is a close examination of the question of purgation through pity and fear, the fourth of the uses of dramatic poetry discussed in the first discourse. Corneille further considered the questions of probability and necessity in the writing of plays. It is readily apparent that the terms and problems under discussion are Aristotelian, and, indeed, the three *Discourses* are an extended exegesis of, or as some critics say, an extended battle with, the *Poetics.* In them Corneille exhibits two contradictory tendencies. He professes a great veneration for Aristotle, claiming that no one has so perfectly followed the rules of the philosopher as he has, and then challenging Aristotle's rules as being out of date and adapted only to the Greek theatre and to Greek civilization. He mentions in this *Discourse* a kind of play which Aristotle did not list among the possible plots for tragedy, promotes it to the first rank among tragedies, and then casually and glibly illustrates the type from one of his own plays. Corneille did not suffer from false modesty, and the reader may easily become irritated that Corneille took almost all his examples of good playwrighting from his own works, but the reader should also remember that it was not in the nature of men of the time to indulge in false modesty. Corneille seems perfectly sincere in using his own plays as examples, and might very well have argued that no other playwright fitted his points so exactly.

Because Corneille's essay is so intimately connected with Aristotle, and because Corneille's quotations are often paraphrases, references to a standard English translation of the *Poetics* have been made in the notes.

Discourse on Tragedy
AND OF THE METHODS OF TREATING IT,
ACCORDING TO PROBABILITY [1]
AND NECESSITY

[1660]

Besides the three uses of a dramatic poem of which I have spoken in the discourse I used as a preface for the first part of this collection, tragedy has this one in particular, "that through pity and fear it purges such passions." [2] These are the terms which Aristotle uses in his definition and which teach us two things: one, that it arouses pity and fear; the other, that by their means it purges such passions. He explains the first at sufficient length, but says nothing about the latter, and of all the terms which he employs in this definition, it is the only one he does not clarify at all. He shows, however, in the last chapter of his *Politics* an intention of speaking of it at a great length in this treatise [the *Poetics*], and it is that which makes most of his interpreters feel that we do not have it complete, because we see nothing at all on this subject.[3] Whatever it might have been, I believe that it is to the point to talk on what he has said before making an effort to divine what he wished to say. The maxims which he establishes for us could lead us to some conjecture on the other [idea of purgation], and on the certainty of what remains we can form a probable opinion of that which has not come down to us.

"We have pity," he says, "for those whom we see suffering a misfortune which they do not deserve, and we fear that a similar misfortune will befall us when we see people like ourselves suffering." [4] This

---

1 The word "probability" is the closest English word to the French *vraisemblable,* which is sometimes taken over intact, or translated as "verisimility," by the seventeenth- and eighteenth-century critics. Cf. Dryden's *Essay of Dramatic Poesy.*

2 Pertinent quotations from Aristotle are given in these notes from the modern translation of Bywater.

". . . with incidents arousing pity and fear, wherewith to accomplish its catharsis of such emotions."—Chap. 6, Ingram Bywater, *Aristotle on the Art of Poetry* (Oxford, 1909), p. 17.

3 Modern scholars are now of the opinion that one or two books of the *Poetics* have been lost, and that Aristotle covered the subject of comedy in one of the missing treatises, but Corneille undoubtedly believed that such a work was never written.

4 ". . . pity is occasioned by undeserved misfortune, and fear by that of one like ourselves."—Chap. 13, Bywater, p. 35.

pity concerns the interest of the person whom we see suffering, the fear which follows it concerns our own person, and this passage alone gives us enough opening to find the manner in which the purging of passions in tragedy is done. The pity for a misfortune, where we see the fall of people similar to ourselves, brings to us a fear of a similar one. This fear brings us to a desire of avoiding it, and this desire to purging, moderating, rectifying, and even eradicating in ourselves the passion which, before our eyes, plunges into this misfortune the persons we pity; for this common, but natural and indubitable reason, that to avoid the effect it is necessary to remove the cause. This explanation will not please those who attach themselves to the commentators of this philosopher. They are troubled by this passage and agree so little with each other that Paul Beny [5] notes twelve or fifteen different opinions which he refutes before giving us his own. His conforms to this one in the reasoning, but differs on this point, that it applies the effect only to kings and princes, perhaps for this reason, that the tragedy can make us fear only the evils which we see happening to those like us, and, in making them happen only to kings and princes, this fear can affect only those of their rank. But, without doubt, he has too literally understood the phrase, *those similar to us,* and has not sufficiently considered that there were no kings in Athens when the poems from which Aristotle takes his examples were shown, and on which he bases his rules. This philosopher would not care to have this thought attributed to him, and would not have used in tragedy a thing whose effect could function so rarely and whose use could be limited to so few people. It is true that ordinarily only kings are introduced for leading characters in tragedy, and the audience has no sceptres with which to resemble them, so that it can have the opportunity of fearing the misfortunes which overtake them; but these kings are men just as the members of the audience, and fall into those misfortunes through the force of passions of which the audience is capable. They even lend an easy argument for making the least of the greatest, and the spectator can easily conceive that if a king, through abandoning himself too much to ambition, to love, to hate, to vengeance, falls into so great disaster that he makes himself pitied in such proportion, he who is only a common man ought to keep these passions in check for fear of falling into a like misfortune. Besides, it is not necessary to put

[5] Paul Beny, or Paolo Beni, an Italian critic of Aristotle.

Pierre Corneille

only the misfortunes of kings in the theatre. Those of other men will find a place if any calamities sufficiently famous and important to deserve it happen to them, and if history takes enough care to teach them to us. Scédase was only a peasant from Leuctres; and I would not hold his woes unworthy of appearing if the purity of our scene could allow that we speak of the effective violation of his two daughters, after the idea of prostitution could not be endured in the person of a saint who had been preserved from it.[6]

To facilitate for us the methods of giving birth to this pity and this fear which Aristotle requires of us, it helps us to choose the characters and the events which can excite both. Also I suppose that it is true that our audience is composed neither of very evil men nor of saints, but people of ordinary goodness, who are not so severely restrained by exact virtue that they are not susceptible to passions but are exposed to the dangers in which passions engage those who yield completely to them. Supposing this, let us examine those characters whom the philosopher excludes from tragedy, in order that we agree with him on those in whom he makes his perfection consist. In the first place, he does not desire "that a completely virtuous man fall from good fortune into bad," and maintains "that this produces neither pity nor fear because this is a completely unjust event."[7] Some interpreters extend the meaning of this Greek word, μιαρόν,[8] which he uses as a name for this happening, to translate it as "abominable"; to which I add that such a success excites more indignation and hate against the man who causes the suffering than pity for the one who suffers, and

6 Voltaire writes on Scédase:
"Kings, emperors, princes, generals of armies, principal heads of republics, it really does not matter. But tragedy must always contain men elevated above common men, not only because the destiny of states depends on the lot of these important persons, but because the ill-fortunes of illustrious men exposed to the regard of nations makes a deeper impression on us than the misfortunes of common men.

"I very much doubt that a peasant of Leuctres, Scédase, by name, whose two daughters had been raped, would be as good a subject for tragedy as Cinna and Iphigenia. Rape, moreover, always has something of the ridiculous, and rarely can be played except among good families, where Corneille pretends that Théodore was set, supposing that this Théodore ever existed, and that the Romans had condemned their women to this form of punishment, which assuredly was neither in their laws nor their customs."

Théodore, by Corneille (1645), failed in production, and was banned because it presented the idea of prostitution.

7 "A good man must not be seen passing from happiness to misfortune. . . . The . . . situation is not fear-imposing or piteous, but simply odious to us."—Chap. 13, Bywater, p. 35.

8 This word implies an offense to our moral or religious feelings. Cf. Bywater, p. 214.

thus this feeling, which is not the right one for tragedy, at least unless well managed, can suffocate the feeling it ought to produce and leave the hearer discontented by the anger which he carries away and which is mingled with compassion which would please him if he took that alone away with him.

Neither does he want "a bad man to pass from disaster to good fortune, because not only can no pity or fear arise from such a success, but it cannot even touch us with the natural feeling of joy with which the prosperity of the first act fills us, to whom our favor attaches itself." [9] The fall of a bad man into misfortune has the material to please us through the aversion which we take for him; but since it is only a just punishment, it does not make us pity, and does not impress fear upon us, in as much as we are not as bad as he, and thus incapable of his crimes, and so cannot fear an equally disastrous outcome.

It remains, therefore, to find a mean between these two extremes, through the choice of a man who is neither entirely good nor entirely bad and who, through a fault or human frailty, falls into a misfortune which he does not deserve. Aristotle gives as examples Oedipus and Thyestes, and I really do not understand his thought at all. The first appears to me to contain no error, even though he kills his father, because he does not know him, and he only contests the way as a man of gallant soul against an unknown who attacks him with superior force. Nevertheless, although the meaning of the Greek word ἁμάρτημα [10] may extend to a simple error of misunderstanding, such as his was, let us admit the example with this philosopher, although I cannot see what passion there is to purge, nor how we can correct ourselves by this example. But, as for Thyestes, I cannot discover this common guilt or error without crime which plunges him into his misfortune. If we look at him before the tragedy which carries his name, he is a committer of incest who violates the wife of his brother; if we consider him in the tragedy, he is a man of good faith who takes the word of his brother with whom he is reconciled. In this first state, he is very much a criminal; in the latter, very much a virtuous man. If

[9] "Nor on the other hand should an extremely bad man be seen falling from happiness into misery. Such a story may arouse the human feeling in us, but it will not move us to either pity or fear."—Chap. 13, Bywater, p. 35.

[10] This word in Aristotle probably refers to an error of judgment. By the New Testament times it has come to mean sin, but the consensus of scholars is that it did not have moral connotations in Aristotle's time.

we attribute his misfortune to his incest, it is a crime of which the spectators are not capable, and the pity which they will feel for him will not include this fear which purges, because they do not resemble him in the least. If we lay his disaster to his good faith, some fear could follow the pity which we will have, but this fear could purge only the easy confidence in the word of a reconciled enemy, which is more the quality of an honest man than a vicious habit; and this purgation would only banish the sincerity of reconciliations. I admit frankly, therefore, that I do not understand the application of this example at all.

I will admit something else. If the purging of passions is accomplished in tragedy, I hold that it works in the way that I have explained, but I doubt that it ever happens, even in those tragedies which have the conditions which Aristotle demands. These conditions are met in Le Cid [11] and caused its great success. Rodrigue and Chimène there have this guilt subject to passions, and these passions cause their misfortune since they are unfortunate only to the extent of their passion for each other. They fall into unhappiness by this human weakness which we share with them. Their misfortune causes pity; this is sure, and that it has wrung many tears from the spectators there is no contesting. This pity ought to give us fear of falling into a like misfortune and purge in us this excess of love which causes their misfortune and makes us feel sorry for them; but I do not know if it gives us this fear, nor if it purges it, and I greatly fear that the reasoning of Aristotle on this point is nothing but a good idea which, in truth, never has its effect. I refer to those who have seen the representation. They can demand an accounting of the secret of their heart, and re-examine that which has touched them in the theatre, to determine whether they have come by that to this reflected fear, and whether they have rectified in themselves the passion which has caused the disgrace which they have pitied. One of the interpreters of Aristotle [12] says that he spoke of this purging of passions in the tragedy only because he wrote after Plato, who banished tragic poets from his republic, because they stirred the people up too strongly. Since he wrote to contradict him and to show that it is not to the point to banish them from civilized states, he wished to find the usefulness in these agitations of the soul, to make them desirable through the same reason that the

---

[11] Corneille's most famous play, produced in 1636 or early 1637.
[12] A fairly common statement, to be found as early as Minturnus' De Poeta, 1559.

other uses to banish them. The qualities that give birth to the impressions which provide the force of the example were not available to him: the punishment of evil actions, the reward of good ones was not the usage of his century as we have made it for ours, and except for those sentences and the didactic discourses which tragedy can pronounce according to its judgment, there is not to be found a solid utility; he has substituted one which is perhaps only imaginary. At least, to produce it requires the conditions it demands; they are met with so rarely that Robertello [13] finds them only in the *Oedipus,* maintaining that this philosopher has not prescribed them to us as so necessary that the lack of them will render a work defective, but only as concepts of perfection in tragedies. Our century has seen these things in *Le Cid,* but I do not know if it has seen them in many others; and if we wish to glance again at that rule, we acknowledge that success has justified many plays in which it is not observed.

The exclusion of completely virtuous persons who fall into misfortune banishes martyrs from our theatre. Polyeucte is a success against this maxim, and Héraclius and Nicomède [14] have pleased even though they impart only pity and give us nothing of fear, nor any passion to purge, since we see them oppressed and near death without any fault on their part from which we can by their example correct ourselves.

The misfortune of a very evil man excites neither pity nor fear; it is unworthy of the former and, as the spectators are not evildoers like him, they do not feel the latter in view of his punishment; but it would be apropos to place some distinction between the crimes. There are those of which honest people are capable by violence of passion, of which the evil outcome can have an effect in the soul of the hearer. An honest man does not go to the edge of the woods to steal, nor commit an assassination in cold blood; but if he is very much in love he may practice deceit on his rival, he may fly into a passion of rage and kill on a first impulse, and ambition may engage him in a crime or in a guilty action. There are few mothers who would murder or poison their children from fear of their making their way in the world as Cléopâtre in *Rodogune;* [15] but there are many who would like to do so, and desist only with reluctance, and at the last possible moment. Even

---

[13] A famous sixteenth-century critic of Aristotle.

[14] The heroes of three famous plays by Corneille. *Polyeucte* (1642 or 1643), *Héraclius* (1646), and *Nicomède* (1651).

[15] *Rodogune* (1644). Cléopâtre is not the famous lover of Antony, but Queen of Syria, who murders her own children.

though they are not capable of so black and so unnatural an action as
that of the Queen of Syria, there are those among them who have some
tincture of that principle, and the view of the just punishment which
she receives from it can make them fear, not a like misfortune, but one
proportional to that which they are capable of committing. It is thus
concerning several other crimes which are not within the scope of our
audience. The reader can make the investigation and application on
that principle.

However, even with such difficulty as there is in finding this effective and lively purgation of passions by means of pity and fear, it is
easy to reconcile ourselves with Aristotle. We have only to say that by
that manner of expressing himself, he did not understand that these
two means always operate together; and that it sufficed according to
him that one of the two make this purgation, with this difference always, that pity *cannot* come without fear, while fear *can* be aroused
without pity. The death of the Count does not do this in *Le Cid,* and
can many times better purge in us that sort of envious pride of the
glory of others than all the compassion we have for Rodogune and for
Chimène [16] can purge the affection for this violent love which causes
them to pity each other. The hearer can have commiseration for
Antiochus,[17] for Nicomède, for Héraclius, but if he continues in it,
and if he cannot believe in his falling into a like misfortune, he is not
cured of any passion. On the contrary, he has none for Cléopâtre, nor
for Prusias,[18] nor for Phocas; [19] but the fear of a similar or approaching
adversity can purge a stubborn mother from dispossessing the well-
being of her children, a husband from great deference toward a second
woman to the prejudice of that of his first bed, everyone from the
avidity of usurping by violence the well-being or dignity of others;
and all that proportional to the condition of each, and as far as he is
capable of understanding. The griefs and irresolutenesses of Auguste
in *Cinna* [20] can cause the last effect by pity and fear together; but, as I
have already said, it does not always happen that those we pity are
unfortunate from their own faults. When they are innocent, our pity
for them inspires no fear, and if we conceive a situation which purges
our passions, it is by the means of another person than the one whom
we pity, and we owe it all to the force of the example.

[16] Chimène and Rodogune are the heroines of Corneille's *Le Cid* and of *Rodogune.*
[17] Antiochus, a character in *Rodogune.*   [18] Prusias, a character in *Nicomède.*
[19] Phocas, a character in *Héraclius.*   [20] *Cinna* (1640).

This explanation finds authorization from Aristotle himself if we wish to weigh well the reason that he gives for the exclusion of events of which he disapproves in tragedy. He never says, "This is not proper because it does not excite pity, and does not give birth to fear, and this other is insupportable because it does not excite fear, and does not give birth to pity," but he rejects them, "because," he says, "they excite neither pity nor fear," [21] thereby making us understand that, because of the lack of the one and the other, they do not please him, and that if they produce one of the two, he does not in the least withhold his approbation. The example of *Oedipus* which he advances confirms me in this thought. If we accept it, it has all the conditions requisite to tragedy; however, his unhappiness excites only pity, and I do not think that, of those who have seen it played, anyone who has pitied has advised himself to fear killing his father or marrying his mother. If this representation can impress some fear, and that fear is capable of purging in us some guilty or vicious inclination, it also purges the curiosity to know the future and prevents us from having recourse to predictions which ordinarily only serve to make us fall into the misfortune predicted to us, by the very pains which we take to avert it; because it is certain that he would not have killed his father nor married his mother, if his father and mother, on hearing the oracle's prediction, had not exposed their fear that this would happen. Moreover, not only would Laïus and Jocasta alone experience this fear, but it would occur merely as the shadow of a crime they had committed forty years before the action presented, and would be impressed on us only by a secondary actor, and by an action outside the tragedy.

To bring this discourse together before passing on to another matter, let us establish for a maxim that the perfection of tragedy consists indeed in exciting pity and fear by means of the leading actor, as Rodrigue in *Le Cid* and Placide in *Théodore*,[22] but that it is not a necessity so absolute that divers persons cannot be used to arouse the two feelings, as in *Rodogune;* and even to bring but one of the two to the audience, as in *Polyeucte,* where the representation forces only pity and no fear. That granted, let us find some moderation in the rigidity of the Rules of the philosopher, or at least some favorable interpretation, so as not to be required to condemn most of the poems we have seen succeed in our theatres.

21 ". . . will not move us to either pity or fear."—Chap. 13, Bywater, p. 35.
22 *Théodore* (1645).

Aristotle does not in the least desire that a completely innocent man should fall into misfortune, because that would be abominable; it excites greater indignation against the persecuter than pity for the misfortunes. No more does he desire that a completely evil man fall into misfortune, because this man cannot evoke pity for a calamity which he deserves, nor arouse fear of a like disaster in the spectators, who do not resemble him; but while the two judgments leave [room for] the example of a good man whose sufferings excite pity greater than our indignation against the one who causes them, or where the punishment of a great crime can correct in us some imperfection which is similar to his, I consider that it is not necessary to raise objections to exposing on the scene very virtuous or very evil men in calamity. Here are two or three ways of doing this, which perhaps Aristotle did not think to anticipate because he saw no examples of them in the theatres of his time.

The first is, when a very virtuous man is persecuted by a very evil one and escapes from the peril while the villain is caught in it, as in *Rodogune* and in *Héraclius;* this could not have been endured if Antiochus and Rodogune had perished in the first, and if Héraclius, Pulchèrie, and Martian in the other, and Cléopâtre and Phocas had triumphed. Their misfortune stirs a pity which is not in the least stifled by aversion toward their oppressors, because it is hoped always that some happy turn will prevent them from succumbing, and, even though the crimes of Phocas and Cléopâtre are great enough to cause the audience to fear committing like ones, the unhappy outcome may have the effects upon the audience of which I have already spoken. It can happen, besides, that a very virtuous man may be persecuted and may even perish at the command of another man, who is not evil enough to arouse much indignation and who shows more weakness than villainy in the persecution which he enforces. If Félix has his son-in-law, Polyeucte, killed, it is not because of an enraged hate toward the Christians which would render him execrable to us, but only because of a shameful timidity that keeps him from daring to save him [Polyeucte] in the presence of Sévère, whose hate and vengeance he [Félix] fears, after the contempt he had shown for him during his ill fortune. We have some aversion for him; we disapprove of his method of working, but this aversion does not remove the pity we have for Polyeucte, and does not prevent his miraculous conversion at the end of the play from reconciling him fully with the audience. We can say the same thing of Prusias in *Nicomède* and of Valeus in *Théodore*. The one mistreats his son, although he is very virtuous, and the other is the cause of the ruin of his, who is no less good, but both have only the weaknesses which do not quite become crimes; and far from exciting an indignation which stifles the pity we have for a generous son, the cowardice of their abasement under the powers they dread, and which they must brave to do well, makes us only have some compassion for them and for their political shame.

To facilitate for us the means of exciting this pity which creates such fine effects in our theatres, Aristotle gives us a clue. "All action," he says, "takes place either between friends, or between enemies, or between people who are indifferent to each other. If an enemy kills or wishes to kill his enemy, that will not produce any commiseration, except in so far as we are moved to learn of or to see the death of a man such as he. When a stranger kills a stranger, that scarcely touches us any further, as long as it does not excite any strife in the soul of him who performs the action; but when these things happen between people whose birth or affection binds them together in interest, as when husband kills or is ready to kill his wife, a mother her children, a brother his sister, it is that which is marvelously suited to tragedy." [23] The reason for this is clear. The opposition of the feelings of nature to the transports of passion, or to the severity of duty, forms powerful emotions which are received with pleasure by the audience; and the audience is easily disposed to pity an unfortunate man oppressed or persecuted by a person who ought to be interested in his salvation and who oftentimes seeks his ruin only with sorrow or, at the least, with repugnance. Horace and Curiace [24] would not be at all to be pitied if they had not been friends and brothers-in-law; nor Rodrigue if he had been persecuted by another than his mistress; and the unhappiness of Antiochus would touch us much less if some other than his mother

[23] "Let us see, then, what kinds of incident strike one as horrible, or rather as piteous. In a deed of this description the parties must necessarily be either friends, or enemies, or indifferent to one another. Now when enemy does it on enemy, there is nothing to move us to pity either in his doing or in his meditating the deed, except so far as the actual pain of the sufferer is concerned; and the same is true when the parties are indifferent to one another. When the tragic deed, however, is done within the family— when murder or the like is done or meditated by brother on brother, by son on father, by mother on son, or son on mother—these are the situations the poet should seek after."—Chap. 14, Bywater, p. 39.   [24] Characters in Corneille's *Horace* (1640).

had demanded the blood of his mistress, or some other than his mistress had demanded the blood of his mother; or if, after the death of his brother, which makes him subject to the fear of a similar thing happening to his own person, he had had to defy others than his mother and his mistress.

The proximity of blood and the intimacy of love or friendship between the persecutor and persecuted, the hunter and the hunted, the one who causes suffering and the one who suffers is, therefore, a great advantage for exciting pity, but there is some evidence that this condition is not as absolute as that of which I have just spoken, and that it concerns only perfect tragedies and nothing more. At least, the Ancients did not always observe it; I do not see it at all in the *Ajax* of Sophocles, nor in his *Philoctetes,* and anyone who wishes to run over that which remains to us of Æschylus and Euripides can find some examples to join to these. When I say that the two conditions are only for perfect tragedies, I do not mean to say that those in which we do not find them are imperfect; that would make it an absolute necessity, and make me contradict myself. But by the phrase "perfect tragedy" I mean the most sublime and moving of the type, so that those which lack one of these two conditions, or both of them, provided that they are regular with this exception, do not fail of being perfect of their type, even though they remain in a less exalted rank, and do not approach the beauty and splendor of the others if they borrow the pomp of verse, or the magnificence of spectacle, or some other agreement which comes with the subject.

In these tragic actions which happen between relatives, it is necessary to consider whether the one who wishes to cause the death of the other recognizes him or does not recognize him, and if he achieves his goal or does not achieve it. The various combinations of these two manners of proceeding form four kinds of tragedy, to which our philosopher attributes varying degrees of perfection. "A person recognizes the one whom he wishes to kill, and actually has him killed, as Medea kills her children, Clytemnestra her husband, Orestes his mother"; and the least kind is this. "A person has another killed without recognizing him, and then recognizes him with grief after having had him killed, and that," he says, "either before the tragedy, or in the tragedy, as the *Alcmeon* of Astydamas, and Telegonus in *Ulysses Wounded,*" two plays which time has not allowed to come to us; and the second kind, according to him, is more elevated than the first. The third is in the highest degree of excellence, "when a person is ready to have one of his relatives killed without knowing him soon enough to save him, as Iphigenia recognizes Orestes for her brother, but must sacrifice him to Diana, and escapes with him." He cites again two examples of this, of Merope in *Cresphontes* and of *Helle,* of which we know nothing. He entirely condemns the fourth species, in which people recognize, undertake, and complete nothing, which he says has something of evil and nothing of tragedy, and gives for example Haemon, who draws his sword against his father in the *Antigone* and uses it only to kill himself,[25] but unless this condemnation is a little modified, it would extend a little far and would envelop not only *Le Cid*, but *Cinna, Rodogune, Héraclius,* and *Nicomède.*

Let us say, then, that this condemnation is only to be understood of those who recognize the person they wish to ruin and desist because of a simple change of will, without any notable happening which obliges their changing, and without any lack of power on their part. I have already indicated this type of denouement as vicious; but when they have done on their side all that they can, and when they are prevented by a superior power from bringing about the result, or by some change in fortunes which causes them to perish, or puts them in the power of those whom they would ruin, it is beyond doubt that such constitutes tragedy, perhaps more sublime than the three kinds Aris-

25 "The deed of horror may be done by the doer knowingly and consciously, as in the old poets, and in Medea's murder of her children in Euripides. Or he may do it, but in ignorance of his relationship, and discover that afterwards, as does the Oedipus in Sophocles. Here the deed is outside the play; but it may be within it, like the act of the Alcmeon in Astydamas, or that of Telegonus in *Ulysses Wounded*. A third possibility is for one meditating some deadly injury to another, in ignorance of his relationship, to make the discovery in time to draw back. . . .

"The worst situation is when the personage is with full knowledge on the point of doing the deed, and leaves it undone. It is odious and also (through the absence of suffering) untragic; hence it is that no one is made to act thus except in some few instances, e.g. Haemon and Creon in Antigone. Next after this comes the actual perpetration of the deed meditated. A better situation than that, however, is for the deed to be done in ignorance, and the relationship discovered afterwards, since there is nothing odious in it, and the Discovery will serve to astound us. But the best of all is the last; what we have in *Cresphontes,* for example, where Merope, on the point of slaying her son, recognizes him in time; in *Iphigenia,* where sister and brother are in a like position; and in *Helle,* where the son recognizes his mother when on the point of giving her up to her enemy."—Chap. 14, Bywater, p. 41.

Cresphontes is a lost play by Euripides; *Ulysses Wounded* was by Sophocles; nothing is known of *Helle;* Astydamas was a tragedian who wrote some 240 tragedies, of which 15 took prizes. He was first produced in B.C. 395.

totle approves; and if he has not spoken of this type at all, it is only because he saw no examples in the theatres of his own time, or it was not the custom to save the good by the ruin of the wicked, unless they have soiled themselves with some crime, as in the case of Electra, who delivers herself from oppression by the death of her mother, encouraging her brother in the crime and facilitating the means for him.

The action of Chimène [26] is then not defective because, after undertaking to ruin Rodrigue, she does not do so even though she could, and all the justice she can obtain from the king is a combat wherein the victory of this deplorable lover imposes silence on her. Cinna and his Émilie do not sin at all against the Rules in not killing Auguste, because the discovered conspiracy makes them impotent, and, if such an unexpected clemency did not dissipate all their hate, it would reveal them as having no tincture of humanity. Who spares Cléopâtre for the ruin of Rodogune? Who forgets Phocas for ridding himself of Héraclius? And if Prusias had remained the master, would not Nicomède have had to go to serve as hostage at Rome, which would have been to him a greater punishment than death? The first two receive punishment for their crimes and fail in their enterprises without recanting; and the last is forced to admit his injustice, after the insurrection of his people and the generosity of that son whom he wished to exalt at the expense of the eldest have prevented it from succeeding.

It is not to refute Aristotle that the writer finds so happy this fourth manner of proceeding, which the philosopher condemns, finds it indeed a new type of tragedy finer than the three which he recommends, and which he would doubtless have preferred had he known it. It is to give honor to our century without impinging in the least on the authority of this philosopher; however, I do not know how to conserve this authority and reverse the order of preference which he established among the three types. Nevertheless, I think it to be well founded in experience to question whether that which he esteems the least of the three is not really the best, and if that which he holds for the best is not the least. The reason is that the last cannot excite pity. A father wishes to kill his son without recognizing him, and regards him only as a stranger and perhaps as an enemy. Let him be accepted as one or the other, his peril is not worth any commiseration, according

[26] Characters in *Le Cid*.

to Aristotle himself, and causes the audience to feel only a certain inner movement of trepidation, to fear that the son will perish before the error is discovered and to wish that it be discovered soon enough for him to escape from death: that which divides interest never prevents us from being interested in the fortune of a man virtuous enough to make himself loved; and when this recognition occurs, it produces only a sentiment of pleasure when we see happen the thing we have wished for.

When this recognition is accomplished only after the death of a stranger, the pity excited by the sorrows of the one who causes him to be killed can have no great depth because it is deferred and is confined in the catastrophe; but when it concerns a discovered face, and they know by whom it is desired, the combat of passions contrary to nature, or of duty against love, occupies the best part of the poem; and from that, brings to birth great and powerful emotions, which renew themselves each moment and redouble the pity. To justify this reasoning by experience, we see that Chimène and Antiochus excite the audience more than does Oedipus in his own person. I say in his own person, because the entire poem excites them perhaps more than *Le Cid* or *Rodogune;* but it owes a part to Dircé, and that which she arouses is only pity borrowed from an episode.

I know that agnition [27] is a fine ornament in tragedies: Aristotle says so, but it is certain that it has its inconveniences. The Italians affect it in the greater part of their poems, and sometimes lose, by the attachment they have for it, many occasions for pathetic sentiments which would have considerable beauties. This manifests itself in *The Death of Crispian*, written by one of their best wits, Jean-Baptiste Ghirardelli, and printed at Rome in the year 1653. [28] The author was at pains to conceal his hero's birth from Constantin, and to make him solely a great captain, who is recognized as the son of Constantin only after the latter has had him put to death. This entire play is so full of wit and fine sentiments that it had enough success to oblige others to write against the author and to censure it as soon as it appeared. But how that birth, hidden without necessity, and contrary to the truth

27 *Agnition* means recognition. Corneille uses this word several times in this meaning, taking it from the Greek word, ἀναγνώρισις. The usual translation is *discovery*.

28 Very little is known about Giovanni-Battista Filippo Ghirardelli. Voltaire mentions him in a note to this discourse. His only surviving work is a tragedy, *Il Costantino*, in prose.

of a known history, has robbed him of finer things than the brilliant ones which he has scattered in this work! The pains, the confusion, the irresolutions, and the griefs of Constantin would have been different in pronouncing a stay of death for his son than for a soldier of fortune. The injustice of his preoccupation would have been more sensible to Crispian on the part of a father than on the part of a master; and the quality of the son, augmenting the grandeur of the crime which had been imposed on him, would at the same time have augmented the grief of seeing a father persuaded. Even Faust [29] would have had more internal struggle in undertaking an incest than in resolving on an adultery; his remorse would have been more living, and his despair more violent. The author has renounced all these advantages by having disdained to treat this subject as P. Stephonius, Jesuit,[30] treated it in our time, and as our Ancients have treated that of Hippolytus; and far from believing that he has elevated it to a type higher than those according to the thought of Aristotle, I am not sure that he has not made it fall below those I have just named.

There is great probability that what this philosopher has said concerning the various degrees of perfection of tragedy had entire justification for his own time and in the presence of his compatriots; I do not wish to question it at all; but I cannot help saying that the taste of our century is not that of his on his preference of one type to the other, or at least that that which pleased his Athenians in the highest degree is not equally pleasing to us French; and I do not know any other method of finding my doubts supportable and remaining completely in the veneration which we owe to all that he has written on poetry.

Before leaving this matter, let us examine his feeling on two questions touching these subjects between related people; the one, if the poet can invent them; the other, if he can change anything in those which he takes from history or fable.

For the first, it is unquestionable that the Ancients took so little liberty with history that they limited their tragedies to a few families because deeds of this kind occurred in so few families; that made this

[29] Corneille is referring to a French translation of *The History of the Damnable Life & Deserved Death of Dr. John Faustus* (1588–94). This work was first published in Paris, translated by Victor Palma Cayet, in 1592. Fifteen editions appeared in the next two hundred years.

[30] Corneille errs in his recording of this name. Bernardus Stephonius, a Jesuit, wrote a tragedy, *Crispus*, in 1634.

philosopher say that fortune furnished the subjects, not art.[31] I believe I said this in another discourse. It seems, however, that he accords poets full right to invention by these words: "They must use what they have received or invent it themselves." [32] These terms would decide the question if they were not so general; but as he has posed three kinds of tragedies, according to the varying times of recognition and the different methods of working, we can review all three to judge if it is not apropos to make some distinction which will restrain that liberty. I have given my opinion on it, however, very boldly, that it may not be imputed to me that I have contradicted Aristotle, provided that I have left completely some one of the three.

I think then in the first place that when it is proposed to have someone killed who is recognized, whether this is achieved or whether it is prevented, the author is not at liberty to invent the principal action, but ought to draw it from history or fable. These enterprises against blood relations are always so criminal and so contrary to nature that they are not credible unless supported by one or the other; and they never have the probability without which invented actions cannot be played.

I dare not decide upon the second type so absolutely. When a man takes up a quarrel with another, and having killed him, comes to recognize him for his father or for his brother and falls into despair, that can be only probable, and by consequence can be invented; however, this circumstance of killing one's father or one's brother without knowing him is so extraordinary and so shocking that we have the right to say that history cannot fail of remembering it when it happens among illustrious persons, and to refuse completely to believe it when history does not record it. The ancient theatre has furnished us only the example of Oedipus, and I do not remember having seen any other among our historians. I know that this event is better suited to fable than to history, and that by consequence, it may have been invented, at least in part, but the history and fable of antiquity have been so mixed that, to escape the danger of making a false distinction, we grant them equal authority in our theatres. It suffices that we invent

---

31 "It was accident rather than art that led the poets in quest of subjects to embody this kind of incidents in their Plots."—Chap. 14, Bywater, p. 41.

32 "In Tragedy . . . they still adhere to the historic names . . . and there are some without a single known name."—Chap. 9, Bywater, pp. 27–29. This is a bad misreading of Aristotle on Corneille's part, for Aristotle says several times that the poet should invent and change for the sake of probability and necessity.

nothing which is not probable, and when invented long since, it must be so well established in the consciousness of the audience that, on the stage, it does not shock the sight. All the *Metamorphoses* of Ovid are manifestly invention; we can draw from them the subjects of tragedy, but we may not invent on their models unless we take episodes of the same character. The reason is that while we can invent only that which is probable, and that these fabulous subjects, such as Andromeda and Phaeton, are not so at all, to invent these episodes is not so much to invent them as it is to add to those which have already been invented; and the episodes find a type of probability in their relation to the principal action, so that one can say that if this could have been done, it must have been done as the poet describes it.

Yet such episodes would not be proper to a historical subject or one of pure invention, because they lack that relation to the principal action and would be less probable than it is. The appearance of Venus and Eolus were well received in *Andromède;* [33] but if I had made Jupiter descend to reconcile Nicomède with his father, or Mercury reveal the conspiracy of Cinna to Augustus, I would have made all my audience revolt, and this miracle would have destroyed all the belief which the rest of the action had obtained. Denouements by gods from a machine are very frequent among the Greeks in tragedies which resemble histories and which are very probable, with that exception. Aristotle does not completely condemn them, and contents himself with preferring those denouements which come from the subject. [34] I do not know what decided the Athenians who were the judges, but the two examples I have just mentioned show sufficiently that it would be dangerous for us to imitate them in this sort of liberty. It has been said to me that these apparitions should not please us because we manifestly know their falsity, and that they would offend our religion, which was not the case among the Greeks. I admit that it is necessary to accommodate oneself to the customs of the audience, and so much the more to its credibility; but it must be conceded to me that we have at least as much faith in the apparition of angels and saints as the Ancients had in their Apollo and their Mercury; but would it be said that I should have used an angel to make Héraclius quarrel with

[33] *Andromède* (1650).
[34] "The Denouement also should arise out of the plot itself, and not depend on stage-artifices, as in *Medea.*"—Chap. 15, Bywater, p. 43.

Martian after the death of Phocas? The poem concerns Christians, and this apparition would have been as fitting there as the gods of antiquity were in those [plays] of the Greeks; it would have been, however, an infallible device for rendering the action ridiculous, and it is necessary only to have a little common sense to keep it in accord. Let me be permitted to say with Tacitus: *Non omnia apud priores meliora, sed nostra quoque aetas multa laudis et artium imitanda posteris tulit.*

I return to tragedies of the second type, where a person does not recognize a father or a son until after he has had him killed; and to conclude in two words after this digression, I would never condemn anyone for having invented it, but I have never allowed it for myself.

Those of the third type admit no difficulty; not only can they be invented, but everything is probable and follows the common manner of natural affections, but I suspect that to oblige poets to take their subjects from history would serve to ban them from the theatres. We do not see anything of that nature among the Greeks which has not the aspect of being invented by their authors. It may be that their story had already been taken from someone. I do not have eyes penetrating enough to pierce such thick obscurities and to determine if the *Iphigenia in Tauris* is the invention of Euripides as his *Helen* and his *Ion,* or if he has taken it from another; but I believe I may say that it is very difficult to find them in history, since such events occur only rarely, and since they do not have enough fame to merit a place. That of Theseus, recognized by the King of Athens, his father, at the time he was about to be killed, is the only one I can remember. Be that as it may, those who love to put them on the stage can invent them without fear of censure. They can thus produce some agreeable suspension in the understanding of the audience, but they need not hope to draw many tears.

The other question, whether it is permitted to change something in the subjects one has drawn from history or fable, seems to be decided in precise enough terms by Aristotle when he says, "that it is not permitted to change subjects as received, and that Clytemnestra ought not to be killed by another than Orestes, nor Eriphyle by another than Alcmeon." [35] This decision, however, is subject to some distinction and some tempering. It is an established fact that these circumstances,

[35] "The traditional stories, accordingly, must be kept as they are, e.g., the murder of Clytemnestra by Orestes and that of Eriphyla by Alcmeon."—Chap. 14, Bywater, p. 39.

or if you like it better, the means of forwarding the action, remain in our power. History does not often note them, or reports them so little that it is necessary to supply them to fill out the poem; and there is the likelihood of presuming that the memory of the auditor, who has read these things elsewhere, will not have them so strongly in his mind that he will notice the change we have made and so accuse us of the sin; this he would not fail to do if he saw that we had changed the principal action. This falsification would cause him to have no faith in all the rest; as, on the contrary, he easily believes all the rest when he sees it lead to the result he knows to be true, when the history has left a strong impression upon him. The example of the death of Clytemnestra can serve to prove what I have just put forward. Sophocles and Euripides have both treated it, but each with a twist and a denouement completely different from the other, and it is this difference which keeps it from being the same play, even though it is the same subject whose principal action they have conserved. It is necessary to conserve this principal action as they did, but it is necessary at the same time to examine it to see if it is so painful or so difficult to represent that it can detract from the belief that the audience owes to the story and that they want to give to the fable by putting it in its place for those who have considered it true. When this inconvenience is to be feared, it is well to hide the outcome from sight, and to make it known by a recitation which shocks less than the spectacle and which impresses us more easily.

It is for this reason that Horace wished that Medea had not killed her children and that Atreus had not roasted those of Thyestes in the sight of the audience.[36] The horror engenders a repugnance to believe these actions as well as the metamorphosis of Progne into a bird and of Cadmus into a serpent, of which the almost impossible representation excites the incredibility when it is hazarded before the eyes of the spectator:

Quodcumque ostendis mihi sic, incredulus odi.

I go on further, and to weaken or alleviate this dangerous horror in a historical action, I would make it happen without the participation of the protagonist, for whom we must always secure the favor of the audience. After Cléopâtre had killed Séleucus, she presented poison

36 Horace, *Ars poetica,* ll. 182–87.

to her other son, Antiochus, on his return from the hunt, and this prince, suspecting what it was, constrained her to take it, and forced her to poison herself.[37] If I had made this action visible without changing it, I would have punished a parricide by another parricide; [38] the audience would have taken an aversion for Antiochus, and it was more pleasant to arrange it that she herself, seeing her shame and black perfidy about to be discovered, poisons herself in her despair, with the design of enveloping the two lovers in her ruin, in removing from them all occasion for caution. This creates two effects. The punishment of this pitiless mother presents a very strong example, because it demonstrates the justice of heaven and not the vengeance of men; on the other hand, Antiochus does not lose anything of the pity and friendly feeling we have for him, which increases more than it diminishes; and finally the action of the history is conserved in spite of the change, since Cléopâtre dies by the same poison which she presents to Antiochus.

Phocas was a tyrant, and slaying him was not a crime; however, it would doubtless have been more suitable to have it happen by the hand of Exupère than by that of Héraclius. We must take care to preserve our heroes from crime so long as it is possible and even to exempt them from drenching their hands in blood except in a just combat. I was very daring in *Nicomède:* Prusias, his father, wanted to have Nicomède assassinated in his army; according to the advice that the latter has had from the assassins themselves, he enters his father's kingdom, seizes it, and compels his unfortunate father to hide in a cavern where the son kills him. I have not pushed history up to that point; and after having drawn Nicomède as too virtuous to indulge in parricide, I believed that I could content myself with making him master for life of those who had persecuted him, without carrying the matter any further.

I would not hide a refinement which I made in the death of Clytemnestra,[39] whom Aristotle proposes to us as an example whose actions ought not to be changed. I believe indeed, with him, that she must die only at the hand of her son Orestes, but I cannot suffer with Sophocles that this son has formed the design of stabbing her while she is on her

37 *Rodogune.*
38 Corneille obviously uses this word to mean any killing of any relative.
39 *Oreste* (1659).

knees before him and imploring him to let her live. I cannot even pardon Electra, who passes for oppressed virtue in the rest of the play, for the inhumanity with which she encourages her brother in this matricide. He is a son who avenges his father, but it is on his mother that he avenges him. Séleucus and Antiochus have as much right to do the same thing in *Rodogune;* but I did not dare give them the least thought of it. Also, our maxim of making protagonists loved was not the usage of the Ancients; these republicans had such a strong hatred of kings that they witnessed with pleasure the crimes committed by the most innocent of their breed. To correct this subject to our fashion, it is necessary that Orestes have a plot only against Ægisthus; that a remnant of respectful tenderness toward his mother makes him leave her punishment to God; that this queen insist on protecting her lover, and that she thrust herself between him and her son in so unfortunate a manner that she receive the blow which the prince meant to deal to the assassin of his father. Thus she perishes by the hand of her son as Aristotle wishes it, without the barbarity of Orestes filling us with horror as in Sophocles, nor does his action require the vengeful furies to torment him, since he remains innocent.

Aristotle himself authorizes us to work in this manner when he teaches us that "the poet is not obliged to treat things as they happen, but as they could or may have happened, according to probability or necessity." [40] He often repeats these last words and never explains them. I have tried to supply this explanation as best I can, and I hope I will be forgiven if I am mistaken.

I say first that this liberty which he allows us of embellishing historical actions by probabilities [41] does not bestow upon us any defense for setting aside probability when we are in distress. It is a privilege he gives us, and not a servitude he imposes upon us. That is clear from his own words. If we can treat things according to probability or according to necessity, we can leave probability to follow necessity; and this alternative supplies the choice of serving that of the two which we judge the more fitting.

This liberty of the poet is found again in more precise terms in the twenty-fifth chapter, which contains the excuses, or rather justifica-

---

[40] "From what we have said, it will be seen that the poet's function is to describe, not the thing that has happened, but a kind of thing that might happen, i.e., what is possible as being probable or necessary."—Chap. 9, Bywater, p. 27.

[41] See note 1, above.

tions, he provides against censure. "It is necessary," he says, "that the poet follow one of the three ways of treating things, and that he represent them as they were, or as it is said they were, or as they ought to have been"; [42] by which he gives the poet the choice either of true history, or of the common opinion on which the fable is founded, or of the probability. He adds then: "If a poet is charged that he has not written things according to truth, let him answer that he has written things as they ought to have been; if they impute to him that he has done neither the one nor the other, let him defend himself on that which is common public opinion, as they have been told of the gods, of which a great deal is not probable." [43] And a little further down, "Often it is better that these things should not be made to happen as they have been described, even though they have happened effectively in that manner," [44] and by consequence, such an alteration is beyond fault. This last passage shows that we are not obliged to set aside truth to give a better form to the actions of tragedy by ornaments of probability, and it shows all the more strongly that it can be taken for granted, according to the second of these three passages, that common opinion suffices to justify us when we do not have the truth, and that we can make some improvement in what we write if we seek for the beauties of this probability. We run by this some risk of a lesser success; but we sin only against the care which we owe to our reputations, and not against the Rules of the theatre.

I will make a second remark on these terms, probability and necessity, whose order is often found reversed in this philosopher, who often says, "according to necessity or probability," and sometimes "according to probability and necessity." From which I draw an inference that there are occasions when probability is to be preferred to necessity, and others when necessity is to be preferred to probability. The reason is that when we employ the latter of these alternative propositions, it is used as a makeshift with which we are forced to content our-

[42] "The poet . . . must necessarily in all instances represent things in one or other of three aspects, either as they were or are, or as they are said or thought to be or to have been, or as they ought to be."—Chap. 25, Bywater, p. 81.

[43] "If the poet's description be criticised as not true to fact, one may urge perhaps that the object ought to be as described. . . . If the description, however, be neither true nor of the thing as it ought to be, the answer must be then, that it is in accordance with opinion."—Chap. 25, Bywater, p. 83.

[44] "Of other statements in poetry one may perhaps say, not that they are better than the truth, but that the fact was so at the time."—Chap. 25, Bywater, p. 83.

selves when we cannot arrive at the other, and that we must make an effort at the first before being reduced to the second, to which we have the right to recourse only in default of the first.

To clarify this mutual preference for probability to necessity, and for necessity to probability, we must distinguish two things in the actions which makᴜ up a tragedy. The first consists of these actions in themselves together with the inseparable circumstances of time and place; the other in their mutual relationship, which makes the one give birth to the other. In the first, probability is to be preferred to necessity; and necessity to probability in the second.

We must place the actions where it is easier and more fitting that they should happen, and make them take place at a reasonable leisure, without accelerating them extraordinarily unless the necessity of confining them to one place and within one day obliges us to do so. I have already made it clear in another Discourse that to conserve the unity of place we often make people who would probably converse in a room talk in a public place; that if the things I have set forth in *Le Cid,* in *Polyeucte,* in *Pompée,* or in *le Menteur* [45] were told in a romance, a little more than one day would have been given to prolong the difficulty. The obeisance which we owe to the Rules of the Unity of Time and Place exempts us sometimes from probability, even though it does not permit us the impossible; but we do not always fall into that necessity; and *La Suivante,*[46] *Cinna, Théodore,* and *Nicomède* have no need of dispensing with probability in time as do these other poems.

This reduction of tragedy to romance [47] is the touchstone for disentangling necessary actions from probable ones. We are limited in the theatre by place, by time, and by the difficulties of the representation, which entirely prevent us from exposing to sight many persons lest they remain without action, or hamper the action of the others. A romance has none of these constraints: it gives the actions which it describes all the leisure necessary for enactment; it places speaker, doer, or dreamer, in a room, in a forest, in a public place—wherever is most appropriate for the particular action; it has an entire palace, an entire city, an entire realm, all the world, where they may perform; and if something happens or is told in the presence of thirty people,

[45] *Le Menteur* (1643).
[46] *La Suivante* (1637).
[47] The French word is *roman,* which usually means *novel* today, but romance is used here as more descriptive of the kind of work Corneille is describing.

the author can describe the various opinions one after the other. It is for this reason that he has no liberty whatever to depart from probability, because he has no legitimate reason or excuse for giving it up.

As the theatre leaves us little facility to reduce everything to probability, because nothing is made known to us except by characters put before us briefly, it exempts us from probability that much more easily. One can maintain that it does not so much exempt as permit us a larger probability; but since Aristotle authorizes us to treat things according to necessity, I would rather say that whatever happens in a way different from the way it happens in a romance, even though well done, has no probability and ought to be counted among necessary actions.

Horace can furnish us several examples of this: the unity of place is exact. Everything takes place in a room. But if we were to write a romance with the same particulars from scene to scene which I have employed, would we make everything transpire in that room? At the end of the first act, Curiace and Camille, his mistress, wish to rejoin the rest of the family, who must be in another room; between the two acts, they receive the news of the election of the three Horaces; at the beginning of the second, Curiace appears in that same room to congratulate them. In the romance, the author would have had these congratulations given in the same place that the news was received, in the presence of all the family; it is not probable that these two would withdraw for their rejoicing, but it is necessary for the theatre; and at least for presenting the sentiments of the three Horaces, of their father, of their sister, of Curiace, and of Sabine, they must all appear together. Romance, which makes nothing visible, easily arrives at the goal; but on the stage, it is necessary to separate the family, to put them in some order and take them one after the other, and to commence with these two, whom I was forced to place in that room at the expense of probability. That having happened, the remainder of the act is completely probable, and nothing need take place in a manner different from the romance. At the end of this act, Sabine and Camille, beside themselves with sorrow, retire from that room in a transport of grief; with probability, they would confine their tears to their room, where the romance makes them remain to receive the news of the battle. However, because of the necessity of having the spectators see these things, Sabine leaves her room at the beginning of the third act and continues to display her sad uneasiness in that room where Camille has found her. After that, the remainder of the act is as probable as the other; and if you wanted to examine the first scenes of the last two with this rigor, you would, perhaps, find the same thing—that if they had once gone out, as they leave at the end of each act, the characters would have been shown in romance elsewhere than in that room.

These examples suffice to explain how an action can be treated according to necessity when it cannot be treated according to probability —which ought always to be preferred to necessity when one considers only the actions themselves.

The connection [48] which makes the one come from the other does not work that way; necessity is, in this case, to be preferred to probability, not that this connection ought not always to be probable, but because it is much better that it be probable and necessary together. The reason for this is easy to conceive. When the connection is only probable without being necessary, the poem can get by with it and it is of no great importance; but when it is probable and necessary, it must be an essential part of the poem, which cannot otherwise exist. You will find in *Cinna* examples of these two kinds of connections: I call this the manner with which one action is produced by another. His conspiracy against Auguste is caused necessarily by the love which he has for Émilie, because he wishes to marry her, and because she will not give herself to him except on that condition. Of these two actions one is true, the other is probable, and their connection is necessary. The benevolence of Auguste gives remorse and irresolution to Cinna: this remorse and irresolution are made to appear probable only by this benevolence, and have a connection with it that is probable only because Cinna can remain firm and arrive at his goal, which is to marry Émilie. He consults her in his irresolution: this consultation is only probable, but it is a necessary effect of his love, because if he had broken off the conspiracy without her consent, he would never have arrived at the goal which he had set for himself, and by consequence there is a necessary connection between two probable actions, or, if you prefer, a necessary creation of a probable action by another equally probable one.

[48] The French word is *liaison.* Dryden uses it without translation. It means the continuity of the action. *Liaison des scènes* refers to the device used so that the stage was never empty. At least one person of a scene would remain to be a character in the next. Cf. Dryden's *Essay of Dramatic Poesy,* pp. 53, 58–59.

Before coming to definitions and divisions of probability and necessity, I think again of the actions which compose tragedy, and I find that we can set off three kinds: some follow history; others interpolate history; the third falsify history. The first are true, the second sometimes probable and sometimes necessary, and the last must always be necessary.

When they are true, it is not necessary to take any pains with probability; they have no need of our help. "All that has happened is manifestly possible," says Aristotle, "because if it could not have happened, it would not have happened." [49] That which we interpolate into history, when it is not approved by this authority, has not this prerogative. "We have a natural propensity," this philosopher goes on to say, "to believe that what has not happened could not have happened"; [50] and it is because of this that we invent a need of a probability more exact than is required to make it credible.

To weigh these two passages well, I believe that I am not violating his thought in the least when I dare say in definition of probability, that it is a thing manifestly possible with propriety, and that it is neither manifestly true nor manifestly false. We can make two divisions, the one of general and particular probability, and the other of ordinary and extraordinary.

General probability is that which is possible and can be rightly done by a king, a general of an army, a lover, an ambitious person, and so on. The particular is that which can or ought to be done by Alexander, Caesar, Alcibiades, compatible with what history tells us of their actions. Thus everything that violates history departs from this probability because it is manifestly false; and it is not probable that Caesar, after the battle of Pharsalia, should remain in good favor with Pompey, or Augustus with Antony after that of Actium, even though, to speak in general terms, it is probable that after a great battle in a civil war the heads of the opposing parties would be reconciled to each other, principally because they are both generous.

This manifest falsity, which destroys probability, can even be encountered in plays which are completely invented. We can falsify history because it has no communication with us, but there are circum-

49 ". . . that which has happened is manifestly possible, else it would not have come to pass."—Chap. 9, Bywater, p. 29.
50 ". . . we are not yet sure as to the possibility of that which has not happened. . . ."—Chap. 9, Bywater, p. 29.

stances, times, and places which can convict an author of falsity when he is gross in his violations. If I introduced a king of France or of Spain under an imaginary name, and if I chose for the time of my action a century of history for which we know the true kings of these two countries, the falsity would be apparent; and it would be even more obvious if I were to place Rome two leagues from Paris so that it would be possible to go there and return in the same day. These are the things over which the poet has no right. He can take some license with history, even regarding particular actions, as those of Caesar or Augustus, and attribute to them actions which they have not performed, or have things happen in a way that they did not do them; but he cannot confuse chronology to make Alexander live in the time of Caesar, and even less can he change the location of places, or the names of kingdoms, provinces, cities, mountains and notable rivers. The reason is that these provinces, these mountains, these rivers, are permanent things. What we know of their situation was so at the beginning of the world; we can presume that they have not changed— at least if they have, that history has noted it—and geography teaches us all the ancient and modern names. Thus a man would be ridiculed for imagining that, in the time of Abraham, Paris was at the foot of the Alps, or that the Seine crossed Spain, and for mixing like grotesque things in an invented play. But history is those things which happen and which succeed each other, each only a moment in duration; and many of these moments escape the knowledge of those who write history. Also we cannot show any history which contains all that happened in the places mentioned, nor all that was done by those whose lives it describes. I do not even except the *Commentaries* of Caesar, who wrote his own history and must have known it completely. We know what countries the Rhone and the Seine flowed through before he went among the Gauls; but we do not know very much, and perhaps nothing at all, of the things that happened there before his arrival. Thus we can indeed place there actions which we pretend took place before that time, but not, under the pretext of poetic fiction and remoteness of the times, change there the natural distance of one place from another. This is the system which Barclay has used in his *Argenis*,[51]

[51] The *Argenis* is an allegorical romance written by John Barclay (1582–1621) dealing with the dangers of political intrigue.

in which he names no city or river of Sicily, or of our provinces, except by its true name, even though all the persons which he places on his tapestry, and their actions, are entirely his invention.

Aristotle seems most indulgent on this subject even though he finds "the poet inexcusable who sins against another art than his, as against medicine or astrology." To which I answer, "he is excusable only under this condition, that he arrives thereby at the goal of his own art, at which he cannot arrive otherwise"; also he goes on to say, "that he sins in that case, and it is better not to sin at all." [52] For my own part, if it is necessary to receive this excuse, I would make a distinction between the arts which can be ignored without shame (because the occasions when it is necessary to speak of them in the theatre happen so rarely), those such as medicine and astrology, which I have just named, and the arts without whose complete or partial cognizance the dramatist cannot establish truth in the play, such as geography and chronology. As he does not know how to represent any action without placing it in some place and in some time, it is inexcusable to make his ignorance apparent in the choice of this place and this time.

I will go on to the other division of probability, ordinary and extraordinary: the ordinary is an action which happens often, or at least as often as its opposite; the extraordinary is an action which happens, in truth, less often than its opposite, but does not fail of having its possibility feasible enough so as not to approach either the miraculous or those rare events which serve as material for bloody tragedies, because of the support they have in history and common opinion, and which can offer an example only for those events which they embody, because they are not believable without having this support. Aristotle gives two ideas or general examples of this extraordinary probability: the one of a subtle and adroit man who finds himself deceived by one

[52] "There is, however, within the limits of poetry itself a possibility of two kinds of error, the one directly, the other only accidentally connected with the art. If the poet meant to describe the thing correctly, and failed through lack of power of expression, his art itself is at fault. But if it was through his having meant to describe it in some incorrect way (e.g. to make the horse in movement have both right legs thrown forward) that the technical error (one in a matter of, say, medicine or some other special science, or impossibilities of whatever kind they may be, have got into his description, his error in that case is not in the essentials of the poetic art.

"If, however, the poetic end might have been as well or better attained without sacrifice of technical correctness in such matters, the impossibility is not to be justified, since the description should be, if it can, entirely free from error."—Chap. 25, Bywater, p. 55.

less subtle than he; the other of a weak man who fights against one stronger than he and who gains the victory,[53] which never fails to be well received when the cause of the simpler or the weaker is the more just. It then seems that the justice of heaven has presided at the success, which finds, accordingly, a much easier belief and satisfies the sympathies of the audience, who always take the part of those whose conduct is the better. Thus the victory of the Cid against the Count is found in this extraordinary probability, though it ought not to be true. "It is probable," says our teacher, "that many things may take place against probability"; [54] and since he thus acknowledges that these extraordinary effects happen against probability, I prefer to call them simply believable and to place them under necessity, expecting that they never be used without necessity.

It can be objected that the same philosopher says "that in regard to poetry, the believable impossible ought to be preferred to the incredible possible," [55] and a critic may conclude thereby that I have little reason for requiring the probable, by the definition which I have just made, when it is manifestly possible for it to be believable, since, according to Aristotle, there are impossible things which are believable.

To resolve this difficulty, and to discover the nature of this impossible-believable, which he does not illustrate, I answer that there are things impossible in themselves which, when looked at in another manner, appear easily possible, and by consequence, believable. These are all those cases wherein we falsify history. It is impossible that they could have happened as we represent them, because they happened otherwise and because it is not in the power of God Himself to change anything which has happened; but they appear manifestly possible when they are within general probability, provided that we look at them detached from history, wishing to forget for the time that history has said the opposite from our invention. All that transpires in *Nicomède* is impossible because history tells us that he had his father

---

[53] "Yet in their Peripeties, as also in their simple plots, the poets I mean show wonderful skill in aiming at the kind of effect they desire—a tragic situation that arouses the human feeling in one, like the clever villain (e.g. Sisyphus) deceived, or the brave wrongdoer worsted."—Chap. 18, Bywater, p. 55.

[54] ". . . there is a probability of things happening against probability."—Chap. 25, Bywater, p. 87.

[55] "For the purposes of poetry, a convincing impossibility is preferable to an unconvincing possibility."—Chap. 25, Bywater, p. 87.

killed without seeing him, and that his brothers of the second marriage were hostages in Rome while he seized the kingdom. All that happens in *Héraclius* is not less so, because he was not the son of Maurice, and even though he had long passed for that of Phocas, and was brought up as such by that tyrant, he comes to overwhelm him by force from the shores of Africa, of which he was governor, and which he perhaps never saw. Nevertheless, we do not consider the incidents of these two tragedies unbelievable; and those who know the departure from history disregard the departure and are pleased at these productions, because they have general probability even though they lack the particular.

All that fable tells us of the gods and their metamorphoses is again impossible and is not allowed by common opinion to be believable, but by this old tradition we have been accustomed to hear them spoken. We even have the right to invent on this model and to join incidents equally impossible to those which the ancient errors have lent us. The hearer is not deceived in his expectations when the title of the poem prepares him to see nothing but the impossible; he finds all completely believable; and, granting this first premise that these are the gods and that they take an interest in and have business with humans, by which all is resolved, he has no difficulty in persuading himself of the remainder.

After having attempted to explain what probability is, it is time that I hazarded a definition of necessity, of which Aristotle speaks so much and which alone authorizes us to change history and exempts us from probability. I say then that necessity, as regards poetry, is nothing other than "the need of the poet to arrive at his goal or to make his actors get there." This definition has its foundation in the diverse interpretations of the Greek word ἀναγχαῖν, which does not always signify that which is absolutely necessary, but also sometimes that which is only useful to bring about something.

The goal of the actors is diverse, according to the varying designs which the variety of subjects gives them. A lover has that of possessing his mistress; an ambitious person, that of seizing a crown; a wronged man, of revenging himself; and so on. The things they must do to bring these ends about constitute the necessity which must be preferred to probability, or to speak more justly, which must be added to probability in the connection of the actions and their dependence on each other. I think that I have already explained myself enough on that above; I will say no more.

The goal of the poet is to please according to the rules of his art. To please, he sometimes has need to heighten the splendor of good actions, and to lessen the horror of disastrous ones. These are the necessities of embellishment when he can violate *particular* probability by some alteration in history, but can only rarely dispense with the *general*, and for things which are of the greatest beauty and so brilliant that they dazzle. Above all, he must not push them beyond extraordinary probability because these ornaments which he adds to his invention are not an absolute necessity, and he does better to give them up entirely than to make his poem appear against every sort of probability. To please according to the rules of his art, he has need to confine his action to the unities of time and place; and as that is an absolute and indispensable necessity, he is permitted more for these two articles than for embellishments.

It is so difficult to find in history or in the imagination of men enough of these events, both illustrious and worthy of tragedy, in which the deliberation and the execution can happen in the same place and on the same day without doing a little violence to the common order of things, that I believe this kind of violence cannot be completely damnable, provided it does not extend to the impossible. There are fine subjects where it cannot be avoided, and a scrupulous author would deprive himself of a fine occasion of glory and the public of much satisfaction if, out of fear of seeing himself forced to make something happen more quickly than probability would permit, he did not venture to put them in the theatre. I would give him in that case advice which perhaps he would find salutary: that is, to prefix no specific time to his poem, and no set place in the location of his actors. The imagination of the audience has greater liberty to go along with the action if it is not fixed by these marks, and the audience would not notice the rapidity of the action if not reminded of it, and thus in spite of itself, the audience would not apply its own knowledge. I have always repented having made the King in *Le Cid* say that he wished Rodrigue would wait an hour or two after having defeated the Moors before fighting Don Sanche: I have thus emphasized that the play takes place in twenty-four hours, and this serves only to advertise to the spectators the difficulties I had in reducing the action to that limit. If I had resolved the conflict without designation of the hour, perhaps they would not have noticed.

I do not think that in comedy the poet is free to compress his action under the necessity of reducing it to the Unity of Time. Aristotle desires that all the actions which go on there be made entirely probable,[56] and does not add the phrase, "or necessary," as for tragedy. Moreover, there is a very great difference between the actions of one and those of the other. Those of comedy show ordinary persons [57] and consist only in intrigues of love and in deceits which develop easily in a day, and very often in Plautus and Terence the time of their duration scarcely exceeds that of their representation; but in tragedy, public affairs are ordinarily combined with the particular interests of the illustrious persons who are made to appear; great battles take place, the capture of cities, great perils, revolutions of states; and all this ill befits the speed which the Rule obliges us to give to what passes on the stage.

If you were to ask me where to extend this liberty of a poet to go against truth and against probability by consideration of his need, I would have trouble in giving you a precise answer. I have made it apparent that there are things over which we have no rights; and for those to which this privilege may apply, it must be more or less reserved according to how well or how little known the subjects are. It is much less permissible in *Horace* and in *Pompée*,[58] of whose history no one is ignorant, than in *Rodogune* and in *Nicomède,* whose names few people knew before I put them into the theatre. The sole rule which can be drawn is that all that is added to history, and all that is changed, should be no more incredible than that which is conserved in the same poem. It is thus that we must understand the verse of Horace touching the fabrication of ornament:

Ficta voluptatis causa sint proxima veris,

and cannot, outside of the subject which he treats, carry the significance of those for which some example can be opened in history or

---

[56] "It is only when their plot is already made up of probable incidents that they give it a basis of proper names instead of writing like the old iambic poets about particular persons."—Chap. 9, Bywater, p. 27.

[57] The old commonplace Renaissance distinction between tragedy and comedy. Corneille attacks this idea in his preface to *Don Sanche d'Aragon* (1650), which is a court comedy.   [58] *Le Morte de Pompée* by Corneille (1633-34).

in fable. The same Horace decides the question, in so far as it can be decided, by this other verse with which I finish this discourse:

. . . *Dabiturque licentia sumpta pudenter.*

Let us furnish it then with discretion, but without qualms; and if possible, let us not furnish it at all; it is more worthy not to have need of grace than to receive it.

Thomas Shadwell
1642?-1692

SHADWELL'S ACTIVITIES as a dramatist extended throughout the Restoration. *The Sullen Lovers* (1668) comes at the beginning of his career, and its preface serves to point out two chief influences on Restoration comedy, that of Jonson and that of Molière. Both authors were plundered by the dramatists, but each was altered to fit the spirit of the times. Jonson's Humours were adapted to the court, and Molière's plots to the Restoration taste. The spirit of both men was discarded in favor of the unvarying theme which so delighted Charles and his nobles. At this stage of his career, Shadwell is the purest disciple of Jonson, but later came to modify his use of the Elizabethan's methods to conform more closely to the temper of his own time.

The Sullen Lovers
[1668; excerpts]
PREFACE

READER—The success of this play, as it was much more than it deserved, so was much more than I expected, especially in this very critical age when every man pretends to be a judge and some that never read three plays in their lives and never understood one are as positive in their judgment of plays as if they were all Jonsons. But had I been used with all the severity imaginable, I should patiently have submitted to my fate; not like the rejected authors of our time, who when their plays are damned will strut and huff it out and laugh at the ignorance of the age. Or, like some other of our modern fops, that declare they are resolved to justify their plays with their swords (though perhaps their courage is as little as their wit), such as peep through their loop-holes in the theatre to see who looks grum upon their plays. And if they spy a gentle squire making faces, he, poor soul, must be hectored till he likes 'em, while the more stubborn Bully Rock damns and is safe. Such is their discretion in the choice of their men. Such gentlemen as these I must confess had need pretend they cannot err. These will huff and look big upon the success of an ill play stuffed full of songs and dances (which have that constraint upon 'em too, that they seldom seem to come in willingly); when in such plays the composer and the dancing-master are the best poets, and yet the unmerciful scribbler would rob them of all the honor.

I am so far from valuing myself (as the phrase is) upon this play that perhaps no man is a severer judge of it than myself; yet if anything could have made me proud of it, it would have been the great favor and countenance it received from His Majesty and their Royal Highnesses.

But I could not persuade myself that they were so favorable to the play for the merit of it, but out of a princely generosity to encourage a young beginner that did what he could to please them and that otherwise might have been balked for ever. 'Tis to this I owe the success of the play and am as far from presumption of my own merits in it as one ought to be who receives an alms.

.   .   .

I have in this play, as near as I could, observed the Three Unities, of Time, Place, and Action. The time of the drama does not exceed six hours, the place is in a very narrow compass, and the main action of the play, upon which all the rest depends, is the sullen love betwixt Stanford and Emilia, which kind of love is only proper to their characters. I have here, as often as I could naturally, kept the scenes unbroken, which (though it be not so much practised, or so well understood by the English) yet among the French poets is accounted a great beauty. But after these frivolous excuses, the want of design in the play has been objected against me; which fault (though I may endeavor a little to extenuate) I dare not absolutely deny. I conceive with all submission to better judgments that no man ought to expect such intrigues in the little actions of a comedy as are required in plays of a higher nature, but in plays of Humour, where there are so many characters as there are in this, there is yet less design to be expected, for if after I had formed three or four forward-prating fops in the play, I had made it full of plot and business, at the latter end, where the

turns ought to be many and suddenly following one another, I must
have let fall the Humour, which I thought would be pleasanter than
intrigues could have been without it, and it would have been easier
to me to have made a plot than to hold up the Humour.

Another objection that has been made by some is that there is the
same thing over and over, which I do not apprehend unless they blame
the unity of the action; yet Horace' *De Arte Poetica* says,

> . . . *sit quod vis, simplex dumtaxat, & unum.*[1]

Or whether it be the carrying on of the Humours to the last which the
same author directs me to do.

> *Si quid inexpertum Scenae committis, & audes*
> *Personam formare novam, Servetur ad Imum*
> *Qualis ab incepto processerit, & sibi constet.*[2]

I have endeavored to represent variety of Humours (most of the
persons of the play differing in their characters from one another),
which was the practice of Ben Jonson, whom I think all dramatic poets
ought to imitate, though none are like to come near; he being the only
person that appears to me to have made perfect representations of
human life. Most other authors that I ever read either have wild romantic tales wherein they strain love and honor to that ridiculous
height that it becomes burlesque, or in their lower comedies content
themselves with one or two Humours at most, and those not near so
perfect characters as the admirable Jonson always made, who never
wrote comedy without seven or eight excellent Humours. I never saw
one, except that of Falstaff, that was in my judgment comparable to
any of Jonson's considerable Humours. You will pardon this digression when I tell you he is the man of all the world I most passionately
admire for his excellency in dramatic poetry.

Though I have known some of late so insolent to say that Ben
Jonson wrote his best plays without wit, imagining that all the wit in
plays consisted in bringing two persons upon the stage to break jests
and to bob one another, which they call repartee, not considering that
there is more wit and invention required in finding out good Humour
and matter proper for it than in all their smart repartees. For, in the
writing of a Humour, a man is confined not to swerve from the character, and obliged to say nothing but what is proper to it, but in the

---

[1] Horace, *Ars poetica*, l. 23.   [2] *Ibid.*, ll. 125–27.

plays which have been wrote of late there is no such thing as perfect character, but the two chief persons are most commonly a swearing, drinking, whoring ruffian for a lover and an impudent, ill-bred tom-rig for a mistress, and these are the fine people of the play, and there is that latitude in this, that almost anything is proper for them to say, but their chief subject is bawdy and profaneness, which they call brisk writing. When the most dissolute of men that relish those things well enough in private are choked at 'em in public, and methinks, if there were nothing but the ill manners of it, it should make poets avoid that indecent way of writing.

John Dryden

1631-1700

IN *An Essay of Dramatic Poesy,* Dryden has summed up and passed judgment upon most of the important critical ideas of his time. The essay is presented in the form of a dialogue, with four friends embarked in a barge on the Thames to witness the naval engagement against the Dutch near the mouth of the river. The conversation soon drifts around to poetry. They agree to limit their discussion to the drama, and once agreed on a definition of tragedy, each argues his own point of view.

The first to speak is Crites, who is Sir Robert Howard, Dryden's brotherin-law, who defends the Ancients—the dramatists of Greece and Rome. He is answered by Eugenius, under which name Lord Buckhurst's opinions are represented. Eugenius upholds the honor of the Moderns in general, by pointing out the flaws of the Ancients, but says practically nothing about the plays of his own time. He and Crites agree to disagree, and Lisideius, a disguise for Sir Charles Sedley, maintains that the French have won the bays in the dramatic art, basing most of his argument on Corneille's Three Discourses on Drama. He is answered by Neander (Dryden himself) who upholds the English against all comers.

Dryden, speaking as Neander, makes several extremely interesting points. He goes back to their agreed definition of drama, "A just and lively image of human nature, representing its Passions and Humours, and the changes of fortune to which it is subject, for the delight and instruction of mankind," and analyzes each point, not quite in order, but tellingly and cogently. It soon becomes apparent in reading these arguments that the chief terms of the disagreement result from two conceptions of the word "Nature." The first, which gives Crites and Lisideius their backing, is that Nature teaches restraint, preciseness, that the artist must imitate the generality of Nature, that is to say, he must present aspects which represent the essence or the class of the feature described. Minor variations are not allowed room, for these peculiarities and individual differences are not a part of the eternal truth that the poet must imitate in Nature. The opposite view is supported by Neander, who follows the idea that Nature teaches variety and copiousness. The poet, in this view, must present Nature in all her aspects, her infinite variety on the single pattern. Yet Dryden was too good an observer of the Rules to allow fancy full rein. He was no romantic engendered a century early. He would set limits to fancy, and his limits still remain pretty well within the neoclassical framework. His feeling of dissatisfaction with the strict limits can be found in several places in his criticism; here, with his statement, "Shakespeare was the Homer, or father of our dramatic poets; Jonson was the Virgil, the pattern of elaborate writing; I admire him but I love Shakespeare"; and in his Preface to *Troilus and Cressida* (1679), where he points out that some critics hold Caliban to be intolerable because he is outside of Nature. He calls Caliban an example of the "copiousness of his invention," but concludes that he is not wholly beyond the bounds of credibility. Thus Dryden has introduced an important factor into neoclassic criticism, that of aesthetic enjoyment on the part of the reader or audience. He means by this something quite different from the delight in a moral show, pleasing to the ideologists and sentimentalists alike; he takes an aesthetic joy in the work of art for its own sake. It is in this sense that he says, "I love Shakespeare," who demonstrably broke the rules of proper dramatic writing.

While the great plague of 1665 was raging, Dryden went to Charlton, the seat of the Earl of Berkshire, his father-in-law, where he remained for about eighteen months. While he was there he wrote this essay, *Annus Mirabilis,* and probably *Secret Love; or, The Maiden Queen.* Three editions of the *Essay of Dramatic Poesy* appeared during Dryden's lifetime.

An Essay of Dramatic Poesy
[1668]

Epistle Dedicatory to the Right Honourable
Charles, Lord Buckhurst

My Lord,—As I was lately reviewing my loose papers, amongst the rest I found this Essay, the writing of which, in this rude and indigested manner wherein your Lordship now sees it, served as an amusement to me in the country, when the violence of the last plague [1] had driven me from the town. Seeing then our theatres shut up, I was engaged in these kind of thoughts with the same delight with which men think upon their absent mistresses. I confess I find many things in this Discourse which I do not now approve; my judgment being not a little altered since the writing of it; but whether for the better or the worse, I know not: neither indeed is it much material, in an Essay, where all

---

[1] The Great Plague of 1665. On June 5, 1665, Charles had ordered the theatres closed to prevent the spreading of the contagion. Dryden went to the country house of his father-in-law, the Earl of Berkshire, and while there wrote this essay.

I have said is problematical. For the way of writing plays in verse,[2] which I have seemed to favour, I have, since that time, laid the practice of it aside, till I have more leisure, because I find it troublesome and slow. But I am no way altered from my opinion of it, at least with any reasons which have opposed it. For your Lordship may easily observe, that none are very violent [3] against it, but those who either have not attempted it, or who have succeeded ill in their attempt. It is enough for me to have your Lordship's example for my excuse in that little which I have done in it; and I am sure my adversaries can bring no such arguments against verse, as those with which the fourth act of *Pompey* [4] will furnish me in its defence. Yet, my Lord, you must suffer me a little to complain of you, that you too soon withdraw from us a contentment, of which we expected the continuance, because you gave it us so early. It is a revolt, without occasion, from your party, where your merits had already raised you to the highest commands, and where you have not the excuse of other men, that you have been ill used, and therefore laid down arms. I know no other quarrel you can have to verse, than that which Spurina had to his beauty, when he tore and mangled the features of his face, only because they pleased too well the sight. It was an honour which seemed to wait for you, to lead out a new colony of writers from the mother nation: and upon the first spreading of your ensigns, there had been many in a readiness to have followed so fortunate a leader; if not all, yet the better part of poets:

> pars, indocili melior grege; mollis et exspes
> Inominata perprimat cubilia.

I am almost of opinion, that we should force you to accept of the command, as sometimes the Praetorian bands have compelled their captains to receive the Empire. The Court, which is the best and surest judge of writing, has generally allowed [5] of verse; and in the town it has found favourers of wit and quality. As for your own particular, my Lord, you have yet youth and time enough to give part of

---

[2] By "verse" Dryden means the rhymed heroic couplet.

[3] A dig at his brother-in-law, Sir Robert Howard, the "Crites" of the Essay. Crites makes an extended argument against the use of rhyme in the latter part of this discussion.

[4] Published in 1664, translated in rhymed couplets by "Certain Persons of Honour," from the French of Corneille.

[5] "Allowed," that is, "approved."

them to the divertisement of the public, before you enter into the serious and more unpleasant business of the world. That which the French poet [6] said of the Temple of Love, may be as well applied to the temple of the Muses. The words, as near as I can remember them, were these:

> Le jeune homme a mauvaise grace,
> N'ayant pas adoré dans le Temple d'Amour;
> Il faut qu'il entre; et pour le sage,
> Si ce n'est pas son vrai séjour,
> C'est un gîte sur son passage.

I leave the words to work their effect upon your Lordship in their own language, because no other can so well express the nobleness of the thought; and wish you may be soon called to bear a part in the affairs of the nation, where I know the world expects you, and wonders why you have been so long forgotten; there being no person amongst our young nobility, on whom the eyes of all men are so much bent. But in the meantime your lordship may imitate the course of Nature, who gives us the flower before the fruit: that I may speak to you in the language of the Muses, which I have taken from an excellent poem to the King:

> As Nature, when she fruit designs, thinks fit
> By beauteous blossoms to proceed to it;
> And while she does accomplish all the spring,
> Birds to her secret operations sing.[7]

I confess I have no greater reason, in addressing this Essay to your Lordship, than that it might awaken in you the desire of writing something, in whatever kind it be, which might be an honour to our age and country. And methinks it might have the same effect on you, which Homer tells us the fight of the Greeks and Trojans before the fleet had on the spirit of Achilles; who, though he had resolved not to engage, yet found a martial warmth to steal upon him at the sight of blows, the sound of trumpets, and the cries of fighting men. For my own part, if, in treating of this subject, I sometimes dissent from the opinion of better wits, I declare it is not so much to combat their opinions, as to defend my own, which were first made public.[8] Some-

---

[6] This poet has never been identified.

[7] By Sir William Davenant, Poet Laureate, 1663.

[8] Refers to a controversy between Dryden and Sir Robert Howard. In the dedication to *The Rival Ladies*, 1664, Dryden had proclaimed the superiority of rhyme to blank verse. Howard answered the next year.

times, like a scholar in a fencing-school, I put forth myself, and show my own ill play, on purpose to be better taught. Sometimes I stand desperately to my arms, like the foot [9] when deserted by their horse; [10] not in hope to overcome, but only to yield on more honourable terms. And yet, my Lord, this war of opinions, you well know, has fallen out among the writers of all ages, and sometimes betwixt friends. Only it has been prosecuted by some, like pedants, with violence of words, and managed by others, like gentlemen, with candour and civility. Even Tully [11] had a controversy with his dear Atticus; and in one of his Dialogues, makes him sustain the part of an enemy in philosophy, who, in his letters, is his confidant of state, and made privy to the most weighty affairs of the Roman senate. And the same respect which was paid by Tully to Atticus, we find returned to him afterwards by Cæsar on a like occasion, who, answering his book in praise of Cato, made it not so much his business to condemn Cato, as to praise Cicero.

But that I may decline some part of the encounter with my adversaries, whom I am neither willing to combat, nor well able to resist; I will give your lordship the relation of a dispute betwixt some of our wits on the same subject, in which they did not only speak of plays in verse, but mingled, in the freedom of discourse, some things of the ancient, many of the modern, ways of writing; comparing those with these, and the wits of our nation with those of others: it is true they differed in their opinions, as it is probable they would: neither do I take upon me to reconcile, but to relate them; and that as Tacitus professes of himself, *sine studio partium, aut ira,* without passion or interest; leaving your lordship to decide it in favour of which part you shall judge most reasonable, and withal, to pardon the many errors of

Your Lordship's

Most obedient humble servant,

JOHN DRYDEN

TO THE READER

THE DRIFT of the ensuing Discourse was chiefly to vindicate the honour of our English writers, from the censure of those who unjustly prefer the French before them. This I intimate, lest any should think me so exceedingly vain, as to teach others an art which they understand much better than myself. But if this incorrect Essay, written in the country

---

[9] Infantry.   [10] Cavalry.   [11] Cicero.

44 John Dryden

without the help of books or advice of friends, shall find any acceptance in the world, I promise to myself a better success of the Second Part, wherein I shall more fully treat of the virtues and faults of the English poets, who have written either in this, the epic, or the lyric way.[12]

An Essay of Dramatic Poesy

It was that memorable day,[13] in the first summer of the late war, when our navy engaged the Dutch; a day wherein the two most mighty and best appointed fleets which any age had ever seen, disputed the command of the greater half of the globe, the commerce of nations, and the riches of the universe: while these vast floating bodies, on either side, moved against each other in parallel lines, and our countrymen, under the happy conduct of his Royal Highness, went breaking, by little and little, into the line of the enemies; the noise of the cannon from both navies reached our ears about the City, so that all men being alarmed with it, and in a dreadful suspense of the event, which they knew was then deciding, every one went following the sound as his fancy led him; and leaving the town almost empty, some took towards the park, some cross the river, others down it; all seeking the noise in the depth of silence.

Among the rest, it was the fortune of Eugenius,[14] Crites,[15] Lisideius,[16] and Neander,[17] to be in company together; three of them persons whom their wit and quality have made known to all the town; and whom I have chose to hide under these borrowed names, that they may not suffer by so ill a relation as I am going to make of this discourse.

Taking then a barge, which a servant of Lisideius had provided for them, they made haste to shoot the bridge, and left behind them that great fall of waters which hindered them from hearing what they desired: after which, having disengaged themselves from many vessels which rode at anchor in the Thames, and almost blocked up the passage towards Greenwich, they ordered the watermen to let fall their oars more gently; and then, every one favouring his own curiosity with a strict silence, it was not long ere they perceived the air to break about them like the noise of distant thunder, or of swallows in a chimney:

[12] The Second Part was never written.   [13] June 3, 1665
[14] Eugenius, Lord Buckhurst.
[15] Crites, Sir Robert Howard, Dryden's brother-in-law.
[16] Lisideius, Sir Charles Sedley.   [17] Neander, Dryden himself.

those little undulations of sound, though almost vanishing before they reached them, yet still seeming to retain somewhat of their first horror, which they had betwixt the fleets. After they had attentively listened till such time as the sound by little and little went from them, Eugenius, lifting up his head, and taking notice of it, was the first who congratulated to the rest that happy omen of our Nation's victory: adding, that we had but this to desire in confirmation of it, that we might hear no more of that noise, which was now leaving the English coast. When the rest had concurred in the same opinion, Crites, a person of a sharp judgment, and somewhat too delicate a taste in wit, which the world have mistaken in him for ill-nature, said, smiling to us, that if the concernment of this battle had not been so exceeding great, he could scarce have wished the victory at the price he knew he must pay for it, in being subject to the reading and hearing of so many ill verses as he was sure would be made on that subject. Adding, that no argument could scape some of those eternal rhymers, who watch a battle with more diligence than the ravens and birds of prey; and the worst of them surest to be first in upon the quarry: while the better able, either out of modesty writ not at all, or set that due value upon their poems, as to let them be often desired and long expected. "There are some of those impertinent people of whom you speak," answered Lisideius, "who to my knowledge are already so provided, either way, that they can produce not only a Panegyric upon the victory, but, if need be, a Funeral Elegy on the Duke; wherein, after they have crowned his valour with many laurels, they will at last deplore the odds under which he fell, concluding that his courage deserved a better destiny." All the company smiled at the conceipt of Lisideius; but Crites, more eager than before, began to make particular exceptions against some writers, and said, the public magistrate ought to send betimes to forbid them; and that it concerned the peace and quiet of all honest people, that ill poets should be as well silenced as seditious preachers.[18] "In my opinion," replied Eugenius, "you pursue your point too far; for as to my own particular, I am so great a lover of poesy, that I could wish them all rewarded who attempt but to do well; at least, I would not have them worse used than one of their brethren was by Sylla the

---

[18] Reference is to three recent Acts of Parliament: the Act of Uniformity (1662), the Conventicle Act (1664), and the Five Mile Act (1665), passed in an effort to control religious fanatics and seditionists.

Dictator:—*Quem in concione vidimus* (says Tully), *cum ei libellum malus poeta de populo subjecisset, quod epigramma in eum fecisset tantummodo alternis versibus longiusculis, statim ex iis rebus quas tunc vendebat jubere ei praemium tribui, sub ea conditione ne quid postea scriberet.*" "I could wish with all my heart," replied Crites, "that many whom we know were as bountifully thanked upon the same condition,—that they would never trouble us again. For amongst others, I have a moral apprehension of two poets,[19] whom this victory, with the help of both her wings, will never be able to escape." " 'Tis easy to guess whom you intend," said Lisideius; "and without naming them, I ask you, if one of them does not perpetually pay us with clenches[20] upon words, and a certain clownish kind of railery? if now and then he does not offer at a catachresis[21] or Clevelandism,[22] wresting and torturing a word into another meaning: in fine, if he be not one of those whom the French would call *un mauvais buffon;* one who is so much a well-willer to the satire, that he intends at least to spare no man; and though he cannot strike a blow to hurt any, yet he ought to be punished for the malice of the action, as our witches are justly hanged, because they think themselves to be such; and suffer deservedly for believing they did mischief, because they meant it." "You have described him," said Crites, "so exactly, that I am afraid to come after you with my other extremity of poetry. He is one of those who, having had some advantage of education and converse, knows better than the other what a poet should be, but puts it into practice more unluckily than any man; his style and matter are every where alike: he is the most calm, peaceable writer you ever read: he never disquiets your passions with the least concernment, but still leaves you in as even a temper as he found you; he is a very Leveller in poetry: he creeps along with ten little words in every line,[23] and helps out his numbers with *For to,* and *Unto,* and all the pretty expletives he can find, till he drags them to the end of another line; while the sense is left tired half way behind it: he doubly starves all his verses, first for want of thought,

---

[19] Robert Wild and Richard Flecknoe. Both wrote triumphal and exceedingly bad poems on the victory.   [20] Puns and other word tricks.   [21] A bad metaphor.
[22] Cleveland was one of the metaphysical poets.
[23] Cf. Pope's *Essay on Criticism,* ll. 346–47:
     While expletives their feeble aid do join
     And ten low words oft creep in one dull line.

and then of expression; his poetry neither has wit in it, nor seems to have it; like him in Martial:

Pauper videri Cinna *vult, et est pauper.*

"He affects plainness, to cover his want of imagination: when he writes the serious way, the highest flight of his fancy is some miserable antithesis, or seeming contradiction; and in the comic he is still reaching at some thin conceit, the ghost of a jest, and that too flies before him, never to be caught; these swallows which we see before us on the Thames are the just resemblance of his wit: you may observe how near the water they stoop, how many proffers they make to dip, and yet how seldom they touch it; and when they do, it is but the surface: they skim over it but to catch a gnat, and then mount into the air and leave it."

"Well, gentlemen," said Eugenius, "you may speak your pleasure of these authors; but though I and some few more about the town may give you a peaceable hearing, yet assure yourselves, there are multitudes who would think you malicious and them injured: especially him whom you first described; he is the very Withers [24] of the city: they have bought more editions of his works than would serve to lay under all their pies at the Lord Mayor's Christmas. When his famous poem first came out in the year 1660, I have seen them reading it in the midst of 'Change time; nay so vehement they were at it, that they lost their bargain by the candles' ends; [25] but what will you say if he has been received amongst great persons? I can assure you he is, this day, the envy of one who is lord in the art of quibbling, and who does not take it well that any man should intrude so far into his province." "All I would wish," replied Crites, "is, that they who love his writings, may still admire him, and his fellow poet: *Qui Bavium non odit, etc.,* is curse sufficient." "And farther," added Lisideius, "I believe there is no man who writes well, but would think he had hard measure, if their admirers should praise anything of his: *Nam quos contemnimus, eorum quoque laudes contemnimus.*" "There are so few who write well in this age," says Crites, "that methinks any praises should be welcome; they neither rise to the dignity of the last age, nor to any of

24 George Wither, chiefly known for doggerel.
25 " 'Change time" was bargaining time on the Royal Exchange. In auctions, bidding was allowed until an inch of candle had burned out, and then the commodity was sold to the last bidder.

the Ancients: and we may cry out of the writers of this time, with more reason than Petronius of his, *Pace vestra liceat dixisse, primi omnium eloquentium perdidistis:* you have debauched the true old poetry so far, that Nature, which is the soul of it, is not in any of your writings."

"If your quarrel," said Eugenius, "to those who now write, be grounded only on your reverence to antiquity, there is no man more ready to adore those great Greeks and Romans than I am: but on the other side, I cannot think so contemptibly of the age in which I live, or so dishonourably of my own country, as not to judge we equal the Ancients in most kinds of poesy, and in some surpass them; neither know I any reason why I may not be as zealous for the reputation of our age as we find the Ancients themselves were in reference to those who lived before them. For you hear your Horace saying,

> *Indignor quidquam reprehendi, non quia crasse*
> *Compositum, illepidève putetur, sed quia nuper.*

And after:

> *Si meliora dies, ut vina, poemata reddit,*
> *Scire velim, pretim chartis quotus arroget annus?*

"But I see I am engaging in a wide dispute, where the arguments are not like to reach close on either side; for Poesy is of so large an extent, and so many both of the Ancients and Moderns have done well in all kinds of it, that in citing one against the other, we shall take up more time this evening than each man's occasions will allow him: therefore I would ask Crites to what part of Poesy he would confine his arguments, and whether he would defend the general cause of the Ancients against the Moderns, or oppose any age of the Moderns against this of ours?"

Crites, a little while considering upon this demand, told Eugenius, that if he pleased, he would limit their dispute to Dramatic Poesy; in which he thought it not difficult to prove, either that the Ancients were superior to the Moderns, or the last age of this of ours.

Eugenius was somewhat surprised, when he heard Crites make choice of that subject. "For ought I see," said he, "I have undertaken a harder province than I imagined; for though I never judged the plays of the Greek or Roman poets comparable to ours, yet, on the other side, those we now see acted come short of many which were written in the last age: but my comfort is, if we are overcome, it will be only by our own countrymen: and if we yield to them in this one part of Poesy, we more surpass them in all the other: for in the epic or lyric way, it will be hard for them to show us one such amongst them, as we have many now living, or who lately were: they can produce nothing so courtly writ, or which expresses so much the conversation of a gentleman, as Sir John Suckling; nothing so even, sweet, and flowing as Mr. Waller,[26] nothing so majestic, so correct, as Sir John Denham; nothing so elevated, so copious, and full of spirit as Mr. Cowley; [27] as for the Italian, French, and Spanish plays, I can make it evident, that those who now write surpass them; and that the drama is wholly ours."

All of them were thus far of Eugenius his opinion, that the sweetness of English verse was never understood or practised by our fathers; even Crites himself did not much oppose it; and every one was willing to acknowledge how much our poesy is improved by the happiness of some writers yet living; who first taught us to mould our thoughts into easy and significant words,—to retrench the superfluities of expression,—and to make our rhyme so properly a part of the verse, that it should never mislead the sense, but itself be led and governed by it.

Eugenius was going to continue this discourse, when Lisideius told him that it was necessary, before they proceeded further, to take a standing measure of their controversy; for how was it possible to be decided who writ the best plays, before we know what a play should be? But, this once agreed on by both parties, each might have recourse to it, either to prove his own advantages, or to discover the failings of his adversary.

He had no sooner said this, but all desired the favour of him to give the definition of a play; and they were the more importunate, because neither Aristotle, nor Horace, nor any other, who had writ of that subject, had ever done it.

Lisideius, after some modest denials, at last confessed he had a rude notion of it; indeed, rather a description than a definition; but which served to guide him in his private thoughts, when he was to make a judgment of what others writ: that he conceived a play ought to be, *A just and lively image of human nature, representing its passions and humours, and the changes of fortune to which it is subject, for the delight and instruction of mankind.*

This definition, though Crites raised a logical objection against it—

26 Edmund Waller.   27 Abraham Cowley.

that it was only *genere et fine*,[28] and so not altogether perfect, was yet
well received by the rest; and after they had given order to the watermen to turn their barge, and row softly, that they might take the cool
of the evening in their return, Crites, being desired by the company to
begin, spoke on behalf of the Ancients, in this manner:—

"If confidence presage a victory, Eugenius, in his own opinion, has
already triumphed over the Ancients: nothing seems more easy to him,
than to overcome those whom it is our greatest praise to have imitated
well; for we do not only build upon their foundations, but by their
models. Dramatic Poesy had time enough, reckoning from Thespis
(who first invented it) to Aristophanes, to be born, to grow up, and to
flourish in maturity. It has been observed of arts and sciences, that in
one and the same century they have arrived to great perfection; and
no wonder, since every age has a kind of universal genius, which in-
clines those that live in it to some particular studies: the work then,
being pushed on by many hands, must of necessity go forward.

"Is it not evident, in these last hundred years, when the study of
philosophy [29] has been the business of all the Virtuosi in Christendom,
that almost a new Nature has been revealed to us? That more errors
of the school have been detected, more useful experiments in philosophy have been made, more noble secrets in optics, medicine, anat-
omy, astronomy discovered, than in all those credulous and doting ages
from Aristotle to us?—so true it is, that nothing spreads more fast than
science, when rightly and generally cultivated.

"Add to this, the more than common emulation that was in those
times of writing well; which though it be found in all ages and all
persons that pretend to the same reputation, yet Poesy, being then in
more esteem than now it is, had greater honours decreed to the professors of it, and consequently the rivalship was more high between
them; they had judges ordained to decide their merit, and prizes to
reward it; and historians have been diligent to record of Æschylus,
Euripides, Sophocles, Lycophron, and the rest of them, both who they
were that vanquished in these wars of the theatre, and how often they
were crowned: while the Asian kings and Grecian commonwealths
scarce afforded them a nobler subject than the unmanly luxuries of a

28 The definition has the class (*genere*) and end or purpose (*fine*), but not the differen-
tiation (*differentia*) which would distinguish it from other forms of writing.
29 Natural philosophy or science. The reference is to The Royal Society.

debauched court, or giddy intrigues of a factious city:—*Alit æmulatio ingenia* (says Paterculus), *et nunc invidia, nunc admiratio incitationem accendit:* Emulation is the spur of wit; and sometimes envy, sometimes admiration, quickens our endeavours.

"But now, since the rewards of honour are taken away, that virtuous emulation is turned into direct malice; yet so slothful, that it contents itself to condemn and cry down others, without attempting to do better: it is a reputation too unprofitable, to take the necessary pains for it; yet, wishing they had it, that desire is incitement enough to hinder others from it. And this, in short, Eugenius, is the reason why you have now so few good poets, and so many severe judges. Certainly, to imitate the Ancients well, much labour and long study is required; which pains, I have already shown, our poets would want encouragement to take, if yet they had ability to go through the work. Those Ancients have been faithful imitators and wise observers of that Nature which is so torn and ill represented in our plays; they have handed down to us a perfect resemblance of her; which we, like ill copiers, neglecting to look on, have rendered monstrous, and disfigured. But, that you may know how much you are indebted to those your masters, and be ashamed to have so ill requited them, I must remember you, that all the rules by which we practise the Drama at this day (either such as relate to the justness and symmetry of the plot, or the episodical ornaments, such as descriptions, narrations, and other beauties, which are not essential to the play), were delivered to us from the observations which Aristotle made, of those poets, who either lived before him, or were his contemporaries: we have added nothing of our own, except we have the confidence to say our wit is better; of which, none boast in this our age, but such as understand not theirs. Of that book which Aristotle has left us, περὶ τῆς Ποιητικῆς, Horace his *Art of Poetry* is an excellent comment, and, I believe, restores to us that Second Book of his concerning *Comedy,* which is wanting in him.

"Out of these two have been extracted the famous Rules, which the French call *Des Trois Unités,* or, The Three Unities, which ought to be observed in every regular play; namely, of Time, Place, and Action.

"The Unity of Time they comprehend in twenty-four hours, the compass of a natural day, or as near as it can be contrived; and the reason of it is obvious to every one,—that the time of the feigned action, or fable of the play, should be proportioned as near as can be to the duration of that time in which it is represented: since, therefore, all plays are acted on the theatre in the space of time much within the compass of twenty-four hours, that play is to be thought the nearest imitation of nature, whose plot or action is confined within that time; and, by the same rule which concludes this general proportion of time, it follows, that all the parts of it are (as near as may be) to be equally subdivided; namely, that one act take not up the supposed time of half a day, which is out of proportion to the rest; since the other four are then to be straitened within the compass of the remaining half: for it is unnatural that one act, which being spoke or written is not longer than the rest, should be supposed longer by the audience; it is therefore the poet's duty, to take care that no act should be imagined to exceed the time in which it is represented on the stage; and that the intervals and inequalities of time be supposed to fall out between the acts.

"This Rule of Time, how well it has been observed by the Ancients, most of their plays will witness; you see them in their tragedies (wherein to follow this rule is certainly most difficult), from the very beginning of their plays, falling close into that part of the story which they intend for the action or principal object of it, leaving the former part to be delivered by narration: so that they set the audience, as it were, at the post where the race is to be concluded; and, saving them the tedious expectation of seeing the poet set out and ride the beginning of the course, they suffer you not to behold him, till he is in sight of the goal, and just upon you.

"For the second Unity, which is that of Place, the Ancients meant by it, that the scene ought to be continued through the play, in the same place where it was laid in the beginning: for, the stage on which it is represented being but one and the same place, it is unnatural to conceive it many,—and those far distant from one another. I will not deny but, by the variation of painted scenes, the fancy, which in these cases will contribute to its own deceit, may sometimes imagine it several places, with some appearance of probability; yet it still carries the greater likelihood of truth if those places be supposed so near each other as in the same town or city; which may all be comprehended under the larger denomination of one place; for a greater distance will bear no proportion to the shortness of time which is allotted, in the acting, to pass from one of them to another; for the observation of this, next to the Ancients, the French are to be most commended. They tie themselves so strictly to the Unity of Place that you never see in any of their plays a scene changed in the middle of an act: if the act begins in a garden, a street, or chamber, 'tis ended in the same place; and that you may know it to be the same, the stage is so supplied with persons, that it is never empty all the time: he who enters second, has business with him who was on before; and before the second quits the stage, a third appears who has business with him. This Corneille calls *la liaison des scènes*, the continuity or joining of the scenes; and 'tis a good mark of a well-contrived play, when all the persons are known to each other, and every one of them has some affairs with all the rest.

"As for the third Unity, which is that of Action, the Ancients meant no other by it than what the logicians do by their *finis*, the end or scope of any action; that which is the first in intention, and last in execution: now the poet is to aim at one great and complete action, to the carrying on of which all things in his play, even the very obstacles, are to be subservient; and the reason of this is as evident as any of the former. For two actions, equally laboured and driven on by the writer, would destroy the unity of the poem; it would be no longer one play, but two: not but that there may be many actions in a play, as Ben Jonson has observed in his *Discoveries*,[30] but they must be all subservient to the great one, which our language happily expresses in the name of *under-plots:* such as in Terence's *Eunuch* is the difference and reconcilement of Thais and Phædria, which is not the chief business of the play, but promotes the marriage of Chærea and Chremes's sister, principally intended by the poet. There ought to be but one action, says Corneille,[31] that is, one complete action, which leaves the mind of the audience in a full repose; but this cannot be brought to pass but by many other imperfect actions, which conduce to it, and hold the audience in a delightful suspense of what will be.

"If by these rules (to omit many others drawn from the precepts and practice of the Ancients) we should judge our modern plays, 'tis probable that few of them would endure the trial: that which should be the business of a day, takes up in some of them an age; instead of one action, they are the epitomes of a man's life; and for one spot of ground, which the stage should represent, we are sometimes in more countries than the map can show us.

[30] Printed in 1641.   [31] From Corneille's *Troisième Discours sur les unités*.

"But if we allow the Ancients to have contrived well, we must acknowledge them to have written better. Questionless we are deprived of a great stock of wit in the loss of Menander among the Greek poets, and of Cæcilius, Afranius, and Varius, among the Romans; we may guess at Menander's excellency by the plays of Terence, who translated some of his; and yet wanted so much of him, that he was called by C. Cæsar the half-Menander; and may judge of Varius, by the testimonies of Horace, Martial, and Velleius Paterculus. 'Tis probable that these, could they be recovered, would decide the controversy; but so long as Aristophanes and Plautus are extant, while the tragedies of Euripides, Sophocles, and Seneca, are in our hands, I can never see one of those plays which are now written but it increases my admiration of the Ancients. And yet I must acknowledge further, that to admire them as we ought, we should understand them better than we do. Doubtless many things appear flat to us, the wit of which depended on some custom or story, which never came to our knowledge; or perhaps on some criticism in their language, which being so long dead, and only remaining in their books, 'tis not possible they should make us understand perfectly. To read Macrobius, explaining the propriety and elegancy of many words in Virgil, which I had before passed over without consideration as common things, is enough to assure me that I ought to think the same of Terence; and that in the purity of his style (which Tully so much valued that he ever carried his works about him) there is yet left in him great room for admiration, if I knew but where to place it. In the meantime I must desire you to take notice that the greatest man of the last age, Ben Jonson, was willing to give place to them in all things: he was not only a professed imitator of Horace, but a learned plagiary of all the others; you track him everywhere in their snow: if Horace, Lucan, Petronius Arbiter, Seneca, and Juvenal, had their own from him, there are few serious thoughts which are new in him: you will pardon me, therefore, if I presume he loved their fashion, when he wore their clothes. But since I have otherwise a great veneration for him, and you, Eugenius, prefer him above all other poets, I will use no farther argument to you than his example: I will produce before you Father Ben, dressed in all the ornaments and colours of the Ancients; you will need no other guide to our party, if you follow him; and whether you consider the bad plays of our age, or regard the good plays of the last, both the best and worst of the modern poets will equally instruct you to admire the Ancients."

Crites had no sooner left speaking, but Eugenius, who had waited with some impatience for it, thus began:

"I have observed in your speech, that the former part of it is convincing as to what the Moderns have profited by the rules of the Ancients; but in the latter you are careful to conceal how much they have excelled them; we own all the helps we have from them, and want neither veneration nor gratitude, while we acknowledge that, to overcome them, we must make use of the advantages we have received from them: but to these assistances we have joined our own industry; for, had we sat down with a dull imitation of them, we might then have lost somewhat of the old perfection, but never acquired any that was new. We draw not therefore after their lines, but those of Nature; and having the life before us, besides the experience of all they knew, it is no wonder if we hit some airs and features which they have missed. I deny not what you urge of arts and sciences, that they have flourished in some ages more than others; but your instance in philosophy makes for me: for if natural causes be more known now than in the time of Aristotle, because more studied, it follows that poesy and other arts may, with the same pains, arrive still nearer to perfection; and, that granted, it will rest for you to prove that they wrought more perfect images of human life than we; which seeing in your discourse you have avoided to make good, it shall now be my task to show you some part of their defects, and some few excellencies of the Moderns. And I think there is none among us can imagine I do it enviously, or with purpose to detract from them; for what interest of fame or profit can the living lose by the reputation of the dead? On the other side, it is a great truth which Velleius Paterculus affirms: *Audita visis libentius laudamus; et præsentia invidia, præterita admiratione prosequimur; et his nos obrui, illis instrui credimus:* that praise or censure is certainly the most sincere, which unbribed posterity shall give us.

"Be pleased then in the first place to take notice that the Greek poesy, which Crites has affirmed to have arrived to perfection in the reign of the Old Comedy,[32] was so far from it that the distinction of it into acts was not known to them; or if it were, it is yet so darkly delivered to us that we cannot make it out.

[32] The type of comedy written by Aristophanes, as distinguished from the New Comedy of Menander. Both kinds are later described in the Essay.

"All we know of it is from the singing of their Chorus; and that too is so uncertain, that in some of their plays we have reason to conjecture they sung more than five times. Aristotle indeed divides the integral parts of a play into four.[33] First, the *Protasis*, or entrance, which gives light only to the characters of the persons, and proceeds very little into any part of the action. Secondly, the *Epitasis*, or working up of the plot; where the play grows warmer, the design or action of it is drawing on, and you see something promising that it will come to pass. Thirdly, the *Catastasis*, called by the Romans, *Status*, the height and full growth of the play: we may call it properly the counter-turn, which destroys that expectation, imbroils the action in new difficulties, and leaves you far distant from that hope in which it found you; as you may have observed in a violent stream resisted by a narrow passage, —it runs round to an eddy, and carries back the waters with more swiftness than it brought them on. Lastly, the *Catastrophe*, which the Grecians called λύσις, the French *le dénouement*, and we the discovery, or unravelling of the plot: there you see all things settling again upon their first foundations; and, the obstacles which hindered the design or action of the play once removed, it ends with that resemblance of Truth and Nature, that the audience are satisfied with the conduct of it. Thus this great man delivered to us the image of a play; and I must confess it is so lively, that from thence much light has been derived to the forming it more perfectly into acts and scenes: but what poet first limited to five the number of the acts, I know not; only we see it so firmly established in the time of Horace, that he gives it for a rule in comedy,—*Neu brevior quinto, neu sit productior actu*. So that you see the Grecians cannot be said to have consummated this art; writing rather by entrances than by acts, and having rather a general indigested notion of a play, than knowing how and where to bestow the particular graces of it.

"But since the Spaniards at this day allow but three acts, which they call *Jornadas*, to a play, and the Italians in many of theirs follow them, when I condemn the Ancients, I declare it is not altogether because they have not five acts to every play, but because they have not confined themselves to one certain number: it is building an house without a model; and when they succeeded in such undertakings, they ought to have sacrificed to Fortune, not to the Muses.

---

[33] Actually this division was made by the Renaissance critic, Julius Caesar Scaliger.

"Next, for the plot, which Aristotle called ὁ μῦθος , and often τῶν πραγμάτων σύνθεσις, and from him the Romans *Fabula;* it has already been judiciously observed by a late writer,[34] that in their tragedies it was only some tale derived from Thebes or Troy, or at least something that happened in those two ages; which was worn so threadbare by the pens of all the epic poets, and even by tradition, itself of the talkative Greeklings (as Ben Jonson calls them), that before it came upon the stage it was already known to all the audience: and the people, so soon as ever they heard the name of Œdipus, knew as well as the poet, that he had killed his father by a mistake, and committed incest with his mother, before the play; that they were now to hear of a great plague, an oracle, and the ghost of Laius: so that they sat with a yawning kind of expectation, till he was to come with his eyes pulled out, and speak a hundred or more verses in a tragic tone, in complaint of his misfortunes. But one Œdipus, Hercules, or Medea, had been tolerable: poor people, they escaped not so good cheap; they had still the *chapon bouillé* set before them, till their appetites were cloyed with the same dish, and, the novelty being gone, the pleasure vanished; so that one main end of Dramatic Poesy in its definition, which was to cause delight, was of consequence destroyed.

"In their comedies, the Romans generally borrowed their plots from the Greek poets; and theirs was commonly a little girl stolen or wandered from her parents, brought back unknown to the city, there got with child by some lewd fellow, who, by the help of his servant, cheats his father; and when her time comes, to cry—*Juno Lucina, fer opem*—one or other sees a little box or cabinet which was carried away with her, and so discovers her to her friends, if some god do not prevent it, by coming down in a machine, and taking the thanks of it to himself.

"By the plot you may guess much of the characters of the persons. An old father, who would willingly, before he dies, see his son well married; his debauched son, kind in his nature to his mistress, but miserably in want of money; a servant or slave, who has so much wit to strike in with him, and help to dupe his father; a braggadocio captain, a parasite, and a lady of pleasure.

"As for the poor honest maid, on whom the story is built, and who ought to be one of the principal actors in the play, she is commonly a

34 Sir Robert Howard, or Ménage.

mute in it: she has the breeding of the old Elizabeth way, which was for maids to be seen and not to be heard; and it is enough you know she is willing to be married, when the fifth act requires it.

"These are plots built after the Italian mode of houses,—you see through them all at once: the characters are indeed the imitation of Nature, but so narrow, as if they had imitated only an eye or an hand, and did not dare to venture on the lines of a face, or the proportion of a body.

"But in how strait a compass soever they have bounded their plots and characters, we will pass it by, if they have regularly pursued them, and perfectly observed those three Unities of Time, Place, and Action; the knowledge of which you say is derived to us from them. But in the first place give me leave to tell you, that the Unity of Place, however it might be practised by them, was never any of their rules: we neither find it in Aristotle, Horace, or any who have written of it, till in our age the French poets first made it a precept of the stage. The Unity of Time, even Terence himself, who was the best and most regular of them, has neglected: his *Heautontimorumenos,* or *Self-Punisher,* takes up visibly two days, says Scaliger; the two first acts concluding the first day, the three last the day ensuing; and Euripides, in tying himself to one day, has committed an absurdity never to be forgiven him; for in one of his tragedies [35] he has made Theseus go from Athens to Thebes, which was about forty English miles, under the walls of it to give battle, and appear victorious in the next act; and yet, from the time of his departure to the return of the Nuntius, who gives the relation of his victory, Æthra and the Chorus have but thirty-six verses; which is not for every mile a verse.

"The like error is as evident in Terence his *Eunuch,* when Laches, the old man, enters by mistake into the house of Thais; where, betwixt his exit and the entrance of Pythias, who comes to give ample relation of the disorders he has raised within, Parmeno, who was left upon the stage, has not above five lines to speak. *C'est bien employer un temps si court,* says the French poet,[36] who furnished me with one of the observations: and almost all their tragedies will afford us examples of the like nature.

"It is true, they have kept the continuity, or, as you called it, *liaison des scènes,* somewhat better: two do not perpetually come in together,

[35] *The Suppliants.*   [36] Corneille.

talk, and go out together; and other two succeed them, and do the same throughout the act, which the English call by the name of single scenes; but the reason is, because they have seldom above two or three scenes, properly so called, in every act; for it is to be accounted a new scene, not only every time the stage is empty; but every person who enters, though to others, makes it so; because he introduces a new business. Now the plots of their plays being narrow, and the persons few, one of their acts was written in a less compass than one of our well-wrought scenes; and yet they are often deficient even in this. To go no further than Terence; you find in the *Eunuch*, Antipho entering single in the midst of the third act, after Chremes and Pythias were gone off; in the same play you have likewise Dorias beginning the fourth act alone; and after she had made a relation of what was done at the Soldiers' entertainment (which by the way was very inartificial, because she was presumed to speak directly to the audience, and to acquaint them with what was necessary to be known, but yet should have been so contrived by the poet as to have been told by persons of the drama to one another, and so by them to have come to the knowledge of the people), she quits the stage, and Phædria enters next, alone likewise: he also gives you an account of himself, and of his returning from the country, in monologue; to which unnatural way of narration Terence is subject in all his plays. In his *Adelphi*, or *Brothers*, Syrus and Demea enter after the scene was broken by the departure of Sostrata, Geta, and Canthara; and indeed you can scarce look unto any of his comedies, where you will not presently discover the same interruption.

"But as they have failed both in laying of their plots, and in the management, swerving from the rules of their own art by misrepresenting Nature to us, in which they have ill satisfied one intention of a play, which was delight; so in the instructive part they have erred worse: instead of punishing vice and rewarding virtue, they have often shewn a prosperous wickedness, and an unhappy piety: they have set before us a bloody image of revenge in Medea, and given her dragons to convey her safe from punishment; a Priam and Astyanax murdered, and Cassandra ravished, and the lust and murder ending in the victory of him who acted them: in short, there is no indecorum in any of our modern plays, which if I would excuse, I could not shadow with some authority from the Ancients.

"And one farther note of them let me leave you: tragedies and comedies were not writ then as they are now, promiscuously, by the same person; but he who found his genius bending to the one, never attempted the other way. This is so plain, that I need not instance to you, that Aristophanes, Plautus, Terence, never any of them writ a tragedy; Æschylus, Euripides, Sophocles, and Seneca, never meddled with comedy: the sock and buskin were not worn by the same poet. Having then so much care to excel in one kind, very little is to be pardoned them, if they miscarried in it; and this would lead me to the consideration of their wit, had not Crites given me sufficient warning not to be too bold in my judgment of it; because, the languages being dead, and many of the customs and little accidents on which it depended lost to us, we are not competent judges of it. But though I grant that here and there we may miss the application of a proverb or a custom, yet a thing well said will be wit in all languages; and though it may lose something in the translation, yet to him who reads it in the original, 'tis still the same: he has an idea of its excellency, though it cannot pass from his mind into any other expression or words than those in which he finds it. When Phædria, in the *Eunuch*, had a command from his mistress to be absent two days, and, encouraging himself to go through with it, said, *Tandem ego non illa caream, si sit opus, vel totum triduum?*—Parmeno, to mock the softness of his master, lifting up his hands and eyes, cries out, as it were in admiration, *Hui! universum triduum!* the elegancy of which *universum*, though it cannot be rendered in our language, yet leaves an impression on our souls: but this happens seldom in him; in Plautus oftener, who is infinitely too bold in his metaphors and coining words, out of which many times his wit is nothing; which questionless was one reason why Horace falls upon him so severely in those verses:

> Sed proavi nostri Plautinos et numeros et
> Laudavere sales, nimium patienter utrumque.
> Ne dicam stolidè.

For Horace himself was cautious to obtrude a new word on his readers, and makes custom and common use the best measure of receiving it into our writings:

> Multa renascentur quæ nunc [jam] cecidere, cadentq[ue]
> Quæ nunc sunt in honore vocabula, si volet usus,
> Quem penes arbitrium est, et jus, et norma loquendi.

"The not observing this rule is that which the world has blamed in our satirist, Cleveland: to express a thing hard and unnaturally, is his new way of elocution. 'Tis true, no poet but may sometimes use a catachresis: Virgil does it—

> Mistaque ridenti colocasia fundet acantho—

in his eclogue of Pollio; and in his seventh Æneid:

> mirantur et undæ,
> Miratur nemus insuetum fulgentia longe
> Scuta virum fluvio pictasque innare carinas.

And Ovid once so modestly, that he asks leave to do it:

> quem, si verbo audacia detur,
> Haud metuam summi dixisse Palatia cæli.

calling the court of Jupiter by the name of Augustus his palace; though in another place he is more bold, where he says,—et longas visent Capitolia pompas. But to do this always, and never be able to write a line without it, though it may be admired by some few pedants, will not pass upon those who know that wit is best conveyed to us in the most easy language; and is most to be admired when a great thought comes dressed in words so commonly received, that it is understood by the meanest apprehensions, as the best meat is the most easily digested: but we cannot read a verse of Cleveland's without making a face at it, as if every word were a pill to swallow: he gives us many times a hard nut to break our teeth, without a kernel for our pains. So that there is this difference betwixt his Satires and Doctor Donne's; that the one gives us deep thoughts in common language, though rough cadence; the other gives us common thoughts in abstruse words: 'tis true, in some places his wit is independent of his words, as in that of the rebel Scot:

> Had Cain been Scot, God would have chang'd his doom;
> Not forc'd him wander, but confin'd him home.[37]

"Si sic omnia dixisset! This is wit in all languages: it is like Mercury, never to be lost or killed:—and so that other—

> For beauty, like white powder, makes no noise,
> And yet the silent hypocrite destroys.[38]

[37] Cleveland's The Rebel Scot, ll. 63–64.
[38] Cleveland's Rupertismus, ll. 39–40.

You see the last line is highly metaphorical, but it is so soft and gentle, that it does not shock us as we read it.

"But, to return from whence I have digressed, to the consideration of the Ancients' writing, and their wit (of which by this time you will grant us in some measure to be fit judges). Though I see many excellent thoughts in Seneca, yet he of them who had a genius most proper for the stage, was Ovid; he had a way of writing so fit to stir up a pleasing admiration and concernment, which are the objects of a tragedy, and to show the various movements of a soul combating betwixt two different passions, that, had he lived in our age, or in his own could have writ with our advantages, no man but must have yielded to him; and therefore I am confident the *Medea* is none of his: for, though I esteem it for the gravity and sententiousness of it, which he himself concludes to be suitable to a tragedy,—*Omne genus scripti gravitate tragædia vincit,*—yet it moves not my soul enough to judge that he, who in the epic way wrote things so near the drama as the story of Myrrha, of Caunus and Biblis, and the rest, should stir up no more concernment where he most endeavoured it. The masterpiece of Seneca I hold to be that scene in the *Troades,* where Ulysses is seeking for Astyanax to kill him: there you see the tenderness of a mother so represented in Andromache, that it raises compassion to a high degree in the reader, and bears the nearest resemblance of anything in the tragedies of the Ancients to the excellent scenes of passion in Shakespeare, or in Fletcher: for love-scenes, you will find few among them; their tragic poets dealt not with that soft passion, but with lust, cruelty, revenge, ambition, and those bloody actions they produced; which were more capable of raising horror than compassion in an audience: leaving love untouched, whose gentleness would have tempered them; which is the most frequent of all the passions, and which, being the private concernment of every person, is soothed by viewing its own image in a public entertainment.

"Among their comedies, we find a scene or two of tenderness, and that where you would least expect it, in Plautus; but to speak generally, their lovers say little, when they see each other, but *anima mea, vita mea;* Ζωὴ καὶ ψυχῆ, as the women in Juvenal's time used to cry out in the fury of their kindness. Any sudden gust of passion (as an ecstasy of love in an unexpected meeting) cannot better be expressed than in a word and a sigh, breaking one another. Nature is dumb on such occasions; and to make her speak would be to represent her un-like herself. But there are a thousand other concernments of lovers, as jealousies, complaints, contrivances, and the like, where not to open their minds at large to each other, were to be wanting to their own love, and to the expectation of the audience; who watch the move-ments of their minds, as much as the changes of their fortunes. For the imaging of the first is properly the work of a poet; the latter he borrows from the historian."

Eugenius was proceeding in that part of his discourse, when Crites interrupted him. "I see," said he, "Eugenius and I are never like to have this question decided betwixt us; for he maintains, the Moderns have acquired a new perfection in writing; I can only grant they have altered the mode of it. Homer described his heroes men of great ap-petites, lovers of beef broiled upon the coals, and good fellows; con-trary to the practice of the French Romances, whose heroes neither eat, nor drink, nor sleep, for love. Virgil makes Æneas a bold avower of his own virtues:

Sum pius Æneas, fama super æthera notus;

which, in the civility of our poets is the character of a fanfaron [39] or Hector: for with us the knight takes occasion to walk out, or sleep, to avoid the vanity of telling his own story, which the trusty 'squire is ever to perform for him. So in their love-scenes, of which Eugenius spoke last, the Ancients were more hearty, were more talkative: they writ love as it was then the mode to make it; and I will grant thus much to Eugenius, that perhaps one of their poets had he lived in our age, *si foret hoc nostrum fato delapsus in ævum* (as Horace says of Lucilius), he had altered many things; not that they were not natural before, but that he might accommodate himself to the age in which he lived. Yet in the meantime, we are not to conclude anything rashly against those great men, but preserve to them the dignity of masters, and give that honour to their memories, *quos Libitina sacravit,* part of which we expect may be paid to us in future times."

This moderation of Crites, as it was pleasing to all the company, so it put an end to that dispute; which Eugenius, who seemed to have the better of the argument, would urge no farther: but Lisideius, after he had acknowledged himself of Eugenius his opinion concerning the

39 A braggart. Hector had come to mean a swaggering bully.

Ancients, yet told him, he had forborne, till his discourse were ended, to ask him why he preferred the English plays above those of other nations? and whether we ought not to submit our stage to the exactness of our next neighbours?

"Though," said Eugenius, "I am at all times ready to defend the honour of my country against the French, and to maintain, we are as well able to vanquish them with our pens, as our ancestors have been with their swords; yet, if you please," added he, looking upon Neander, "I will commit this cause to my friend's management; his opinion of our plays is the same with mine, and besides, there is no reason, that Crites and I, who have now left the stage, should re-enter so suddenly upon it; which is against the laws of comedy."

"If the question had been stated," replied Lisideius, "who had writ best, the French or English, forty years ago, I should have been of your opinion, and adjudged the honour to our own nation; but since that time" (said he, turning towards Neander), "we have been so long together bad Englishmen [40] that we had not leisure to be good poets. Beaumont, Fletcher, and Jonson (who were only capable of bringing us to that degree of perfection which we have), were just then leaving the world; as if in an age of so much horror, wit, and those milder studies of humanity, had no farther business among us. But the Muses, who ever follow peace, went to plant in another country: it was then that the great Cardinal Richelieu began to take them into his protection; and that, by his encouragement, Corneille, and some other Frenchmen, reformed their theatre (which before was as much below ours, as it now surpasses it and the rest of Europe). But because Crites in his discourse for the Ancients has prevented me, by observing many rules of the stage which the Moderns have borrowed from them, I shall only, in short, demand of you, whether you are not convinced that of all nations the French have best observed them? In the Unity of Time you find them so scrupulous that it yet remains a dispute among their poets, whether the artificial day of twelve hours, more or less, be not meant by Aristotle, rather than the natural one of twenty-four; and consequently, whether all plays ought not to be reduced into that compass. This I can testify, that in all their dramas writ within these last twenty years and upwards, I have not observed any that have extended the time to thirty hours: in the Unity of Place they are full as

[40] An allusion to the period of the Commonwealth.

scrupulous; for many of their critics limit it to that very spot of ground where the play is supposed to begin; none of them exceed the compass of the same town or city. The Unity of Action in all plays is yet more conspicuous; for they do not burden them with under-plots, as the English do: [41] which is the reason why many scenes of our tragi-comedians carry on a design that is nothing of kin to the main plot; and that we see two distinct webs in a play, like those in ill-wrought stuffs; and two actions, that is, two plays, carried on together, to the confounding of the audience; who, before they are warm in their concernments for one part, are diverted to another; and by that means espouse the interest of neither. From hence likewise it arises that the one half of our actors are not known to the other. They keep their distances, as if they were Montagues and Capulets, and seldom begin an acquaintance till the last scene of the fifth act, when they are all to meet upon the stage. There is no theatre in the world has anything so absurd as the English tragi-comedy; 'tis a drama of our own invention, and the fashion of it is enough to proclaim it so; here a course of mirth, there another of sadness and passion, and a third of honour and a duel: thus, in two hours and a half, we run through all the fits of Bedlam. The French affords you as much variety on the same day, but they do it not so unseasonably, or *mal à propos,* as we: our poets present you the play and the farce together; and our stages still retain somewhat of the original civility of the Red Bull: [42]

> *Atque ursum et pugiles media inter carmina poscunt.*

The end of tragedies or serious plays, says Aristotle, is to beget admiration, compassion, or concernment; but are not mirth and compassion things incompatible? and is it not evident that the poet must of necessity destroy the former by intermingling of the latter? that is, he must ruin the sole end and object of his tragedy, to introduce somewhat that is forced into it, and is not of the body of it. Would you not think that physician mad, who, having prescribed a purge, should immediately order you to take restringents?

"But to leave our plays, and return to theirs. I have noted one great advantage they have had in the plotting of their tragedies; that is, they are always grounded upon some known history: according to

---

[41] This practice is particularly noticeable in Fletcher and in many other writers between 1600 and 1642.

[42] A popular playhouse built about 1606 and demolished after the Restoration.

that of Horace, *Ex noto fictum carmen sequar;* and in that they have so imitated the Ancients that they have surpassed them. For the Ancients, as was observed before, took for the foundation of their plays some poetical fiction, such as under that consideration could move but little concernment in the audience, because they already knew the event of it. But the French goes farther:

> *Atque ita mentitur, sic veris falsa remiscet*
> *Primo ne medium, medio ne discrepet imum.*

He so interweaves truth with probable fiction that he puts a pleasing fallacy upon us; mends the intrigues of fate, and dispenses with the severity of history, to reward that virtue which has been rendered to us there unfortunate. Sometimes the story has left the success so doubtful that the writer is free, by the privilege of a poet, to take that which of two or more relations will best suit with his design: as for example, in the death of Cyrus, whom Justin and some others report to have perished in the Scythian war, but Xenophon affirms to have died in his bed of extreme old age. Nay more, when the event is past dispute, even then we are willing to be deceived, and the poet, if he contrives it with appearance of truth, has all the audience of his party; at least during the time his play is acting: so naturally we are kind to virtue, when our own interest is not in question, that we take it up as the general concernment of mankind. On the other side, if you consider the historical plays of Shakespeare, they are rather so many chronicles of kings, or the business many times of thirty or forty years, cramped into a representation of two hours and a half; which is not to imitate or paint Nature, but rather to draw her in miniature, to take her in little; to look upon her through the wrong end of a perspective, and receive her images not only much less, but infinitely more imperfect than the life: this, instead of making a play delightful, renders it ridiculous:—

> *Quodcunque ostendis mihi sic, incredulus odi.*

For the spirit of man cannot be satisfied but with truth, or at least verisimility; and a poem is to contain, if not τὰ ἔτυμα, yet ἐτύμοισιν ὁμοῖα as one of the Greek poets has expressed it.

"Another thing in which the French differ from us and from the Spaniards, is that they do not embarrass, or cumber themselves with too much plot; they only represent so much of a story as will constitute one whole and great action sufficient for a play; we, who undertake more, do but multiply adventures which, not being produced from one another, as effects from causes, but rarely following, constitute many actions in the drama, and consequently make it many plays.

"But by pursuing closely one argument, which is not cloyed with many turns, the French have gained more liberty for verse, in which they write; they have leisure to dwell on a subject which deserves it; and to represent the passions (which we have acknowledged to be the poet's work), without being hurried from one thing to another, as we are in the plays of Calderon, which we have seen lately upon our theatres under the name of Spanish plots. I have taken notice but of one tragedy of ours whose plot has that uniformity and unity of design in it, which I have commended in the French; and that is *Rollo*,[43] or rather, under the name of Rollo, the Story of Bassianus and Geta in Herodian: there indeed the plot is neither large nor intricate, but just enough to fill the minds of the audience, not to cloy them. Besides, you see it founded upon the truth of history,—only the time of the action is not reduceable to the strictness of the Rules; and you see in some places a little farce mingled, which is below the dignity of the other parts, and in this all our poets are extremely peccant: even Ben Jonson himself, in *Sejanus*[44] and *Catiline*,[45] has given us this oleo[46] of a play, this unnatural mixture of comedy and tragedy; which to me sounds just as ridiculously as the history of David with the merry humours of Golia's. In *Sejanus* you may take notice of the scene betwixt Livia and the physician which is a pleasant satire upon the artificial helps of beauty: in *Catiline* you may see the parliament of women; the little envies of them to one another; and all that passes betwixt Curio and Fulvia: scenes admirable in their kind, but of an ill mingle with the rest.

"But I return again to the French writers, who, as I have said, do not burden themselves too much with plot, which has been reproached to them by an ingenious person of our nation as a fault; for, he says, they commonly make but one person considerable in a play; they dwell on him, and his concernments, while the rest of the persons are only subservient to set him off. If he intends this by it,—that there is one person in the play who is of greater dignity than the rest, he must tax, not only

43 *The Bloody Brother; or, Rollo, Duke of Normandy*, a tragedy by Fletcher (and Jonson?), printed in 1639; probably written about 1619.
44 *Sejanus His Fall*, 1603. 45 *Catiline His Conspiracy*, 1611.
46 A mixture or hodgepodge.

John Dryden

theirs, but those of the Ancients, and which he would be loth to do, the best of ours; for it is impossible but that one person must be more conspicuous in it than any other, and consequently the greatest share in the action must devolve on him. We see it so in the management of all affairs; even in the most equal aristocracy, the balance cannot be so justly poised but some one will be superior to the rest, either in parts, fortune, interest, or the consideration of some glorious exploit; which will reduce the greatest part of business into his hands.

"But, if he would have us to imagine, that in exalting one character the rest of them are neglected, and that all of them have not some share or other in the action of the play, I desire him to produce any of Corneille's tragedies, wherein every person, like so many servants in a well-governed family, has not some employment, and who is not necessary to the carrying on of the plot, or at least to your understanding it.

"There are indeed some protatic [47] persons in the Ancients, whom they make use of in their plays, either to hear or give the relation: but the French avoid this with great address, making their narrations only to, or by such, who are some way interested in the main design. And now I am speaking of relations, I cannot take a fitter opportunity to add this in favour of the French, that they often use them with better judgment and more à propos than the English do. Not that I commend narrations in general,—but there are two sorts of them. One, of those things which are antecedent to the play, and are related to make the conduct of it more clear to us. But 'tis a fault to choose such subjects for the stage as will force us on that rock because we see they are seldom listened to by the audience and that is many times the ruin of the play; for, being once let pass without attention, the audience can never recover themselves to understand the plot: and indeed it is somewhat unreasonable that they should be put to so much trouble, as that, to comprehend what passes in their sight, they must have recourse to what was done, perhaps, ten or twenty years ago.

"But there is another sort of relations, that is, of things happening in the action of the play, and supposed to be done behind the scenes; and this is many times both convenient and beautiful; for by it the French avoid the tumult to which we are subject in England, by repre-

---

[47] A term employed by Corneille to refer to characters who are used to give information to the audience, but who take no part in the plot.

senting duels, battles, and the like; which renders our stage too like the theatres where they fight prizes. For what is more ridiculous than to represent an army with a drum and five men behind it; all which the hero of the other side is to drive in before him; or to see a duel fought, and one slain with two or three thrusts of the foils, which we know are so blunted that we might give a man an hour to kill another in good earnest with them.

"I have observed that in all our tragedies, the audience cannot forbear laughing when the actors are to die; it is the most comic part of the whole play. All *passions* may be lively represented on the stage, if to the well-writing of them the actor supplies a good commanded voice, and limbs that move easily, and without stiffness; but there are many *actions* which can never be imitated to a just height: dying especially is a thing which none but a Roman gladiator could naturally perform on the stage, when he did not imitate or represent, but do it; and therefore it is better to omit the representation of it.

"The words of a good writer, which describe it lively, will make a deeper impression of belief in us than all the actor can insinuate into us, when he seems to fall dead before us; as a poet in the description of a beautiful garden, or a meadow, will please our imagination more than the place itself can please our sight. When we see death represented, we are convinced it is but fiction; but when we hear it related, our eyes, the strongest witnesses, are wanting, which might have undeceived us; and we are all willing to favour the sleight, when the poet does not too grossly impose on us. They therefore who imagine these relations would make no concernment in the audience, are deceived, by confounding them with the other, which are of things antecedent to the play: those are made often in cold blood, as I may say, to the audience; but these are warmed with our concernments, which were before awakened in the play. What the philosophers say of motion, that, when it is once begun, it continues of itself, and will do so to eternity, without some stop put to it, is clearly true on this occasion: the soul being already moved with the characters and fortunes of those imaginary persons, continues going of its own accord; and we are no more weary to hear what becomes of them when they are not on the stage, than we are to listen to the news of an absent mistress. But it is objected, that if one part of the play may be related, then

why not all? I answer, some parts of the action are more fit to be represented, some to be related. Corneille says [48] judiciously that the poet
is not obliged to expose to view all particular actions which conduce
to the principal: he ought to select such of them to be seen, which will
appear with the greatest beauty, either by the magnificence of the
show, or the vehemence of passions which they produce, or some other
charm which they have in them; and let the rest arrive to the audience
by narration. 'Tis a great mistake in us to believe the French present
no part of the action on the stage; every alteration or crossing of a
design, every new-sprung passion, and turn of it, is a part of the action,
and much the noblest, except we conceive nothing to be action till
the players come to blows; as if the painting of the hero's mind were
not more properly the poet's work than the strength of his body. Nor
does this anything contradict the opinion of Horace, where he tells
us,

> Segnius irritant animos demissa per aurem,
> Quam quæ sunt oculis subjecta fidelibus.

For he says immediately after,

> Non tamen intus
> Digna geri promes in scenam; multaq[ue] tolles
> Ex oculis, quæ mox narret facundia præsens.

Among which many he recounts some:

> Nec pueros coram populo Medea trucidet,
> Aut in avem Progne mutetur, Cadmus in anguem, etc.

That is, those actions which by reason of their cruelty will cause aversion in us, or by reason of their impossibility, unbelief, ought either
wholly to be avoided by a poet, or only delivered by narration. To
which we may have leave to add, such as, to avoid tumult (as was before hinted), or to reduce the plot into a more reasonable compass of
time, or for defect of beauty in them, are rather to be related than
presented to the eye. Examples of all these kinds are frequent, not
only among all the Ancients, but in the best received of our English
poets. We find Ben Jonson using them in his *Magnetic Lady*,[49] where
one comes out from dinner, and relates the quarrels and disorders of
it, to save the undecent appearance of them on the stage, and to abbre-
viate the story; and this in express imitation of Terence, who had done

---

[48] *Discours des trois unités.*   [49] *Magnetic Lady*, 1632.

the same before him in his *Eunuch,* where Pythias makes the like relation of what had happened within at the Soldiers' entertainment. The relations likewise of Sejanus's death, and the prodigies before it, are remarkable; the one of which was hid from sight, to avoid the horror and tumult of the representation; the other, to shun the introducing of things impossible to be believed. In that excellent play, *The King and No King,*[50] Fletcher goes yet farther; for the whole unravelling of the plot is done by narration in the fifth act, after the manner of the Ancients; and it moves great concernment in the audience, though it be only a relation of what was done many years before the play. I could multiply other instances, but these are sufficient to prove that there is no error in choosing a subject which requires this sort of narrations; in the ill management of them, there may.

"But I find I have been too long in this discourse, since the French have many other excellencies not common to us; as that you never see any of their plays end with a conversion, or simple change of will, which is the ordinary way which our poets use to end theirs. It shows little art in the conclusion of a dramatic poem, when they who have hindered the felicity during the four acts, desist from it in the fifth, without some powerful cause to take them off their design; and though I deny not but such reasons may be found, yet it is a path that is cautiously to be trod, and the poet is to be sure he convinces the audience that the motive is strong enough. As for example, the conversion of the Usurer in *The Scornful Lady*[51] seems to me a little forced; for, being an Usurer, which implies a lover of money to the highest degree of covetousness,—and such the poet has represented him,—the account he gives for the sudden change is, that he has been duped by the wild young fellow; which in reason might render him more wary another time, and make him punish himself with harder fare and coarser clothes, to get up again what he had lost: but that he should look on it as a judgment, and so repent, we may expect to hear in a sermon, but I should never endure it in a play.

"I pass by this; neither will I insist on the care they take that no person after his first entrance shall ever appear, but the business which brings him upon the stage shall be evident; which rule, if ob-

50 *King and No King,* 1611. This play was often presented in the Restoration theatres.
51 *The Scornful Lady,* by Beaumont and Fletcher, c. 1613, was a favorite comedy in Dryden's time.

served, must needs render all the events in the play more natural; for there you see the probability of every accident, in the cause that produced it; and that which appears chance in the play, will seem so reasonable to you, that you will there find it almost necessary: so that in the exit of the actor you have a clear account of his purpose and design in the next entrance (though, if the scene be well wrought, the event will commonly deceive you); for there is nothing so absurd, says Corneille,[52] as for an actor to leave the stage only because he has no more to say.

"I should now speak of the beauty of their rhyme, and the just reason I have to prefer that way of writing in tragedies before ours in blank verse; but because it is partly received by us, and therefore not altogether peculiar to them, I will say no more of it in relation to their plays. For our own, I doubt not but it will exceedingly beautify them; and I can see but one reason why it should not generally obtain, that is, because our poets write so ill in it. This indeed may prove a more prevailing argument than all others which are used to destroy it, and therefore I am only troubled when great and judicious poets, and those who are acknowledged such, have writ or spoke against it: as for others, they are to be answered by that one sentence of an ancient author: [53]—*Sed ut primo ad consequendos eos quos priores ducimus, accendimur, ita ubi aut praeteriri, aut aequari eos posse desperavimus, studium cum spe senescit: quod, scilicet, assequi non potest, sequi desinit; . . . praeteritoque eo in quo eminere non possumus, aliquid in quo nitamur, conquirimus.*"

Lisideius concluded in this manner; and Neander, after a little pause, thus answered him:

"I shall grant Lisideius, without much dispute, a great part of what he has urged against us; for I acknowledge that the French contrive their plots more regularly, and observe the laws of comedy, and decorum of the stage (to speak generally), with more exactness than the English. Farther, I deny not but he has taxed us justly in some irregularities of ours, which he has mentioned; yet, after all, I am of opinion that neither our faults nor their virtues are considerable enough to place them above us.

"For the lively imitation of Nature being in the definition of a play, those which best fulfil that law ought to be esteemed superior to the others. 'Tis true, those beauties of the French poesy are such

52 *Discours des trois unités.*   53 Velleius Paterculus.

as will raise perfection higher where it is, but are not sufficient to give it where it is not: they are indeed the beauties of a statue, but not of a man, because not animated with the soul of Poesy, which is imitation of humour and passions: and this Lisideius himself, or any other, however biassed to their party, cannot but acknowledge, if he will either compare the humours of our comedies, or the characters of our serious plays, with theirs. He who will look upon theirs which have been written till these last ten years, or thereabouts, will find it a hard matter to pick out two or three passable humours amongst them. Corneille himself, their arch-poet, what has he produced except *The Liar*,[54] and you know how it was cried up in France; but when it came upon the English stage, though well translated, and that part of Dorant acted to so much advantage as I am confident it never received in its own country, the most favourable to it would not put it in competition with many of Fletcher's or Ben Jonson's. In the rest of Corneille's comedies you have little humour; he tells you himself, his way is, first to show two lovers in good intelligence with each other; in the working up of the play to embroil them by some mistake, and in the latter end to clear it, and reconcile them.

"But of late years Molière, the younger Corneille, Quinault, and some others, have been imitating afar off the quick turns and graces of the English stage. They have mixed their serious plays with mirth, like our tragi-comedies, since the death of Cardinal Richelieu; which Lisideius and many others not observing have commended that in them for a virtue which they themselves no longer practise. Most of their new plays are, like some of ours, derived from the Spanish novels. There is scarce one of them without a veil, and a trusty Diego, who drolls much after the rate of *The Adventures*.[55] But their Humours, if I may grace them with that name, are so thin-sown, that never above one of them comes up in any play. I dare take upon me to find more variety of them in some one play of Ben Jonson's than in all theirs together; as he who has seen *The Alchemist*,[56] *The Silent Woman*,[57] or *Bartholomew-Fair*,[58] cannot but acknowledge with me.

"I grant the French have performed what was possible on the

54 Written in 1642. Translated in 1661 and played at the Theatre Royal in Vere Street with Hart as Dorant.
55 *The Adventures of Five Hours*, by Sir Samuel Tuke, produced at Lincoln's Inn Fields in January, 1662-63. Diego is the comic servant.
56 *The Alchemist*, 1610.   57 *Epicœne; or, The Silent Woman*, 1609.
58 *Bartholomew Fair*, 1614.

ground-work of the Spanish plays; what was pleasant before, they have made regular: but there is not above one good play to be writ on all those plots; they are too much alike to please often; which we need not the experience of our own stage to justify. As for their new way of mingling mirth with serious plot, I do not, with Lisideius, condemn the thing, though I cannot approve their manner of doing it. He tells us, we cannot so speedily recollect ourselves after a scene of great passion and concernment, as to pass to another of mirth and humour, and to enjoy it with any relish: but why should he imagine the soul of man more heavy than his senses? Does not the eye pass from an unpleasant object to a pleasant in a much shorter time than is required to this? and does not the unpleasantness of the first commend the beauty of the latter? The old rule of logic might have convinced him, that contraries, when placed near, set off each other. A continued gravity keeps the spirit too much bent; we must refresh it sometimes, as we bait in a journey that we may go on with greater ease. A scene of mirth, mixed with tragedy, has the same effect upon us which our music has betwixt the acts; which we find a relief to us from the best plots and language of the stage, if the discourses have been long. I must therefore have stronger arguments, ere I am convinced that compassion and mirth in the same subject destroy each other; and in the meantime cannot but conclude, to the honour of our nation, that we have invented, increased, and perfected a more pleasant way of writing for the stage, than was ever known to the Ancients or Moderns of any nation, which is tragi-comedy.

"And this leads me to wonder why Lisideius and many others should cry up the barrenness of the French plots above the variety and copiousness of the English. Their plots are single; they carry on one design, which is pushed forward by all the actors, every scene in the play contributing and moving towards it. Our plays, besides the main design, have under-plots or by-concernments, of less considerable persons and intrigues, which are carried on with the motion of the main plot: as they say the orb of the fixed stars, and those of the planets, though they have motions of their own, are whirled about by the motion of the *primum mobile*,[59] in which they are contained. That simili-

---

[59] The tenth and outermost sphere in Ptolemaic astronomy, which controlled the movements of all the others. The "First Mover" in the same sentence refers to the same thing.

tude expresses much of the English stage; for if contrary motions may be found in Nature to agree; if a planet can go east and west at the same time;—one way by virtue of his own motion, the other by the force of the First Mover;—it will not be difficult to imagine how the under-plot, which is only different, not contrary to the great design, may naturally be conducted along with it.

"Eugenius has already shown us, from the confession of the French poets, that the Unity of Action is sufficiently preserved, if all the imperfect actions of the play are conducing to the main design; but when those petty intrigues of a play are so ill ordered, that they have no coherence with the other, I must grant that Lisideius has reason to tax that want of due connection; for co-ordination in a play is as dangerous and unnatural as in a state. In the meantime he must acknowledge, our variety, if well ordered, will afford a greater pleasure to the audience.

"As for his other argument, that by pursuing one single theme they gain an advantage to express and work up the passions, I wish any example he could bring from them would make it good; for I confess their verses are to me the coldest I have ever read. Neither, indeed, is it possible for them, in the way they take, so to express passion, as that the effects of it should appear in the concernment of an audience, their speeches being so many declamations, which tire us with the length; so that instead of persuading us to grieve for their imaginary heroes, we are concerned for our own trouble, as we are in tedious visits of bad company; we are in pain till they are gone. When the French stage came to be reformed by Cardinal Richelieu, those long harangues were introduced to comply with the gravity of a churchman. Look upon the *Cinna* [60] and the *Pompey;* [61] they are not so properly to be called plays, as long discourses of reason of state; and *Polyeucte* [62] in matters of religion is as solemn as the long stops upon our organs. Since that time it is grown into a custom, and their actors speak by the hour-glass, like our parsons; nay, they account it the grace of their parts, and think themselves disparaged by the poet, if they may not twice or thrice in a play entertain the audience with a speech of an hundred lines. I deny not but this may suit well enough with the French; for as we, who are a more sullen people, come to be diverted

---

[60] *Cinna; ou, La Clémence d'Auguste,* 1640.   [61] *La Mort de Pompée,* 1641.
[62] *Polyeucte, Martyr, tragédie chrétienne,* 1640.

at our plays, so they, who are of an airy and gay temper, come thither to make themselves more serious: and this I conceive to be one reason why comedies are more pleasing to us, and tragedies to them. But to speak generally: it cannot be denied that short speeches and replies are more apt to move the passions and beget concernment in us, than the other; for it is unnatural for any one in a gust of passion to speak long together, or for another in the same condition to suffer him, without interruption. Grief and passion are like floods raised in little brooks by a sudden rain; they are quickly up; and if the concernment be poured unexpectedly in upon us, it overflows us: but a long sober shower gives them leisure to run out as they came in, without troubling the ordinary current. As for comedy, repartee is one of its chiefest graces; the greatest pleasure of the audience is a chase of wit, kept up on both sides, and swiftly managed. And this our forefathers, if not we, have had in Fletcher's plays, to a much higher degree of perfection than the French poets can reasonably hope to reach.

"There is another part of Lisideius his discourse, in which he rather excused our neighbors than commended them; that is, for aiming only to make one person considerable in their plays. 'Tis very true what he has urged, that one character in all plays, even without the poet's care, will have advantage of all the others; and that the design of the whole drama will chiefly depend on it. But this hinders not that there may be more shining characters in the play: many persons of a second magnitude, nay, some so very near, so almost equal to the first, that greatness may be opposed to greatness, and all the persons be made considerable, not only by their quality, but their action. 'Tis evident that the more the persons are, the greater will be the variety of the plot. If then the parts are managed so regularly, that the beauty of the whole be kept entire, and that the variety become not a perplexed and confused mass of accidents, you will find it infinitely pleasing to be led in a labyrinth of design, where you see some of your way before you, yet discern not the end till you arrive at it. And that all this is practicable, I can produce for examples many of our English plays: as *The Maid's Tragedy*,[63] *The Alchemist*,[64] *The Silent Woman:* [65] I was going to have named *The Fox*,[66] but that the unity of design seems not exactly observed in it; for there appear two actions

[63] *The Maid's Tragedy*, by Beaumont and Fletcher, written between 1608 and 1611.
[64] See note 56.   [65] See note 57.   [66] *Volpone; or, The Fox*, by Jonson, 1605-6.

in the play; the first naturally ending with the fourth act; the second forced from it in the fifth; which yet is the less to be condemned in him, because the disguise of Volpone, though it suited not with his character as a crafty or covetous person, agreed well enough with that of a voluptuary; and by it the poet gained the end at which he aimed, the punishment of vice, and the reward of virtue, both which that disguise produced. So that to judge equally of it, it was an excellent fifth act, but not so naturally proceeding from the former.

"But to leave this, and pass to the latter part of Lisideius his discourse, which concerns relations: I must acknowledge with him, that the French have reason to hide that part of the action which would occasion too much tumult on the stage, and to choose rather to have it made known by narration to the audience. Farther, I think it very convenient, for the reasons he has given, that all incredible actions were removed; but whether custom has so insinuated itself into our countrymen, or Nature has so formed them to fierceness, I know not; but they will scarcely suffer combats and other objects of horror to be taken from them. And indeed, the indecency of tumults is all which can be objected against fighting: for why may not our imagination as well suffer itself to be deluded with the probability of it, as with any other thing in the play? For my part, I can with as great ease persuade myself that the blows are given in good earnest, as I can that they who strike them are kings or princes, or those persons which they represent. For objects of incredibility,—I would be satisfied from Lisideius, whether we have any so removed from all appearance of truth, as are those of Corneille's *Andromède*,[67] a play which has been frequented the most of any he has writ. If the Perseus, or the son of a heathen god, the Pegasus, and the Monster, were not capable to choke a strong belief, let him blame any representation of ours hereafter. Those indeed were objects of delight; yet the reason is the same as to the probability: for he makes it not a ballet or masque, but a play, which is to resemble truth. But for death, that it ought not to be represented, I have, besides the arguments alleged by Lisideius, the authority of Ben Jonson, who has forborne it in his tragedies; for both the death of Sejanus and Catiline are related: though in the latter I cannot but observe one irregularity of that great poet; he has removed the scene in the same act from Rome to Catiline's army, and from thence again

67 *Andromède*, a comedy, 1650.

to Rome; and besides, has allowed a very inconsiderable time, after Catiline's speech, for the striking of the battle, and the return of Petreius, who is to relate the event of it to the senate: which I should not animadvert on him, who was otherwise a painful observer of τὸ πρέπον, or the *decorum* of the stage, if he had not used extreme severity in his judgment on the incomparable Shakespeare for the same fault.—To conclude on this subject of relations; if we are to be blamed for showing too much of the action, the French are as faulty for discovering too little of it: a mean betwixt both should be observed by every judicious writer, so as the audience may neither be left unsatisfied by not seeing what is beautiful, or shocked by beholding what is either incredible or undecent.

"I hope I have already proved in this discourse, that though we are not altogether so punctual as the French in observing the laws of comedy, yet our errors are so few, and little, and those things wherein we excel them so considerable, that we ought of right to be preferred before them. But what will Lisideius say, if they themselves acknowledge they are too strictly bounded by those laws, for breaking which he has blamed the English? I will allege Corneille's words, as I find them in the end of his Discourse of the Three Unities: *Il est facile aux spéculatifs d'estre sévères, etc.* ' 'Tis easy for speculative persons to judge severely; but if they would produce to public view ten or twelve pieces of this nature, they would perhaps give more latitude to the rules than I have done, when by experience they had known how much we are limited and constrained by them, and how many beauties of the stage they banished from it.' To illustrate a little what he has said: By their servile observations of the Unities of Time and Place, and integrity of scenes, they have brought on themselves that dearth of plot, and narrowness of imagination, which may be observed in all their plays. How many beautiful accidents might naturally happen in two or three days, which cannot arrive with any probability in the compass of twenty-four hours? There is time to be allowed also for maturity of design, which, amongst great and prudent persons, such as are often represented in Tragedy, cannot, with any likelihood of truth, be brought to pass at so short a warning. Farther; by tying themselves strictly to the Unity of Place, and unbroken scenes, they are forced many times to omit some beauties which cannot be shown where the act began; but might, if the scene were interrupted, and the stage

cleared for the persons to enter in another place; and therefore the
French poets are often forced upon absurdities; for if the act begins in
a chamber, all the persons in the play must have some business or other
to come thither, or else they are not to be shown that act; and sometimes their characters are very unfitting to appear there: as, suppose
it were the king's bed-chamber; yet the meanest man in the tragedy
must come and dispatch his business there, rather than in the lobby
or courtyard (which is fitter for him), for fear the stage should be
cleared, and the scenes broken. Many times they fall by it in a greater
inconvenience; for they keep their scenes unbroken, and yet change
the place; as in one of their newest plays,[68] where the act begins in the
street. There a gentleman is to meet his friend; he sees him with his
man, coming out from his father's house; they talk together, and the
first goes out: the second, who is a lover, has made an appointment
with his mistress; she appears at the window, and then we are to
imagine the scene lies under it. This gentleman is called away, and
leaves his servant with his mistress; presently her father is heard from
within; the young lady is afraid the serving-man should be discovered,
and thrusts him into a place of safety, which is supposed to be her
closet. After this, the father enters to the daughter, and now the
scene is in a house; for he is seeking from one room to another for
this poor Philipin,[69] or French Diego, who is heard from within, drolling and breaking many a miserable conceit on the subject of his sad
condition. In this ridiculous manner the play goes forward, the stage
being never empty all the while: so that the street, the window, the
houses, and the closet, are made to walk about, and the persons to
stand still. Now what, I beseech you, is more easy than to write a
regular French play, or more difficult than to write an irregular English one, like those of Fletcher, or of Shakespeare?

"If they content themselves, as Corneille did, with some flat design,
which, like an ill riddle, is found out ere it be half proposed, such plots
we can make every way regular, as easily as they; but whenever they
endeavour to rise to any quick turns and counterturns of plot, as
some of them have attempted, since Corneille's plays have been less
in vogue, you see they write as irregularly as we, though they cover it

[68] Corneille's *L'Amour à la mode*, a comedy, 1651. Translated into heroic verse by
John Bulteel under the title *Amorous Orontes, or; The Love in Fashion*, and acted at
the Theatre Royal in Bridges Street in 1664.
[69] Actually a character in this play, but a common type-name for the comic servant.

more speciously. Hence the reason is perspicuous why no French plays, when translated, have, or ever can succeed on the English stage. For, if you consider the plots, our own are fuller of variety; if the writing, ours are more quick and fuller of spirit; and therefore 'tis a strange mistake in those who decry the way of writing plays in verse, as if the English therein imitated the French. We have borrowed nothing from them; our plots are weaved in English looms: we endeavour therein to follow the variety and greatness of characters which are derived to us from Shakespeare and Fletcher; the copiousness and well-knitting of the intrigues we have from Jonson; and for the verse itself we have English precedents of elder date than any of Corneille's plays. Not to name our old comedies before Shakespeare, which were all writ in verse of six feet, or Alexandrines, such as the French now use—I can show in Shakespeare many scenes of rhyme together, and the like in Ben Jonson's tragedies: in *Catiline* and *Sejanus* sometimes thirty or forty lines—I mean besides the Chorus, or the monologues; which, by the way, showed Ben no enemy to this way of writing, especially if you read his *Sad Shepherd*,[70] which goes sometimes on rhyme, some-times on blank verse, like an horse who eases himself on trot and amble. You find him likewise commending Fletcher's pastoral of *The Faithful Shepherdess*,[71] which is for the most part rhyme, though not refined to that purity to which it hath since been brought. And these examples are enough to clear us from a servile imitation of the French.

"But to return whence I have digressed: I dare boldly affirm these two things of the English drama; First, that we have many plays of ours as regular as any of theirs, and which, besides, have more variety of plot and characters; and secondly, that in most of the irregular plays of Shakespeare or Fletcher (for Ben Jonson's are for the most part regular), there is a more masculine fancy and greater spirit in the writing than there is in any of the French. I could produce, even in Shakespeare's and Fletcher's works, some plays which are almost ex-actly formed; as *The Merry Wives of Windsor*,[72] and *The Scornful Lady:* but because (generally speaking) Shakespeare, who writ first, did not perfectly observe the laws of comedy, and Fletcher, who came nearer to perfection, yet through carelessness made many faults; I will

---

[70] *The Sad Shepherd*, by Jonson. Uncompleted; first published in Folio in 1640.
[71] *The Faithful Shepherdess*, 1608–9.
[72] The action of this play covers three days only.

take the pattern of a perfect play from Ben Jonson, who was a careful and learned observer of the dramatic laws, and from all his comedies I shall select *The Silent Woman;* of which I will make a short examen, according to those rules which the French observe."

As Neander was beginning to examine *The Silent Woman,* Eugenius, earnestly regarding him; "I beseech you, Neander," said he, "gratify the company, and me in particular, so far, as before you speak of the play, to give us a character of the author; and tell us frankly your opinion, whether you do not think all writers, both French and English, ought to give place to him."

"I fear," replied Neander, "that in obeying your commands I shall draw some envy on myself. Besides, in performing them, it will be first necessary to speak somewhat of Shakespeare and Fletcher, his rivals in poesy; and one of them, in my opinion, at least his equal, perhaps his superior.

"To begin, then, with Shakespeare. He was the man who of all modern, and perhaps ancient poets, had the largest and most comprehensive soul. All the images of Nature were still present to him, and he drew them, not laboriously, but luckily; when he describes anything, you more than see it, you feel it too. Those who accuse him to have wanted learning, give him the greater commendation: he was naturally learned; he needed not the spectacles of books to read Nature; he looked inwards, and found her there. I cannot say he is everywhere alike; were he so, I should do him injury to compare him with the greatest of mankind. He is many times flat, insipid; his comic wit degenerating into clenches,[73] his serious swelling into bombast. But he is always great, when some great occasion is presented to him; no man can say he ever had a fit subject for his wit, and did not then raise himself as high above the rest of poets,

Quantum lenta solent inter viburna cupressi.

The consideration of this made Mr. Hales of Eton [74] say, that there was no subject of which any poet ever writ, but he would produce it much better done in Shakespeare; and however others are now generally preferred before him, yet the age wherein he lived, which had contemporaries with him Fletcher and Jonson, never equalled them to him in their esteem: and in the last king's court, when Ben's repu-

---

[73] See note 20.   [74] A well-known Fellow of Eton.

tation was at highest, Sir John Suckling, and with him the greater part of the courtiers, set our Shakespeare far above him.

"Beaumont and Fletcher, of whom I am next to speak, had, with the advantage of Shakespeare's wit, which was their precedent, great natural gifts, improved by study: Beaumont especially being so accurate a judge of plays, that Ben Jonson, while he lived, submitted all his writings to his censure, and, 'tis thought, used his judgment in correcting, if not contriving, all his plots. What value he had for him, appears by the verses he writ to him; and therefore I need speak no farther of it. The first play that brought Fletcher and him in esteem was their *Philaster:* [75] for before that, they had written two or three very unsuccessfully, as the like is reported of Ben Jonson,[76] before he writ *Every Man in his Humour.*[77] Their plots were generally more regular than Shakespeare's, especially those which were made before Beaumont's death; and they understood and imitated the conversation of gentlemen much better; whose wild debaucheries, and quickness of wit in repartees, no poet before them could paint as they have done. Humour, which Ben Jonson derived from particular persons, they made it not their business to describe: they represented all the passions very lively, but above all, love. I am apt to believe the English language in them arrived to its highest perfection: what words have since been taken in, are rather superfluous than ornamental. Their plays are now the most pleasant and frequent entertainments of the stage; two of theirs being acted through the year for one of Shakespeare's or Jonson's: the reason is, because there is a certain gaiety in their comedies, and pathos in their more serious plays, which suit generally with all men's humours. Shakespeare's language is likewise a little obsolete, and Ben Jonson's wit comes short of theirs.

"As for Jonson, to whose character I am now arrived, if we look upon him while he was himself (for his last plays were but his dotages), I think him the most learned and judicious writer which any theatre ever had. He was a most severe judge of himself, as well as others. One cannot say he wanted wit, but rather that he was frugal of it. In his works you find little to retrench or alter. Wit, and language, and humour also in some measure, we had before him; but something of

---

[75] *Philaster; or, Love Lies A-Bleeding,* by Beaumont and Fletcher, 1608–9.

[76] Ben Jonson wrote several plays for Henslowe, which have not survived. Among them are *Page of Plymouth, Richard Crookback,* and *Robert II, King of Scots.*

[77] *Every Man in His Humour,* 1598.

art was wanting to the Drama till he came. He managed his strength to more advantage than any who preceded him. You seldom find him making love in any of his scenes, or endeavouring to move the passions; his genius was too sullen and saturnine to do it gracefully, especially when he knew he came after those who had performed both to such an height. Humour was his proper sphere; and in that he delighted most to represent mechanic people. He was deeply conversant in the Ancients, both Greek and Latin, and he borrowed boldly from them: there is scarce a poet or historian among the Roman authors of those times whom he has not translated in *Sejanus* and *Catiline*. But he has done his robberies so openly, that one may see he fears not to be taxed by any law. He invades authors like a monarch; and what would be theft in other poets is only victory in him. With the spoils of these writers he so represents old Rome to us, in its rites, ceremonies, and customs, that if one of their poets had written either of his tragedies, we had seen less of it than in him. If there was any fault in his language, 'twas that he weaved it too closely and laboriously, in his comedies especially: perhaps, too, he did a little too much Romanise our tongue, leaving the words which he translated almost as much Latin as he found them: wherein, though he learnedly followed their language, he did not enough comply with the idiom of ours. If I would compare him with Shakespeare, I must acknowledge him the more correct poet, but Shakespeare the greater wit. Shakespeare was the Homer, or father of our dramatic poets; Jonson was the Virgil, the pattern of elaborate writing; I admire him, but I love Shakespeare. To conclude of him; as he has given us the most correct plays, so in the precepts which he has laid down in his *Discoveries,* we have as many and profitable rules for perfecting the stage, as any wherewith the French can furnish us.

"Having thus spoken of the author, I proceed to the examination of his comedy, *The Silent Woman.*

EXAMEN OF *The Silent Woman*

"To begin first with the length of the action; it is so far from exceeding the compass of a natural day,[78] that it takes not up an artificial one. 'Tis all included in the limits of three hours and a half, which is no more than is required for the presentment on the stage: a beauty

---

[78] Twenty-four hours. The artificial day was twelve hours.

perhaps not much observed; if it had, we should not have looked on the Spanish translation of *Five Hours* [79] with so much wonder. The scene of it is laid in London; the latitude of place is almost as little as you can imagine; for it lies all within the compass of two houses, and after the first act, in one. The continuity of scenes is observed more than in any of our plays, except his own *Fox* and *Alchemist*. They are not broken above twice or thrice at most in the whole comedy; and in the two best of Corneille's plays, the *Cid* [80] and *Cinna*, they are interrupted once. The action of the play is entirely one; the end or aim of which is the settling Morose's estate on Dauphine. The intrigue of it is the greatest and most noble of any pure unmixed comedy in any language; you see in it many persons of various characters and humours, and all delightful. As first, Morose, or an old man, to whom all noise but his own talking is offensive. Some who would be thought critics, say this humour of his is forced: but to remove that objection, we may consider him first to be naturally of a delicate hearing, as many are, to whom all sharp sounds are unpleasant; and secondly, we may attribute much of it to the peevishness of his age, or the wayward authority of an old man in his own house, where he may make himself obeyed; and to this the poet seems to allude in his name Morose. Besides this, I am assured from divers persons, that Ben Jonson was actually acquainted with such a man, one altogether as ridiculous as he is here represented. Others say, it is not enough to find one man of such an humour; it must be common to more, and the more common the more natural. To prove this, they instance in the best of comical characters, Falstaff. There are many men resembling him; old, fat, merry, cowardly, drunken, amorous, vain, and lying. But to convince these people, I need but tell them that humour is the ridiculous extravagance of conversation, wherein one man differs from all others. If then it be common, or communicated to many, how differs it from other men's? or what indeed causes it to be ridiculous so much as the singularity of it? As for Falstaff, he is not properly one humour, but a miscellany of humours or images, drawn from so many several men: that wherein he is singular is his wit, or those things he says *præter expectatum,* unexpected by the audience; his quick evasions, when you imagine him surprised, which, as they are extremely diverting of themselves, so receive a great addition from his person; for

[79] See note 55.   [80] *Le Cid,* 1637; *Cinna,* 1640.

the very sight of such an unwieldy old debauched fellow is a comedy alone. And here, having a place so proper for it, I cannot but enlarge somewhat upon this subject of humour into which I am fallen. The Ancients had little of it in their comedies; for the τὸ γελοῖον of the Old Comedy, of which Aristophanes was chief, was not so much to imitate a man, as to make the people laugh at some odd conceit, which had commonly somewhat of unnatural or obscene in it. Thus, when you see Socrates brought upon the stage, you are not to imagine him made ridiculous by the imitation of his actions, but rather by making him perform something very unlike himself; something so childish and absurd, as by comparing it with the gravity of the true Socrates, makes a ridiculous object for the spectators. In their New Comedy which succeeded, the poets sought indeed to express the ἦθος, as in their tragedies the πάθος of mankind. But this ἦθος contained only the general characters of men and manners; as old men, lovers, serving-men, courtezans, parasites, and such other persons as we see in their comedies; all which they made alike: that is, one old man or father, one lover, one courtezan, so like another, as if the first of them had begot the rest of every sort: *Ex homine hunc natum dicas.* The same custom they observed likewise in their tragedies. As for the French, though they have the word *humeur* among them, yet they have small use of it in their comedies or farces; they being but ill imitations of the *ridiculum,* or that which stirred up laughter in the Old Comedy. But among the English 'tis otherwise: where by humour is meant some extravagant habit, passion, or affection, particular (as I said before) to some one person, by the oddness of which, he is immediately distinguished from the rest of men; which being lively and naturally represented, most frequently begets that malicious pleasure in the audience which is testified by laughter; as all things which are deviations from customs are ever the aptest to produce it: though by the way this laughter is only accidental, as the person represented is fantastic or bizzare; but pleasure is essential to it, as the imitation of what is natural. The description of these humours, drawn from the knowledge and observation of particular persons, was the peculiar genius and talent of Ben Jonson; to whose play I now return.

"Besides Morose, there are at least nine or ten different characters and humours in *The Silent Woman;* all which persons have several concernments of their own, yet are all used by the poet to the conducting of the main design to perfection. I shall not waste time in commending the writing of this play; but I will give you my opinion, that there is more wit and acuteness of fancy in it than in any of Ben Jonson's. Besides that he has here described the conversation of gentlemen in the persons of True-Wit, and his friends, with more gaiety, air, and freedom, than in the rest of his comedies. For the contrivance of the plot, 'tis extreme, elaborate, and yet withal easy; for the λύσις, or untying of it, 'tis so admirable, that when it is done, no one of the audience would think the poet could have missed it; and yet it was concealed so much before the last scene, that any other way would sooner have entered into your thoughts. But I dare not take upon me to commend the fabric of it, because it is altogether so full of art, that I must unravel every scene in it to commend it as I ought. And this excellent contrivance is still the more to be admired, because 'tis comedy, where the persons are only of common rank, and their business private, not elevated by passions or high concernments, as in serious plays. Here every one is a proper judge of all he sees, nothing is represented but that with which he daily converses: so that by consequence all faults lie open to discovery, and few are pardonable. 'Tis this which Horace has judiciously observed:

> Creditur, ex medio quia res arcessit, habere
> Sudoris minimum; sed habet Comedia tanto
> Plus oneris, quanto veniæ minus.

"But our poet who was not ignorant of these difficulties has made use of all advantages; as he who designs a large leap takes his rise from the highest ground. One of these advantages is that which Corneille has laid down [81] as the greatest which can arrive to any poem, and which he himself could never compass above thrice in all his plays; viz., the making choice of some signal and long-expected day, whereon the action of the play is to depend. This day was that designed by Dauphine for the settling of his uncle's estate upon him; which to compass, he contrives to marry him. That the marriage had been plotted by him long beforehand, is made evident by what he tells True-Wit in the second act, that in one moment he had destroyed what he had been raising many months.

"There is another artifice of the poet, which I cannot here omit, because by the frequent practice of it in his comedies he has left it to

[81] Discours des trois unités.

us almost as a rule; that is, when he has any character or humour wherein he would show a *coup de Maistre,* or his highest skill, he recommends it to your observation by a pleasant description of it before the person first appears. Thus, in *Bartholomew-Fair* he gives you the pictures of Numps and Cokes, and in this those of Daw, Lafoole, Morose, and the Collegiate Ladies; all which you hear described before you see them. So that before they come upon the stage, you have a longing expectation of them, which prepares you to receive them favourably; and when they are there, even from their first appearance you are so far acquainted with them, that nothing of their humour is lost to you.

"I will observe yet one thing further of this admirable plot; the business of it rises in every act. The second is greater than the first; the third than the second; and so forward to the fifth. There too you see, till the very last scene, new difficulties arising to obstruct the action of the play; and when the audience is brought into despair that the business can naturally be effected, then, and not before, the discovery is made. But that the poet might entertain you with more variety all this while, he reserves some new characters to show you, which he opens not till the second and third act; in the second Morose, Daw, the Barber, and Otter; in the third the Collegiate Ladies: all which he moves afterwards in by-walks, or under-plots, as diversions to the main design, lest it should grow tedious, though they are still naturally joined with it, and somewhere or other subservient to it. Thus, like a skilful chess-player, by little and little he draws out his men, and makes his pawns of use to his greater persons.

"If this comedy and some others of his were translated into French prose (which would now be no wonder to them, since Molière has lately given them plays out of verse, which have not displeased them), I believe the controversy would soon be decided betwixt the two nations, even making them the judges. But we need not call our heroes to our aid. Be it spoken to the honour of the English, our nation can never want in any age such who are able to dispute the empire of wit with any people in the universe. And though the fury of a civil war, and power for twenty years together abandoned to a barbarous race of men, enemies of all good learning, had buried the Muses under the ruins of monarchy; yet, with the restoration of our happiness, we see revived Poesy lifting up its head, and already shaking off the rubbish which lay so heavy on it. We have seen since his Majesty's return, many dramatic poems which yield not to those of any foreign nation, and which deserve all laurels but the English. I will set aside flattery and envy: it cannot be denied but we have had some little blemish either in the plot or writing of all those plays which have been made within these seven years; (and perhaps there is no nation in the world so quick to discern them, or so difficult to pardon them, as ours:) yet if we can persuade ourselves to use the candour of that poet, who, though the most severe of critics, has left us this caution by which to moderate our censures—

> *ubi plura nitent in carmine, non ego paucis*
> *Offendar maculis;—*

if, in consideration of their many and great beauties, we can wink at some slight and little imperfections, if we, I say, can be thus equal to ourselves, I ask no favour from the French. And if I do not venture upon any particular judgment of our late plays, 'tis out of the consideration which an ancient writer gives me: *vivorum, ut magna admiratio, ita censura difficilis:* betwixt the extremes of admiration and malice, 'tis hard to judge uprightly of the living. Only I think it may be permitted me to say, that as it is no lessening to us to yield to some plays, and those not many, of our own nation in the last age, so can it be no addition to pronounce of our present poets, that they have far surpassed all the Ancients, and the modern writers of other countries."

This was the substance of what was then spoken on that occasion; and Lisideius, I think, was going to reply, when he was prevented thus by Crites: "I am confident," said he, "that the most material things that can be said have been already urged on either side; if they have not, I must beg of Lisideius that he will defer his answer till another time: for I confess I have a joint quarrel to you both, because you have concluded, without any reason given for it, that rhyme is proper for the stage. I will not dispute how ancient it hath been among us to write this way; perhaps our ancestors knew no better till Shakespeare's time. I will grant it was not altogether left by him, and that Fletcher and Ben Jonson used it frequently in their Pastorals, and sometimes in other plays. Farther—I will not argue whether we received it originally from our own countrymen, or from the French; for that is an inquiry of as little benefit, as theirs who, in the midst of the great plague, were not so solicitous to provide against it, as to know whether we had it from the malignity of our own air, or by transportation from Holland. I have therefore only to affirm, that it is not allowable in serious plays; for comedies, I find you already concluding with me. To prove this, I might satisfy myself to tell you, how much in vain it is for you to strive against the stream of the people's inclination; the greatest part of which are prepossessed so much with those excellent plays of Shakespeare, Fletcher, and Ben Jonson, which have been written out of rhyme, that except you could bring them such as were written better in it, and those too by persons of equal reputation with them, it will be impossible for you to gain your cause with them, who will still be judges. This it is to which, in fine, all your reasons must submit. The unanimous consent of an audience is so powerful, that even Julius Cæsar (as Macrobius reports of him), when he was perpetual dictator, was not able to balance it on the other side; but when Laberius, a Roman Knight, at his request contended in the *Mime* with another poet, he was forced to cry out, *Etiam favente me victus es, Laberi*. But I will not on this occasion take the advantage of the greater number, but only urge such reasons against rhyme, as I find in the writings of those who have argued for the other way. First, then, I am of opinion that rhyme is unnatural in a play, because dialogue there is presented as the effect of sudden thought: for a play is the imitation of Nature; and since no man, without premeditation, speaks in rhyme, neither ought he to do it on the stage. This hinders not but the fancy may be there elevated to an higher pitch of thought than it is in ordinary discourse; for there is a probability that men of excellent and quick parts may speak noble things *extempore:* but those thoughts are never fettered with the numbers or sound of verse without study, and therefore it cannot be but unnatural to present the most free way of speaking in that which is the most constrained. For this reason, says Aristotle, 'tis best to write tragedy in that kind of verse which is the least such, or which is nearest prose: and this amongst the Ancients was the Iambic, and with us is blank verse, or the measure of verse kept exactly without rhyme. These numbers therefore are fittest for a play; the others for a paper of verses, or a poem; blank verse being as much below them as rhyme is improper for the Drama. And if it be objected that neither are blank verses made *extempore,* yet, as nearest Nature, they are still to be preferred. But there are two particular exceptions, which many besides myself have had to verse; by which it will appear yet more plainly how improper it is in plays. And the first of them is grounded on that very reason for which some have commended rhyme; they say, the quickness of repartees in argumentative scenes receives an ornament from verse. Now what is more unreasonable than to imagine that a man should not only light upon the Wit, but the rhyme too, upon the sudden? This nicking [82] of him who spoke before both in sound and measure, is so great an happiness, that you must at least suppose the persons of your play to be born poets: *Arcades omnes, et cantare pares, et respondere parati:* they must have arrived to the degree of *quicquid conabar dicere;* to make verses almost whether they will or no. If they are anything below this, it will look rather like the design of two, than the answer of one: it will appear that your actors hold intelligence together; that they perform their tricks like fortune-tellers, by confederacy. The hand of art will be too visible in it, against that maxim of all professions—*Ars est celare artem;* that it is the greatest perfection of art to keep itself undiscovered. Nor will it serve you to object, that however you manage it, 'tis still known to be a play; and, consequently, the dialogue of two persons understood to be the labour of one poet. For a play is still an imitation of Nature; we know we are to be deceived, and we desire to be so; but no man ever was deceived but with a probability of truth; for who will suffer a gross lie to be fastened on him? Thus we sufficiently understand that the scenes which represent cities and countries to us are not really such, but only painted on boards and canvas; but shall that excuse the ill painture or designment of them? Nay, rather ought they not be laboured with so much the more diligence and exactness, to help the imagination? since the mind of man does naturally tend to truth; and therefore the nearer anything comes to the imitation of it, the more it pleases.

"Thus, you see, your rhyme is incapable of expressing the greatest thoughts naturally, and the lowest it cannot with any grace: for what is more unbefitting the majesty of verse, than to call a servant, or bid a door be shut in rhyme? and yet you are often forced on this miserable necessity. But verse, you say, circumscribes a quick and luxuriant fancy, which would extend itself too far on every subject, did not the

[82] To come in precisely.

labour which is required to well-turned and polished rhyme, set bounds to it. Yet this argument, if granted, would only prove that we may write better in verse, but not more naturally. Neither is it able to evince that; for he who wants judgment to confine his fancy in blank verse, may want it as much in rhyme: and he who has it will avoid errors in both kinds. Latin verse was as great a confinement to the imagination of those poets as rhyme to ours; and yet you find Ovid saying too much on every subject. *Nescivit* (says Seneca) *quod bene cessit relinquere:* of which he gives you one famous instance in his description of the deluge:

> *Omnia pontus erat, deerant quoque litora ponto.*
>
> Now all was sea, nor had that sea a shore.

Thus Ovid's fancy was not limited by verse, and Virgil needed not verse to have bounded his.

"In our own language we see Ben Jonson confining himself to what ought to be said, even in the liberty of blank verse; and yet Corneille, the most judicious of the French poets, is still varying the same sense an hundred ways, and dwelling eternally on the same subject, though confined by rhyme. Some other exceptions I have to verse; but since these I have named are for the most part already public, I conceive it reasonable they should first be answered."

"It concerns me less than any," said Neander (seeing he had ended), "to reply to this discourse; because when I should have proved that verse may be natural in plays, yet I should always be ready to confess, that those which I have written in this kind come short of that perfection which is required. Yet since you are pleased I should undertake this province, I will do it, though with all imaginable respect and deference, both to that person from whom you have borrowed your strongest arguments,[83] and to whose judgment, when I have said all, I finally submit. But before I proceed to answer your objections, I must first remember you, that I exclude all comedy from my defence; and next that I deny not but blank verse may be also used; and content myself only to assert, that in serious plays where the subject and characters are great, and the plot unmixed with mirth, which might allay or divert these concernments which are produced, rhyme is there as natural and more effectual than blank verse.

[83] Sir Robert Howard, who has just been speaking in his *alter ego* as Crites.

"And now having laid down this as a foundation—to begin with Crites—I must crave leave to tell him, that some of his arguments against rhyme reach no farther than, from the faults or defects of ill rhyme, to conclude against the use of it in general. May not I conclude against blank verse by the same reason? If the words of some poets who write in it are either ill chosen, or ill placed, which makes not only rhyme, but all kind of verse in any language unnatural, shall I, for their vicious affectation, condemn those excellent lines of Fletcher, which are written in that kind? Is there anything in rhyme more constrained than this line in blank verse?—*I heaven invoke, and strong resistance make;* where you see both the clauses are placed unnaturally, that is, contrary to the common way of speaking, and that without the excuse of a rhyme to cause it: yet you would think me very ridiculous, if I should accuse the stubbornness of blank verse for this, and not rather the stiffness of the poet. Therefore, Crites, you must either prove that words, though well chosen, and duly placed, yet render not rhyme natural in itself; or that, however natural and easy the rhyme may be, yet it is not proper for a play. If you insist on the former part, I would ask you, what other conditions are required to make rhyme natural in itself, besides an election of apt words, and a right disposition of them? For the due choice of your words expresses your sense naturally, and the due placing them adapts the rhyme to it. If you object that one verse may be made for the sake of another, though both the words and rhyme be apt, I answer, it cannot possibly so fall out; for either there is a dependence of sense betwixt the first line and the second, or there is none: if there be that connection, then in the natural position of the words the latter line must of necessity flow from the former; if there be no dependence, yet still the due ordering of words makes the last line as natural in itself as the other: so that the necessity of a rhyme never forces any but bad or lazy writers to say what they would not otherwise. 'Tis true, there is both care and art required to write in verse. A good poet never establishes the first line till he has sought out such a rhyme as may fit the sense, already prepared to heighten the second: many times the close of the sense falls into the middle of the next verse, or farther off, and he may often prevail himself of the same advantages in English which Virgil had in Latin—he may break off in the hemistich, and begin another line. Indeed, the not observing these two last things makes plays which are writ in verse so tedious: for though, most commonly, the sense is to be confined to the couplet, yet nothing that does *perpetuo tenore fluere*, run in the same channel, can please always. 'Tis like the murmuring of a stream, which not varying in the fall, causes at first attention, at last drowsiness. Variety of cadences is the best rule; the greatest help to the actors, and refreshment to the audience.

"If then verse may be made natural in itself, how becomes it unnatural in a play? You say the stage is the representation of Nature, and no man in ordinary conversation speaks in rhyme. But you foresaw when you said this, that it might be answered—neither does any man speak in blank verse, or in measure without rhyme. Therefore you concluded, that which is nearest Nature is still to be preferred. But you took no notice that rhyme might be made as natural as blank verse, by the well placing of the words, etc. All the difference between them, when they are both correct, is, the sound in one, which the other wants; and if so, the sweetness of it, and all the advantage resulting from it, which are handled in the Preface to *The Rival Ladies*,[84] will yet stand good. As for that place of Aristotle, where he says, plays should be writ in that kind of verse which is nearest prose, it makes little for you; blank verse being properly but measured prose. Now measure alone, in any modern language, does not constitute verse; those of the Ancients in Greek and Latin consisted in quantity of words, and a determinate number of feet. But when, by the inundation of the Goths and Vandals into Italy, new languages were introduced, and barbarously mingled with the Latin, of which the Italian, Spanish, French, and ours (made out of them and the Teutonic) are dialects, a new way of poesy was practised; new, I say, in those countries, for in all probability it was that of the conquerors in their own nations: at least we are able to prove, that the eastern people have used it from all antiquity. This new way consisted in measure or number of feet, and rhyme; the sweetness of rhyme, and observation of accent, supplying the place of quantity in words, which could neither exactly be observed by those barbarians, who knew not the rules of it, neither was it suitable to their tongues, as it had been to the Greek and Latin. No man is tied in modern poesy to observe any farther rule in the feet of his verse, but that they be dissyllables;

---

[84] *The Rival Ladies,* a tragi-comedy by Dryden, produced in the Theatre Royal in Bridges Street, c. May, 1664.

whether Spondee, Trochee, or Iambic, it matters not; only he is
obliged to rhyme: neither do the Spanish, French, Italian, or Germans,
acknowledge at all, or very rarely, any such kind of poesy as blank
verse amongst them. Therefore, at most 'tis but a poetic prose, a
sermo pedestris; and as such, most fit for comedies, where I acknowledge rhyme to be improper. Farther; as to that quotation of Aristotle,
our couplet verses may be rendered as near prose as blank verse itself,
by using those advantages I lately named—as breaks in an hemistich,
or running the sense into another line—thereby making art and order
appear as loose and free as nature: or not tying ourselves to couplets
strictly, we may use the benefit of the Pindaric way [85] practised in *The
Siege of Rhodes;* [86] where the numbers vary, and the rhyme is disposed
carelessly, and far from often chiming. Neither is that other advantage
of the Ancients to be despised, of changing the kind of verse when they
please, with the change of the scene, or some new entrance; for they
confine not themselves always to iambics, but extend their liberty to
all lyric numbers, and sometimes even to hexameter. But I need not
go so far to prove that rhyme, as it succeeds to all other offices of Greek
and Latin verse, so especially to this of plays, since the custom of nations at this day confirms it; the French, Italian, and Spanish tragedies
are generally writ in it; and sure the universal consent of the most
civilised parts of the world, ought in this, as it doth in other customs,
to include the rest.

"But perhaps you may tell me, I have proposed such a way to make
rhyme natural, and consequently proper to plays, as is unpracticable;
and that I shall scarce find six or eight lines together in any play, where
the words are so placed and chosen as is required to make it natural.
I answer, no poet need constrain himself at all times to it. It is enough
he makes it his general rule; for I deny not but sometimes there may
be a greatness in placing the words otherwise; and sometimes they may
sound better; sometimes also the variety itself is excuse enough. But
if, for the most part, the words be placed as they are in the negligence
of prose, it is sufficient to denominate the way practicable; for we
esteem that to be such, which in the trial oftener succeeds than misses.
And thus far you may find the practice made good in many plays:

---

[85] Irregular in length of line and rhyme scheme.

[86] *The Siege of Rhodes,* by William Davenant (1656) was the first play produced in a
public way after the closing of the theatres in 1642.

where you do not, remember still, that if you cannot find six natural rhymes together, it will be as hard for you to produce as many lines in blank verse, even among the greatest of our poets, against which I cannot make some reasonable exception.

"And this, Sir, calls to my remembrance the beginning of your discourse, where you told us we should never find the audience favourable to this kind of writing, till we could produce as good plays in rhyme as Ben Jonson, Fletcher, and Shakespeare had writ out of it. But it is to raise envy to the living, to compare them with the dead. They are honoured, and almost adored by us, as they deserve; neither do I know any so presumptuous of themselves as to contend with them. Yet give me leave to say thus much, without injury to their ashes; that not only we shall never equal them, but they could never equal themselves, were they to rise and write again. We acknowledge them our fathers in wit; but they have ruined their estates themselves, before they came to their children's hands. There is scarce an humour, a character, or any kind of plot, which they have not used. All comes sullied or wasted to us: and were they to entertain this age, they could not now make so plenteous treatments out of such decayed fortunes. This therefore will be a good argument to us, either not to write at all, or to attempt some other way. There is no bays to be expected in their walks: *tentanda via est, quà me quoque possum tollere humo.*

"This way of writing in verse they have only left free to us; our age is arrived to a perfection in it, which they never knew; and which (if we may guess by what of theirs we have seen in verse, as *The Faithful Shepherdess*, and *Sad Shepherd*) 'tis probable they never could have reached. For the genius of every age is different; and though ours excel in this, I deny not but to imitate Nature in that perfection which they did in prose, is a greater commendation than to write in verse exactly. As for what you have added—that the people are not generally inclined to like this way—if it were true, it would be no wonder, that betwixt the shaking off an old habit, and the introducing of a new, there should be difficulty. Do we not see them stick to Hopkins' and Sternhold's [87] psalms, and forsake those of David, I mean Sandys [88] his translation of them? If by the people you understand the multitude,

87 Popular doggerel translations of the Psalms.
88 George Sandys' translation of the Psalms, published in 1636, was popular with cultured readers, whereas the vulgar preferred Hopkins and Sternhold.

the οἱ πολλοί, 'tis no matter what they think; they are sometimes in the right, sometimes in the wrong: their judgment is a mere lottery. *Est ubi plebs rectè putat, est ubi peccat.* Horace says it of the vulgar, judging poesy. But if you mean the mixed audience of the populace and the noblesse, I dare confidently affirm that a great part of the latter sort are already favourable to verse; and that no serious plays written since the King's return have been more kindly received by them than *The Siege of Rhodes*, the *Mustapha*,[89] *The Indian Queen*,[90] and *Indian Emperor*.[91]

"But I come now to the inference of your first argument. You said that the dialogue of plays is presented as the effect of sudden thought, but no man speaks suddenly, or *extempore*, in rhyme; and you inferred from thence, that rhyme, which you acknowledge to be proper to epic poesy, cannot equally be proper to dramatic, unless we could suppose all men born so much more than poets, that verses should be made in them, not by them.

"It has been formerly urged by you, and confessed by me, that since no man spoke any kind of verse *extempore*, that which was nearest Nature was to be preferred. I answer you, therefore, by distinguishing betwixt what is nearest to the nature of Comedy, which is the imitation of common persons and ordinary speaking, and what is nearest the nature of a serious play: this last is indeed the representation of Nature, but 'tis Nature wrought up to a higher pitch. The plot, the characters, the wit, the passions, the descriptions, are all exalted above the level of common converse, as high as the imagination of the poet can carry them, with proportion to verisimility. Tragedy, we know, is wont to image to us the minds and fortunes of noble persons, and to portray these exactly; heroic rhyme is nearest Nature, as being the noblest kind of modern verse.

> *Indignatur enim privatis et prope socco*
> *Dignis carminibus narrari cæna Thyestæ*

says Horace: and in another place,

> *Effutire leves indigna tragœdia versus.*

---

[89] *The Tragedy of Mustapha, Son of Solyman the Magnificent*, by Roger Boyle, Earl of Orrey, produced at Lincoln's Inn Fields in 1664 and in a revised version at the same theatre in 1665.

[90] *The Indian Queen*, by Dryden and Sir Robert Howard, produced in the Theatre Royal in January, 1663/4.

[91] *The Indian Emperor; or, The Conquest of Mexico by the Spaniards, Being the Sequel of the Indian Queen*, by Dryden, produced in the Theatre Royal c. April, 1665.

Blank verse is acknowledged to be too low for a poem, nay more, for a paper of verses; but if too low for an ordinary sonnet,[92] how much more for Tragedy, which is by Aristotle, in the dispute betwixt the epic poesy and the dramatic, for many reasons he there alleges, ranked above it?

"But setting this defence aside, your argument is almost as strong against the use of rhyme in poems as in plays; for the epic way is everywhere interlaced with dialogue, or discoursive scenes; and therefore you must either grant rhyme to be improper there, which is contrary to your assertion, or admit it into plays by the same title which you have given it to poems. For though Tragedy be justly preferred above the other, yet there is a great affinity between them, as may easily be discovered in that definition of a play which Lisideius gave us. The *genius* of them is the same—a just and lively image of human nature, in its actions, passions, and traverses of fortune: so is the end—namely, for the delight and benefit of mankind. The characters and persons are still the same, viz., the greatest of both sorts; only the manner of acquainting us with those actions, passions, and fortunes, is different. Tragedy performs it *viva voce*, or by action, in dialogue; wherein it excels the Epic Poem, which does it chiefly by narration, and therefore is not so lively an image of human nature. However, the agreement betwixt them is such, that if rhyme be proper for one, it must be for the other. Verse, 'tis true, is not the effect of sudden thought; but this hinders not that sudden thought may be represented in verse, since those thoughts are such as must be higher than Nature can raise them without premeditation, especially to a continuance of them, even out of verse; and consequently you cannot imagine them to have been sudden either in the poet or in the actors. A play, as I have said, to be like Nature, is to be set above it; as statues which are placed on high are made greater than the life, that they may descend to the sight in their just proportion.

"Perhaps I have insisted too long on this objection; but the clearing of it will make my stay shorter on the rest. You tell us, Crites, that rhyme appears most unnatural in repartees, or short replies: when he who answers (it being presumed he knew not what the other would say, yet) makes up that part of the verse which was left incomplete, and supplies both the sound and measure of it. This, you say, looks rather like the confederacy of two, than the answer of one.

92 Any short poem.

"This, I confess, is an objection which is in every man's mouth, who loves not rhyme: but suppose, I beseech you, the repartee were made only in blank verse, might not part of the same argument be turned against you? for the measure is as often supplied there as it is in rhyme; the latter half of the hemistich as commonly made up, or a second line subjoined as a reply to the former; which any one leaf in Jonson's plays will sufficiently clear to you. You will often find in the Greek tragedians, and in Seneca, that when a scene grows up into the warmth of repartees, which is the close fighting of it, the latter part of the trimeter is supplied by him who answers; and yet it was never observed as a fault in them by any of the ancient or modern critics. The case is the same in our verse, as it was in theirs; rhyme to us being in lieu of quantity to them. But if no latitude is to be allowed a poet, you take from him not only his licence of *quidlibet audendi*, but you tie him up in a straiter compass than you would a philosopher. This is indeed *Musas colere severiores*. You would have him follow Nature, but he must follow her on foot: you have dismounted him from his Pegasus. But you tell us, this supplying the last half of a verse, or adjoining a whole second to the former, looks more like the design of two, than the answer of one. Suppose we acknowledge it: how comes this confederacy to be more displeasing to you, than in a dance which is well contrived? You see there the united design of many persons to make up one figure: after they have separated themselves in many petty divisions, they rejoin one by one into a gross: the confederacy is plain amongst them, for chance could never produce anything so beautiful; and yet there is nothing in it that shocks your sight. I acknowledge the hand of art appears in repartee,[93] as of necessity it must in all kind of verse. But there is also the quick and poignant brevity of it (which is an high imitation of Nature in those sudden gusts of passion) to mingle with it; and this, joined with the cadency and sweetness of the rhyme, leaves nothing in the soul of the hearer to desire. 'Tis an art which appears; but it appears only like the shadowings of painture, which being to cause the rounding of it, cannot be absent; but while that is considered, they are lost: so while we attend to the other beauties of the matter, the care and labour of the rhyme is carried from us, or at least drowned in its own sweetness, as bees are some-

---

[93] Stichomythia, or dialogue in verse between two or more persons, each with one-line speeches.

times buried in their honey. When a poet has found the repartee, the last perfection he can add to it, is to put it into verse. However good the thought may be, however apt the words in which 'tis couched, yet he finds himself at a little unrest, while rhyme is wanting: he cannot leave it till that comes naturally and then is at ease, and sits down contented.

"From replies, which are the most elevated thoughts of verse, you pass to those which are most mean, and which are common with the lowest of household conversation. In these, you say, the majesty of verse suffers. You instance in the calling of a servant, or commanding a door to be shut, in rhyme. This, Crites, is a good observation of yours, but no argument: for it proves no more but that such thoughts should be waived, as often as may be, by the address of the poet. But suppose they are necessary in the places where he uses them, yet there is no need to put them into rhyme. He may place them in the beginning of a verse, and break it off, as unfit, when so debased, for any other use: or granting the worst—that they require more room than the hemistich will allow, yet still there is a choice to be made of the best words, and least vulgar (provided they be apt), to express such thoughts. Many have blamed rhyme in general, for this fault, when the poet with a little care might have redressed it. But they do it with no more justice than if English Poesy should be made ridiculous for the sake of the Water-poet's [94] rhymes. Our language is noble, full, and significant; and I know not why he who is master of it may not clothe ordinary things in it as decently as the Latin, if he use the same diligence in his choice of words: *delectus verborum origo est eloquentiæ.* It was the saying of Julius Cæsar, one so curious in his, that none of them can be changed but for a worse. One would think, *unlock the door,* was a thing as vulgar as could be spoken; and yet Seneca could make it sound high and lofty in his Latin:

> *Reserate clusos regii postes laris.*
>
> Set wide the palace gates.

"But I turn from this conception, both because it happens not above twice or thrice in any play that those vulgar thoughts are used; and then too (were there no other apology to be made, yet), the necessity of them, which is alike in all kind of writing, may excuse them. For

[94] John Taylor, a prolific writer of rather poor verse. He got his name from his earlier career as a waterman on the Thames.

if they are little and mean in rhyme, they are of consequence such in blank verse. Besides that the great eagerness and precipitation with which they are spoken, makes us rather mind the substance than the dress; that for which they are spoken, rather than what is spoken. For they are always the effect of some hasty concernment, and something of consequence depends on them.

"Thus, Crites, I have endeavoured to answer your objections; it remains only that I should vindicate an argument for verse, which you have gone about to overthrow. It had formerly been said [95] that the easiness of blank verse renders the poet too luxuriant, but that the labour of rhyme bounds and circumscribes an over-fruitful fancy; the sense there being commonly confined to the couplet, and the words so ordered that the rhyme naturally follows them, not they the rhyme. To this you answered, that it was no argument to the question in hand; for the dispute was not which way a man may write best, but which is most proper for the subject on which he writes.

"First, give me leave, Sir, to remember you that the argument against which you raised this objection was only secondary: it was built on this hypothesis—that to write in verse was proper for serious plays. Which supposition being granted (as it was briefly made out in that discourse, by showing how verse might be made natural), it asserted, that this way of writing was an help to the poet's judgment, by putting bounds to a wild overflowing fancy. I think, therefore, it will not be hard for me to make good what it was to prove on that supposition. But you add, that were this let pass, yet he who wants judgment in the liberty of his fancy, may as well show the defect of it when he is confined to verse; for he who has judgment will avoid errors, and he who has it not, will commit them in all kinds of writing.

"This argument, as you have taken it from a most acute person,[96] so I confess it carries much weight in it: but by using the word judgment here indefinitely, you seem to have put a fallacy upon us. I grant, he who has judgment, that is, so profound, so strong, or rather so infallible a judgment, that he needs no helps to keep it always poised and upright, will commit no faults either in rhyme or out of it. And on the other extreme, he who has a judgment so weak and crazed that no helps can correct or amend it, shall write scurvily out of rhyme, and worse in it. But the first of these judgments is nowhere to be found,

[95] Epistle Dedicatory to *The Rival Ladies*.   [96] Sir Robert Howard.

and the latter is not fit to write at all. To speak therefore of judgment as it is in the best poets; they who have the greatest proportion of it, want other helps than from it, within. As for example, you would be loth to say that he who is endued with a sound judgment has no need of History, Geography, or Moral Philosophy, to write correctly. Judgment is indeed the master-workman in a play; but he requires many subordinate hands, many tools to his assistance. And verse I affirm to be one of these; 'tis a rule and line by which he keeps his building compact and even, which otherwise lawless imagination would raise either irregularly or loosely; at least, if the poet commits errors with this help, he would make greater and more without it: 'tis, in short, a slow and painful, but the surest kind of working. Ovid, whom you accuse for luxuriancy in verse, had perhaps been farther guilty of it, had he writ in prose. And for your instance of Ben Jonson, who, you say, writ exactly without the help of rhyme; you are to remember, 'tis only an aid to a luxuriant fancy, which his was not: as he did not want imagination, so none ever said he had much to spare. Neither was verse then refined so much, to be an help to that age, as it is to ours. Thus then the second thoughts being usually the best, as receiving the maturest digestion from judgment, and the last and most mature product of those thoughts being artful and laboured verse, it may well be inferred, that verse is a great help to a luxuriant fancy; and this is what that argument which you opposed was to evince."

Neander was pursuing this discourse so eagerly that Eugenius had called to him twice or thrice, ere he took notice that the barge stood still, and that they were at the foot of Somerset Stairs,[97] where they had appointed it to land. The company were all sorry to separate so soon, though a great part of the evening was already spent; and stood a-while looking back on the water, upon which the moonbeams played, and made it appear like floating quicksilver: at last they went up through a crowd of French people, who were merrily dancing in the open air, and nothing concerned for the noise of guns which had alarmed the town that afternoon. Walking thence together to the Piazze,[98] they parted there; Eugenius and Lisideius to some pleasant appointment they had made, and Crites and Neander to their several lodgings.

97 At the west end of old Somerset House.
98 An open arcade at Covent Garden, built by Inigo Jones in 1663–64.

Saint-Évremond

1610-1703

Charles de Marguetel de Saint-Denis, Seigneur de Saint-Évremond represents the aristocratic Frenchman of the seventeenth century at its best. There was, it may be said, a great gap between his mental life and ideas and his actual way of living, for in the one he was a staunch admirer of the old Roman republicans and in the other he was a refined dallier, creator of measured *bon mots,* in a world of salons and amorous intrigues. His early years were occupied by activity in the army and in political matters. The disgrace of Fouquet forced him into exile in England where he spent the last half of his life. It was during this period that most of his writing was done. Much of Saint-Évremond's writing concerned the theatre, where he was a lifelong admirer of Corneille, even though as a disciple of Gassendi he was an Epicurean and consequently, in theory, opposed to Corneille, who had leanings toward Stoicism. The strength of his attitudes is to be found in their flavor rather than in their substance. His prose style is among the best of his century.

The "Dissertation on the Tragedy of Racine's Entitled *Alexander the Great*" first appeared in 1666 and was revised in 1668. The "Ancient and Modern Tragedy" appeared in 1672. The works of Saint-Évremond were translated into English in 1713 by M. des Maizeaux, but since this translation is loose, a new one has been prepared here.

Dissertation on the Tragedy of Racine's Entitled
ALEXANDER THE GREAT
[1666: Revised in 1668]

Now that I have read the *Grand Alexandre,* Corneille's old age gives me fewer alarms, and I no longer have so many fears that tragedy will come to an end with him. But I might wish that he would, before his death, adopt the author of this play in order to develop his true successor with the tenderness of a father. I would like to have him give him the fine taste for antiquity he possesses so advantageously, so that he could make him enter into the genius of those dead nations and understand soundly the character of the heroes who are no more. To my way of thinking this is the only thing lacking to this fine talent. He has thoughts that are strong and bold, expressions that equal the force of his thoughts; but after that you will permit me to tell you that he has not understood either Alexander or Porus. It appears that he wanted to give us a greater idea of Porus than of Alexander, in which it was not possible to succeed; for the history of Alexander, entirely true though it is, has indeed the air of a romance, and to make a greater hero is to border on the fabulous; it is to deprive one's work not only of the credit of truth but also of the charm of probability. Let us not then imagine anything greater than this master of the universe or our imaginations will be too vast and too exalted. If we wish to have other heroes excel him, let us take from them the vices that he had and give them the virtues that he did not have. Let us not show Scipio greater, even though there was never seen among the Romans a mind as elevated as his; it is necessary to show him more just, leaning more to the good, more moderate, more temperate and more virtuous.

Do not let the contenders for Caesar against Alexander claim in his favor either passion for glory, or grandeur of mind, or firmness of courage. These qualities are so plain in the Greek that to have more of them would be to have too much. But let them make the Roman wiser in his enterprises, more skillful in affairs, with more extensive interests, more the master of his passions.

One very exacting judge of the merit of men contented himself with comparing anyone of whom he had an exalted opinion with Alexander: he did not dare to attribute to him any greater qualities; he merely did not include Alexander's bad ones: *Magno illi Alexandro, sed sobrio neque iracundo simillimus.**

Perhaps our author has entered into these considerations in some way; perhaps in order to make Porus bigger without getting into the fabulous, he chose the line of weakening his Alexander. If that has been his design, he could not have succeeded better, for he has created a prince who is so ordinary that a hundred others could get the better of him. It is not that Ephestion does not give a good picture of him, or that Taxile or even Porus does not speak favorably of his

* Velleius Paterculus (*History*, Book II, Chapter 41), speaking of Caesar.

greatness, but when he appears himself, he does not have the force to sustain it, unless through modesty he wishes to appear to be a simple man among the inhabitants of India in just repentance for having wished to pass for a god among the Persians. To speak seriously, I do not recognize anything about Alexander here except the name alone: his genius, his temperament, his qualities I do not find anywhere. I search in an impetuous hero for extraordinary actions that will stir me, and I find a prince who is so little animated that he leaves me as cold as I already was. I would expect to find in Porus a grandeur of mind that would be more a stranger to us: the hero of the Indies ought to have a character different from ours. There, so to speak, another sky, another sun, another earth produce other animals and other fruits: the men there seem to be unlike us in appearance, and still more, I dare say, in diversity of mind: a morality and a wisdom peculiar to the region seems to rule there and to guide alien minds in an alien world. Porus, however, whom Quintus Curtius depicts as totally foreign to the Greeks and the Persians, is here entirely French. In place of our being carried to the Indies, he is brought into France, where he adjusts himself so well to our temperament that he seems to have been born among us or at least to have lived here all his life.

Those who wish to represent some hero of the old centuries ought to enter into the genius of the nation of which he was, into the genius of the time when he lived, and particularly into his own genius. It is necessary to depict a king of Asia in a different way from a Roman consul. The one will talk like an absolute monarch who disposes of his subjects like slaves; the other like a magistrate who loves only the laws and makes their authority respected by a free people. It is necessary to give a different kind of picture for an old Roman who is zealous for the public good and moved by a savage liberty than for a flatterer of the time of Tiberius who exhibits the self-interest that submits to servitude. Different persons of the same condition and of the same time must be differently depicted when history gives them different kinds of characters. It would be ridiculous to give the same portrait of Cato as of Caesar, of Catiline as of Cicero, of Brutus as of Mark Antony, under the notion that they lived in the Republic at the same time. The spectator who sees these Ancients represented on our stages uses the same rules to judge properly of them that the poet uses in depicting them well, and to succeed better in the task he puts his mind at a remove from everything that he sees around him that pertains to his own customs, tries to free himself from the taste of his time, and renounces his own nature, if it differs from that of the characters represented; for the dead cannot make themselves what we are, but reason, which belongs to all times, can allow us to take part in what they have been.

One of the great faults of our nation is to judge everything by itself even to considering as alien to his own country anyone who does not have either French airs or manners. From that fact it follows that we can be justly reproached for an inability to judge things except in terms of the rapport that they have with us, of which Corneille had an unjust and painful experience in his *Sophonisbe*.[1] Mairet,[2] who had depicted his Sophonisba as unfaithful to the old Syphax and enamored of the young and victorious Massinissa, pleased everybody generally for having matched the taste of the women and the true spirit of the courtiers. But Corneille—who made his Greeks speak better than Greeks, Romans than Romans, and Carthaginians better than the Carthaginians ever spoke themselves—Corneille, who almost alone had the good taste of antiquity, has had the misfortune of displeasing our century, because he entered into the genius of those nations and conserved the true character of the daughter of Hasdrubal.

Thus, to the shame of our judgments, this author who has surpassed all our others, and who perhaps here surpassed himself in rendering to the great names all that is their due, has been unable to oblige us to render unto him what is his due, enslaved as we are by custom to the things that are in use with us, and little disposed by reason to have esteem for qualities and sentiments that do not agree with ours.

Let us conclude, after so extended a consideration, that Alexander and Porus ought to retain their characters entirely; that it is our business to see them on the banks of Hydapses as they were, and not for them to come, on the banks of the Seine, to learn our nature and adopt our sentiments. The speech of Porus ought to contain something more foreign and rare. If Quintus Curtius is admired in his harangue

1 Corneille's *Sophonisbe* was first acted in 1663.
2 Mairet (1604–86), *Sophonisbe* (1634).

of the Scythians for creating thoughts and expressions natural to that nation, the author could make himself as much a marvel by making us see, so to speak, the strangeness of the genius of another world.

The difference in character of these two kings, each showing so well what he owes to his own environment, and revealing virtue differently exercised in the diversity of fortune, attracted the attention of historians and obliged them to leave us a picture of them. The poet, who could add to the truth of things or at least adorn them with all the ornaments of poetry, has, instead of employing the colors and figures of poetry to embellish them, taken much away from their beauty; and whether because the fear of saying too much kept him from saying enough or, whether because of dryness and sterility, he remains much below the true. He could enter into the interior and draw their most secret motivations from the recesses of these great souls, as Corneille did, but he scarcely looks at the plain exteriors, barely concerned with noticing what appears, less deep in penetrating what is hidden.

I would have wished that the strength of the piece had been to present these great men to us, and that, in a scene fully worthy of the magnificence of the subject, the grandeur of these great minds were allowed to expand as far as they could go. If the conversation of Sertorius and Pompey so much filled our minds,* what should be hoped for from that between Alexander and Porus, on so uncommon a subject? I would have wished also that the author had given us a fuller idea of that war. In short, that crossing of the River Hydaspes, so strange that it can scarcely be conceived: a great army on the other side with terrible chariots and frightful elephants, lightning flashes, thunder, storms that threw everything into confusion at a time when such a large river had to be crossed on simple skins; a hundred astonishing things that were terrifying to the Macedonians and that could make Alexander say that finally he had found a peril worthy of him; all of that ought to enflame the imagination of the poet, both in the description of the trappings and in the account of the battle.

However, the poet hardly speaks of the camps of the two kings, who are deprived of their own temperaments to be made attendants upon princesses who are purely imaginary. That whole most precious and greatest desire of man, the defence of one's country and the salvation

* *Sertorius* by Corneille, Act III, Scene 1.

of a kingdom, does not excite Porus to combat. He is moved only by the beautiful eyes of Axiane, and the only goal of his valor is to recommend himself in her eyes. Thus are knights-errant depicted when they undertake an adventure; and the greatest wit of all Spain, in my opinion, never has Don Quixote entered a combat without first paying his respects to Dulcinea.

A romance maker can form his heroes in accordance with his fancy and it is not particularly important to give a true picture of an obscure prince whose reputation is barely known to us: but the great personalities of antiquity, so celebrated in their age and better known among us even than the living—the Alexanders, the Scipios, the Caesars—ought not lose their characters at our hands, for even the least sensitive spectator knows that they are injured when they are given faults that they do not possess, when they are deprived of virtues which had made an agreeable impression upon his mind. Once established in us, their virtues concern our self-love in the same way that our own real merits do. The introduction of the least alteration will make us feel the change violently. Especially, they must not be made lesser warriors so that they may glitter more as lovers. We can give them mistresses of our own invention, we can inject passion into their glory, but let us refrain from turning an Alexander into an Antony, and let us not ruin a hero whose reputation has been established for so many centuries, in favor of the lover whom we form in our own fancy.

To reject love from our tragedies as unworthy of heroes is to remove what can league us with them by a secret bond, by I do not know what connection that still remains between their minds and ours; but in resurrecting them for us, do not let them sink below themselves; do not spoil what they possess above the generality of men. With this reservation, I avow that there are no subjects in which a general passion that nature has given us all cannot participate painlessly and without violence. Besides, since women are as necessary on the stage as men, it is proper to have them speak as much as possible of that which is most natural to them, and upon which subject they speak better than upon any other. If you forbid some of them the expression of amorous sentiments and others the secret conversation in which confidences are exchanged, you will generally reduce them to boring speeches. Almost all their actions, like their speech, ought to be the effect of their passion; their joys, their sorrows, their fears, and their desires ought all to show a little love if they are to please us.

If you introduce a mother who rejoices over the happiness of her dear son or who suffers from the misfortunes of her poor daughter, her satisfaction or her pain will make little impression on the minds of the spectators. To be touched by the tears and the complaints of this sex, we should see a woman who weeps for the death of a lover and not a woman who is desolate at the loss of a husband. The precious and tender sorrow of mistresses touches us much more than the concocted and interested bereavements of a widow, who, entirely sincere though she may sometimes be, provides us always with a dismal suggestion of burials and their lugubrious ceremonies.

Of all the widows who have ever appeared on the stage I have enjoyed seeing only Cornelia,* because here instead of being forced to imagine children without a father and a woman without a husband, my entirely Roman sensibilities recall to my mind the spirit of ancient Rome and of the great Pompey.

That is all that can be reasonably granted to love on our stage; but let us be content with this advantage, in which even regularity may be concerned; and may even the stoutest partisans of love not believe that the principal end of tragedy should be to excite little tendernesses in our hearts. In truly heroic subjects grandeur of mind ought to be retained above all other things. What would be gentle and tender in the mistress of an ordinary man is often weak and shameful in the lover of a hero. When she is alone she may speak to herself of internal conflicts that she feels in herself; she may sigh in secret about her torment, or confide to her dear but trusted confidante all her fears and sorrows; but, sustained by her glory and fortified by her reason, she ought always to remain mistress of her impassioned feelings, and incite her lover to do great things through her resolution, instead of keeping him from them through her weakness.

In fact, it is an unworthy spectacle to see the courage of a hero debilitated by sighs and tears, and if he proudly scorns the tears of a beautiful woman who loves him, his scorn appears to be less the firmness of his spirit than the hardness of his mind.

To avoid this difficulty, Corneille paid as much attention to the characters of his illustrious women as to those of his heroes. Emilia

* In *Pompée* by Corneille.

animates Cinna to the execution of their plan and penetrates his heart to confound all his feelings that were opposed to the death of Augustus.* Cleopatra felt a passion for Caesar and tried everything to save Pompey; † she would have been unworthy of Caesar had she not opposed the cowardice of her brother, and Caesar unworthy of her had he been capable of approving that infamy. Dircé in *Oedipe*, contests with Theseus in greatness of courage, turning on him the dismal explanation of the oracle which he wished to be applied to his love for her.

But we must consider Sophonisba,‡ whose character would have been the envy even of the Romans. We must see her sacrificing the young Massinissa for the old Syphax for the good of her country. We must see her listen as little to the demands of duty in leaving Syphax as she listened to the expression of his love when she left Massinissa. We must see her subordinate all sorts of attachments, all that binds us together, all that unites us, the strongest chains, the sweetest passions, to her love for Carthage and her hate of Rome. And finally we must see her, at a time when everyone has abandoned her, not fail herself, and among the worthless hearts that she has won over, to save her country, able to draw from her own heart a final succor to save its glory and its liberty.

Corneille makes his heroes speak with so much propriety that he would never have given us the conversation between Caesar and Cleopatra had Caesar believed that he had the business in Alexandria that he had; § however fine it might have been, as the presentation of the conversation of an agreeable lover to the indifferent persons who listen to it, he would have done without it assuredly, at least until Caesar could see the battle of Pharsalia completely won, Pompey dead, and the remainder of his partisans in flight. As Caesar then believed himself master of everything, he acted as one with a glory acquired and a power apparently assured; but when he discovers the conspiracy of Ptolemy and sees his affairs in bad state and his own life in danger, no longer do we have the lover who talks with his mistress about his passion; it is the Roman general who speaks to the queen of the peril that faces them and leaves her suddenly to go to look out for their common safety.

---

* See *Cinna*, Act I, Scene III.   † Corneille's *Pompée*.
‡ In Corneille's *Sophonisbe*.   § Corneille, *Pompée*, Act IV, Scene III.

It is, then, ridiculous to busy Porus with love alone on the point of a great combat which was going to decide everything for him; it is not less so to make Alexander run away when his enemies rally. He should be made to come forward with dispatch to encounter Porus, and not withdraw precipitately to hurry to see Cléophile again: he who never had any such amorous impatience, and to whom victory never seemed full enough until he had either destroyed or pardoned. That which I find to be most pitiful for him is that he is made to lose much on one side without gaining anything on the other. He is as little a hero of love as of war. History is disfigured without the romance being embellished: a warrior whose glory contains nothing stirring to excite our ardor, a lover whose passion produces nothing to touch our sensibilities.

That is what I have to say on Alexander and Porus. If I have not applied myself in regular fashion to an exact critique, it is because I have less wished to examine the play in detail than to elaborate on the decorum that one should maintain in making heroes speak, on the discernment that it is necessary to have of the difference between characters, on the good and bad uses of the softness of love in tragedy, rejected too austerely by those who allot all space to the movements of fear and pity, and sought after with too much delicacy by those who have the taste for sentiments of this sort.

Of Ancient and Modern Tragedy
[1672]

NEVER have there been seen so many Rules for the making of good tragedies—at a time when so few of them are being written that it is necessary to put the old ones on the stage. I remember that the Abbé d'Aubignac composed one according to the laws that he had imperiously laid down for the stage.* It did not succeed; and at a time when he was boasting everywhere that he was the only one of our authors who had followed the precepts of Aristotle, M. the Prince said, "I

---

* François Hédelin, the Abbé d'Aubignac, was born in 1604 and died in 1676. In 1657 he published his treatise, the *Pratique du théâtre*. Some time later he wrote a tragedy in prose, *Zénobie*, which did not succeed.

am indebted to M. d'Aubignac for having followed the Rules of Aristotle so well, but I cannot pardon the Rules of Aristotle for having caused M. d'Aubignac to make such a bad tragedy."

We must agree that Aristotle's *Poetics* is an excellent work. However, there is nothing so perfect in it that it should set the Rules for all nations and all times. Descartes and Gassendi have discovered truths that Aristotle did not know. Corneille has found beauties for the stage that were not known to him; our philosophers have pointed out errors in his *Physics;* our poets have seen faults in his *Poetics,* at least to our way of thinking, all things being as much changed as they are.

Gods and goddesses brought about everything that was great and extraordinary in the plays of the Ancients, either because of their hate or their protection, and out of so many supernatural happenings nothing seemed fabulous to the people who had the opinion that gods and men formed one society. The gods were motivated almost always by human passions; men undertook nothing without getting the advice of the gods and executed nothing without their assistance. Thus, in this mixture of divinity and humanity, there was nothing that could not be believed.

But today all these marvels are mythical. The gods fail us and we fail them. And if, wishing to imitate the Ancients somehow, an author should introduce angels and saints on the stage, he would scandalize the devout as a profane man and would appear an imbecile in the eyes of the libertines. The preachers would not allow confusion of the pulpit with the theatre, or that one should go to learn from the mouths of actors what is retailed with authority in the churches to the whole population.

Besides, this would give a great advantage to the libertines, who could, in the theatre, turn into ridicule the same things that they receive with apparent submission in the churches, either out of respect for the place in which these things are said or through reverence for the persons who speak them.

But let us suppose that our learned men should abandon all holy matters to the liberty of the stage; let us somehow arrange it so that the least devout should listen to them with all the docility that the most submissive persons could have; even then it is certain that from the most holy doctrine, the most Christian actions, and the most useful truths, the tragedies that would be made would be those that would please the least.

The spirit of our religion is directly opposed to that of tragedy. The humility and patience of our saints are too directly contrary to the virtue of the kind of hero that the stage demands. With what zeal and what strength did Heaven inspire Néarque and Polyeucte: [3] and what did these new Christians not do to respond to these happy inspirations? The love and the charms of a dearly loved young spouse made no impression on the mind of Polyeucte. The political considerations of Félix, as being less touching, made even a smaller impression. Undaunted by either prayers or threats, Polyeucte strove harder to die for God than other men strive to live for themselves. Nevertheless, what would have made a good sermon made a bad tragedy, or would have if the dialogues between Pauline and Sévère had not saved for the author a reputation that the Christian virtues of our martyrs would have lost for him.

The stage loses all that is pleasing in it when it represents holy subjects, and the holy subjects lose most of the religious respect owing to them, when they are presented on the stage.

In truth, the stories of the Old Testament are much more useful on our stages. Moses, Samson, and Joshua had quite a different effect there than Polyeucte and Néarque. The amount of the marvelous that they can bring to it has something that is more proper for the stage. But it seems to me that the priests would not fail to cry out against the profanation of these sacred stories with which they fill their ordinary conversations, their books, and their sermons. And, to speak sensibly, the miraculous crossing of the Red Sea, Joshua's stopping the sun in its course by prayer, Samson defeating armies with the jawbone of an ass—all these marvels, I say, would not be believed in a play, because in the Bible one adds faith to them, but soon the Bible would be doubted too because none of this would be believed in the play.

If what I say is founded on good and solid reasons, we will have to content ourselves with purely natural but extraordinary things, and choose for our heroes principal traits which we can consider human and which evoke admiration as being rare and elevated above others.

3 Corneille's *Polyeucte* (1640).

In short, we must have nothing but the great, yet human; in the human, the mediocre must be avoided; in the great, the fabulous.

I do not wish to compare the *Pharsalia* to the *Aeneid:* I know clearly the difference in their value; but in the respect of their elevation, Pompey, Caesar, Cato, Curio, and Labienus did more for Lucan than Jupiter, Mercury, Juno, Venus and all the rest of the other gods and goddesses did for Virgil.[4]

The pictures that Lucan gives us of his great men are truly more beautiful and more affecting than those that Virgil gives of his immortals. The latter has dressed his gods in our weaknesses, to bring them to the threshold of man; the former raises his heroes to the point where they can bear comparison with gods.

Victrix causa diis placuit, sed victa Catoni.[5]

In Virgil the gods are not the equivalent of heroes; in Lucan the heroes are the equivalent of gods.

To impart to you my true feeling, I believe that the tragedies of the Ancients could happily have lost their gods with their oracles and soothsayers.

It was because of these gods, oracles, and soothsayers that there reigned on the stage a spirit of superstition and terror capable of infecting the human race with a thousand errors and afflicting it even more with woes. And in considering the common impressions that tragedy made in Athens on the minds of the spectators, it can be said that Plato was more right in prohibiting the practice than was Aristotle in advising it; for did not tragedy, which consisted of excessive rousing of fear and pity, make the stage a school of fright and compassion at which one learned to be frightened at all perils and to grieve at all misfortunes?

I can only with difficulty be persuaded that a mind accustomed to being frightened at what concerns the woes of another can be entirely easy in the presence of the woes that concern itself. It is perhaps there that the Athenians became so susceptible to the impressions of fear, and that spirit of terror, inspired in the theatre with so much art, became only too natural in the army.

In Sparta and at Rome, where the stage exposed to the eyes of the citizens only examples of valor and fortitude, the people were not

[4] Lucan's *Pharsalia* had the civil wars in Rome for subject matter.
[5] Lucan, *Pharsalia*, Bk. I, l. 128.

less haughty and brave in combat than firm and constant in the calamities of the Republic. Since in Athens this art of fearing and lamenting had been learned, there were exhibited in war those same unhappy emotions that had been learned at the performances.

Thus the spirit of superstition caused the rout of armies and that of lamentation made them content themselves with weeping about their great misfortunes, when they should have been finding some remedy. But how would they not have learned to grieve, in that school of commiseration? The characters represented were examples of ultimate misery and mediocre virtue.

Such was the desire to lament that fewer virtues were shown than troubles, for fear that a mind raised to the admiration of a hero would be less able to abandon itself to pity for a wretched man, and, in order to better impress the sentiments of fear and affliction on the spectators, choruses of children, virgins, and old men were always on the stage, to furnish their frights or their tears for each event.

Aristotle was fully aware of the harm that this could do to the Athenians, but he thought he had found a sufficient remedy for it in establishing a certain "purgation," which no one up to now has understood and which, in my judgment, he did not understand very well himself; for is there anything so ridiculous as to found a science which surely brings on sickness in order to establish another which uncertainly effects its cure—that of putting a perturbation in a mind in order to try afterwards to calm it by the reflections that it can make to itself on the shameful state in which it finds itself?

Among a thousand persons present at a play, there would be perhaps six philosophers who would be capable of becoming tranquil again through these wise and useful meditations; but the multitude would make no reflections, and one can be almost assured that by getting accustomed to seeing certain things on the stage, the spectator will form a habit of one of these deplorable emotions.

The same disturbing elements are not to be found in our plays as in the plays of the Ancients, since our fear never reaches the point of that superstitious terror that had such bad effects on courage. Our fear is most often only a pleasant disturbance that consists in keeping our minds in suspense; it is a fond interest taken by our minds in the subjects that attract their attention.

About the same thing can be said of our kind of pity. We deprive it of all its weakness and leave it all that it can possess of the charitable and humane. I love to see pitied the misfortune of a great man who is unhappy; I am glad that he attracts compassion and that he on occasion makes himself master of our tears; but I wish that these tender and generous tears would come from his misfortunes and his virtues together, and that along with the sad feeling of pity we might have the sensation of a lively admiration which should give birth in our minds of a lover's desire to imitate it.

We still have to mix a little love into the new kind of tragedy in order to rid ourselves the better of the black thoughts that the ancient kind left through superstition and terror. And, in truth, there is no passion that excites us more than a good love for anything that is noble and generous. Some men, who will abandon themselves in cowardly fashion to the insults of a scarcely formidable enemy, will defend the objects of their love until death against the attacks of the most valiant. The weakest and most timid animals, those animals formed by nature to be always timorous and always running away, will stand up fiercely against whatever they fear the most, to guard the objects of their love. Love has a warmth that serves as courage for those who have the least of it. But, to confess the truth, our authors have made a rather bad use of this splendid passion, which the Ancients did not make with their fear and pity, for, except for eight or ten plays in which its movements have been managed happily, we do not have any in which lovers and love are not equally disfigured.

We put an affected tenderness where we should put the most noble sentiments. We give softness to what should be the most touching, and sometimes in intending to express the graces of nature naively, we fall into a simplicity that is low and shameful.

While attempting to make kings and emperors into perfect lovers, we make ridiculous princes out of them; and by reason of their pleadings and their sighs where there is nothing to plead or sigh about, we turn them into imbeciles both as lovers and as princes. Often on our stages our great heroes love like shepherds, and the innocence of a kind of pastoral love takes the place of all glory and all virtue.

If an actress possesses the art of complaining and weeping in a touching manner, we will shed tears for her in moments that demand gravity; and because she pleases better when she is capable of feeling, she will incite some kind of sorrow at every point.

We require a love that is sometimes naive, sometimes tender, and sometimes sorrowful without caring who wants the naiveté, or tenderness, or sorrow; that comes from the fact that, wanting love to be everywhere, we seek for a diversity in manners and almost never base it in passion.

I hope that someday we shall find the true use for this passion that has become too ordinary. This emotion that ought to be the agent for making more gentle whatever is either too barbarous or too dismal, that ought to affect our hearts nobly, animate our courage and raise our spirits, will not always be the object of an affected tenderness or of an imbecile simplicity. When that time comes we shall make the Ancients envious of us. Unless a poet has an excessive love for the Ancients or is too much disgusted with his own century, he will use no tragedies of Sophocles or Euripides as models for the plays of our time.

I am not saying that their tragedies did not have what they needed to please the taste of the Athenians; but I dare assure whoever would translate into French in all its force even *Oedipus,* the masterpiece of the Ancients, that nothing in the world would appear more barbarous, more depressing, more opposed to the true sentiments that ought to be held.

Our century has this advantage at least, that it is permitted to hate vices freely, and to have love for virtue. Since the gods committed great crimes in the plays of the Ancients, the crimes won the respect of the spectators, and no one dared to consider bad what was really abominable. When Agamemnon sacrificed his own daughter—a daughter tenderly loved—to appease the anger of the gods, that barbarous sacrifice was regarded as a pious obedience, as the ultimate sign of a religious submission.

At that time, whoever wanted to retain the true feelings of humanity had to murmur against the cruelty of the gods, in an impious fashion; and whoever wished to be devout in respect to the gods had to be cruel and barbarous toward men. It was necessary to do, like Agamemnon, complete violence to nature and love:

Tantum religio potuit suadere malorum,[6]

says Lucretius concerning this barbarous sacrifice.

[6] Lucretius, *De rerum natura,* Bk. I, l. 101: "To such evil deeds does religion persuade men."

Today we see men presented to us without the intervention of the gods, a hundredfold more useful to the public and to the individual. For in our tragedies there are no criminals who are not detested and no heroes who cannot be admired. Few crimes go unpunished there; few virtues are not rewarded. With the good examples that we give the public from the stage, with the pleasing emotions of love and admiration added to a rectified pity and fear, we will arrive at the perfection that Horace desired:

Omne tulit punctum qui miscuit utile dulci,[7]

which could never be, in accordance with the rules of the Ancients.

I shall close with a bold and new thought: it is that tragedy should seek above all things to show a greatness of mind well expressed that excites a tender admiration in us. In this kind of admiration there is a delight for the mind: our courage is heightened by it and our soul is touched.

[7] Horace, *Ars poetica,* l. 343: "He gets every vote who mixes the useful with the pleasant."

John Milton
1608-1674

JOHN MILTON is too well known to need introduction here, but his contribution to dramatic criticism is perhaps less familiar to readers than his
contribution to poetry. In the Ancients-Moderns quarrel, Milton takes the
side of the Ancients, drawing his dramatic ideas from the Greeks rather
than from the French whom English tragedians were favoring. It may be
argued that Milton's precepts lack validity because *Samson Agonistes* was
not intended for the stage, but the ideas he expounds found considerable
acceptance in the eighteenth century.

Samson Agonistes
[1671]

PREFACE

OF THAT SORT OF DRAMATIC POEM WHICH IS CALLED TRAGEDY

TRAGEDY, as it was anciently composed, hath been ever held the
gravest, moralest, and most profitable of all other poems; therefore
said by Aristotle to be of power by raising pity and fear or terror, to
purge the mind of those and such like passions, that is to temper and
reduce them to just measure with a kind of delight, stirred up by
reading or seeing those passions well imitated. Nor is Nature wanting in her own effects to make good his assertion: for so in physic
things of melancholic hue and quality are used against melancholy,
sour against sour, salt to remove salt humours. Hence philosophers
and other gravest writers, as Cicero, Plutarch, and others, frequently
cite out of tragic poets, both to adorn and illustrate their discourse.
The Apostle Paul himself thought it not unworthy to insert a verse
of Euripides into the text of Holy Scripture, I *Cor.* 15. 33 and Paraeus
commenting on the Revelation, divides the whole book as a tragedy,

into acts distinguished each by a Chorus of Heavenly Harpings and Song between. Heretofore men in highest dignity have laboured not a little to be thought able to compose a tragedy. Of that honour Dionysius the elder was no less ambitious than before of his attaining to the tyranny. Augustus Caesar also had begun his *Ajax*, but unable to please his own judgment with what he had begun, left it unfinished. Seneca the philosopher is by some thought the author of those tragedies (at least the best of them) that go under that name. Gregory Nazianzen, a father of the Church, thought it not unbeseeming the sanctity of his person to write a tragedy, which he entitled, *Christ Suffering*. This is mentioned to vindicate tragedy from the small esteem, or rather infamy, which in the account of many it undergoes at this day with other common interludes; happening through the poets' error of intermixing comic stuff with tragic sadness and gravity; or introducing trivial and vulgar persons, which by all judicious hath been counted absurd; and brought in without discretion, corruptly to gratify the people. And though ancient tragedy use no prologue, yet using sometimes in case of self defence or explanation that which Martial calls an Epistle; in behalf of this tragedy coming forth after the ancient manner, much different from what among us passes for best, thus much before-hand may be epistled; that Chorus is here introduced after the Greek manner, not ancient only but modern, and still in use among the Italians. In the modelling therefore of this poem, with good reason, the Ancients and Italians are rather followed, as of much more authority and fame. The measure of verse used in the Chorus is of all sorts, called by the Greeks Monostrophic, or rather Apolelymenon, without regard had to Strophe, Antistrophe, or Epode, which were a kind of stanzas framed only for the music then used with the Chorus that sung; not essential to the poem, and therefore not material; or being divided into Stanzas or pauses, they may be called Allaeostropha. Division into act and scene referring chiefly to the stage (to which this work never was intended) is here omitted.

It suffices if the whole drama be found not produced beyond the fifth act, of the style and uniformity, and that commonly called the plot, whether intricate or explicit, which is nothing indeed but such economy or disposition of the fable as may stand best with verisimilitude and decorum; they only will best judge who are not unacquainted with Aeschylus, Sophocles, and Euripides, the three tragic poets unequalled yet by any, and the best rule to all who endeavour to write tragedy. The circumscription of time wherein the whole drama begins and ends, is according to ancient rule, and best example, within the space of 24 hours.

René Rapin

1621-1687

THE YEAR 1674 is an important one in the history of literary criticism in France, for in it appeared Boileau's *Art poétique* and two works by René Rapin that were destined to have great influence upon the century that followed. The first of these, his translation into French of Longinus's *On the Sublime,* had much to do with creating a vogue for sublimity as an intended effect in literary productions and with originating speculation on aesthetic questions. The second, his *Reflections on Aristotle's Poetics,* entitled him to a place alongside Le Bossu and Dacier, in the trio of French Aristotelian formalists who were the authorized interpreters of the neoclassic code in drama. Actually, Rapin was less a defender of the Ancients than his reputation might indicate. Both Le Bossu and Rapin were responsive to new ideas, caught the tone of their time with shrewd accuracy. Of the two, Rapin was the one who reflected the new ideas and new tone that Racine had brought to the stage. In Rapin are to be found seeds of critical doctrine that were to develop into more than one kind of sentimentalism in the eighteenth century. Especially important in this connection are the ideas that the rousing of passions is in itself pleasant and his interpretation of the Aristotelian catharsis, which became, with some modification, the standard interpretation among the sentimentalists of the eighteenth century.

Thomas Rymer found a kindred spirit in Rapin and his translation of the Frenchman's work appeared very shortly after the original publication in 1674.

Reflections on the POETICS *of Aristotle* [1]

[1674; excerpts]

REFLECTIONS IN GENERAL

VII

IT IS NOT easily decided what the nature and what precisely is the end of this art; the interpreters of Aristotle differ in their opinions. Some

1 This translation is by Thomas Rymer (q.v.), 1674.

will have the end to be delight, and that 'tis on this account it labors to move the passions, all whose motions are delightful, because nothing is more sweet to the soul than agitation; it pleases itself in changing the objects to satisfy the immensity of its desires. 'Tis true, delight is the end poetry aims at, but not the principal end, as others pretend. In effect, poetry being an art, ought to be profitable by the quality of its own nature, and by the essential subordination that all arts should have to polity, whose end in general is the public good. This is the judgment of Aristotle, and of Horace, his chief interpreter.

X

FOR NO OTHER END is poetry delightful than that it may be profitable. Pleasure is only the means by which the profit is conveyed; and all poetry, when 'tis perfect, ought of necessity to be a public lesson of good manners for the instruction of the world. Heroic poesy proposes the example of great virtues and great vices, to excite men to abhor these, and to be in love with the other. It gives us an esteem for Achilles in Homer, and contempt for Thersites. It begets in us a veneration for the piety of Aeneas in Virgil and horror for the profaneness of Mezentius. Tragedy rectifies the use of passions, by moderating our fear and our pity which are obstacles of virtue; it lets men see that vice never escapes unpunished, when it represents Aegysthus in the *Electra* of Sophocles punished after the ten years enjoyment of his crime. It teaches us that the favors of fortune and the grandeurs of the world are not always true goods when it shews on the theatre a queen so unhappy as Hecuba deploring with that pathetic air her misfortunes in Euripides. Comedy, which is an image of common conversation, corrects the public vices by letting us see how ridiculous they are in particulars. Aristophanes does not mock at the foolish vanity of Praxagora (in his *Parliament of Women*)[2] but to cure the vanity of the other Athenian women; and it was only to teach the Roman soldiers in what consisted true valor that Plautus exposed in public the extravagence of false bravery in his Braggadocio Captain, in that comedy of the *Glorious Soldier*.[3]

XI

BUT BECAUSE poetry is only profitable so far as it is delightful, 'tis of greatest importance in this art to please; the only certain way to

[2] Aristophanes' *Ecclesiazusae*.　　　　[3] Plautus, *Miles Gloriosus*.

please is by Rules. These therefore are to be established, that a poet may not be left to confound all things, imitating those extravagances which Horace so much blames; that is to say, by joining things naturally incompatible, mixing tigers with lambs, birds with serpents, to make one body of different species, and thereby authorize fancies more indigested than the dreams of sick men; for unless a man adhere to principles, he is obnoxious to all extravagances and absurdities imaginable; unless he go by Rule, he slips at every step towards Wit and falls into errors as often as he sets out. . . .

XII

ARISTOTLE drew the platform of these Rules from the poems of Homer and other Poets of his time by the reflections he had a long time made on their works. I pretend not by a long discourse to justify the necessity, the justness, and the truth of these Rules, nor to make an history of Aristotle's *Treatise of Poesy;* or examine whether it is complete, which many others have done: all these things I suppose; only I affirm that these Rules well considered, one shall find them made only to reduce Nature into method, to trace it step by step, and not suffer the least mark of it to escape us. 'Tis only by these Rules that the verisimility in fictions is maintained, which is the soul of poesy. For unless there be the Unity of Place, of Time, and of the Action in the great poems, there can be no verisimility. In fine, 'tis by these Rules that all becomes just, proportionate, and natural; for they are founded upon good sense and sound reason, rather than authority and example. Horace's *Book of Poesy,* which is but an interpretation of that of Aristotle, discovers sufficiently the necessity of being subject to Rules, by the ridiculous Absurdities one is apt to fall into who follows only his fancy; for though poesy be the effect of fancy, yet if this fancy be not regulated, 'tis a mere caprice, not capable of producing anything reasonable.

REFLECTIONS IN PARTICULAR

XVII

TRAGEDY, of all parts of poesy, is that which Aristotle has most discussed, and where he appears most exact. He alleges that tragedy is a public lecture, without comparison more instructive than philosophy; because it teaches the mind by the sense, and rectifies the passions by the passions themselves, calming by their emotion the troubles they excite in the heart. The philosopher had observed two important faults in man to be regulated, pride and hardness of heart, and he found for both vices a cure in tragedy. For it makes man modest by representing the great masters of the earth humbled; and it makes him tender and merciful by shewing him on the theatre the strange accidents of life, and the unforeseen disgraces to which the most important persons are subject. But because man is naturally timorous and compassionate, he may fall into another extreme, to be either too fearful or too full of pity; the too much fear may shake the constancy of mind, and the too great compassion may enfeeble the equity. 'Tis the business of tragedy to regulate these two weaknesses; it prepares and arms him against disgraces by shewing them so frequent in the most considerable persons; and he shall cease to fear ordinary accidents, when he sees such extraordinary [ones] happen to the highest part of mankind. But as the end of tragedy is to teach men not to fear too weakly the commonly misfortunes and manage their fear, it makes account also to teach them to spare their compassion for objects that deserve it. For there is an injustice in being moved at the afflictions of those who deserve to be miserable. One may see without pity Clytemnestra slain by her son, Orestes, in Aeschylus because she had cut the throat of Agamemnon, her husband; and one cannot see Hippolytus die by the plot of his stepmother, Phaedra, in Euripides, without compassion, because he died not but for being chaste and virtuous. This to me seems, in short, the design of tragedy, according to the system of Aristotle, which to me appears admirable, but which has not been explained as it ought by his interpreters; they have not, it may seem, sufficiently understood the mystery to unfold it well.

XVIII

BUT IT IS NOT ENOUGH that tragedy be furnished with all the most moving and terrible adventures that history can afford to stir in the heart those motions it pretends, to the end it may cure the mind of those vain fears that may annoy it, and those childish compassions that may soften it. 'Tis also necessary, says the philosopher, that every poet employ these great objects of terror and pity as the two most powerful springs in art, to produce that pleasure which tragedy may yield. And this pleasure, which is properly of the mind, consists in the agitation of the soul moved by the passions. Tragedy cannot be delightful to the spectator unless he become sensible to all that is represented; he must enter into all the different thoughts of the actors, interest himself in the adventures, fear, hope, afflict himself, and rejoice with them. The theatre is dull and languid when it ceases to produce these motions in the soul of those that stand by. But as of all passions, fear and pity are those that make strongest impressions on the heart of man by the natural disposition he has of being afraid and of being mollified. Aristotle has chosen these amongst the rest to move more powerfully the soul by the tender sentiments they cause when the heart admits and is pierced by them. In effect, when the soul is shaken by motions so natural and so humane, all the impressions it feels becomes delightful; its trouble pleases, and the emotion it finds is a kind of charm to it, which does cast it into a sweet and profound meditation, and which insensibly does engage it in all the interests that are managed on the theatre. 'Tis then that the heart yields itself over to all the objects that are proposed, that all images strike it, that it espouses the sentiments of all those that speak, and becomes susceptible of all the passions that are presented because 'tis moved. And in this agitation consists all the pleasure that one is capable to receive from tragedy: for the spirit of man does please itself with the different situations caused by the different objects, and the various passions that are represented.

x x

MODERN TRAGEDY turns on other principles; the genius of our [French] nation is not strong enough to sustain an action on the theatre by moving only terror and pity. These are machines that will not play as they ought but by great thoughts and noble expressions, of which we are not indeed altogether so capable as the Greeks. Perhaps our nation, which is naturally gallant, has been obliged by the necessity of our character to frame for ourselves a new system of tragedy to suit with our humor. The Greeks, who were popular estates and who hated monarchy, took delight in their spectacles to see kings humbled and high fortunes cast down, because the exaltation grieved them. The English, our neighbors, love blood in their sports by the quality of their temperament; these are insulaires, separated from the rest of men; we are more humane. Gallantry, moreover, agrees with our manners, and our poets believed that they could not succeed well on the theatre but by sweet and tender sentiments; in which, perhaps, they had some reason. For, in effect, the passions represented become deformed and insipid, unless they are founded on sentiments conformable to those of the spectator. 'Tis this that obliges our poets to stand up so strongly for the privilege of gallantry on the theatre, and to bend all their subjects to love and tenderness; the rather, to please the women, who have made themselves judges of these divertisements, and usurped the right to pass sentence. And some besides have suffered themselves to be prepossessed and led by the Spaniards, who make all their Cavaliers amorous. 'Tis by them that tragedy began to degenerate; and we by little and little accustomed to see heroes on the theatre smitten with another love than that of glory, and that by degrees all the great men of antiquity have lost their characters in our hands. 'Tis likewise perhaps by this gallantry that our age would devise a color to excuse the feebleness of our wit; not being able to sustain always the same action by the greatness of words and thoughts. However it be, for I am not hardy enough to declare myself against the public, 'tis to degrade tragedy from that majesty which is proper to it, to mingle in it love, which is of a character always light, and little suitable to that gravity of which tragedy makes profession. Hence it proceeds that these tragedies mixed with gallantries never makes such admirable impressions on the spirit as did those of Sophocles and Euripides; for all the bowels were moved by the great objects of terror and pity which they proposed. 'Tis likewise for this that the reputation of our modern tragedies so soon decays and yields but small delight at two years end; whereas the Greek please yet to those that have a good taste after two thousand years, because what is not grave and serious on the theatre, though it give delight at present, after a short time grows distasteful and unpleasant, and because, what is not proper for great thoughts and great figures in tragedy cannot support itself. The Ancients who perceived this, did not interweave their gallantry and love, save in comedy. For love is of a character that always degenerates from that heroic air, of which tragedy must never divest itself. And nothing to me shews so mean and senseless as for one to amuse himself with whining about frivolous kindnesses when he may be admirable by great and noble thoughts and sublime expressions. But I dare not presume so far on my own capacity and credit to oppose myself of my own head against a usage so established. I must be content modestly to propose my doubts, and that may serve to exercise the wits in an age that only wants matter. But to end this reflection with a touch of Christianism, I am persuaded that the innocence of the theatre might be better preserved according to the idea of the ancient tragedy, because the new is become too effeminate by the softness of latter ages; and the Prince de Conty who signalized his zeal against the modern tragedy by his treatise on that subject would, without doubt, have allowed the ancient, because that has nothing that may seem dangerous.[4]

X X V

COMEDY is an image of common life; its end is to shew on the stage the faults of particulars, in order to amend the faults of the public, and to correct the people through a fear of being rendered ridiculous. So that which is most proper to excite laughter is that which is most essential to comedy. One may be ridiculous in words, or ridiculous in things. There is an honest laughter and a buffoon laughter. 'Tis merely a gift of Nature to make everything ridiculous. For all the actions of human life have their fair and wrong side, their serious and ridiculous. But Aristotle, who gives precepts to make men weep, leaves none to make them laugh. This proceeds purely from the genius; art and method have little to do with it, 'tis the work of Nature alone. The Spaniards have a genius to discern the ridiculous of things much better than the French; and the Italians, who are naturally comedians, express it better; their tongue is more proper for it, by a drolling tone peculiar to Terence, that he made one Latin comedy of two when their language has attained its perfection. Finally, that pleasant turn, that gaiety which can sustain the delicacy of his character, without falling into coldness, nor into buffoonry; that fine raillery which is the flower of Wit, is the talent which comedy demands; but it must always be observed that the true ridiculous of art for the entertainment on the theatre ought to be no other but the copy of the ridiculous that is found in Nature. Comedy is as it should be when the spectator believes himself really in the company of such persons as he has represented, and takes himself to be in a family whilst he is at the theatre; and that he there sees nothing but

[4] The Prince of Conty. Armand de Bourbon, Prince de Conti, was a sponsor of Molière. He attacked the theatre in his *Traité de la comédie et des spectacles selon les traditions de l'Église* (1667).

what he sees in the world. For comedy is worth nothing at all unless he know and can compare the manners that are exhibited on the stage with those of such persons as he has conversation withal. 'Twas by this that Menander had so great success amongst the Grecians; and the Romans thought themselves in conversation whilst they sat beholding the comedies of Terence; for they perceived nothing but what they had been accustomed to find in ordinary companies. 'Tis the great art of comedy to keep close to Nature and never leave it; to have common thoughts and expressions fitted to the capacity of all the world. For it is most certainly true, that the most gross strokes of Nature, whatever they be, please always more than the most delicate, that are not natural; nevertheless base and vulgar terms are not to be permitted on the theatre, unless supported by some kind of Wit. The proverbs and wise sayings of the people ought not to be suffered unless they have some pleasant meaning, and unless they are natural. This is the most general principle of comedy; by which, whatever is represented, cannot fail to please; but without it, nothing. 'Tis only by adhering to Nature that the probability can be maintained, which is the sole infallible guide that may be followed in the theatre. Without probability all is lame and faulty; with it all goes well. None can run astray who follow it; and the most ordinary faults of comedy happen from thence, that the decencies are not well observed, nor the incidents enough prepared. 'Tis likewise necessary to take heed that the colors employed to prepare the incidents be not too gross, to leave to the spectator the pleasure of finding out himself what they signify. But the most ordinary weakness of our comedies is the unravelling; scarce ever any succeed well in that, by the difficulty there is in untying happily that knot which had been tied. It is easy to wind up an intrigue, 'tis only the work of fancy; but the unravelling is the pure and perfect work of the judgment. 'Tis this that makes the success difficult, and if one would thereon make a little reflection, he might find that the most universal fault of comedies is that the catastrophe is not natural. It rests to examine, whether in comedy the images may be drawn greater than the natural, the more to move the minds of the spectators by more shining portraits, and by stronger impressions? That is to say, whether a poet may make a miser more covetous, a morose man more morose and troublesome than the original? To which I answer, that Plautus, who studied to please the common people, made them so; but Terence, who would please the better sort, confined himself within the bounds of Nature, and he represented vices without making them either better or worse. Notwithstanding these extravagant characters, such as the Citizen turned Gentleman,[5] and the Sick in Imagination [6] of Molière, failed not of success a little while ago at court, where all the tastes are so delicate; but all things there are well received, even to the divertisements of the provinces, if they have any air of pleasantry; for there they love to laugh rather than to admire. These are the most important rules of comedy. . . .

[5] Molière's *Le Bourgeois gentilhomme* (1670).
[6] Molière's *Le Malade imaginaire* (1673).

René Le Bossu
1631-1680

RENÉ LE BOSSU is known to history only for his *Treatise of the Epic Poem*, first published in 1675: but although as a man he remains an obscure and unimportant figure, his book was widely read, was widely quoted, and was responsible for the growth of an attitude toward the structuring of a play that was popular for almost a century. This was the attitude that a play should be built around a fable, should, in fact, be an expanded and concrete fable. The last part of the seventeenth century was a period in which there was much interest in fables, and one of the distinguishing features of neoclassical criticism was its emphasis upon the abstract or general idea in literature in relation to concrete or particular fact. Thus, although Le Bossu was writing primarily about the epic, his thoughts were important in dramatic criticism as well.

This work was translated into English by "W. J." in 1695.

Treatise of the Epic Poem
[1675; excerpt]

CHAPTER VII. THE METHOD OF COMPOSING A FABLE

THE FIRST THING we are to begin with for composing a fable is to choose the instruction and the point of morality which is to serve as its foundation, according to the design and end we propose to ourselves.

I would, for instance, exhort two brothers, or any other persons who hold an estate in common, to agree well together the better to preserve it: and this is the end of the fable and the first thing I thought on.

For this purpose I endeavor to imprint upon their minds this maxim: "that a misunderstanding between friends is the ruin of families and of all sorts of societies." This maxim which I make choice of is the point of morality and the truth which serves as a foundation to the fable I would compose.

In the next place this moral truth must be reduced into action, and a general action must be feigned in imitation of the true and singular actions of those who have been ruined by a misunderstanding that has happened among them. I say then, that several persons were engaged together to look after an estate which they hold in common. They fall out with one another, and this difference leaves them defenceless to the will of an enemy who ruins them.

This is the first platform of a fable. The action which this recital presents us with has four qualifications: it is universal, it is imitated, it is feigned, and it contains allegorically a moral truth. This model then comprehends the two essential parts which compose the fable; *viz*, the truth and the fiction. All this is common to all sorts of fables.

The names that are given to the personages do first specify a fable. Æsop gives them the names of beasts. "Once upon a time," says he, "two dogs were set to keep a flock of sheep; they fight with one another and leave the sheep without defence to the mercy of the wolf that commits what ravage he pleases among them." These names are the meanest of any. The action is still general, and the fiction is altogether apparent.

We may disguise the fiction, render the action more singular, and make it a rational fable by the names of men invented at pleasure. "Pridamont and Orontes, two brothers by a second marriage, were left very rich by their father's last will and testament. They could not agree in sharing their estates and were so obstinately bent one against the other that to provide for their common interest against Clitander (their elder brother by a former marriage) was the very least of their care. He very dextrously foments their quarrel and keeps them from minding the design he has upon them by pretending he expected nothing but a small gratuity by the accommodations which he daily proposes but never urges home to them. In the meantime he gains upon the judges and all others who were intrusted with this affair; he procures the will to be cancelled and becomes master of all that estate he pretended he would have gratified his brothers with, though to his own prejudice."

This fable is a rational and probable fable; but because the names are feigned as well as the things and the action is only particular and the families ordinary, it is neither an epic nor tragic fable and can only be managed in comedy. For Aristotle informs us, "that comic poets invent both the names and the things." *

* *Poetics*, Chap. 9.

In order to make this an *à la mode* comic fable, some girl or another should have been promised to Clitander, but the will should have put the father upon altering his design, and he should have obliged her to have married one of these two rich coxcombs for whom she had not the least fancy. And here the comical part might have been carried on very regularly even as the poet pleased. But to return.

The fiction might be so disguised under the truth of history that those who are ignorant of the poet's art would believe that he had made no fiction. But the better to carry on this disguise, search must be made in history for the names of some persons to whom this feigned action might either probably or really have happened; and then must the action be rehearsed under these known names with such circumstances that alter nothing of the essence either of the fable or the moral, as in the following example:

"In the war King Philip the Fair had with the Flemings in the year 1302, he sent out his army under the command of Robert, Earl of Artois, his general, and Ralph of Nesle, his constable. When they were in the Plain of Courtray in sight of the enemy, the Constable says, ' 'Twas so easy to starve them that it would be advisable not to hazard the lives of so many brave men against such vile and despicable fellows.' The Earl very haughtily rejects this advice, charging him with cowardice and treachery. 'We will see,' replies the Constable in a rage, 'which of us has the most loyalty and bravery'; and with that away he rides directly towards the enemy, drawing all the French cavalry after him. This precipitation and the dust they raised hindered them from discovering a large and deep river beyond which the Flemings were posted. The French were miserably cast away in the torrent. At this loss the infantry were so startled that they suffered themselves to be cut in pieces by the enemy."

'Tis by this means that the fiction may have some agreement with the truth itself, and the precepts of the art do not contradict one another, though they order us to begin by feigning an action and then advise us to draw it from history. As for the fiction and fable, it signifies little whether the persons are dogs, or Orontes and Pridamont, or Robert d'Artois and the Earl of Nesle, or lastly Achilles and Agamemnon. . . .

Thomas Rymer
1641-1713

THOMAS RYMER is remembered chiefly for his bad criticism of Shakespeare and for his invention of the term "poetic justice," a convenient name for the age-old duty of a writer to punish vice and to reward virtue. The term became common in discussions of sentimentalism and is often heard even today.

A careful, fastidious man, but completely without literary sensitivity, Rymer represents the ultimate development of the theoretical critics of the Renaissance. His weakness is not one of logic but rather of fundamental premise. He laid down, or called upon, rules of criticism and flayed mercilessly any deviation from them. Not only the tragedies of Shakespeare were thus derided; all except those of the Ancients came under attack.

It is easy to perceive Rymer's view of the ideal type of tragedy from his sketch of the *Invincible Armado* included in the excerpts reprinted here. This exhibits no knowledge of theatrical requirements; it is a good example of the type of play which ought to have been liked but never was. It is interesting to note that the *Invincible Armado* is completely free of the "love and honor" theme so dear to the hearts of the tragedians of the time.

Rymer's doctrine of poetic justice was set forth in his *Tragedies of the Last Age Considered* (1678). Dryden spoke favorably of this work but rejected Rymer's position after the appearance of *A Short View of Tragedy* (1693).

A Short View of Tragedy
[1693; excerpts]

CHAPTER ONE

WHAT REFORMATION may not we expect, now that in France they see the necessity of a chorus to their tragedies? Boyer and Racine, both of the Royal Academy, have led the dance; they have tried the success in the last plays that were presented by them.

The chorus was the root and original and is certainly always the most necessary part of tragedy.

The spectators thereby are secured that their poet shall not juggle or put upon them in the matter of place and time, other than is just and reasonable for the representation.

And the poet has this benefit: the chorus is a goodly show, so that he need not ramble from his subject out of his wits for some foreign toy or hobby-horse to humor the multitude.

Aristotle * tells us of two senses that must be pleased, our sight and our ears. And it is in vain for a poet (with Bays in the *Rehearsal*) [1] to complain of injustice and the wrong judgment in his audience unless these two senses be gratified.

The worst on it is that most people are wholly led by these two senses, and follow them upon content without ever troubling their noddle farther.

How many plays owe all their success to a rare show? Even in the days of Horace, enter on the stage a person in a costly, strange habit—Lord! what clapping, what noise and thunder as Heaven and earth were coming together! yet not one word spoken.

> *Dixit adhuc aliquid? nil, sane, quid placit ergo?*
> *Lana Terentino violas imitata veneno.*
>
> Was there ought said? troth no, What then did touch ye?
> Some Prince of *Bantham*, or a *Mamamouche*.

It matters not whether there be any plot and characters, any sense or a wise word from one end to the other, provided in our play we have the Senate of Rome, the Venetian Senate in their Pontificalibus,[2] or a blackamoor ruffian, or Tom Dove,[3] or other four legged hero of the Bear Garden.[4]

The eye is a quick sense, will be in with our fancy, and prepossesses the head strangely. Another means whereby the eye misleads our judgment is the action. We go to see a play acted; in tragedy is represented a memorable action; so the Spectators are always pleased to

* *Poetica.*

---

[1] *The Rehearsal* (1671), by the Duke of Buckingham and others, is a famous burlesque of the heroic tragedy. The part of Bays, the author of the tragedy being rehearsed, is a satire on Dryden, but the attack is by no means confined to him.
[2] Pontificalibus: Vestments or Robes of Office.
[3] Tom Dove: a well-known performing bear.
[4] Four-Legged Hero of the Bear Garden: the animals used in baiting.

see action and are not often so ill-natured to pry into and examine whether it be proper, just, natural, in season, or out of season. Bays in the *Rehearsal* well knew this secret: the two Kings are at their Coranto; nay, the Moon and the Earth dance the hey—anything in Nature or against Nature, rather than allow the serious council or other dull business to interrupt or obstruct action.

This thing of action finds the blind side of human kind an hundred ways. We laugh and weep with those that laugh or weep; we gape, stretch, and are very dotterels [5] by example.

. . .

Many, peradventure, of the tragical scenes in Shakespeare cried up for the action might do yet better without words. Words are a sort of heavy baggage that were better out of the way at the push of action, especially in his bombast circumstance where the words and action are seldom akin, generally are inconsistent, at cross purposes, embarrass or destroy each other; yet to those who take not the words distinctly, there may be something in the buzz and sound that like a drone to a bagpipe may serve to set off the action. For an instance of the former, would not a rap at the door better express Iago's meaning than

> . . . *Call aloud.*
> *Iago.* Do with like timorous accent, and dire yell,
> As when by night and negligence the fire
> Is spied in populous cities? [6]

For, "What ship? Who is arrived?" The answer is,

> 'Tis one Iago, Ancient to the General.
> He has had most favorable and happy speed;
> Tempests themselves, high seas, and howling winds,
> The guttered rocks, and congregated sands,
> Traitors ensteep'd, to clog the guiltless keel,
> As having sense of beauty, do omit
> Their common natures, letting go safely by
> The divine Desdemona.[7]

Is this the language of the exchange or the Insuring Office? Once in a man's life he might be content at Bedlam to hear such rapture. In a play one should speak like a man of business, his speech must be Πολιτινος, which the French render *Agrissante;* the Italians, *Negotiosa*

---

[5] Dotterels: silly persons, dotards.   [6] *Othello,* I, i, 75–77.

[7] *Ibid.,* II, i, 78–85. In line 82, Ff. and modern eds. read "mortal" in place of "common."

and *Operativa;* but by this gentleman's talk one may well guess he has nothing to do. And he has many companions that are

> . . . Hey day!
> I know not what to do, nor what to say.*

It was then a strange imagination in Ben Jonson to go stuff out a play [8] with Tully's orations. And in Seneca, to think his dry morals and a tedious train of sentences might do feats or have any wonderful operation in the drama.

Some go to see, others to hear a play. The poet should please both, but be sure that the spectators be satisfied whatever entertainment he give his audience.

But if neither the show nor the action cheats us, there remains still a notable vehicle to carry off nonsense, which is pronunciation.

> By the loud trumpet, which our courage aids;
> We learn that sound as well as sense persuades.†

Demosthenes ‡ had a good stock of sense, was a great master of words, could turn a period, and draw up his tropes [9] in a line of battle, and fain would he have seen some effect of his orations; nobody was moved, nobody minded him. He goes to the playhouse, bargains with an actor, and learned of him to speak roundly and gracefully. From that time: who but Demosthenes? Never such a leading man! Whenever he spake, no division; not a vote to the contrary, the whole house were with him, *nemine contradicente.* This change observed, a friend went to him for the secret: "Tell me," says he, "your nostrum, tell me your receipt; what is the main ingredient that makes an orator?" Demosthenes answered, "Pronunciation." "What then the next thing?" "Pronunciation." "Pray then, what the third?" Still the answer was, Pronunciation.

Now this was at Athens, where want of Wit was never an objection against them. So that it is not in song only that a good voice diverts us from the Wit and Sense. From the stage, the bar, or the pulpit a good voice will prepossess our ears, and having seized that pass, is in a fair way to surprise our judgment.

---

* *Rehearsal.* [II, iv, 86].
† Waller. [Edmund Waller, "Upon the Earl of Roscommon's Translation of Horace"].
‡ Plutarch, *Demosthenes.*

---

[8] *Catiline His Conspiracy,* by Jonson, 1611.
[9] Figures of speech.

Considering then what power the show, the action, and the pronunciation have over us, it is no wonder that wise men often mistake and give an hasty judgment, which upon a review is justly set aside.

Horace divides the judges into *majores numero,* and the few or better sort, and these for the most part were of different judgments. The like distinction may hold in all other nations; only at Athens there was a third sort who were Judges upon * Oath, Judges in Commission, by the Government sworn to do right and determine the merits of a play without favor or affection.

But amongst the Moderns, never was a cause canvassed with so much heat between the play judges as that in France about Corneille's tragedy of the *Cid.*[10] The majority were so fond of it that with them it became a proverb. *Cela est plus beau que la Cid.*† On the other side, Cardinal Richelieu damned it and said, "All the pudder about it was only between the ignorant people and the men of judgment."

Yet this Cardinal with so nice a taste had not many years before been several times to see acted the *Tragedy of Sir Thomas More* [11] and as often wept at the representation. Never were known so many people ‡ crowded to death as at that play. Yet was it the Manufacture of Jehan de Serre, one about the form of our Flecknoe,[12] or Thomas Jordan. The same de Serre that dedicated a Book of Meditations to K. Charles I and went home with pockets full of medals and reward.

By this instance we see a man the most sharp and of the greatest penetration was imposed upon by these cheating senses, the eyes and the ears, which greedily took in the impression from the show, the action, and from the emphasis and pronunciation, though there was no great matter of fable, no manners, no fine thoughts, no language —that is, nothing of a tragedy, nothing of a poet all the while.

Horace was very angry with these empty shows and vanity which the gentlemen of his time ran like mad after:

—Insanos oculos, et gaudia vana.

What would he had said to the French opera of late so much in vogue? There it is for you to bewitch your eyes and to charm your

* Plutarch, *Cimon.* † Pelisson, *Hist. Acad.* ‡ *Parnasse Reform.*

10 Published in 1636.
11 Jean Puget de la Serre, *Thomas Morus, tragédie en prose,* 1642.
12 Richard Flecknoe was satirized so severely by Dryden that his name came to be used as a term for a shabby dramatist. Cf. *Macflecknoe* by Dryden.

ears. There is a cup of enchantment, there is music and machine; [13] Circe and Calipso in conspiracy against Nature and good sense. 'Tis a debauch the most insinuating, and the most pernicious; none would think an opera and civil reason should be the growth of one and the same climate. But shall we wonder at anything for a sacrifice to the Grand Monarch? Such worship, such idol. All flattery to him is insipid unless it be prodigious; nothing reasonable or within compass can come near the matter. All must be monstrous, enormous, and outrageous to Nature to be like him or give any echo on his appetite.

Were Rabelais alive again, he would look on his Gargantua as but a pigmy.

The hero's Race excels the poet's thought.*

The Academy Royal may pack up their modes and methods, & *pensées ingenienses;* the Racines and the Corneilles must all now dance to the tune of *Baptista.* Here is the opera; here is machine and *Baptista;* farewell Apollo and the Muses.

Away with your opera from the theatre; better had they become the Heathen temples for the Corybantian Priests and (*Semiviros Gallos*) the old capons of Gaul, than a people that pretend from Charlemagne or descend from the undoubted loins of German and Norman conquerers.

In the French not many years before was observed the like vicious appetite, and immoderate passion for *vers burlesque.*

They were current in Italy an hundred years ere they passed to this side the Alps. But once they had their turn in France, so right to their humor, they overran all; nothing wise or sober might stand in their way.† All were possessed with the spirit of burlesque from Doll in the dairy to the matrons at Court and the maids of honor. Nay, so far went the frenzy that no bookseller would meddle on any terms without burlesque, insomuch that *Ann.* 1649 was at Paris printed a serious treatise with this title,

La Passion de Nostre Seigneur, En vers Burlesque.[14]

If we cannot rise to the perfection of intrigue in Sophocles, let us

---

* [Edmund] Waller, "These Verses were Writ in the Tasso of Her Royal Highness."
† Pelisson, *Histor. Acad.*

13 Machine: used not only of a mechanical contrivance, but also of a turn in the plot in much the same sense as the modern word "device."
14 Rymer is not exaggerating this fashion for *vers burlesque;* this title actually exists.

sit down with the honesty and simplicity of the first beginners in
tragedy: As for example.

One of the most simple now extant is the *Persians* by Æschylus.

Some ten years after that Darius had been beaten by the Greeks,
Xerxes (his Father Darius being dead) brought against them such
forces by sea and land, the like never known in history. Xerxes went
also in person, with all the Maison de Roi, Satrapie, and Gendarmerie;
all were routed. Some forty years afterwards the poet takes hence his
subject for tragedy.

The place is Darius's tomb, in the Metropolis of Persia.

The time is the night, an hour or two before day break.

First, on the stage are seen 15 persons in robes, proper for the
Satrapa, or Chief Princes in Persia. Suppose they met so early at the
tomb, then sacred, and ordinarily resorted to by people troubled in
mind, on the accounts of dreams or anything not boding good. They
talk of the state of affairs: of Greece, and of the expedition. After
some time, take upon them to be the Chorus.

The next on the stage comes Atossa, the Queen Mother of Persia.
She could not lie in bed for a dream that troubled her; so in a fit of
devotion comes to her husband's tomb, there luckily meets with so
many wise men and counsellors to ease her mind by interpreting her
dream. This with the Chorus makes the Second Act.

After this, their disorder, lamentation, and wailing is such that
Darius is disturbed in his tomb, so his ghost appears, and belike stays
with them till day break. Then the Chorus concludes the act.

In the Fourth Act come the messengers with sad tidings, which, with
the reflections and troubles thereupon, and the Chorus, fill out this
act.

In the last, Xerxes himself arrives, which gives occasion of con-
doling, howling, and distraction enough, to the end of the tragedy.[15]

One may imagine how a Grecian audience that loved their country and gloried in the virtue of their ancestors would be affected with
this representation.

Never appeared on the stage a ghost of greater consequence. The
Grand Monarch Darius, who had been so shamefully beaten by those
petty provinces of the united Grecians, could not now lie quiet in

15 Aeschylus, *Persians,* 472 B.C.

his grave for them; but must be raised from the dead again to be witness of his son's disgrace and of their triumph.

Were a tragedy after this model to be drawn for our stage, Greece and Persia are too far from us. The scene must be laid nearer home. As at the Louvre, and instead of Xerxes, we might take John, King of France, and the Battle of Poictiers. So if the Germans or Spaniards were to compose a play on the Battle of Pavia and King Francis there taken prisoner, the scene should not be laid at Vienna, or at Madrid, but at the Louvre. For there the tragedy would principally operate, and there all the lines most naturally center.

But perhaps the memorable Adventure of the Spaniards in [15]88 against England may better resemble that of Xerxes. Suppose then a tragedy called the *Invincible Armado*.

The place, then, for the action may be at Madrid by some tomb or solemn place of resort; or if we prefer a turn in it from good to bad fortune, then some drawing-room in the Palace near the King's bed-chamber.

The time to begin, twelve at night.

The scene opening presents 15 grandees of Spain with their most solemn beards and accoutrements, met there (suppose) after some ball or other public occasion. They talk of the state of affairs, the greatness of their power, the vastness of their dominions, and prospect to be infallibly, ere long, lords of all. With this prosperity and goodly thoughts transported, they at last form themselves into the Chorus, and walk such measures, with Music, as may become the gravity of such a Chorus.

Then enter two or three of the Cabinet Council, who now have leave to tell the secret; that the preparations and the Invincible Armado was to conquer England. These, with part of the Chorus, may communicate all the particulars, the provisions, and the strength by sea and land; the certainty of success, the advantages by that accession; and the many ton of tar barrels for the heretics. These topics may afford matter enough, with the Chorus, for the second act.

In the third act, these gentlemen of the Cabinet cannot agree about sharing the preferments of England, and a mighty broil there is amongst them. One will not be content unless he is King of Man; another will be Duke of Lancaster. One, that had seen a coronation in England, will by all means be Duke of Aquitaine, or else Duke of

Normandy. And on this occasion two competitors have a juster occasion to work up and shew the muscles of their passion than Shakespeare's Cassius and Brutus. After, the Chorus.

The fourth act may, instead of Atossa, present some old dames of the Court, used to dream dreams and to see sprights, in their night-rails and forehead cloths, to alarm our gentlemen with new apprehensions, which make distraction and disorders sufficient to furnish out this act.

In the last act the King enters, and wisely discourses against dreams and hobgoblins to quiet their minds: And the more to satisfy them and take off their fright, he lets them to know what St. Loyola had appeared to him, and assured him that all is well. This said, comes a messenger of the ill news; his account is lame, suspected; he sent to prison. A second messenger, that came away long after, but had a speedier passage, his account is distinct, and all their loss credited. So in fine, one of the Chorus concludes with that of Euripides; Thus you see the gods bring things to pass often otherwise than was by man proposed.

In this draught we see the fable, and the characters or manners of Spaniards, and room for fine thoughts and noble expressions, as much as the poet can afford.

The first act gives a review, or ostentation of their strength in battle-array.

In the second, they are in motion for the attack, and we see where the action falls.

In the third, they quarrel about dividing the spoil.

In the fourth, they meet with a repulse; are beaten off by a vanguard of dreams, goblins, and terrors of the night.

In the fifth, they rally under their King in person, and make good their ground, till overpowered by fresh troops of conviction; and mighty Truth prevails.

For the First Act, a painter would draw Spain hovering and ready to strike at the universe.

In the Second, just taking England in her pounces.

But it must not be forgotten, in the Second Act, that here be some Spanish-Friar or Jesuit, as St. Xavier (for he may drop in by miracle, anywhere) to ring in their ears the Northern Heresy, like Iago in Shakespeare, *Put money in thy purse*, I say, *Put money in thy purse*. So often may he repeat the Northern Heresy. Away with your secular advantages; I say the Northern Heresy. There is roastmeat for the Church; Veto a Christo, the Northern Heresy.

If Mr. Dryden might try his pen on this subject, doubtless to an audience that heartily love their country and glory in the virtue of their ancestors, his imitation of Æschylus would have better success, and would [fill] pit, box, and gallery far beyond any thing now in possession of the stage, however wrought up by the unimitable Shakespeare.

CHAPTER VII [EXCERPTS]

BUT EARLY under Queen Elizabeth, our dramatic poetry grew to something of a just symmetry and proportion. In 1566 Geo. Gascoigne of Grays Inn translated the *Supposes* from Ariosto, which was acted, as also his *Jocasta* [16] Englished from Euripides, the Epilogue written by Chr. Telverton.

And after that were reckoned for comedy, Edward, Earl of Oxford; for tragedy, amongst others, Thomas, Lord of Buckhurst, whose *Gorboduc* [17] is a fable, doubtless better turned for tragedy than any on this side the Alps in his time, and might have been a better direction to Shakespeare and Ben Jonson than any guide they have had the luck to follow.

Here is a King, the Queen, and their two sons. The King divides his realm and gives it betwixt his two sons. They quarrel. The elder brother kills the younger, which provokes the mother to kill the elder. Thereupon, the King kills the mother. And then to make a clear stage, the people rise and dispatch old Gorboduc.

It is objected by our neighbors against the English that we delight in bloody spectacles. Our poets who have not imitated *Gorboduc* in the regularity and roundness of the design have not failed on the theatre to give us the *atrocité* and blood enough in all conscience. From this time dramatic poetry began to thrive with us and flourish wonderfully. The French confess they had nothing in this kind considerable until 1635 that the Academy Royal was founded. Long before which time we had from Shakespeare, Fletcher, and Ben Jonson whole volumes at this day in possession of the stage, and acted with greater applause than ever. Yet after all, I fear what Quintilian

[16] 1566.　　　　　[17] 1562.

pronounced concerning the Roman comedy may as justly be said of English tragedy: *In tragoedia maxime claudicamus, vix levem consequimur umbram.* In tragedy we come short extremely; hardly have we a slender shadow of it.

CHAPTER VIII [EXCERPTS]

FROM ALL the tragedies acted on our English stage, *Othello* is said to bear the bell away. The subject is more of a piece, and there is indeed something like, there is, as it were, some phantom of a fable. The fable is always accounted the soul of tragedy. And it is the fable which is properly the poet's part. Because the other three parts of tragedy, to wit, the characters are taken from the moral philosopher; the thoughts or sense, from them that teach rhetoric; and the last part, which is the expression, we learn from the grammarians.

The fable is drawn from a novel, composed in Italian by Geraldi Cinthio, who also was a writer of tragedies, and to that use employed such of his tales as he judged proper for the stage. But with this of the Moor, he meddled no farther.

Shakespeare alters it from the original in several particulars, but always, unfortunately, for the worse. He bestows a name on his Moor, and styles him the Moor of Venice, a note of pre-eminence which neither history nor heraldry can allow him. Cinthio, who knew him best, and whose creature he was, calls him simply a Moor. We say the Piper of Strasburg, the Jew of Florence, and, if you please, the Pindar of Wakefield—all upon record and memorable in their places. But we see no such cause for the Moor's preferment to that dignity. And it is an affront to all chroniclers and antiquaries to top upon 'em a Moor with that mark of renown who yet had never fallen within the sphere of their cognisance.

Then is the Moor's wife, from a simple citizen in Cinthio, dressed up with her topknots, and raised to be Desdemona, a Senator's daughter. All this is very strange and therefore pleases such as reflect not on the improbability. This match might well be without the parent's consent. Old Horace long ago forbade the bans.

Sed non ut placidis Coeant immitia, non ut
Serpentes avibus geminentur, tigribus agni.

THE FABLE

OTHELLO, a blackamoor captain, by talking of his prowess and feats of war, makes Desdemona, a Senator's daughter, to be in love with him and to be married to him without her parent's knowledge. And having preferred Cassio to be his lieutenant (a place which his Ensign Iago sued for), Iago in revenge works the Moor into a jealousy that Cassio cuckolds him, which he effects by stealing and conveying a certain handkerchief which had at the wedding been by the Moor presented to his bride. Hereupon, Othello and Iago plot the deaths of Desdemona and Cassio. Othello murders her, and soon after is convinced of her innocence. And as he is about to be carried to prison in order to be punished for the murder, he kills himself.

Whatever rubs or difficulty may stick on the bark, the moral, sure, of this fable is very instructive.

1. First, this may be a caution to all maidens of quality how, without their parents' consent, they run away with blackamoors.

Di non si accompagnare con huomo, cui la natura & il cielo, & il modo della vita, disgiunge da noi.—Cinthio.

Secondly, this may be a warning to all good wives, that they look well to their linen.

Thirdly, this may be a lesson to husbands that before their jealousy be tragical, the proofs may be mathematical.

Cinthio affirms that *She was not overcome by a womanish appetite, but by the virtue of the Moor.* It must be a good-natured reader that takes Cinthio's word in this case, though in a novel. Shakespeare, who is accountable both to the eyes and to the ears, and to convince the very heart of an audience, shews that Desdemona was won by hearing Othello talk.

> . . . I spake of most disastrous chances,
> Of moving accidents, by flood and field:
> Of hair-breadth 'scapes i'th' imminent deadly breach;
> Of being taken by the insolent foe;
> And sold to slavery; of my redemption thence,
> And portents in my travel's history,
> Wherein of antars vast, and deserts idle,
> Rough quarries, rocks, and hills, whose heads touch Heaven,
> It was my hint to speak, such was my process;
> And of the Cannibals that each other eat;

The Anthropophagi, and men whose heads
Do grow beneath their shoulders—[18]

This was the charm, this was the philtre, the love-powder that took
the daughter of this noble Venetian. This was sufficient to make the
blackamoor white and reconcile all, though there had been a cloven
foot into the bargain.

A meaner woman might be as soon taken by Aqua Tetrachymagogon.[19]

Nodes, cataracts, tumors, chilblains, carnosity, shankers, or any cant
in the bill of an High German Doctor is as good fustian circumstance
and as likely to charm a Senator's daughter. But, it seems, the noble
Venetians have an other sense of things. The Doge himself tells us:

I think this tale would win my daughter too.[20]

Horace tells us,

Intererit Multum—
Colchus an Assyrius, Thebis nutritus, an Argis.

Shakespeare in this play calls 'em the super-subtle Venetians. Yet
examine throughout the tragedy there is nothing in the noble Desdemona that is not below any country chambermaid with us.

And the account he gives of their noblemen and Senate can only
be calculated for the latitude of Gotham.

The character of that state is to employ strangers in their wars. But
shall a poet thence fancy that they will set a Negro to be their general, or trust a Moor to defend them against the Turk? With us a
blackamoor might rise to be a trumpeter, but Shakespeare would
not have him less than a lieutenant-general. With us a Moor might
marry some little drab or small-coal wench; Shakespeare would provide him the daughter and heir of some great lord or Privy councellor.
And all the town should reckon it a very suitable match. Yet the English are not bred up with that hatred and aversion to the Moors as are
the Venetians, who suffer by a perpetual hostility from them,

Littora littoribus contraria.

Nothing is more odious in Nature than an improbable lie. And
certainly never was any play fraught like this of *Othello,* with improbabilities.

[18] I, iii, 157–68. Text varies slightly from modern readings.
[19] Aqua Tetrachymagogon: a medicine intended to stimulate the flow of the four
humours.   [20] I, iii, 195.

The characters or manners, which are the second part in a tragedy, are not less unnatural and improper than the fable was improbable and absurd.

Othello is made a Venetian general. We see nothing done by him, nor related concerning him that comports with the condition of a general, or, indeed, of a man, unless the killing of himself, to avoid a death the law was about to inflict upon him. When his jealousy had wrought him up to a resolution of's taking revenge for the supposed injury, he sets Iago to the fighting part to kill Cassio, and chooses himself to murder the silly woman, his wife, that was like to make no resistance.

His love and his jealousy are no part of a soldier's character, unless for comedy.

But what is most intolerable is Iago. He is no blackamoor soldier, so we may be sure he should be like other soldiers of our acquaintance, yet never in tragedy, nor in comedy, nor in Nature was a soldier with his character; take it in the author's own words,

> *Em.* . . . some eternal villain,
> Some busy and insinuating rogue,
> Some cogging, cozening slave, to get some office.[21]

Horace describes a soldier otherwise.

> *Impiger, iracundus, inexorabilis, acer.*

Shakespeare knew his character of Iago was inconsistent. In this very play, he pronounces:

> If . . . thou dost deliver more or less than truth,
> Thou art no soldier.[22]

This he knew, but to entertain the audience with something new and surprising, against common sense and Nature, he would pass upon us a close, dissembling, false, insinuating rascal, instead of an open-hearted, frank, plain-dealing soldier, a character constantly worn by them for some thousands of years in the world.

Tiberius Caesar * had a poet arraigned for his life because *Agamemnon* was brought on the stage by him, with a character unbecoming a soldier.

Our ensigns and subalterns, when disgusted by the captain throw

* *Sueton* in Tib.

---

[21] IV, ii, 154–6.   [22] II, ii, 243–5.

up their commissions, bluster, and are bare-faced. Iago, I hope, is not brought on the stage in a red coat. I know not what livery the Venetians wear, but am sure they hold not these conditions to be *alla soldatesca.*

Non sia egli perfare la vendetta con infidie, ma con la spada in mano.
—Cinthio.

Nor is our poet more discreet in his Desdemona. He had chosen a soldier for his knave, and a Venetian lady is to be the fool.

This Senator's daughter runs away to a carrier's inn, the Sagittary, with a blackamoor; is no sooner wedded to him, but the very night she beds him is importuning and teasing him for a young smock-faced lieutenant, Cassio. And though she perceives the Moor jealous of Cassio, yet will she not forbear, but still rings Cassio, Cassio, in both his ears.

Roderigo is the cully [23] of Iago, brought in to be murdered by Iago that Iago's hands might be the more in blood, and be yet the more abominable villain, who without that was too wicked on all conscience, and had more to answer for than any tragedy or furies could inflict upon him. So there can be nothing in the characters either for the profit or to delight an audience.

The third thing to be considered is the thoughts. But from such characters we need not expect many that are either true, or fine, or noble.

And without these, that is, without sense or meaning, the fourth part of tragedy, which is the expression can hardly deserve to be treated on distinctly. The verse rumbling in our ears are of good use to help off the action.

In the neighing of an horse or in the growling of a mastiff there is a meaning, there is as lively expression, and, may I say, more humanity than many times in the tragical flights of Shakespeare.

The first we see are Iago and Roderigo by night in the streets of Venice. After growling a long time together, they resolve to tell Brabantio that his daughter is run away with the blackamoor. Iago and Roderigo were not of quality to be familiar with Brabantio, nor had any provocation from him to deserve a rude thing at their hands. Brabantio was a noble Venetian, one of the sovereign lords and principal persons in the Government, peer to the most Serene Doge,

[23] Gull, or dupe.

148   Thomas Rymer

one attended with more state, ceremony, and punctillio than any English duke or nobleman in the Government will pretend to. This misfortune in his daughter is so prodigious, so tender a point, as might puzzle the finest wit of the most super-subtle Venetian to touch upon it or break the discovery to her father. See then how delicately Shakespeare minces the matter.

> *Rod.* What ho, Brabantio, Signior Brabantio, ho.
> *Iago.* Awake, what ho, Brabantio,
> Thieves, thieves, thieves:
> Look to your house, your daughter, and your bags.
> Thieves, thieves.
> > [Brabantio at a window.]
> *Bra.* What is the reason of this terrible summons?
> What is the matter there?
> *Rod.* Signior, is all your family within?
> *Iago.* Are your doors locked?
> *Bra.* Why, wherefore ask you this?
> *Iago.* [Zounds], Sir, you are robb'd, for shame put on your gown;
> Your heart is burst, you have lost half your soul.
> Even now, very now, an old black ram
> Is tupping your white ewe. Arise, arise!
> Awake the snorting citizens with the bell,
> Or else the Devil will make a grandsire of you.
> Arise, I say! [24]

Nor have they yet done. Amongst other ribaldry, they tell him.

> *Iago.* Sir, you are one of those that will not serve God, if the Devil bid you; because we come to do you service, you think us ruffians, you'll have your daughter covered with a Barbary stallion. You'll have your nephews neigh to you; you'll have coursers for cousins, and gennets for germans.
> *Bra.* What profane wretch art thou?
> *Iago.* I am one, Sir, that comes to tell you your daughter and the Moor are now making the beast with two backs. [25]

In former days there wont to be kept at the courts of princes somebody in a fool's coat that in pure simplicity might let slip something which made way for the ill news and blunted the shock which otherwise might have come too violent upon the party.

Aristophanes puts Nicias and Demosthenes in the disguise of serv-

[24] The word "Zounds" is omitted in Rymer, and the line "your Gown," is misplaced and put at the end of Brabantio's speech.—I, i, 85–100.
[25] I, i, 121–9. The word "germans" means cousins or near relations.

ants that they might without indecency be drunk. And drunk he must make them that they might without reserve lay open the Arcana of state and the knavery of their ministers.

After King Francis had been taken prisoner at Pavia, Rabelais tells of a drunken bout between Gargantua and Friar John, where the valiant Friar, bragging over his cups, amongst his other flights, says he, "Had I lived in the days of Jesus Christ, I would ha' guarded Mount Olivet that the Jews should never ha' tane him. The Devil fetch me, if I would not have ham stringed those Mr. Apostles that after their good supper ran away so scurvily and left their Master to shift for himself. I hate a man should run away when he should play at sharps. Pox on't, that I should not be King of France for an hundred years or two. I would curtail all our French dogs that ran away at Pavia."

This is address, this is truly satire, where the preparation is such that the thing principally designed falls in as it only were of course.

But Shakespeare shews us another sort of address; his manners and good breeding must not be like the rest of the civil world. Brabantio was not in masquerade, was not incognito; Iago well knew his rank and dignity.

> *Iago.* The Magnifico is much beloved,
> And hath in his effect a voice potential
> As double as the Duke—— [26]

But besides the manners to a magnifico, humanity cannot bear that an old gentleman in his misfortune should be insulted over with such a rabble of scoundrel language when no cause or provocation. Yet thus it is on our stage: this is our school of good manners, and the *Speculum Vitae.*

But our Magnifico is here in the dark, nor are yet his robes on. Attend him to the Senate House, and there see the difference, see the effects of purple.

.   .   .

But pass we to something of a more serious air and complexion. Othello and his bride are the first night no sooner warm in bed together but a drunken quarrel happening in the garrison, two soldiers fight, and the General rises to part the fray. He swears.

[26] I, ii, 14–6.

> *Othel.* Now, by Heaven,
> My blood begins my safer guides to rule,
> And passion, having my best judgment cool'd,
> Essays to lead the way. If once I stir,
> Or do but lift this arm, the best of you
> Shall sink in my rebuke. Give me to know
> How this foul rout began, who set it on,
> And he that is approv'd in this offence,
> Though he had twinn'd with me both at a birth,
> Should lose me. What, in a town of war,
> Yet wild, the people's hearts brimful of fear,
> To manage private and domestic quarrels,
> In night, and on the court, and guard of safety.
> 'Tis Monstrous. Iago, who began? [27]

In the days of yore, soldiers did not swear in this fashion. What should a soldier say farther when he swears unless he blaspheme? Action should speak the rest. What follows must be *ex ore gladis*. He is to rap out an oath, not wire-draw and spin it out. By the style one might judge that Shakespeare's soldiers were never bred in a camp, but rather had belonged to some Affidavit Office. Consider also throughout this whole scene how the Moorish General proceeds in examining into this rout; no Justice Clod-pate could go on with more phlegm and deliberation. The very first night that he lies with the divine Desdemona to be thus interrupted might provoke a man's Christian patience to swear in another style. But a Negro General is a man of strange mettle. Only his Venetian bride is a match for him. She understands that the soldiers in the garrison are by th'ears together, and presently she at midnight is in amongst them.

· · ·

The last act begins with Iago and Roderigo who a little before had been upon the huff.

> *Rod.* I say it is not very well. I will make myself known to Desdemona. If she will return me my jewels, I will give over my suit, and repent my unlawful solicitation, if not, assure yourself, I'll seek satisfaction of you. [28]

Roderigo, a noble Venetian, had sought Desdemona in marriage, is troubled to find the Moor had got her from him, advises with Iago, who wheedles him to sell his estate and go over the sea to Cyprus in expectation to cuckold Othello; there having cheated Roderigo of all

[27] II, ii, 229–42. [28] IV, ii, 223–32.

his money and jewels on pretence of presenting them to Desdemona, our gallant grows angry and would have satisfaction from Iago, who sets all right by telling him Cassio is to be Governor, Othello is going with Desdemona into Mauritania. To prevent this, you are to murder Cassio, and then all may be well.

Iago. He goes into Mauritania, and takes away with him the fair Desdemona, unless his abode be lingered here by some accident, wherein none can be so determinate, as the removing of Cassio.[29]

Had Roderigo been one of the Banditi, he might not much stick at the murder. But why Roderigo should take this for payment and risk his person where the prospect of advantage is so very uncertain and remote, nobody can imagine. It had need be a super-subtle Venetian that this plot will pass upon. Then after a little spurt of villainy and murder, we are brought to the most lamentable that ever appeared on any stage. A noble Venetian lady is to be murdered by our poet in sober sadness purely for being a fool. No pagan poet but would have found some machine [30] for her deliverance. Pegasus would have strained hard to have brought old Perseus on his back, time enough to rescue this Andromeda from so foul a monster. Has our Christian poetry no generosity, nor bowels? Ha, Sir Lancelot! Ha, St. George! Will no ghost leave the shades for us in extremity to save a distressed damosel?

But for our comfort, however felonious is the heart, hear with what soft language he does approach her with a candle in his hand:

> *Oth.* Put out the light, and then put out the light;
> If I quench thee, thou flaming minister,
> I can again thy former light restore—— [31]

Who would call him barbarian, monster, savage? Is this a blackamoor?

> *Soles occidere & redire possunt——*

The very soul and quintessence of Sir George Etherege.

One might think the General should not glory much in this action, but make an hasty work on't, and have turned his eyes away from so unsoldierly an execution, yet is he all pause and deliberation, handles her as calmly and is as careful of her soul's health as it had been her Father Confessor. "Have you prayed tonight, Desdemona?" But the

[29] IV, ii, 257–61.   [30] See note 13.   [31] V, ii, 9–11.

suspense is necessary that he might have a convenient while so to roll his eyes and so to gnaw his nether lip to the spectators. Besides the greater cruelty—*sub tam lentis maxillis.*

But hark, a most tragical thing laid to her charge.

> *Oth.* That handkerchief that I so lov'd, and gave thee,
> Thou gav'st to Cassio.
> *Desd.* No, by my life and soul,
> Send for the man and ask him.
> *Oth.* —By Heaven I saw my handkerchief in his hand—
> —I saw the handkerchief.[32]

So much ado, so much stress, so much passion and reputation about an handkerchief! Why was not this called the *Tragedy of the Handkerchief?* What can be more absurd than (as Quintilian expresses it) *in parvis litibus has tragoedias movere?* We have heard of Fortunatus his purse, and of the invisible cloak, long ago worn threadbare, and stowed up in the wardrobe of obsolete romances; one might think that were a fitter place for this handkerchief than that it, at this time of day, be worn on the stage, to raise everywhere all this clutter and turmoil. Had it been Desdemona's garter, the sagacious Moor might have smelt a rat, but the handkerchief is so remote a trifle, no booby on this side Mauritania could make any consequence from it.

We may learn here that a woman never loses her tongue, even though after she is stifled.

> *Desd.* O falsly, falsly murder'd.
> *Em.* Sweet Desdemona, O sweet mistress, speak.
> *Desd.* A guiltless death I die.
> *Em.* O who has done the deed?
> *Desd.* Nobody. I myself. Farewell.
> Commend me to my kind lord, O, farewell.[33]

This Desdemona is a black swan, or an old blackamoor is a bewitching bedfellow. If this be Nature, it is a *lascheté* below what the English language can express.

For Lardella, to make love like an humble bee was, in the *Rehearsal,* thought a fancy odd enough.

But hark what follows:

> *Oth.* —O heavy hour!
> Methinks it should be now a huge eclipse
> Of sun and moon, and that the affrighted globe
> Should yawn at alteration.[34]

[32] V, ii, 59–81.   [33] V, ii, 147–56.   [34] V, ii, 124–7.

This is wonderful. Here is poetry to elevate and amuse. Here is found all-sufficient. It would be uncivil to ask Flamsteed [35] if the sun and moon can both together be so hugely eclipsed in any heavy hour whatsoever. Nor must the spectators consult Gresham College [36] whether a body is naturally frighted till he yawn again. The fortune of Greece is not concerned with these matters. These are physical circumstances a poet may be ignorant in without any harm to the public. These slips have no influence on our manners and good life, which are the poets' province.

Rather may we ask here what unnatural crime Desdemona or her parents had committed to bring this judgment down upon her, to wed a blackamoor, and innocent to be thus cruelly murdered by him. What instruction can we make out of this catastrophe? Or whither must our reflection lead us? Is not this to envenom and sour our spirits to make us repine and grumble at Providence and the government of the world? If this be our end, what boots it to be virtuous?

Desdemona dropt the handkerchief and missed it that very day after her marriage. It might have been rumpled up with her wedding sheets. And this night that she lay in her wedding sheets, the Fairy Napkin (whilst Othello was stifling her) might have started up to disarm his fury and stop his ungracious mouth. Then might she (in a trance for fear) have lain as dead. Then might he, believing her dead, touched with remorse, have honestly cut his own throat, by the good leave and with the applause of all the spectators, who might thereupon have gone home with a quiet mind, admiring the beauty of Providence, fairly and truly represented on the theatre.

.   .   .

But from this scene to the end of the play we meet with nothing but blood and butchery described much-what to the style of the last speeches and confessions of the persons executed at Tyburn. With this difference; that there we have the *fact* and the due course of justice, whereas our poet, against all justice and reason, against all law, humanity, and Nature, in a barbarous, arbitrary way, executes and makes havoc of his subjects, hab-nab, as they come to hand. Desdemona dropped her handkerchief; therefore she must be stifled. Othello, by law to be broken on the wheel, by the poet's cunning

35 Flamsteed—John Flamsteed, the first Astronomer Royal (1646–1719).
36 The meeting-place of The Royal Society.

escapes with cutting his own throat. Cassio, for I know not what, comes off with a broken shin. Iago murders his benefactor, Roderigo, as this were poetical gratitude. Iago is not yet killed because yet never was such a villain alive. The Devil, if once he brings a man to be dipped in a deadly sin, lets him alone to take his course. And now when the Foul Fiend had done with him, our wise authors take the sinner into their poetical service, there to accomplish him, and do the Devil's drudgery.

Philosophy tells us it is a principle in the Nature of man to be grateful.

History may tell us that John an Oaks, John a Stiles, or Iago were ungrateful. Poetry is to follow Nature; philosophy must be his guide. History and fact in particular cases of John an Oaks, or John of Styles are no warrant or direction for a poet. Therefore, Aristotle is always telling us that poetry is σπουδιότερον και φιλοποφωτερον, is more general and abstracted, is led more by the philosophy, the Reason and Nature of things, than history, which only records things higglety-pigglety, right or wrong, as they happen. History might without any preamble or difficulty say that Iago was ungrateful. Philosophy then calls him unnatural. But the poet is not, without huge labor and preparation to expose the monster, and after shew the divine vengeance executed upon him. The poet is not to add willful murder to his ingratitude; he has not antidote enough for the poison; his hell and furies are not punishment sufficient for one single crime of that bulk and aggravation.

> *Em.* O, thou dull Moor, that handkerchief thou speakest on,
> I found by fortune, and did give my husband.
> For often with a solemn earnestness,
> (More than indeed belong'd to such a trifle)
> He begg'd of me to steal it.[37]

Here we see the meanest woman in the play takes this handkerchief for a trifle below her husband to trouble his head about it. Yet we find it entered into our poet's head to make a tragedy of this trifle.

Then for the unravelling of the plot as they call it, never was old deputy recorder in a country town, with his spectacles in summoning up the evidence, at such a puzzle, so blundered and bedoltefied, as is our poet, to have a good riddance, and get the catastrophe off his hands.

[37] V, ii, 280–84.

What can remain with the audience to carry home with them from this sort of poetry, for their use and edification? How can it work, unless (instead of settling the mind, and purging our passions) to delude our senses, disorder our thoughts, addle our brain, pervert our affections, have our imaginations, corrupt our appetite, and fill our head with vanity, confusion, *Tintamarre,* and jingle-jangle, beyond what all the parish clerks of London, with their Old Testament farces and interludes in Richard the Second's time could ever pretend to? Our only hopes, for the good of their souls, can be that these people go to the playhouse as they do to church, to sit still, look on one another, make no reflection, nor mind the play, more than they would a sermon.

There is in this play some burlesque, some humour, and ramble of comical Wit, some shew, and some mimicry to divert the spectators, but the tragical part is plainly none other than a bloody farce, without salt or savour.

The Tragedies of the Last Age Considered
[1678; selection]

IN FORMER TIMES poetry was another thing than history or than the law of the land. Poetry discovered crimes the law could never find out, and punished those the law had acquitted. The Areopagus cleared Orestes, but with what furies did the poets haunt and torment him? And what a wretch made they of Oedipus when the casuist excused his invincible ignorance?

The poets considered that naturally men were affected with pity when they saw others suffer more than their fault deserved, and vice, they thought, could never be painted too ugly and frightful; therefore, whether they would move pity or make vice detested, it concerned them to be somewhat of the severest in the punishments they inflicted. Now, because their hands were tied, that they could not punish beyond such a degree, they were obliged to have a strict eye on their malefactor that he transgressed not too far, that he committed not two crimes when but responsible for one, nor, indeed, be so far guilty as by the law to deserve death. For though historical justice might rest there, yet poetical justice could not be so content. It would require that the satisfaction be complete and full ere the malefactor goes off the stage, and nothing left to God Almighty and another world. Nor will it suffer that the spectators trust the poet for a hell behind the scenes; the fire must roar in the conscience of the criminal, the fiends and furies be conjured up to their faces with a world of machine and horrid spectacles, and yet the criminal could never move pity. Therefore, amongst the Ancients we find no malefactors of this kind; a willful murderer is with them as strange and unknown as a parricide to the old Romans. Yet need we not fancy that they were squeamish or unacquainted with any of these great lumping crimes in that age when we remember their Oedipus, Orestes, or Medea. But they took care to wash the viper, to cleanse away the venom, and with such art to prepare the morsel they made it all junket to the taste, and all physic in the operation.

They so qualified, so allayed, and covered the crime with circumstance that little could appear on the stage but wither the causes and provocations before it, or the remorse and penitence, the despairs and horrors of conscience which followed, to make the criminal every way a fit object for pity. Nor can we imagine their stage so rarely endured any bloodshed and that the sight was displeasing because the spectators were some sort of effeminate, unfighting fellows, when we remember the battles of Marathon and Salamin, and with what small number these very spectators had routed Xerxes and the greatest armies in the world. For now it was that the arms of the Athenians (as well as their arts) shined in their greatest glory.

The truth is, the poets were to move pity, and this pity was to be moved for the living who remained, and not for the dead. And they found in Nature that men could not so easily pardon a crime committed before their faces and consequently could not be so easily disposed to bestow that pity on the criminal which the poets labored for. The poets, I say, found that the sight of the face made so strong an impression as no art of theirs could afterwards fully conquer.

John Dryden

DRYDEN's "Heads of an Answer to Rymer" was never printed in his life-time, for it comes from notes he scribbled in his copy of Rymer's *Short View of Tragedy*. It was first published by Jacob Tonson in the 1711 edition of *The Works of Beaumont and Fletcher*, and later, with the paragraphs in a different order, by Johnson in the "Life of Dryden" in his *Lives of the English Poets*. Dryden's copy of Rymer's book has been destroyed, so these texts, and one printed by Saintsbury, are all that we have. The present version comes from Johnson.

These notes cannot be considered as a finished essay, but rather as the line Dryden would have taken had he actually completed his answer to Rymer. Certain ideas from the *Essay of Dramatic Poesy* are repeated, but Dryden's thinking goes farther, and he makes several significant anticipations of the battlegrounds of the eighteenth century. In spite of the importance of this work, it remains one of the most neglected pieces of Dryden's criticism.

Heads of an Answer to Rymer
[1693]

THAT WE MAY less wonder why pity and terror are not now the only springs on which our tragedies move, and that Shakespeare may be more excused, Rapin confesses that the French tragedies now all run on the *tendre;* and gives the reason, because love is the passion which most predominates in our souls, and that therefore the passions represented become insipid, unless they are comfortable to the thoughts of the audience. But it is to be concluded that this passion works not now amongst the French so strongly as the other two did amongst the Ancients. Amongst us, who have a stronger genius for writing, the operations from the writing are much stronger; for the raising of Shakespeare's passions is more from the excellency of the words and thoughts than the justness of the occasion; and if he has been able to pick single occasions, he has never founded the whole reasonably; yet, by the genius of poetry in writing, he has succeeded.

Rapin attributes more to the *dictio*, that is, to the words and discourse of a tragedy, than Aristotle has done, who places them in the last rank of beauties; perhaps only last in order because they are the last product of the design, of the disposition or connection of its parts; of the characters, of the manners of those characters, and of the thoughts proceeding from those manners. Rapin's words are remarkable: " 'Tis not the admirable intrigue, the surprising events, and extraordinary incidents that make the beauty of a tragedy: 'tis the discourses, when they are natural and passionate: so are Shakespeare's."

The parts of a poem, tragic or heroic, are,

1. The fable itself.
2. The order or manner of its contrivance, in relation of the parts to the whole.
3. The manners or decency of the characters, in speaking or acting what is proper for them, and proper to be shown by the poet.
4. The thoughts which express the manners.
5. The words which express those thoughts.

In the last of these, Homer excels Virgil; Virgil all the other ancient poets; and Shakespeare all modern poets.

For the second of these, the order: the meaning is, that a fable ought to have a beginning, middle, and an end, all just and natural; so that that part, *e.g.*, which is the middle could not naturally be the beginning or end, and so of the rest: all depend on one another, like the links of a curious chain. If terror and pity are only to be raised, certainly this author follows Aristotle's rules, and Sophocles' and Euripides' example; but joy may be raised too, and that doubly, either by seeing a wicked man punished or a good man at last fortunate; or perhaps indignation, to see wickedness prosperous and goodness depressed: both these may be profitable to the end of a tragedy, reformation of manners; but the last improperly, only as it begets pity in the audience; though Aristotle, I confess, places tragedies of this kind in the second form.

He who undertakes to answer this excellent critique of Mr. Rymer,[1] in behalf of our English poets against the Greek, ought to do it in this manner: either by yielding to him the greatest part of what he contends for, which consists in this, that the μῦδος, *i.e.*, the design and

[1] *A Short View of Tragedy*, 1693.

conduct of it, is more conducing in the Greeks to those ends of tragedy which Aristotle and he propose, namely, to cause terror and pity; yet the granting this does not set the Greeks above the English poets.

But the answerer ought to prove two things: First. That the fable is not the greatest masterpiece of a tragedy, though it be the foundation of it.

Secondly. That other ends as suitable to the nature of tragedy may be found in the English, which were not in the Greek.

Aristotle places the fable first; not *quoad dignitatem, sed quoad fundamentum:* for a fable never so movingly contrived to those ends of his, pity and terror, will operate nothing on our affections, except the characters, manners, thoughts, and words are suitable.

So that it remains for Mr. Rymer to prove, that in all those, or the greatest part of them, we are inferior to Sophocles and Euripides; and this he has offered at, in some measure; but, I think, a little partially to the Ancients.

For the fable itself, 'tis in the English more adorned with episodes, and larger than in the Greek poets; consequently more diverting. For, if the action be but one, and that plain, without any counterturn of design or episode, *i.e.,* underplot, how can it be so pleasing as the English, which have both underplot and a turned design, which keeps the audience in expectation of the catastrophe? whereas in the Greek poets we see through the whole design at first.

For the characters, they are neither so many nor so various in Sophocles and Euripides as in Shakespeare and Fletcher: only they are more adapted to those ends of tragedy which Aristotle commends to us, pity and terror.

The manners flow from the characters, and consequently must partake of their advantages and disadvantages.

The thoughts and words, which are the fourth and fifth beauties of tragedy, are certainly more noble and more poetical in the English than in the Greek, which must be proved by comparing them somewhat more equitably than Mr. Rymer has done.

After all, we need not yield that the English way is less conducing to move pity and terror, because they often show virtue oppressed and vice punished: where they do not both, or either, they are not to be defended.

And if we should grant that the Greeks performed this better, perhaps it may admit of dispute whether pity and terror are either the prime or at least the only ends of tragedy.

'Tis not enough that Aristotle had said so; for Aristotle drew his models of tragedy from Sophocles and Euripides; and if he had seen ours might have changed his mind. And chiefly we have to say (what I hinted on pity and terror, in the last paragraph save one), that the punishment of vice and reward of virtue are the most adequate ends of tragedy, because most conducing to good example of life. Now, pity is not so easily raised for a criminal (and the ancient tragedy always represents its chief person such) as it is for an innocent man; and the suffering of innocence and punishment of the offender is of the nature of English tragedy: contrarily, in the Greek, innocence is unhappy often, and the offender escapes. Then we are not touched with the sufferings of any sort of men so much as of lovers; and this was almost unknown to the Ancients: so that they neither administered poetical justice, of which Mr. Rymer boasts, so well as we; neither knew they the best commonplace of pity, which is love.

He therefore unjustly blames us for not building on what the Ancients left us; for it seems upon consideration of the premises, that we have wholly finished what they began.

My judgment on this piece is this: that it is extremely learned, but that the author of it is better read in the Greek than in the English poets; that all writers ought to study this critique, as the best account I have ever seen of the Ancients; that the model of tragedy he has here given is excellent and extremely correct; but that it is not the only model of all tragedy, because it is too much circumscribed in plot, characters, etc.; and, lastly, that we may be taught here justly to admire and imitate the Ancients, without giving them the preference with this author, in prejudice to our own country.

Want of method in this excellent treatise makes the thoughts of the author sometimes obscure.

His meaning, that pity and terror are to be moved, is, that they are to be moved as the means conducing to the ends of tragedy, which are pleasure and instruction.

And these two ends may be thus distinguished. The chief end of the poet is to please; for his immediate reputation depends on it.

The great end of the poem is to instruct, which is performed by making pleasure the vehicle of that instruction; for poesy is an art, and all arts are made to proiil.—*Rapin.*

The pity, which the poet is to labor for, is for the criminal, not for those or him whom he has murdered, or who have been the occasion of the tragedy. The terror is likewise in the punishment of the same criminal, who, if he be represented too great an offender, will not be pitied; if altogether innocent, his punishment will be unjust.

Another obscurity is, where he says Sophocles perfected tragedy by introducing the third actor; that is, he meant three kinds of action: one company singing or speaking; another playing on the music; a third dancing.

To make a true judgment in this competition betwixt the Greek poets and the English, in tragedy:

Consider, first, how Aristotle has defined a tragedy. Secondly, what he assigns the end of it to be. Thirdly, what he thinks the beauties of it. Fourthly, the means to attain the end proposed.

Compare the Greek and English tragic poets justly, and without partiality, according to those rules.

Then, secondly, consider whether Aristotle has made a just definition of tragedy; of its parts, of its ends, and of its beauties; and whether he, having not seen any others but those of Sophocles, Euripides, etc., had or truly could determine what all the excellences of tragedy are, and wherein they consist.

Next, show in what ancient tragedy was deficient; for example, in the narrowness of its plots and fewness of persons; and try whether that be not a fault in the Greek poets; and whether their excellency was so great, when the variety was visibly so little; or whether what they did was not very easy to do.

Then make a judgment on what the English have added to their beauties; as, for example, not only more plot, but also new passions; as, namely, that of love, scarcely touched on by the Ancients, except in this one example of Phaedra, cited by Mr. Rymer; and in that how short they were of Fletcher!

Prove also that love, being an heroic passion, is fit for tragedy, which cannot be denied, because of the example alleged of Phaedra; and how far Shakespeare has outdone them in friendship, etc.

To return to the beginning of this inquiry: consider if pity and terror be enough for tragedy to move; and I believe, upon a true definition of tragedy, it will be found that its work extends farther and that it is to reform manners, by a delightful representation of human life in great persons, by way of dialogue. If this be true, then not only pity and terror are to be moved, as the only means to bring us to virtue, but generally love to virtue and hatred to vice, by showing the rewards of one and punishments of the other; at least, by rendering virtue always amiable, though it be shown unfortunate; and vice detestable, though it be shown triumphant.

If, then, the encouragement of virtue and discouragement of vice be the proper ends of poetry in tragedy, pity and terror, though good means, are not the only. For all the passions, in their turns, are to be set in a ferment; as joy, anger, love, fear are to be used as the poet's commonplaces; and a general concernment for the principal actors is to be raised by making them appear such in their characters, their words, and actions, as will interest the audience in their fortunes.

And if, after all, in a larger sense, pity comprehends this concernment for the good, and terror includes detestation for the bad, then let us consider whether the English have not answered this end of tragedy as well as the Ancients, or perhaps better.

And here Mr. Rymer's objections against these plays are to be impartially weighed, that we may see whether they are of weight enough to turn the balance against our countrymen.

It is evident those plays which he arraigns have moved both those passions in a high degree upon the stage.

To give the glory of this away from the poet, and to place it upon the actors, seems unjust.

One reason is, because whatever actors they have found the event has been the same; that is, the same passions have been always moved; which shows that there is something of force and merit in the plays themselves, conducing to the design of raising these two passions: and suppose them ever to have been excellently acted, yet action only adds grace, vigor, and more life upon the stage; but cannot give it wholly where it is not first. But, secondly, I dare appeal to those who have never seen them acted, if they have not found these two passions moved within them; and if the general voice will carry it, Mr. Rymer's prejudice will take off his single testimony.

This, being matter of fact, is reasonably to be established by this appeal; as, if one man says it is night when the rest of the world conclude it to be day, there needs no farther argument against him that it is so.

If he urge that the general taste is depraved, his arguments to prove this can at best but evince that our poets took not the best way to raise those passions; but experience proves against him that those means which they have used have been successful, and have produced them.

And one reason of that success is, in my opinion, this: that Shakespeare and Fletcher have written to the genius of the age and nation in which they lived; for though nature, as he objects, is the same in all places, and reason too the same, yet the climate, the age, the disposition of the people to whom a poet writes may be so different that what pleased the Greeks would not satisfy an English audience.

And if they proceed upon a foundation of truer reason to please the Athenians than Shakespeare and Fletcher to please the English, it only shows that the Athenians were a more judicious people; but the poet's business is certainly to please the audience.

Whether our English audience have been pleased hitherto with acorns, as he calls it, or with bread, is the next question; that is, whether the means which Shakespeare and Fletcher have used, in their plays, to raise those passions before-named, be better applied to the ends by the Greek poets than by them. And perhaps we shall not grant him this wholly: let it be yielded that a writer is not to run down with the stream, or to please the people by their unusual methods, but rather to reform their judgments, it still remains to prove that our theatre needs this total reformation.

The faults which he has found in their design are rather wittily aggravated in many places than reasonably urged; and as much may be returned on the Greeks by one who were as witty as himself.

They destroy not, if they are granted, the foundation of the fabric; only take away from the beauty of the symmetry; for example, the faults in the character of the King, in *King and No King*,[2] are not, as he calls them, such as render him detestable, but only imperfections which accompany human nature, and are for the most part excused by

2 *King and No King,* by Beaumont and Fletcher, 1611.

the violence of his love; so that they destroy not our pity or concern-ment for him: this answer may be applied to most of his objections of that kind.

And Rollo [3] committing many murders, when he is answerable but for one, is too severely arraigned by him; for it adds to our horror and detestation of the criminal; and poetic justice is not neglected neither; for we stab him in our minds for every offence which he commits; and the point, which the poet is to gain on the audience, is not so much in the death of an offender as the raising a horror of his crimes.

That the criminal should neither be wholly guilty nor wholly in-nocent, but so participating of both as to move both pity and terror, is certainly a good rule, but not perpetually to be observed; for that were to make all tragedies too much alike; which objection he foresaw, but has not fully answered.

To conclude therefore: if the plays of the Ancients are more cor-rectly plotted, ours are more beautifully written. And if we can raise passions as high on worse foundations, it shows our genius in tragedy is greater; for in all other parts of it the English have manifestly ex-celled them.

[3] *The Bloody Brothers; or, Rollo, Duke of Normandy,* by Fletcher and Jonson(?), 1619.

André Dacier
1651-1722

For much of the eighteenth century, the text and commentaries of Aristotle's *Poetics* by André Dacier were standard, and Dacier's reputation probably exceeds his actual performance. Dacier was a classic scholar, the editor of many classical texts. His wife, the translator of Homer into French prose, was another of the famous classicists of the neoclassic period. Although Dacier was always sure that Aristotle was right, his approach was that of the rationalist: Aristotle was right only because what he said always conformed with reason. As a writer on drama, Dacier had little to offer that was original, but he organized and codified much that had been said, and it is understandable that his commentaries became the Bible of the neoclassic critic. His work became known in England through an anonymous translation in 1705.

Notes to *Aristotle's* POETICS [1]

[1692]

I. Preface [EXCERPT]

We come now to the first consequence which we draw from what we have established, and shall endeavor to prove that our laws and what pleases can never be opposite, since the Rules were made only for what pleases and tend only to show the way you must walk in to do so. By this we shall destroy the false maxim, that all that pleases is good, and assert that we ought on the contrary to say, that all that is good pleases or ought to please. For the goodness of any work whatsoever does not proceed from this, that it gives us pleasure, but the pleasure that we have proceeds from its goodness, unless our deluded eyes and corrupt imaginations mislead us, for that which causes our mistakes is not where is, but what is not.

[1] English translation, London, 1705.

If the Rules and what pleased were things opposite, you would never arrive at the giving pleasure but by mere chance, which is absurd. There must for that reason be a certain way which leads thither, and that way is the Rule which we ought to learn. But what is that Rule? 'Tis a precept which, being drawn from the pleasant and profitable leads us to their source. Now what is the pleasant and profitable? 'Tis that which pleases naturally; in all arts 'tis this we consult; 'tis the most sure and perfect model we can imitate. In it we find perfect Unity and Order, for itself is order, or to speak more properly, the effect of order and the rule which conducts us thither. There is but one way to find order, but a great many to fall into confusion.

There would be nothing bad in the world if all that pleased were good, for there is nothing so ridiculous but what will have its admirers. You may say, indeed, 'tis no truer that what is good pleases, because we see every day disputes about the Good and Pleasant, that the same thing pleases some and displeases others; nay, it pleases and displeases the very same persons at different times. From whence then proceeds this difference? It comes either from an absolute ignorance of the Rule or that the passions alter it. Rightly to clear this truth, I believe I may lay down this maxim, that all sensible objects are of two sorts; some may be judged of by sense independently for reason. I call sense that impression which the animal spirits make on the soul. Others can't be judged of but by Reason exercised in science. Things simply agreeable or disagreeable are of the first sort. All the world may judge alike of these; for example, the most ignorant in music perceives very well when a player on the lute strikes one string for another, because he judges by his sense, and that sense is the rule. In such occasions we may therefore very well say that all that pleases is good, because that which is good doth please, or that which is evil never fails to displease; for neither the passions nor ignorance dull the senses; on the contrary, they sharpen them. 'Tis not so in things which spring from reason. Passion and ignorance act very strongly on it and oftentimes choke it. This is the reason why we ordinarily judge so ill and differently concerning those things of which that is the rule and the cause. Why what is bad often pleases and that which is good doth not always so, 'tis not the fault of the object; 'tis the fault of him who judges. But what is good will infallibly please those who can judge, and that's sufficient. By this we may see that a play that shall bring those things which are to be judged of by reason within the Rules, as also what is to be judged of by the sense, shall never fail to please, for it will please both the learned and ignorant. Now this conformity of suffrages is the most sure or, according to Aristotle, the only mark of the good and pleasant, whether they are followed methodically and with design or by hazard only. For 'tis certain there are many persons who are entirely ignorant of these Rules and yet don't fail to succeed in several affairs. This is far from destroying the Rules, and serves to show their beauty, and proves how far they are conformable to Nature, since those often follow them who know nothing of 'em. In the Remarks you shall find many examples of the vast difference the observance or neglect of the Rules make in the same subject and by that be thoroughly convinced that they are the two only causes of good or bad works and that there can never be any occasion where the perfect harmony which is between the Rules and what pleases should be broken.

II. Remarks on Chapter VI of Aristotle's *Poetics*

This the "purgation" passage is, as has already been said, the most important place of the definition, as also the most difficult; for what the commentators have said to explain it serves only to render it more obscure. There are several explications of it to be found among them, but the true one is not there. And this is what very much embarrassed Mr. Corneille, who after a long search understood but one small part of it and had only a glimpse of that neither, since he doubts whether tragedy, though it has all the conditions Aristotle requires, would refine the passions. "I am afraid," says he, "that the reasoning of this philosopher is only a fine idea and that it never was effectually true." [2] He is not far from the opinion of one of Aristotle's interpreters, who thinks he speaks of this refining of the passions only to contradict Plato, who had condemned tragedy and banished it from his Commonwealth, because in imitating all sorts of actions, as well bad as good, it insinuated itself into the minds of the spectators by its agreeableness and revived those passions which it ought to extinguish. Aristotle is then desirous to show that 'tis to no purpose to banish it from well regulated states, and to succeed in that design he finds the advantage of it in these agitations of the soul and endeavors to render this poem

[2] See Corneille's *Discourse on Tragedy*, p. 6.

commendable by the very same reason which Plato used to have it banished.[3] If we had the second book of this Art of Poetry, in which Aristotle explains himself at length, as he had promised in the last chapter of his *Politics*, we should not have been obliged at this time to defend him against these unjust suppositions; but since that book is lost, we must endeavor to supply the want of it as well as we can and to show that there is nothing more true than what Aristotle says here of the refining of the passions, which is the only end that tragedy proposes to itself and which is only found fault with because it is not understood. There are two things to examine in these words: "And which by the means of compassion and terror perfectly refines in us all sorts of passions and whatever else is like them." [4]

First then, we must see how tragedy can refine terror and compassion in exciting them; and afterwards how in refining them it refines also at the same time those other passions which would make us fall into the same calamities. For in this the difficulty doth consist, but before we proceed to that, 'tis convenient to explain the term, "to refine the passions." The Academics, and afterwards the Stoics, made use of it to say "to drive out, to root them out of the soul." In this sense 'tis false to say that tragedy can refine the passions, for it is out of its power. But the Peripatetics, being persuaded that 'twas only the excess was vicious and that the passions when regulated were useful, nay necessary, they meant only by "to refine the passions" to curb the excess by which they erred and to reduce them to a just moderation. And this is the end they attribute to tragedy as the only one it can attain to.

Now let us see how it excites in us terror and compassion in order to refine them. This is not very difficult. It excites them then by setting before our eyes the calamities into which those who are like ourselves have fallen by involuntary faults, and it refines them by rendering those very misfortunes familiar to us, because it teaches us by that not to fear them nor to be too much concerned when they do really happen to us. Aristotle is not the only man who has had this idea of tragedy; the emperor Marcus Aurelius, however Stoical he was, passed the same judgment on this art. Chap. 6th of the 9th book of his Re-

---

[3] Plato's *Republic*, Bk. X.
[4] Note the difference between Dacier's translation and that of a modern scholar, I. Bywater (*Aristotle on the Art of Poetry*, Oxford, 1909, p. 17): "with incidents arousing pity and fear, wherewith to accomplish its catharsis of such emotions."

flections: his words are very remarkable. "Tragedies," says he, "were first introduced to put men in mind of those accidents which happen in their lives, to inform them that they must necessarily come, and teach them that those things which they see with so much delight on the stage should not appear insupportable in the Grand Theatre of the World; for you see plainly that such ought to be the catastrophe of all pieces, and those who cry so much on the theatre, *Oh Cytheron*, do not deliver themselves from their own evils."

This is then the first effect of tragedy; it refines terror and compassion by themselves. The advantage it brings to mankind by this is sufficiently great, since it prepares them to bear the most unlucky accidents courageously and disposes the most miserable to think themselves happy when they compare their own misfortunes with those which tragedy has represented to them. In whatsoever condition a man may be, yet when he shall see an Oedipus, a Philoctetes, an Orestes, he can but think his own afflictions light in comparison with theirs.

But tragedy does not stop here. In refining terror and compassion, it refines at the same time all those other passions which can precipitate us into the same miseries. For in laying before us the crimes which have drawn those unhappy ones into the pains they suffer, it teaches us to stand on our guard, that we may not fall into them, and to moderate and refine that passion which was the only cause of their loss. This is what Aristotle thought, and this is the aim of tragedy. To take away this is to despoil it of its character and to make it lose the very name of a *fable,* since there is no fable which was not invented to form the manners by instructions disguised under the allegory of an action. Our tragedy may succeed well enough—in the first part, that is. It may excite and refine terror and compassion. But it rarely arrives at the last, which is, nevertheless, the most advantageous. It refines few of the other passions, and as it runs generally on love-intrigues, if it refined any, it must be that only. So we must expect but very little benefit. We must not admire if Mr. Corneille thought that this refining of the passions was imaginary. But you may say that if it was not, how comes it to pass that Plato judged otherwise and that he considered tragedy as the engagement and *boutefeu* of the passions? Plato considered tragedy only in its separate parts and judged of its effects by those which it produced on the spot, for 'tis true that in the very moment it rouses and excites the passions, as Aristotle also agrees. Aristotle considered it thoroughly and judged of it by the effects it produced after the representation was over, for 'tis certain that when the violent motions which the actions have stirred up begin to abate, we naturally profit by those crimes we have seen committed and which had drawn on the heads of their authors such horrible calamities. We may compare Plato and Aristotle on this occasion to two physicians, one of which condemns a remedy that the other approves. The first may argue with some show of reason that it will immediately put all the humours in motion and that by so doing it will cause in the body an intestine war which is capable of destroying it; and the other, after having examined more narrowly the causes and consequences of this disorder shall maintain his opinion by the great advantage which will accrue from this evacuation, it being only of those noxious humours which were the cause of the malady. This is exactly the difference which is between Plato and Aristotle. Tragedy is a true medicine which purges the passions, since it teaches the ambitious to moderate his ambition, the wicked to fear God, the passionate to restrain his anger, etc., but it is a very agreeable medicine and works only by pleasure.

William Congreve

1670-1729

WILLIAM CONGREVE is best known for his comedies; and, in *The Way of the World*, is credited with bringing the Restoration Comedy of Manners to its peak. In his comedies we sense, however, a turning away from the lusciousness of writers like Etherege and the early Dryden, and from the bitterness of Wycherley, to a cold intellectualism, a treatment of comedy as an art, expressing a life which was no longer lived, which never had been lived, but which is refined above life. The difference can be illustrated in two quotations. Charles II declared at one time, "I believe no man honest, and no woman continent out of principle." Congreve polishes this same idea, and elevates it to art when he writes in *Love for Love*,

> He alone won't betray in whom none will confide,
> And the nymph may be chaste that has never been tried.[1]

In the following selection we gain some insight into Congreve's methods of characterization, and some very useful information on the meaning of the words "Humour" and "Wit." This letter first appeared in a volume entitled *Letters on Several Occasions: written by and Between Mr. Dryden, Mr. Wycherley, Mr.——, Mr. Congreve, and Mr. Dennis*, which was issued in 1696.

Concerning Humour in Comedy

[1695]

DEAR SIR,[2] You write to me that you have entertained yourself two or three days with reading several comedies of several authors, and your observation is that there is more of Humour in our English writers than in any of the other comic poets, ancient or modern. You desire to know my opinion, and at the same time my thought of that which is generally called Humour in comedy.

---

[1] I am indebted to Professor Joseph Wood Krutch for this example, H. H. A.

[2] This letter is addressed to John Dennis (1657–1734), a noted English critic and writer of some obscure tragedies. See pp. 193–210.

I agree with you in an impartial preference of our English writers in that particular. But if I tell you my thoughts of Humour, I must at the same time confess that what I take for true Humour has not been so often written even by them as is generally believed. And some who have valued themselves and have been esteemed by others for that kind of writing have seldom touched upon it. To make this appear to the world would require a long and labored discourse, and such as I neither am able nor willing to undertake. But such little remarks as may be continued within the compass of a letter, and such unpremeditated thoughts as may be communicated between friend and friend, without incurring the censure of the world, or setting up for a dictator you shall have from me since you have enjoined it.

To define Humour, perhaps, were as difficult as to define Wit, for like that, it is of infinite variety. To enumerate the several Humours of men were a work as endless as to sum up their several opinions. And in my mind the *Quot homines tot Sententiae* might have been more properly interpreted of Humour, since there are many men of the same opinion in many things who are yet quite different in Humours. But tho' we cannot certainly tell what Wit is, or, what Humour is, yet we may go near to shew something which is not Wit or not Humour, and yet often mistaken for both. And since I have mentioned Wit and Humour together, let me make the first distinction between them and observe to you that *Wit is often mistaken for Humour.*

I have observed that when a few things have been wittily and pleasantly spoken by any character in a comedy it has been very usual for those who make their remarks on a play while it is acting to say, *Such a thing is very Humourously spoken. There is a great deal of Humour in that part.* Thus the character of the person speaking, maybe, surprisingly and pleasantly, is mistaken for a character of Humour which indeed is a character of Wit. But there is a great difference between a comedy wherein there are many things *humourously,* as they call it which is *pleasantly,* spoken, and one where there are several characters of Humour distinguished by the particular and different Humours appropriated to the several persons represented and which naturally arise from the different constitutions, complexions, and dispositions of men. The saying of humourous things does not distinguish characters, for every person in a comedy may be allowed to speak them. From a witty man they are expected, and even a fool may be permitted to stumble on 'em by chance. Tho' I make a difference betwixt Wit and Humour, yet I do not think that humourous characters exclude Wit. No, but the manner of Wit should be adapted to the Humour. As for instance, a character of splenetic and peevish Humour should have a satirical Wit. A jolly and sanguine Humour should have a facetious Wit. The former should speak positively; the latter, carelessly, for the former observes and shews things as they are; the latter, rather overlooks Nature and speaks things as he would have them; and his Wit and Humour have both of them a less alloy of judgment than the others.

As Wit, so its opposite, *folly, is sometimes mistaken for Humour.*

When a poet brings a character on the stage committing a thousand absurdities and talking impertinencies, roaring aloud and laughing immoderately on every, or rather, upon no occasion, this is a character of Humour.

Is anything more common than to have a pretended comedy stuffed with such grotesques, figures, and farce fools? Things that either are not in Nature, or if they are, are monsters and births of mischance, and consequently as such should be stifled and huddled out of the way like Sooterkins,[3] that mankind may not be shocked with an appearing possibility of the degeneration of a God-like species. For my part, I am as willing to laugh as anybody, and am as easily diverted with an object truly ridiculous, but at the same time, I can never care for seeing things that force me to entertain low thoughts of my Nature. I don't know how it is with others, but I confess freely to you, I could never look long upon a monkey without very mortifying reflections, tho' I never heard anything to the contrary why that creature is not originally of a distinct species. As I don't think Humour exclusive of Wit, neither do I think it inconsistent with Folly, but I think the Follies should be only such as men's Humours may incline 'em to, and not Follies entirely abstracted from both Humour and Nature.

Sometimes *personal defects are misrepresented for Humours.*

I mean, sometimes characters are barbarously exposed on the stage, ridiculing natural deformities, casual defects in the senses, and infirmities of age. Sure the poet must both be very ill-natured himself

3 A false birth or abortion.

and think his audience so when he proposes by shewing a man deformed, or deaf, or blind, to give them an agreeable entertainment, and hopes to raise their mirth by what is truly an object of compassion. But much need not be said upon this head to anybody, especially to you, who in one of your letters to me concerning Mr. Jonson's *Fox* have justly excepted against this immoral part of ridicule in Corbaccio's [4] character; and there I must agree with you to blame him, whom otherwise I cannot enough admire for his great mastery of true Humour in comedy.

External habit of body is often mistaken for Humour.

By external habit I do not mean the ridiculous dress or clothing of a character, tho' that goes a good way in some received characters. (But undoubtedly a man's Humour may incline him to dress differently from other people.) But I mean a singularity of manners, speech, and behavior peculiar to all, or most, of the same country, trade, profession, or education. I cannot think that a Humour which is only a habit or disposition contracted by use or custom; for by a disuse or compliance with other customs it may be worn off or diversified.

Affectation is generally mistaken for Humour.

These are indeed so much alike that at a distance they may be mistaken one for the other. For what is Humour in one may be Affectation in another, and nothing is more common than for some to affect particular ways of saying and doing things peculiar to others whom they admire and would imitate. Humour is the life, Affectation the picture. He that draws a character of Affectation shews Humour at the second hand; he at best but publishes a translation and his pictures are but copies.

But as these two last distinctions are the nicest,[5] so it may be most proper to explain them by particular instances from some author of reputation. Humour I take either to be born with us, and so of a natural growth, or else to be grafted into us by some accidental change in the constitution or revolution of the internal habit of body, by which it becomes, if I may so call it, naturalized.

Humour is from Nature, Habit from custom, and Affectation from industry.

---

[4] One of the hangers-on of Volpone in Jonson's *Volpone; or, The Fox*, 1606.
[5] Finest, or most subtle.

Humour shews us as we are.

Habit shews us as we appear under a forcible impression.

Affectation shews us what we would be under a voluntary disguise.

Tho' here I would observe by the way that a continued Affectation may in time become a Habit.

The character of Morose in the *Silent Woman* [6] I take to be a character of Humour. And I choose to instance this character to you from many others of the same author because I know it has been condemned by many as unnatural and farce. And you have yourself hinted some dislike of it for the same reason in a letter to me concerning some of Jonson's plays.

Let us suppose Morose to be a man naturally splenetic and melancholy; is there anything more offensive to one of such a disposition than noise and clamour? Let any man that has the spleen (and there are enough in England) be judge. We see common examples of this Humour in little every day. 'Tis ten to one but three parts in four of the company that you dine with are discomposed and startled at the cutting of a cork or scratching a plate with a knife. It is a proportion of the same Humour that makes such or any other noise offensive to the person that hears it, for there are others who will not be disturbed at all by it. Well. But Morose you will say is so extravagant he cannot bear any discourse or conversation above a whisper. Why, it is his excess of this Humour that makes him become ridiculous and qualifies his character for comedy. If the poet had given him but a moderate proportion of that Humour, 'tis odds but half the audience would have sided with the character and have condemned the author for exposing a Humour which was neither remarkable nor ridiculous. Besides, the distance of the stage requires the figure represented to be something larger than the life, and sure a picture may have features larger in proportion and yet be very like the original. If this exactness of quality were to be observed in Wit, as some would have it in Humour, what would become of those characters that are designed for men of Wit? I believe if a poet should steal a dialogue of any length from the extempore discourse of the two wittiest men upon earth, he would find the scene but coldly received by the town. But to the purpose.

The character of Sir John Daw in the same play is a character of

---

[6] *Epicœne; or, The Silent Woman*, by Jonson, 1609.

Affectation. He everywhere discovers an Affectation of learning, when he is not only conscious to himself but the audience also plainly perceives that he is ignorant. Of this kind are the characters of Thraso in the *Eunuch* of Terence, and Pyrgopolinices in the *Miles Gloriosus* of Plautus. They affect to be thought valiant when both themselves and the audience know they are not. Now such boasting of valor in men who were really valiant would undoubtedly be a Humour, for a fiery disposition might naturally throw a man into the same extravagance which is only affected in the characters I have mentioned.

The character of Cob in *Every Man in His Humour* [7] and most of the under-characters in *Bartholomew Fair* [8] discover only a singularity of manners appropriated to the several educations and professions of the persons represented. They are not Humours but Habits contracted by custom. Under this head may be ranged all country clowns, sailors, tradesmen, jockeys, gamesters, and such like who make use of cants or peculiar dialects in their several arts and vocations. One may almost give a receipt for the composition of such a character, for the poet has nothing to do but to collect a few proper phrases and terms of art and to make the person apply them by ridiculous metaphors in his conversation with characters of different natures. Some late characters of this kind have been very successful, but in my mind they may be painted without much art or labor, since they require little more than a good memory and superficial observation. But true Humour cannot be shewn without a dissection of Nature and a narrow search to discover the first seeds from whence it has its root and growth.

If I were to write to the world, I should be obliged to dwell longer upon each of these distinctions and examples, for I know that they would not be plain enough to all readers. But a bare hint is sufficient to inform you of the notions which I have on this subject. And I hope by this time you are of my opinion that Humour is neither Wit, nor Folly, nor personal defect, nor Affectation, nor Habit, and yet that each and all of these have been both written and received for Humour.

I should be unwilling to venture even on a bare description of Humour, much more, to make a definition of it, but now my hand is in, I'll tell you what serves me instead of either. I take it to be, *A singular and unavoidable manner of doing or saying anything, pecul-*

[7] First acted in 1598.   [8] First acted in 1614.

iar and natural to one man only, by which his speech and actions are distinguished from those of other men.

Our Humour has relation to us, and to what proceeds from us, as the accidents have to a substance; it is a color, taste, and smell diffused through all; tho' our actions are never so many and different in form, they are all splinters of the same wood and have naturally one complexion, which tho' it may be disguised by art, yet cannot be wholly changed. We may paint it with other colors, but we cannot change the grain. So the natural sound of an instrument will be distinguished, tho' the notes expressed by it are never so various and the diversions never so many. Dissimulation may, by degrees, become more easy to our practice, but it can never absolutely transubstantiate us into what we would seem. It will always be in some proportion a violence upon Nature.

A man may change his opinion, but I believe he will find it a difficulty to part with his Humour, and there is nothing more provoking than the being made sensible of that difficulty. Sometimes one shall meet with those who, innocently enough, but at the same time impertinently, will ask the question, "Why are you not merry?" "Why are you not gay, pleasant, and cheerful?" Then instead of answering, could I ask such one, "Why are you not handsome? Why have you not black eyes and a better complexion?" Nature abhors to be forced.

The two famous philosophers of Ephesus and Abdera [9] have their different sects at this day. Some weep and others laugh at one and the same thing.

I don't doubt but you have observed several men laugh when they are angry, others who are silent, some that are loud. Yet I cannot suppose that it is the passion of anger which is in itself different, or more or less in one than t'other, but that it is the Humour of the man that is predominant and urges him to express it in that manner. Demonstrations of pleasure are as various; one man has a Humour of retiring from all company when anything has happened to please him beyond expectation; he hugs himself alone, and thinks it an addition to the pleasure to keep it secret. Another is upon thorns till he has made proclamation of it, and must make other people sensible of his happiness before he can be so himself. So it is in grief and other

[9] Heraclitus of Ephesus was the "weeping philosopher," as contrasted with Democritus of Abdera, the "laughing philosopher."

passions. Demonstrations of love and the effects of that passion upon several Humours are infinitely different, but here the ladies who abound in servants [10] are the best judges. Talking of the ladies, methinks something should be observed of the Humour of the fair sex, since they are sometimes so kind as to furnish out a character for comedy. But I must confess I have never made any observation of what I apprehend to be true Humour in women. Perhaps passions are too powerful in that sex to let Humour have its course, or maybe by reason of their natural coldness, Humour cannot exert itself to that extravagant degree which it often does in the male sex. For if ever anything does appear comical or ridiculous in a woman, I think it is little more than an acquired Folly or an Affectation. We may call them the weaker sex, but I think the true reason is because our Follies are stronger and our faults more prevailing.

One might think that the diversity of Humour, which must be allowed to be diffused throughout mankind, might afford endless matter for the support of comedies. But when we come closely to consider that point, and nicely to distinguish the difference of Humours, I believe we shall find the contrary. For tho' we allow every man something of his own and a peculiar Humour, yet every man has it not in quantity to become remarkable by it. Or if many do become remarkable by their Humours, yet all those Humours may not be diverting. Nor is it only requisite to distinguish what Humour will be diverting, but also how much of it, what part of it to shew in light and what to cast in shades, how to set it off by preparatory scenes, and by opposing other Humours to it in the same scene. Thro' a wrong judgment, sometimes, men's Humours may be opposed when there is really no specific difference between them, only a greater proportion of the same in one than t'other, occasioned by his having more phlegm, or choler, or whatever the constitution is, from whence their Humours derive their source.

There is infinitely more to be said on this subject, tho' perhaps I have already said too much; but I have said it to a friend, who I am sure will not expose it if he does not approve of it. I believe the subject is entirely new and was never touched upon before; and if I would have anyone to see this private essay, it should be someone who might be provoked by my errors in it to publish a more judicious treatise on the subject. Indeed I wish it were done, that the world being a little

[10] Lovers, or gallants.

acquainted with the scarcity of true Humour, and the difficulty of finding and shewing it might look a little more favorably on the labors of them who endeavour to search into Nature for it and lay it open to the public view.

I don't say but that very entertaining and useful characters, and proper for comedy, may be drawn from Affectations and those other qualities which I have endeavored to distinguish from Humour; but I would not have such imposed on the world for Humour, nor esteemed of equal value with it. It were perhaps the work of a long life to make one comedy true in all its parts, and to give every character in it a true and distinct Humour. Therefore, every poet must be beholding to other helps to make out his number of ridiculous characters. But I think such a one deserves to be broke who makes all false musters, who does not shew one true Humour in a comedy, but entertains his audience to the end of the play with everything out of Nature.

I will make but one observation to you more, and have done; and that is grounded upon an observation of your own, and which I mentioned at the beginning of my letter, *viz.*, that there is more of Humour in our English comic writers than in any others. I do not at all wonder at it, for I look upon Humour to be almost of English growth; at least, it does not seem to have found such increase on any other soil. And what appears to me to be the reason of it is the great freedom, privilege, and liberty which the common people of England enjoy. Any man that has a Humour is under no restraint or fear of giving it a vent; they have a proverb among them which, maybe, will shew the bent and genius of the people as well as a longer discourse. "He that will have a May Pole shall have a May Pole." This is a maxim with them and their practice is agreeable to it. I believe something considerable too may be ascribed to their feeding so much on flesh, and the grossness of their diet in general. But I have done; let the physicians agree that. Thus you have my thoughts of Humour to my power of expressing them in so little time and compass. You will be kind to shew me wherein I have erred, and as you are very capable of giving me instruction, so I think I have a very just title to demand it from you, being without reserve,

Your real Friend,
and humble Servant,
W. Congreve

July 10, 1695

Jeremy Collier
1650-1726

JEREMY COLLIER, whose onslaught on the stage set off a major literary
controversy, was a nonjuring, puritanical divine who sought not merely
the reform of the theatres but their complete extinction. His *Short View
of the Profaneness and Immorality of the English Stage* (1698) fused and
broadcast the growing discontent with the licentiousness of the plays written up to that time, and materially affected dramatic writing for many
years. Collier was too astute to make a frontal attack on the stage as an
institution, so with a great display of learning he paraded the views of
the ancient critics to show that the function of drama was "to recommend
virtue and discountenance vice." Through five of his six chapters, he proves
that the contemporary stage could not by any stretch of the imagination
be considered as doing either of these tasks. In his sixth chapter, Collier
allows his real opinions to come to the fore and attempts to make out a
case for the permanent closing of all theatres. This chapter, however, is of
little importance in the controversy which followed.

His outburst made itself felt throughout the literary world, and the
playwrights made several attempts to answer him. Congreve, Vanbrugh,
and many others replied in pamphlets, but to little avail. Collier promptly
answered, adducing more evidence of a sort which could not be denied.
Other pamphleteers flocked to offer support where none was needed. The
playwrights and their defenders were lost, because they conceded Collier's
terms. Apparently no one of the regular dramatists had evolved a theory
of comedy for comedy's sake; yet they wrote comedy of no other sort.
Restoration comedy was one of cynical wit, a cruel comedy of manners,
not of moral purpose. Yet in answering Collier, Vanbrugh and Congreve
attempted to show that their fine rakes were intended to be objects of
ridicule. This idea was so patently false that Collier had little trouble
disposing of their arguments. Only Farquhar had some understanding of
the problem, for in his *Discourse upon Comedy,* he attempted to view
comedy from the light of common sense. His ideas were inchoate, but it
was the only way that Collier could in any sense be answered.

Collier weakened part of his argument, however, by his extreme sensitivity to *double entendre* and to profanity. While it is easy to find an abundance of objectionable passages in the plays, Collier saved some of his
heaviest barrages for lines that strike the modern reader as comparatively

innocent. Another ground on which Collier could be attacked was the use he made of Rymer's idea of Decorum. He spent pages in demonstrating that the members of the clergy should be displayed according to the type— sincere, passionless, devout, and pure. The clergymen as depicted in Restoration drama were affronts to him and to all other clergymen. In vain the writers protested that individual clergymen might be licentious and corrupt. Rymer had insisted on Decorum, and Collier was adamant. Perhaps the fact that he was himself a member of the clergy had something to do with the strength of his views.

The *Short View of the Profaneness and Immorality of the English Stage* did not single-handed do the job of reforming the stage, but it undoubtedly accelerated the process. The tradition he was attacking had vanished from the court and was hanging on in the theatre merely as an art form which was becoming less and less connected with real life. After his book, many plays such as *The Way of the World, The Recruiting Officer,* and *The Beaux' Stratagem* carried on the old tradition, but time and the respectability of Queen Anne were on Collier's side.[1]

A Short View of the Profaneness and Immorality of the English Stage

[1698; excerpts]

INTRODUCTION

THE BUSINESS of plays is to recommend virtue and discountenance vice; to shew the uncertainty of human greatness, the sudden turns of fate, and the unhappy conclusions of violence and injustice; 'tis to expose the singularities of pride and fancy, to make folly and falsehood contemptible, and to bring everything that is ill under infamy and neglect. This design has been oddly pursued by the English stage. Our poets write with a different view and are gone into another interest. 'Tis true, were their intentions fair, they might be serviceable to this purpose. They have in great measure the springs of thought and inclination in their power. Show, music, action, and rhetoric are moving entertainments; and, rightly employed, would be very significant. But force and motion are things indifferent, and the use lies chiefly in the application. These advantages are now in the enemies'

---

[1] The best account and a full bibliography of the Collier controversy can be found in Joseph Wood Krutch's *Comedy and Conscience after the Restoration,* New York, 1949.

hand and under a very dangerous management. Like cannon seized, they are pointed the wrong way; and by the strength of the defence, the mischief is made the greater. That this complaint is not unreasonable I shall endeavor to prove by shewing the misbehavior of the stage with respect to morality and religion. Their liberties in the following particulars are intolerable, *viz.*, their smuttiness of expression; their swearing, profaneness, and lewd application of Scripture; their abuse of the clergy, their making their top characters libertines and giving them success in their debauchery. This charge, with some other irregularities, I shall make good against the stage and shew both the novelty and scandal of the practice. And, first, I shall begin with the rankness and indecency of their language.

CHAPTER I: THE IMMODESTY OF THE STAGE

IN TREATING of this head, I hope the reader does not expect that I should set down chapter and page and give him the citations at length. To do this would be a very unacceptable and foreign employment. Indeed the passages, many of them, are in no condition to be handled. He that is desirous to see these flowers, let him do it in their own soil. 'Tis my business rather to kill the root than transplant it. But that the poets may not complain of injustice, I shall point to the infection at a distance, and refer in general to play and person.

Now among the curiosities of this kind we may reckon Mrs. Pinchwife, Horner, and Lady Fidget in the *Country Wife;* [2] Widow Blackacre and Olivia in the *Plain Dealer.* [3] These, though not all the exceptionable characters, are the most remarkable. I'm sorry the author should stoop his wit thus low and use his understanding so unkindly. Some people appear coarse and slovenly out of poverty. They can't well go to the charge of sense. They are offensive, like beggars, for want of necessaries. But this is none of the *Plain Dealer's* case; he can afford his Muse a better dress when he pleases. But then the rule is, where the motive is the less, the fault is the greater. To proceed. Jacinta, Elvira, Dalinda, and Lady Pliant, in the *Mock Astrologer,* [4] *Spanish Friar,* [5] *Love Triumphant,* [6] and *Double Dealer,* [7] forget themselves extremely; and almost all the characters in the *Old Batchelor* [8]

[2] By William Wycherley, 1675.
[4] By John Dryden, 1668.
[6] By John Dryden, 1694.
[8] By William Congreve, 1693.

[3] By William Wycherley, 1676.
[5] By John Dryden, 1680.
[7] By William Congreve, 1693.

are foul and nauseous. *Love for Love* [9] and the *Relapse* [10] strike sometimes upon this sand, and so likewise does *Don Sebastian*.[11]

I don't pretend to have read the stage through; neither am I particular to my utmost. Here is quoting enough unless 'twere better.
Besides, I may have occasion to mention somewhat of this kind afterwards. But from what has been hinted already, the reader may be over-
furnished. Here is a large collection of debauchery; such pieces are
rarely to be met with. 'Tis sometimes painted at length too and appears in great variety of progress and practice. It wears almost all sorts
of dresses to engage the fancy and fasten upon the memory and keep
up the charm from languishing. Sometimes you have it in image and
description; sometimes by way of allusion; sometimes in disguise; and
sometimes without it. And what can be the meaning of such a representation unless it be to tincture the audience, to extinguish shame, and
make lewdness a diversion? This is the natural consequence, and therefore one would think 'twas the intention too. Such licentious discourse tends to no point but to stain the imagination, to awaken folly,
and to weaken the defenses of virtue. It was upon the account of these
disorders that Plato banished poets his Commonwealth. And one of
the Fathers calls poetry, *Vinum Daemonum,* an intoxicating draught
made up of the Devil's dispensatory.

I grant the abuse of a thing is no argument against the use of it.
However, young people particularly should not entertain themselves
with a lewd picture, especially when 'tis drawn by a masterly hand.
For such a liberty may probably raise those passions which can neither
be discharged without trouble, nor satisfied without a crime. 'Tis not
safe for a man to trust his virtue too far, for fear it should give him
the slip. But the danger of such an entertainment is but part of the
objection; 'tis all scandal and meanness into the bargain. It does in
effect degrade human nature; sinks reason into appetite, and breaks
down the distinctions between man and beast. Goats and monkeys, if
they could speak, would express their brutality in such language as
this.

To argue the matter more at large.

Smuttiness is a fault in behavior as well as in religion. 'Tis a very
coarse diversion, the entertainment of those who are generally least

---

[9] By William Congreve, 1695.   [10] By John Vanbrugh, 1696.
[11] By John Dryden, 1690.

both in sense and station. The looser part of the mob have no true relish of decency and honor, and want education and thought to furnish out a genteel conversation. Barrenness of fancy makes them often take up with those scandalous liberties. A vicious imagination may blot a great deal of paper at this rate with ease enough. And 'tis possible convenience may sometimes invite to the expedient. The modern poets seem to use smut as the old ones did machines, to relieve a fainting invention. When Pegasus is jaded and would stand still, he is apt like other tits to run into every puddle.

Obscenity in any company is a rustic, uncreditable talent, but among women 'tis particularly rude. Such talk would be very affrontive in conversation and not endured by any lady of reputation. Whence then comes it to pass that those liberties which disoblige so much in conversation should entertain upon the stage? Do women leave all the regards to decency and conscience behind them when they come to the playhouse? Or does the place transform their inclinations and turn their former aversions into pleasure? Or were their pretences to sobriety elsewhere nothing but hypocrisy and grimace? Such suppositions as these are all satire and invective. They are rude imputations upon the whole sex. To treat the ladies with such stuff is no better than taking their money to abuse them. It supposes their imagination vicious and their memories ill-furnished, that they are practiced in the language of the stews and pleased with the scenes of brutishness. When at the same time the customs of education and the laws of decency are so very cautious and reserved in regard to women —I say so very reserved—that 'tis almost a fault for them to understand they are ill-used. They can't discover their disgust without disadvantage, nor blush without disservice to their modesty. To appear with any skill in such cant looks as if they had fallen upon ill conversation or managed their curiosity amiss. In a word, he that treats the ladies with such discourse must conclude either that they like it or they do not. To suppose the first is a gross reflection upon their virtue. And as for the latter case, it entertains them with their own aversion, which is ill-nature, and ill-manners enough in all conscience. And in this particular custom and conscience, the forms of breeding and the maxims of religion are on the same side. In other instances vice is often too fashionable. But here a man can't be a sinner without being a clown.

In this respect the stage is faulty to a scandalous degree of nauseousness and aggravation. For:

1. The poets make women speak smuttily. Of this the places beforementioned are sufficient evidence, and if there was occasion they might be multiplied to a much greater number. Indeed the comedies are seldom clear of these blemishes. And sometimes you have them in tragedy. For instance, the *Orphan's* [12] Monimia makes a very improper description, and the Royal Leonora in the *Spanish Friar,* runs a strange length in the history of love. And do princesses use to make their reports with such fulsome freedoms? Certainly this Leonora was the first queen of her family. Such raptures are too luscious for Joan of Naples. Are these the tender things Mr. Dryden says the ladies call on him for? I suppose he means the ladies that are too modest to show their faces in the pit.[13] This entertainment can be fairly designed for none but such. Indeed it hits their palate exactly. It regales their lewdness, graces their character, and keeps up their spirits for their vocation. Now to bring women under such misbehavior is violence to their native modesty, and a misrepresentation of their sex. For modesty, as Mr. Rapin observes,* is the character of women.[14] To represent them without this quality is to make monsters of them and throw them out of their kind. Euripides, who was no negligent observer of human nature, is always careful of this Decorum. Thus Phaedra,† when possessed with an infamous passion, takes all imaginable pains to conceal it. She is as regular and reserved in her language as the most virtuous matron. 'Tis true, the force of shame and desire, the scandal of satisfying, and the difficulty of parting with her inclinations disorder her to distraction. However, her frenzy is not lewd; she keeps her modesty even after she has lost her wits. Had Shakespeare secured this point for his young virgin, Ophelia, the play ‡ had been better contrived. Since he was resolved to drown the lady like a kitten, he should have set her a swimming a little sooner. To keep her alive only to sullen her reputation and discover the rankness of her breath was very cruel. But it may be said the freedoms of distraction go for nothing, a fever has no faults, and a man *non compos,* may kill without murder. It may be so; but then such people ought to be kept in

* *Reflections upon Aristotle, &c.*
† Euripides, *Hippolitus.*   ‡ *Hamlet.*

---

[12] By Thomas Otway, 1680.   [13] Prostitutes wore masks to the theatre.
[14] A reference to Rymer's idea of Decorum. See p. 146.

dark rooms and without company. To shew them or let them loose is somewhat unreasonable. But after all, the modern stage seems to depend upon this expedient. Women are sometimes represented silly, and sometimes mad, to enlarge their liberty and screen their impudence from censure. This politic contrivance we have in Marcella, Hoyden, and Miss Prue.* However, it amounts to this confession, that women, when they have their understanding about them, ought to converse otherwise. In fine, modesty is the distinguishing virtue of that sex and serves both for ornament and defence; modesty was designed by providence as a guard to virtue, and that it might be always at hand 'tis wrought into the mechanism of the body. 'Tis likewise proportioned to the occasions of life and strongest in youth when passion is so too. 'Tis a quality as true to innocence as the senses are to health; whatever is ungrateful to the first is prejudicial to the latter. The enemy no sooner approaches, but the blood rises in opposition and looks defiance to an indecency. It supplies the room of reasoning and collection. Intuitive knowledge can scarcely make a quicker impression; and what, then, can be a surer guide to the unexperienced? It teaches by sudden instinct and aversion. This is both a ready and a powerful method of instruction. The tumult of the blood and spirits and the uneasiness of the sensation are of singular use. They serve to awaken reason and prevent surprise. Thus the distinctions of good and evil are refreshed, and the temptation kept at a proper distance.

2. They represent their single ladies and persons of condition under these disorders of liberty. This makes the irregularity still more monstrous and a greater contradiction to Nature and probability. But rather than not be vicious, they will venture to spoil a character. This mismanagement we have partly seen already. Jacinta [15] and Belinda † are farther proof; and the *Double Dealer* is particularly remarkable. There are but four Ladies in this play, and three of the biggest of them are whores. A great compliment to quality to tell them there is not above a quarter of them honest! This was not the Roman breeding. Terence and Plautus his strumpets were little people; but of this more hereafter.

3. They have oftentimes not so much as the poor refuge of a double

---

* *Don Quixote*. [By Thomas D'Urfey, 1694; in two parts.] *Relapse, Love for Love.*
† *Mock Astrologer. Old Batchelor.*

[15] John Dryden, *An Evening's Love; or, The Mock Astrologer*, 1668.

meaning to fly to. So that you are under a necessity either of taking ribaldry or nonsense. And when the sentence has two handles, the worst is generally turned to the audience. The matter is so contrived that the smut and scum of the thought now arises uppermost, and, like a picture drawn to sight, looks always upon the company.

4. And which is still more extraordinary, the prologues and epilogues are sometimes scandalous to the last degree.* I shall discover them for once, and let them stand like rocks in the margin. Now here, properly speaking, the actors quit the stage and remove from fiction into life. Here they converse with the boxes and pit and address directly to the audience. These preliminary and concluding parts are designed to justify the conduct of the play, and bespeak the favor of the company. Upon such occasions one would imagine, if ever, the ladies should be used with respect and the measures of decency observed. But here we have lewdness without shame or example. Here the poet exceeds himself. Here are such strains as would turn the stomach of an ordinary debauchee and be almost nauseous in the stews. And to make it the more agreeable, women are commonly picked out for this service. Thus the poet courts the good opinion of the audience. This is the dessert he regales the ladies with at the close of the entertainment. It seems, he thinks, they have admirable palates! Nothing can be a greater breach of manners than such liberties as these. If a man would study to outrage quality and virtue, he could not do it more effectually. But:

5. Smut is still more insufferable with respect to religion. The heathen religion was in a great measure a mystery of iniquity. Lewdness was consecrated in the temples as well as practiced in the stews. Their deities were great examples of vice and worshipped with their own inclination. 'Tis no wonder therefore their poetry should be tinctured with their belief, and that the stage should borrow some of the liberties of their theology. This made Mercury's procuring and Jupiter's adultery the more passable in *Amphytrion*.† Upon this score, Gimnausium is less monstrous in praying the gods to send her store of gallants. And thus Chaerea defends his adventure by the precedent of Jupiter and Danae.‡ But the Christian religion is quite of another complexion. Both its precepts and authorities are the

---

* *Mock Astrologer. Country Wife. Cleomenes* [*The Spartan Hero*, by John Dryden, 1692], *Old Batchelor*.

† Plautus.   ‡ Cisteller. Terence, *Eunuch*.

highest discouragement to licentiousness. It forbids the remotest tendencies to evil, banishes the follies of conversation, and obliges up to sobriety of thought. That which might pass for raillery and entertainment in heathenism is detestable in Christianity. The restraint of the precept and the quality of the Deity and the expectations of futurity quite alter the case.

But notwithstanding the latitudes of paganism, the Roman and Greek theatres were much more inoffensive than ours.

.   .   .

To come home and near our own times. The English theatre from Queen Elizabeth to King Charles II will afford us something not inconsiderable to our purpose.

As for Shakespeare, he is too guilty to make an evidence. But I think he gains not much by his misbehavior; he has commonly Plautus's fate: where there is most smut, there is least sense.

Ben Jonson is much more reserved in his plays and declares plainly for modesty in his *Discoveries:* [16] some of his words are these.

A just writer, whom he calls a true artificer, will avoid obscene and effeminate phrase. Where manners and fashions are corrupted, language is so too. The excess of feasts and apparel are the notes of a sick state, and the wantonness of language of a sick mind. A little after he returns to the argument, and applies his reasoning more particularly to the stage. *Poetry* (says he) *and picture both behold pleasure and profit as their common object, but should abstain from all base pleasures, lest they should wholly err from their end; and, while they seek to better men's minds, destroy their manners. Insolent and obscene speeches and jests upon the best men are most likely to excite laughter. But this is truly leaping from the stage to the tumbril again, reducing all Wit to the original dung-cart.** More might be cited to this purpose, but that may serve for another occasion. In the meantime I shall go on to Beaumont and Fletcher.

Fletcher's *Faithful Shepherdess* [17] is remarkably moral and a sort of exhortation to chastity. This play met with ill judges; 'twas hissed before half-acted, and seems to have suffered on the account of its

---

* *Discoveries,* pp. 700, 701, 706, 717.

[16] Jonson's *Discoveries* were a collection of miscellaneous observations on poetry, posthumously published in 1640.
[17] By John Fletcher (1608).

innocence. Soon after, Ben Jonson and Beaumont appear and justify the author in a copy of verses. And as Beaumont commends modesty in Fletcher, so he is commended himself by Mr. Earl for the same quality.

> Such passions, such expressions meet my eye,
> Such wit untainted with obscenity.

And as I remember, Jasper Main has some strokes to the same purpose. Fletcher is still more full for the cause. Indeed nothing can be more express. He delivers himself by way of prologues where the poet speaks in his own person. The Prologue to the *Woman-Hater* very frankly lets the audience know what they are to expect. *If there be any amongst you* (says he) *that come to hear lascivious scenes, let them depart; For I do pronounce this, to the utter discomfort of all two-penny gallery men, you shall hear no bawdry in it.* We find in those days smut was the expectation of a coarse palate and relished by none but two-penny customers. In the *Knight of the Burning Pestle,*[18] part of the Prologue runs thus. *They were banished the theatre at* Athens, *and from* Rome *hissed, that brought parasites on the stage with apish actions, or fools with uncivil habits, or courtesans with immodest words.* Afterwards, Prologue, who represents a person gives us more to the same purpose.

> . . . . Fly far from hence
> All private taxes, immodest phrases,
> Whatever may but look like vicious.
> For wicked mirth never true pleasure brings;
> For honest minds are pleased with honest things.

I have quoted nothing but comedy in this author. The *Coronation* [19] is another. And the Prologue tells you there is

> No undermirth, such as does lard the scene
> For coarse delight, the language here is clean.
> And confident our poet bade me say,
> He'll bate you but the folly of a play.
> For which, altho' dull souls his pen despise,
> Who think it yet too early to be wise;
> The nobles yet will thank his Muse, at least
> Excuse him, 'cause his thought aimed at the best.

[18] By Francis Beaumont and John Fletcher (1607).
[19] *The Coronation* (1635) was actually by James Shirley but was included in the second folio of Beaumont and Fletcher in 1679. Since Collier probably used this edition, the ascription there led him astray.

Thus these poets are in their judgments clearly ours. 'Tis true, their hand was not always steady. But thus much may be averred, that Fletcher's later plays are the most inoffensive. This is either a sign of the poet's reformation, or that the exceptionable passages belonged to Beaumont, who died first.

To these authorities of our own nation, I shall add a considerable testimony out of Mr. Corneille. This author was sensible that though the expression of his *Théodore* [20] was altogether unsmutty,

Yet the bare idea of prostitution uneffected shocked the audience and made the play miscarry. The poet protests he took great care to alter the natural complexion of the image and to convey it decently to the fancy and delivered only some part of the history as inoffensively as possible. And after all his screening and conduct, the modesty of the audience would not endure that little the subject forced him upon. He is positive the comedies St. Augustine declaimed against were not such as the French. For theirs are not spectacles of turpitude, as that Father justly calls those of his time. The French, generally speaking, containing nothing but examples of innocence, piety, and virtue.

In this citation we have the opinion of the poet, the practice of the French theatre, and the sense of that nation, and all very full to our purpose.

To conclude this chapter. By what has been offered, it appears that the *present English stage* is superlatively scandalous. It exceeds the liberties of all times and countries. It has not so much as the poor plea of a precedent to which most other ill things may claim a pretence. 'Tis mostly mere discovery and invention; a new world of vice found out and planted with all the industry imaginable. Aristophanes himself, how bad soever in other respects, does not amplify and flourish and run through all the topics of lewdness like these men. The miscellany poems are likewise horribly licentious. They are sometimes collections from antiquity, and often the worst parts of the worst poets. And to mend the matter, the Christian translation is more nauseous than the pagan original. Such stuff, I believe, was never seen and suffered before. In a word, if poverty and diseases, the dishonor of families, and the debauching of kingdoms are such valuable advantages, then I confess these books deserve encouragement. But if the case is otherwise, I humbly conceive the proceeding should be so too.

[20] See Corneille, p. 4.

Sir John Vanbrugh
1664-1726

Sır John Vanbrugh is known both as a playwright and as an architect. Blenheim Palace is a worthy example of his heavy, massive architectural style. But there is nothing heavy about his plays. He was quick to see through the essential falsity of sentimentalism, and made his objection known in his play, *The Relapse* (1696), in which the rake who had reformed at the end of Colley Cibber's *Love's Last Shift* (1696) falls from grace. *The Relapse* was one of the plays singled out for special attack by Collier in his *Short View*, and to defend his position, Vanbrugh published the pamphlet here excerpted. Vanbrugh's answer, fairly representative of many offered by the defenders of the stage, reveals its weakness by trying to pretend that Restoration comedy was something it was not—that is, moral. Like most of his fellows, Vanbrugh accepted Collier's basic premise, that comedy has a moral purpose, and thus was reduced to saying that his play really was not as morally offensive as it seemed. Restoration comedy cannot be defended on moral grounds, and the pose that it is all a satire is but rationalization. Collier had little trouble in disposing of such arguments as this.

A Short Vindication of THE RELAPSE *and* THE PROVOK'D WIFE *from Immorality and Profaneness*
[1698; excerpts]

When first I saw Mr. Collier's performance upon the irregularities of the stage (in which amongst the rest of the gentlemen, he's pleased to afford me some particular favors), I was far from designing to trouble either my self or the town with a vindication; I thought his charges against me for immorality and profaneness were grounded upon so much mistake that every one (who had had the curiosity to see the plays, or on this occasion should take the trouble to read 'em) would easily discover the root of the invective, and that 'twas the quarrel of his gown and not of his God that made him take arms against me.

I found the opinion of my friends and acquaintances the same (at least they told me so), and the righteous as well as the unrighteous persuaded me the attack was so weak the town would defend it self; that the general's head was too hot for his conduct to be wise; his shot too much at random ever to make a breach; and that the siege would be raised, without my taking the field.

I easily believed what my laziness made me wish, but I have since found that by the industry of some people whose temporal interest engages 'em in the squabble, and the natural propensity of others to be fond of anything that's abusive, this lampoon has got credit enough in some places to brand the persons it mentions with almost as bad a character as the author of it has fixt upon himself by his life and conversation in the world.

I think 'tis therefore now a thing no farther to be laughed at. Should I wholly sit still, those people who are so much mistaken to think I have been busy to encourage immorality may double their mistake and fancy I profess it: I will therefore endeavor in a very few pages to convince the world I have brought nothing upon the stage that proves me more an atheist than a bigot.

I may be blind in what relates to my self; 'tis more than possible, for most people are so: but if I judge right, what I have done is in general a discouragement to vice and folly; I am sure I intended it, and I hope I have performed it. Perhaps I have not gone the common road nor observed the strictest prescriptions, but I believe those who know this town will agree that the rules of a college of divines will in an infinity of cases fall as short of the disorders of the mind as those of the physicians do in the diseases of the body, and I think a man may vary from 'em both without being a quack in either.

The real query is whether the way I have varied be likely to have a good effect or a bad one? That's the true state of the case; which if I am cast in, I don't question however to gain the least thus much of my cause, that it shall be allowed I aimed at the mark, whether I hit it or not. This, if it won't vindicate my sense, will justify my morals; and shew the world that this honest gentleman in stretching his malice and curtailing his charity has played a part which would have much better become a licentious poet than a reverend divine.

Tho' I resolve to use very few words, I would willingly observe some method, were it possible, that the world, who is the judge, might sum up the evidence the easier and bring the right and wrong into the shorter (and by consequence the clearer) view; but his play is so wild, I must be content to take the ball as it comes, and return it if I can, which whether I always do or not, however, I believe will prove no great matter, since I hope 'twill appear where he gives me the rest he makes but a wide chase: his most threatening strokes end in nothing at all; when he cuts, he's under line; when he forces, he's up in the nets. But to leave tennis and come to the matter.

· · ·

The next chapter is upon the encouragement of immorality by the stage: and here Constant [1] is fallen upon for pretending to be a fine gentleman without living up to the exact rules of religion. If Mr. Collier excludes everyone from that character that does not, I doubt he'll have a more general quarrel to make up with the gentlemen of England than I have with the Lords, tho' he tells 'em I have highly affronted 'em.

But I would fain know after all, upon what foundation he lays so positive a position that Constant is my model for a fine gentleman; and that he is brought upon the stage for imitation.

He might as well say, if I brought his character upon the stage, I designed it a model to the clergy: and yet I believe most people would take it t'other way. O, but these kind of fine gentlemen, he says, are always prosperous in their undertakings, and their vice under no kind of detection, for in the fifth act of the play, they are usually rewarded with a wife or a mistress. And suppose I should reward him with a bishopric in the fifth act, would that mend his character? I have too great a veneration for the clergy to believe that would make 'em follow his steps. And yet (with all due respect to the ladies) take one amour with another, the bishopric may prove as weighty a reward as a wife or a mistress either. He says Mr. Bull was abused upon the stage, yet he got a wife and a benefice too. Poor Constant has neither, nay, he has not got even his mistress yet, he had not, at least, when the play was last acted. But this honest doctor, I find, does not yet understand the nature of comedy, tho' he has made it his study

1 The hero of *The Provoked Wife* (1697).

so long. For the business of comedy is to shew people what they should do, by representing them upon the stage doing what they should not. Nor is there any necessity a philosopher should stand by, like an interpreter at a puppet-show, to explain the moral to the audience. The mystery is seldom so deep but the pit and boxes can dive into it, and 'tis their example out of the playhouse that chiefly influences the galleries. The stage is a glass for the world to view itself in; people ought therefore to see themselves as they are; if it makes their faces too fair, they won't know they are dirty and by consequence will neglect to wash 'em. If therefore I have shewed Constant upon the stage, what generally the thing called a fine gentleman is off on't, I think I have done what I should do. I have laid open his vices as well as his virtues. 'Tis the business of the audience to observe where his flaws lesses his value; and by considering the deformity of his blemishes, become sensible how much a finer thing he would be without 'em. But after all, Constant says nothing to justify the life he leads, except where he's pleading with Lady Brute to debauch her; and sure nobody will suppose him there to be speaking much of his mind. Besides, his mistress in all her answers makes the audience observe the fallacy of his arguments. And I think young ladies may without much penetration make this use of the dialogue, that they are not to take. all for Gospel men tell 'em upon such occasions.

John Dennis
1657-1734

Both for the volume and penetration of his critical labors, John Dennis deserves to be known as the most important English critic of the early years of the eighteenth century. The title "The Critic" that was given him in his lifetime was by no means always one of derision, as is often thought. The students of literature who adopt the sides taken by the great names in literary quarrels are apt to look at Dennis through the eyes of Pope and suppose him to be a "dunce" unworthy of the attention of the serious reader. Such is far from the case.

In the seventeenth century it was commonly believed that all emotionality is bad, that a man can live a good life only by extirpating his passions or rigidly subjecting them to the rule of reason. At the turn of the century Dennis was fighting the battle for more faith in emotion and in imagination. At the same time, he was concerned with working out more definite principles upon which dramatic art should be based, to effect a comprehensive dramaturgy, to take the chaos out of English drama. In the course of many debates he came, perhaps, to put too much emphasis upon Aristotle and was nearsighted in his belief in poetic justice. But it must be noted that many of his critical ideas were new, invigorating, and important; and that even his understanding of poetic justice was more profound than that of many of his contemporaries.

Dennis's own plays were only mildly successful. This fact alone made him susceptible to attack when his criticism obviously went beyond his practice. His critical books and pamphlets were often occasioned by specific controversies. *The Impartial Critic* (1693), in dialogue form, was a reply to Thomas Rymer's *A Short View of Tragedy* (1693); *The Usefulness of the Stage* (1698) represents Dennis's participation in the Collier controversy. Since Addison, in his *Spectator* No. 40, was attacking Dennis's conception of poetic justice, Dennis's "To the Spectator, upon His Essay on the 16th of April" is a rebuttal. A considerable degree of personal animosity can be found in the attacks upon Addison's *Cato* and upon Steele's *Conscious Lovers*. *The Advancement and Reformation of Modern Poetry* (1701), one of Dennis's most pretentious critical works, is an exception, for in it Dennis developed the thesis that religious enthusiasm must be reintroduced into modern poetry.

John Dennis

The Impartial Critic

[1693]

DIALOGUE IV

BEAUMONT, FREEMAN

Freem. So, I have now got loose and have secured us against more interruption.

Beaum. Now then, let me hear your objections to Mr. Rymer's design,[1] for nothing can seem more commendable to me than his intention, which is to restore tragedy to its primitive purity by reestablishing the ancient method and reviving the Rules of Aristotle.

Freem. I am for observing the Rules of Aristotle as much as any man living as far as it can be done without reestablishing the ancient method. But because the Ancients' tragedies had little love in them that therefore ours must have little too; because the ancient tragedies had a Chorus that therefore we must ridiculously ape them—this is what I cannot endure to hear of.

Beaum. But why *ridiculously* ape them? Mr. Rymer pretends that the chorus is necessary; nay, that it is almost the most necessary part of a tragedy, that the French have lately seen the necessity of it, and that the success of their last plays has sufficiently justified the wisdom of their late reformation.

Freem. 'Tis very inexcusable in a man of sense to make any conclusion from success. The French before now have damned a very good play and consequently may like an ill one. *J'ai vu* (says Saint-Évremond) *Corneille perdre sa réputation (s'il est possible qu'il la perdit) à la représentation d'une de ses meilleures pièces.* I have seen, says he, Corneille lose his reputation (if it had been possible for him to lose it) at the acting of one of his best plays. Which he speaks to condemn the changeable relish of the Parisians. Nor is it true that the French saw any necessity for the restoring the Chorus. Monsieur Racine, in his preface to *Esther,* which was the first tragedy that has been lately writ with a Chorus, says that he was put upon the handling that subject in that method by those who had the Superintendency

---

[1] Thomas Rymer, a prominent critic of the late seventeenth century. The reference here is to his *Short View of Tragedy* (q.v.).

of the House of St. Cyr; that is, by Madame de Maintenon. So that
what Mr. R[ymer] calls a necessity was but at the best a conveniency.

Beaum. A conveniency!

Freem. Aye, for upon the writing this religious play with a Chorus,
the cloistered beauties of that blooming Society had a favorable occasion of showing their parts in a religious way to the French court.

Beaum. Let me die, if thou hast not been reading the scandalous
Chronicle.

Freem. Many an honest, well-meaning text has met with a wicked
comment.

Beaum. But what does it signify whether the French found the
Chorus necessary or only found it convenient? Mr. Rymer, whom all
the world allows to be a competent judge of these matters, not only
affirms it to be necessary but the most necessary part of a tragedy.

Freem. That it is not the most necessary part of a tragedy I shall
prove by an argument, which, if Mr. Rymer admits of Aristotle's
Rules, will amount to a demonstration. For tragedy, according to
Aristotle, is the imitation of an important action. Now an action may
be imitated without the Chorus but not without the episode.

Beaum. What is it that you call episode?

Freem. All that was between the singing of the Chorus, which is
all our modern tragedy. But further, fable is the very soul of tragedy,
according to Mr. Rymer himself. Now nothing is more plain than
this, that the fable in tragedy may subsist without the Chorus but
not without the episode. From whence it necessarily follows that the
episode is always the most necessary part of a tragedy, for without it
tragedy can have no soul and consequently can have no being.

Beaum. This, I must confess, is something.

Freem. Something? Well, to complete your conviction, I shall add
the authority of Dacier, who has these words in his comment upon
Aristotle's *Treatise of Poetry,* Chap. 12. Sect. 6.

*La tragédie n'étoit dans son origine q'un choeur sans acteurs. Ensuite
on ajouta les acteurs pour délasser le choeur, et tout ce que ces acteurs
disoient entre deux chants de choeur s'appelloit épisode, comme qui
diroit partie ajoutée, parce que ces récits étoient pièces étrangères et
surajoutées à une cérémonie dont elles ne faisoient point partie: mais
quand la tragédie eut commencé à se former et que les récits qui*

n'étoient que les parties accessoires furent dévenues les principales alors, etc.[2]

So that it is plain, according to the sense of Dacier, that though the Chorus was at first the foundation of tragedy, it is now the least necessary part of it.

Beaum. Well, you seem to have proved that the Chorus is not the most necessary part of a tragedy. However, it may be necessary and therefore ought to be restored. Mr. Rymer affirms particularly that it is necessary to confine a poet to unity of place.

Freem. There he is so far mistaken that Monsieur Racine, who in several of his former tragedies has with religion observed that unity, has not tied himself to it so scrupulously in the very first tragedy which he writ with a Chorus, which he owns himself in his preface to *Esther* and is plain to anyone who reads that tragedy. And whereas Mr. R[ymer] affirms that the Chorus is not to be lost out of sight, let him but consult the first scene of the second act of *Esther* and the seventh scene of the third act of *Athaliah* (which is the second play that Racine writ with a Chorus) and he will find that in those scenes the stage is without a Chorus.

Beaum. But has not Racine in that deviated from the ways of the Ancients?

Freem. I must confess I believe he has, for having read over the *Oedipus* and *Antigone* of Sophocles, I find that in those two plays the Chorus is always in sight. However, this may serve as an argument to prove two things: first, that if a poet will be irregular, he may as well break the Unity of Place with a Chorus as without it; secondly, it may prove that Racine undertook to write his *Esther* purely out of compliance with Madame de Maintenon. For if he had done it with a design of conforming to the Ancients, he would doubtless have conformed in everything; but he has been so far from doing that that his *Esther*, you know, has but three acts, which is directly contrary to the precept of Horace,

[2] "In its origin, tragedy was only a chorus without actors. Afterwards, actors were added to give the chorus a rest, and everything said by the actors between two songs was called 'episode,' or as one might say 'added part,' because these speeches were parts that were extraneous and additional to the ceremony in which they played a part; but when tragedy had begun to take form as such, and when the speeches which were only accessory parts had become the chief parts, then, etc."

and to the practice of the Ancients.

Beaum. Why, as far as I can remember, Sophocles and Euripides never distinguished their plays by acts.

Freem. They did not make use of the word "act" to denote their distinctions as the Romans afterwards did; but, however, the Chorus sung four times in the intervals of the episode as the music plays four times in the intervals of the acts with us.

Beaum. You affirm then that the Chorus is necessary upon no account.

Freem. I cannot conceive how the Chorus can be necessary if tragedy can attain its end without it. Now the end of tragedy according to Aristotle is to excite compassion and terror in order to the purging of those and the like passions.[4] And terror and compassion may be excited without a Chorus, perhaps better than with it.

Beaum. Pray, why so?

Freem. Because the Chorus in some measure must calm an audience which the episode disturbed by its sublimity and by its pathetic, and therefore he who makes use of a Chorus in tragedy seems to me to do like a physician who prescribing a dose for the evacuation of peccant humours should afterwards order restringents to be taken in the midst of its kind operation. The song of the Chorus must be foreign from the matter or pertinent. If foreign from the matter, it must not only calm the mind in some measure but take it off from the subject. But if it is never so pertinent, it must very much cool a reader, if not a spectator, though I make no question but it must have the same effect upon both.

Beaum. But you ought to prove that it must have the same effect upon both.

Freem. If it has not, it must be wholly unprofitable, for the design of the Chorus is to give good advice, to preach up morality, to extol virtue, to praise or pray to the gods.

> *Ille bonis faveatq[ue]; et consilietur amice,*
> *Et regat iratos et amet peccare timentis;*

[3] Horace, *Ars poetica,* ll. 189–90.
[4] ". . . with incidents arousing pity and fear, wherewith to accomplish its catharsis of such emotions." Chap. 6, Bywater, p. 17.

Ille dapes laudet mensae brevis: ille salubrem
Justitiam legesq[ue], et apertis otia portis.
Ille tegat commissa, deosq[ue] precetur et oret
Ut redeat miseris abeat fortuna superbis.[5]
Horat. *Art. Poet.*

Now I would fain know how an audience that is extremely disturbed with terror or with compassion can be capable of harkening to good advice, of apprehending the reasonableness of good instruction, or of performing religious duties.

Beaum. But pray, if terror and compassion must be raised to such a height without receiving any check, how can they be said to be purged?

Freem. Dacier has given us a very sensible account of that. For as the humours in some distempered body are raised in order to the evacuating that which is redundant or peccant in them, so tragedy excites compassion and terror to the same end; for, the play being over, an audience becomes serene again and is less apt to be moved at the common accidents of life after it has seen the deplorable calamities of heroes and sovereign princes.[6]

Beaum. Now here I have an objection to make which must be confessed to be of some importance. Aristotle has given rules for the Chorus, which he would not have done unless he had believed it necessary. Horace has followed his steps. Dacier, who is Aristotle's best interpreter, has endeavored its restoration. He has declared the necessity of it for teaching morality to the people; he has told us that Racine was convinced that there was a necessity for it; and he has commended him for reviving it in his last tragedies.[7]

Freem. But pray, sir, how came you to know what Dacier says? I thought you had told me you had not conversed with the critics lately.

Beaum. I read this in Dacier's preface but now, when you left me alone.

Freem. Indeed, it must be confessed that Aristotle has mentioned the Chorus and discoursed of the different parts of it. But then, consider how large a space the Chorus took up in the ancient tragedy and how little Aristotle has said of it, and you will be obliged to own that

[5] Horace, *Ars poetica*, ll. 196–201.
[6] See *Aristotle's Art of Poetry together with Mr. D'Acier's Notes,* English translation, London, 1705, pp. 78–79. See Dacier, pp. 165–70.
[7] See Dacier's Preface to *Aristotle's Art of Poetry,* English translation, London, 1705, B1, verso.

he slighted it and would have made no mention of it if he could have avoided it; but he could not do that, being engaged to treat of the whole art of the stage. Nor could he in prudence condemn the use of it if you consider that it was religious in its office and institution. The same answer will serve for Horace, because his religion and design were the same with Aristotle's. Dacier shall answer himself. For if he declares a Chorus to be necessary in his Preface, he tells you in his comment upon the Sixth Chapter of Aristotle that he scarce believes it to be natural and that, having several times wondered how so delicate and so ingenious a people as the Athenians must be allowed to be could think it agreeable to Nature or probability that a Chorus who represented the spectators of a tragical action should sing and dance upon such extraordinary and moving events, he was obliged to attribute it to the inclinations and superstitions of the Greeks, who, as they were the people of the world the most inclined to singing and dancing (which natural bent of theirs was fortified by education), so were they the most bigoted of all nations. And singing and dancing, which helped to constitute the ceremonials of their religion, were held as sacred by them and of divine institution. So that when Dacier, who tells us in his comment upon the Sixth Chapter that he could not have believed the Chorus natural if it had not been so adapted to the superstition and musical temper of the Greeks, declares it to be necessary in his Preface, he must do it out of belief that his own countrymen were as airy bigots as the Greeks.

Beaum. And, faith, he was very much in the right of it. How many Frenchmen have we seen who between the first and second courses have risen from table and danced to their own damned voices? I must confess they do not dance at church, but they have several apish gesticulations there which one may easily mistake for dancing and which are as entertaining to the full. But for singing, it is both their diversion and duty.

Freem. Well then, all this considered, it is no wonder that Dacier should tell us that Racine, being to write upon a religious subject, saw a necessity for a Chorus; that is, for a great deal of singing and dancing; for without it there had been two inconveniences: first, the religion of the stage had been more free from superstition than that of the altar; and secondly, a play had been more insipid than High Mass.

Beaum. Yet Dacier has given us two reasons for the necessity of a

Chorus that have nothing to do with Racine. For a Chorus, says he, is necessary, first, to deliver moral sentiments to the people, and secondly, to reflect upon what is vicious and commendable in the characters of the primary actors, in which he is certainly in the right. Now, the Chorus being retrenched from our modern tragedy, morality must be retrenched at the same time. For the principal actors being shaken by violent passions cannot be made sententious, for sentences require reflection and that requires serenity, at least some degree of serenity. How then can our theatre, the Chorus being retrenched, be said to be the school of virtue? Or how can anyone be the better for modern tragedy?

Freem. Our theatre may be said to be the school of virtue upon two accounts. First, because it removes the greatest obstructions to virtue by reducing the passions to a just mediocrity from their violence and irregularity. And secondly, because it teaches some moral doctrine by the fable which must always be allegorical and universal.

Beaum. This answer is something satisfactory. But what can you answer to the second pretended necessity for restoring the Chorus? which is, that the stage may be furnished with persons who may commend or blame anything that may be vicious or excellent in the characters of the primary actors? For there may be a necessity sometimes for their speaking profanely and impiously, which may be of dangerous consequence without the reflections of the Chorus.

Freem. Nothing that is said can be of pernicious consequence in a tragedy if it is writ as it ought to be. That is, if it is what Horace calls *Fabula recte morata.*[8]

Beaum. Pray what may that be?

Freem. A tragedy is *Fabula recte morata* in which the manners are well painted; so that every actor discovers immediately by what he says his inclinations, his designs, and the very bottom of his character; then if anything is said impiously, an audience not only knows that it is spoken by an impious man but by one that is upon the point of being punished for his impiety.

Beaum. This seems to be sensible enough. But now good sense requires that we should think of our dinner, for a hungry Sophister who disputes at the time he may eat does but defraud his own genius to put a cheat upon another man's reason. Therefore, let's to the

---

8 Horace, *Ars poetica*, ll. 319–20.

Cock, and I'll send for Jack Wild to make a third man, who shall very dogmatically tell you that there can be no tragedy without a Chorus.

Freem. But can he prove it?

Beaum. That you shall judge when you have heard him.

Freem. Well, I'll follow you.

The Usefulness of the Stage
[1698; excerpt]

CHAPTER I

For REASON may often afflict us and make us miserable by setting our impotence or our guilt before us, but that which it generally does is the maintaining us in a languishing state of indifference, which perhaps is more removed from pleasure than it is from affliction, and which may be said to be the ordinary state of men.

It is plain then that Reason, by maintaining us in that state, is an impediment to our pleasure, which is our happiness; for to be pleased a man must come out of his ordinary state. Now nothing in this life can bring him out of it but passion alone, which Reason pretends to combat.

Nothing but passion, in effect, can please us, which everyone may know by experience; for when any man is pleased, he may find by reflection that at the same time he is moved. The pleasure that any man meets with oftenest is the pleasure of sense. Let anyone examine himself in that, and he will find that the pleasure is owing to passion; for the pleasure vanishes with the desire and is succeeded by loathing, which is a sort of grief.

Since nothing but pleasure can make us happy, it follows that to be very happy we must be much pleased; and since nothing but passion can please us, it follows that to be very much pleased we must be very much moved. This needs no proof, or if it did experience would be a very convincing one, since anyone may find when he has a great deal of pleasure that he is extremely moved.

And that very height and fullness of pleasure which we are promised in another life must, we are told, proceed from passion, or something which resembles passion. At least, no man has so much as pretended that it will be the result of Reason. For we shall then be delivered from these mortal organs, and Reason shall then be no more. We shall then no more have occasion from premises to draw conclusions and a long train of consequences, for, becoming all spirit and all knowledge, we shall see things as they are. We shall lead the glorious life of angels, a life exalted above all Reason, a life consisting of ecstasy and intelligence.

Thus it is plain that the happiness both of this life and the other is owing to passion and not to Reason. But though we can never be happy by the force of Reason, yet while we are in this life we cannot possibly be happy without it or against it. For since man is by his nature a reasonable creature, to suppose man happy against Reason is to suppose him happy against Nature, which is absurd and monstrous. We have shown that a man must be pleased to be happy, and must be moved to be pleased, and that to please him to a height you must move him in proportion. But then the passions must be raised after such a manner as to take Reason along with them. If Reason is quite overcome, the pleasure is neither long, nor sincere, nor safe. For how many that have been transported beyond their Reason have never recovered it? If Reason resists, a man's breast becomes the seat of civil war, and the combat makes him miserable. For the passions, which are in their nature so very troublesome, are only so because their motions are always contrary to the motions of the will, as grief, sorrow, shame, and jealousy. And that which makes some passions in their natures pleasant is because they move with the will, as love, joy, pity, hope, terror, and sometimes anger. But this is certain, that no passion can move in a full consent with the will unless at the same time it be approved of by the understanding. And no passion can be allowed of by the understanding that is not raised by its true springs and augmented by its just degrees. Now in the world it is so very rare to have our passions thus raised and so improved that that is the reason why we are so seldom thoroughly and sincerely pleased. But in the drama the passions are false and abominable unless they are moved by their true springs and raised by their just degrees. Thus are they moved, thus are they raised, in every well-writ tragedy, till they come to as great a height as Reason can very well bear. Besides, the very motion has a tendency to the subjecting them to Reason, and the very raising purges and moderates them. So that the passions are seldom anywhere so pleasing and nowhere so safe as they are in tragedy. Thus have I shown that to be happy is to be pleased, and to be pleased is to be moved in such a manner as is allowed of by Reason. I have shown too that tragedy moves us thus and consequently pleases us, and consequently makes us happy. Which was the thing to be proved.

The Advancement and Reformation of Modern Poetry

[1701; excerpt]

THERE IS NOTHING in Nature that is great and beautiful without rule and order, and the more rule and order and harmony we find in the objects that strike our senses, the more worthy and noble we esteem them. I humbly conceive that it is the same in art and particularly in poetry, which ought to be an exact imitation of Nature. Now Nature, taken in a stricter sense, is nothing but that rule and order and harmony which we find in the visible creation. The universe owes its admirable beauty to the proportion, situation, and dependence of its parts. And the little world which we call man owes not only its health and ease and pleasure, nay the continuance of its very being, to the regularity of the mechanical motion, but even the strength too of its boasted Reason and the piercing force of those aspiring thoughts which are able to pass the bounds that circumscribe the universe. As Nature is order and rule and harmony in the visible world, so Reason is the very same throughout the invisible creation. For Reason is order and the result of order. And nothing that is irregular, as far as it is irregular, ever was or ever can be either natural or reasonable. Whatever God created, he designed it regular; and as the rest of the creatures cannot swerve in the least from the eternal laws preordained for them without becoming fearful or odious to us; so man, whose mind is a law to itself, can never in the least transgress that law without lessening his Reason and debasing his Nature. In fine, whatever is irregular either in the visible or invisible world

is to the person who thinks right, except in some very extraordinary
cases, either hateful or contemptible.

But as both Nature and Reason, which two in a larger acceptation
is Nature, owe their greatness, their beauty, their majesty to the
perpetual order, for order at first made the face of things so beautiful, and the cessation of that order would once more bring in chaos;
so poetry, which is an imitation of Nature, must do the same thing.
It can neither have greatness nor real beauty if it swerves from the
laws which Reason severely prescribes it, and the more irregular any
poetical composition is, the nearer it comes to extravagance and confusion, and to nonsense, which is nothing.

To the Spectator, upon His Paper on the 16th of April [Spectator No. 40, Addison]

[1712; excerpt]

"POETICAL JUSTICE" . . . [says Addison] "has no foundation in
Nature and Reason, because we find that good and evil happen alike
to all men on this side the grave." [9] In answer to which he must give
me leave to tell him that this is not only a very false but a dangerous
assertion, that we neither know what men really are nor what they
really suffer.

'Tis not always that we know men's crimes, but how seldom do we
know their passions, and especially their darling passions? And as
passion is the occasion of infinitely more disorder in the world than
malice, for where one man falls a sacrifice to inveterate malice, a
thousand become victims to revenge and ambition, and whereas
malice has something that shocks human nature, passion is pleasingly
catching and contagious. Can anything be more just than that that
Providence which governs the world should punish men for indulging
their passions as much as for obeying the dictates of their most en-
venomed hatred and malice?

Thus you see, for aught we know, good and evil does not happen
alike to all men on this side the grave, because 'tis for the most part
by their passions that men offend, and 'tis by their passions for the

9 See below, p. 243.

most part that they are punished. But this is certain, that the more virtue a man has the more he commands his passions, but the virtuous alone command them. The wicked take the utmost care to dissemble and conceal them, for which reason we neither know what our neighbors are nor what they really suffer. Man is too finite, too shallow, and too empty a creature to know another man thoroughly, to know the creature of an infinite Creator; but dramatical persons are creatures of which a poet is himself the creator. And though a mortal is not able to know the Almighty's creatures, he may be allowed to know his own, to know the utmost extent of their guilt, and what they ought to suffer; nay, he must be allowed not only to know this himself but to make it manifest and unquestionable to all his readers and hearers. The creatures of a poetical creator have no dissimulation and no reserve. We see their passions in all their height and in all their deformity, and when they are unfortunate we are never to seek for the cause.

But suppose I should grant that there is not always an equal distribution of affliction and happiness here below. Man is a creature who was created immortal and a creature consequently that will find a compensation in futurity for any seeming inequality in his destiny here. But the creatures of a poetical creator are imaginary and transitory; they have no longer duration than the representation of their respective fables. And consequently, if they offend, they must be punished during that representation. And therefore we are very far from pretending that poetical justice is an equal representation of the justice of the Almighty.

We freely confess that 'tis but a very narrow and a very imperfect type of it, so very narrow and so very imperfect that 'tis forced by temporal to represent eternal punishments; and therefore when we show a man unfortunate in tragedy for not restraining his passions, we mean that everyone will, for such neglect, unless he timely repents, be infallibly punished by infinite justice either here or hereafter.

Remarks upon Addison's CATO, A TRAGEDY

[1713; excerpt]

PROBABILITY ought certainly to reign in every tragical action; but though it ought everywhere to predominate, it ought not to exclude the wonderful, as the wonderful which ought everywhere to predominate in epic poetry ought not to exclude the probable. We shall then treat of the improbabilities of this tragedy when we come to speak of the absurdities with which it throughout abounds from the indiscreet and injudicious observance of some of the Rules of Aristotle. We are at present showing what beauties are wanting to it from the not observing others of those Rules. Here then are none of those beautiful surprises which are to be found in some of the Grecian tragedies and in some of our own, and consequently here is nothing wonderful, nothing terrible or deplorable, which all three are caused by surprise. Now as tragedy is the imitation of an action which excites compassion and terror, and as that alone can be justly accounted a very fine tragical scene which excites one of those two passions, or both, in a very great degree, and as it is impossible either of 'em can be excited in a very great degree without a very great surprise, and there is in this tragedy no very great surprise, we find there is not in this tragedy no not so much as one very fine tragical scene, no not so much as one scene with which we are extremely moved. I sit with indolence from the opening of the play to the very catastrophe; and when at length the catastrophe comes, instead of vehemently shaking with terror or dissolving with melting pity, I rather burn with indignation and I shudder with horror.

Remarks on a Play Called THE CONSCIOUS LOVERS, A COMEDY [10]

[1723; excerpts]

WHEN Sir Richard says that anything that has its foundation in happiness and success must be the subject of comedy, he confounds comedy with that species of tragedy which has a happy catastrophe.

10 *The Conscious Lovers* (1723) was a sentimental comedy by Sir Richard Steele.

When he says that 'tis an improvement of comedy to introduce a joy
too exquisite for laughter, he takes all the care that he can to show
that he knows nothing of the nature of comedy. Does he really believe
that Molière, who, in the opinion of all Europe, excepting that small
portion of it which is acquainted with Ben Jonson, had borne away
the prize of comedy from all nations and from all ages if for the sake
of his profit he had not descended sometimes too much to buffoonry?
Let Sir Richard or anyone look into that little piece of Molière called
La Critique de l'école des femmes, and he shall find there that in
Molière's opinion 'tis the business of a comic poet to enter into the
ridicule of men and to expose the blind sides of all sorts of people
agreeably; that he does nothing at all if he does not draw the pictures
of his contemporaries and does not raise the mirth of the sensible part
of an audience, which, says he, 'tis no easy matter to do. This is the
sense of Molière, though the words are not his exactly.

When Sir Richard talks of a joy too exquisite for laughter, he seems
not to know that joy, generally taken, is common, like anger, indignation, love, to all sorts of poetry: to the epic, the dramatic, the lyric;
but that that kind of joy which is attended with laughter is the characteristic of comedy, as terror or compassion, according as the one or
the other is predominant, makes the characteristic of tragedy, as admiration does of epic poetry.

When Sir Richard says that weeping upon the sight of a deplorable
object is not a subject for laughter but that 'tis agreeable to good
sense and to humanity, he says nothing but what all the sensible part
of the world has always granted; but then all that sensible part of the
world have always denied that a deplorable object is fit to be shown
in comedy. When Sir George Etherege, in his comedy of *Sir Fopling
Flutter,* [11] shows Loveit in all the height and violence of grief and
rage, the judicious poet takes care to give those passions a ridiculous
turn by the mouth of Dorimant. Besides that, the subject is at the bottom ridiculous; for Loveit is a mistress who has abandoned herself
to Dorimant, and by falling into these violent passions only because
she fancies that something of which she is very desirous has gone beside her makes herself truly ridiculous. Thus is the famous scene in
the second act of *Sir Fopling* by the character of Loveit and the dex-
trous handling of the subject kept within the bounds of comedy. But

[11] George Etherege, *The Man of Mode; or, Sir Fopling Flutter* (1676).

the scene of the discovery in the *Conscious Lovers* is truly tragical. Indiana was strictly virtuous. She had indeed conceived a violent passion for Bevil, but all young people in full health are liable to such a passion, and perhaps the most sensible and the most virtuous are more than others liable. But besides that she kept this passion within the bounds of honor, it was the natural effect of her esteem for her benefactor and of her gratitude; that is, of her virtue. These considerations rendered her case deplorable and the catastrophe downright tragical, which of a comedy ought to be the most comical part for the same reason that it ought to be the most tragical part of a tragedy.

George Farquhar
1678-1707

In a sense, George Farquhar's *Discourse upon Comedy* (1702) might be considered as an answer to Collier, but in a larger sense it represents the light of practicality and common sense cutting through a dense fog of critical thinking. The only way Collier could be successfully attacked was to challenge the premises he took from the critics, and no responsible critic had dared very seriously to question the authority of the Rules and the purpose of comedy, which was, according to the best thought of the day, to correct the conduct of mankind by depicting his weaknesses and foibles unfavorably. The business of comedy, according to Collier, is to expose vice and make virtue attractive. To Farquhar, comedy is an agreeable fable, with the same kind of moral that Æsop's fables have, to the point, but not necessarily moral in an ethical sense.

Farquhar was a successful, practical playwright, and, with considerable justification, urged that only those who know the theatre should do serious criticism of the drama. If pushed too far, his position can result in absurdities as palpable as some of the absurdities to which he objected. However, to read this essay after a long subjection to the more orthodox critics is to step into the fresh air after a long session in the smoke-filled atmosphere of Will's Coffee House.

A Discourse upon Comedy
IN REFERENCE TO THE ENGLISH STAGE
IN A LETTER TO A FRIEND [1]
[1702]

With submission, sir, my performance in the practical part of poetry is no sufficient warrant for your pressing me in the speculative. I have no foundation for a legislator; and the two or three little plays I have written are cast carelessly into the world, without any bulk of preface,

[1] This "friend" is not known, if, indeed, Farquhar really addressed the letter to anyone.

because I was not so learned in the laws as to move in defence of a bad case. Why, then, should a compliment go farther with me than my own interest? Don't mistake me, sir; here is nothing that could make for my advantage in either preface or dedication; no speculative curiosities nor critical remarks; only some present sentiments, which hazard, not study, brings into my head, without any preliminary method or cogitation.

Among the many disadvantages attending poetry, none seems to bear a greater weight than that so many set up for judges when so very few understand a tittle of the matter. Most of our other arts and sciences bear an awful distance in their prospect, or with a bold and glittering varnish dazzle the eyes of the weak-sighted vulgar. The divine stands wrapt up in his cloud of mysteries, and the amused laity must pay tithes and veneration to be kept in obscurity, grounding their hopes of future knowledge on a competent stock of present ignorance (in the greater part of the Christian world this is plain). With what deference and resignation does the bubbled client commit his fees and cause into the clutches of the law, where assurance beards justice by prescription, and the wrong side is never known to make its patron blush. Physic and logic are so strongly fortified by their impregnable terms of art, and the mathematician lies so cunningly intrenched within his lines and circles, that none of those of their party dare peep into their puzzling designs.

Thus the generality of mankind is held at a gazing distance, whose ignorance, not presuming, perhaps, to an open applause, is yet satisfied to pay a blind veneration to the very faults of what they don't understand.

Poetry alone, and chiefly the drama, lies open to the insults of all pretenders; she was one of Nature's eldest offsprings, whence, by her birthright and plain simplicity, she pleads a genuine likeness to her mother; born in the innocence of time, she provided not against the assaults of succeeding ages, and, depending altogether on the generous end of her invention, neglected those secret supports and serpentine devices used by other arts that wind themselves into practice for more subtle and politic designs. Naked she came into the world, and, 'tis to be feared, like its professors, will go naked out.

'Tis a wonderful thing that most men seem to have a great veneration for poetry, yet will hardly allow a favorable word to any piece of it that they meet; like your virtuosos in friendship, that are so ravished with the notional nicety of the virtue that they can find no person worth their intimate acquaintance. The favor of being whipt at school for Martial's *Epigrams* or Ovid's *Epistles* is sufficient privilege for turning pedagogue and lashing all their successors; and it would seem, by the fury of their correction, that the ends of the rod were still in their buttocks. The scholar calls upon us for Decorums and Economy; [2] the courtier cries out for wit and purity of style; the citizen for humor and ridicule; the divines threaten us for immodesty, [3] and the ladies will have an intrigue. Now here are a multitude of critics, whereof the twentieth person only has read *quae genus,* and yet every one is a critic after his own way—that is, such a play is best because I like it. A very familiar argument, methinks, to prove the excellence of a play, and to which an author would be very unwilling to appeal for his success. Yet such is the unfortunate state of dramatic poetry that it must submit to such judgments; and by the censure or approbation of such variety [4] it must either stand or fall. But what salvo, what redress for this inconvenience? Why, without all dispute, an author must endeavor to pleasure that part of the audience who can lay the best claim to a judicious and impartial reflection. But before he begins, let him well consider to what division that claim does most properly belong. The scholar will be very angry at me for making that the subject of a question which is self-evident without any dispute; for, says he, who can pretend to understand poetry better than we, who have read Homer, Virgil, Horace, Ovid, &c., at the university? What knowledge can outstrip ours, that is founded upon the criticisms of Aristotle, Scaliger, Vossius, and the like? We are the better sort and therefore may claim this as a due compliment to our learning; and if a poet can please us, who are the nice and severe critics, he cannot fail to bring in the rest of an inferior rank.

I should be very proud to own my veneration for learning, and to acknowledge any compliment due to the better sort upon that foundation; but I'm afraid the learning of the better sort is not confined to college studies; for there is such a thing as reason without syllogism,

---

[2] Decorums and economy are obsolete critical terms. Decorums means the rules of propriety, and economy means rules of structure and proportion.

[3] A reference to the Collier attack which was still having its repercussions even at this late date.

[4] Of critics.

knowledge without Aristotle, and languages besides Greek and Latin. We shall likewise find in the court and city several degrees superior to those at commencements. From all which I must beg the scholar's pardon for not paying him the compliment of the better sort (as he calls it); and, in the next place, inquire into the validity of his title from his knowledge of criticism and the course of his studies.

I must first beg one favor of the graduate. Sir, here is a pit full of Covent Garden gentlemen, a gallery full of citts, a hundred ladies of court education, and about two hundred footmen of nice morality, who having been unmercifully tiezed with a parcel of foolish, impertinent, irregular plays all this last winter, make it their humble request that you would oblige them with a comedy of your own making, which they don't question will give them entertainment. "O, sir," replies the square cap, "I have long commiserated the condition of the English audience, that has been forced to take up with such wretched stuff as lately has crowded the stage; your *Jubilees* and your *Foppingtons*,[5] and such irregular impertinence that no man of sense could bear the perusal of 'em. I have long intended, out of pure pity to the stage, to write a perfect piece of this nature; and now, since I am honored by the commands of so many, my intensions shall immediately be put in practice."

So to work he goes; old Aristotle, Scaliger, with their commentators, are lugged down from the high shelf, and the moths are dislodged from their tenement of years; Horace, Vossius, Heinsius, Hedelin, Rapin, with some half a dozen more, are thumbed and tossed about to teach the gentleman, forsooth, to write a comedy; and here is he furnished with Unity of Action, Continuity of Action, Extent of Time, Preparation of Incidents, Episodes, Narrations, Deliberations, Didactics, Pathetics, Monologues, Figures, Intervals, Catastrophes, Choruses, Scenes, Machines, Decorations, &c.—a stock sufficient to set up any mountebank in Christendom. And if our new author would take an opportunity of reading a lecture upon his play in these terms, by the help of a zany and a joint-stool,[6] his scenes might go off as well as the doctors' packets; but the misfortune of it is, he scorns all application

---

[5] Farquhar's *The Constant Couple; or, A Trip to the Jubilee* (1699). Lord Foppington appears in Cibber's *Love's Last Shift* (1696), in *The Relapse* by Vanbrugh (1696), and in Cibber's *The Careless Husband* (1704).

[6] A zany was a clown. A joint-stool was a carefully fitted stool, not rough-hewn, made by a joiner. Probably the zany used the joint-stool as a property in his act.

to the vulgar, and will please the better sort, as he calls his own sort. Pursuant, therefore, to his philosophical dictates, he first chooses a single plot, because most agreeable to the regularity of criticism, no matter whether it affords business enough for diversion or surprise. He would not for the world introduce a song or dance, because his play must be one entire action. We must expect no variety of incidents, because the exactness of his three hours won't give him time for their preparation. The Unity of Place admits no variety of painting and prospect, by which mischance, perhaps, we shall lose the only good scenes in the play. But no matter for that; this play is a regular play; this play has been examined and approved by such and such gentlemen, who are stanch critics, and masters of art; and this play I will have acted. Lookee, Mr. Rich,[7] you may venture to lay out a hundred and fifty pound for dressing this play, for it was written by a great scholar, and fellow of a college.

Then a grave dogmatical prologue is spoken to instruct the audience what should please them; that this play has a new and different cut from the farce they see every day; that this author writes after the manner of the Ancients, and here is a piece according to the model of the Athenian drama. Very well! This goes off Hum drum, so-so. Then the players go to work on a piece of hard, knotty stuff, where they can no more show their art than a carpenter can upon a piece of steel. Here is the lamp and the scholar in every line, but not a syllable of the poet. Here is elaborate language, sounding epithets, flights of words that strike the clouds, whilst the poor sense lags after, like the lanthorn in the tail of the kite, which appears only like a star while the breath of the players' lungs has strength enough to bear it up in the air.

But the audience, willing perhaps to discover his ancient model and the Athenian drama, are attentive to the first act or two; but not finding a true genius of poetry, nor the natural air of free conversation, without any regard to his regularity, they betake themselves to other work; not meeting the diversion they expected on the stage, they shift for themselves in the pit; and for default of entertainment now, they strike up for more diverting scenes when the play is done. And though the play be regular as Aristotle, and modest as Mr. Collier could wish, yet it promotes more lewdness in the consequence and procures more

7 Christopher Rich, Patentee of Theatre Royal.

effectually for intrigue than any *Rover*,[8] *Libertine*,[9] or *Old Batchelor* [10] whatsoever. At last comes the epilogue, which pleases the audience very well, because it sends them away and terminates the fate of the poet; the patentees rail at him, the players curse him, the town damns him, and he may bury his copy in Paul's, for not a bookseller about will put it in print.

This familiar account, sir, I would not have you charge to my invention, for there are precedents sufficient in the world to warrant it in every particular. The town has been often disappointed in those critical plays, and some gentlemen that have been admired in their speculative remarks have been ridiculed in the practic. All the Authorities, all the Rules of Antiquity have proved too weak to support the theatre, whilst others, who have dispensed with the critics and taken latitude in the economy of their plays have been the chief supporters of the stage and the ornament of the drama. This is so visibly true that I need bring in no instances to enforce it; but you say, sir, 'tis a paradox that has often puzzled your understanding, and you lay your commands upon me to solve it, if I can.

Lookee, sir, to add a value to my complaisance to you, I must tell you, in the first place, that I run as great a hazard in nibbling at this paradox of poetry as Luther did by touching Transubstantiation; 'tis a mystery that the world has sweetly slept in so long that they take it very ill to be wakened; especially being disturbed for their rest when there is no business to be done. But I think that Bellarmin [11] was once as orthodox as Aristotle; and since the German doctor has made a shift to hew down the cardinal, I will have a tug with *ipse dixit*,[12] though I die for't.

But in the first place I must beg you, sir, to lay aside your superstitious veneration for Antiquity, and the usual expressions on that score—that the present age is illiterate, or their taste is vitiated; that we live in the decay of time,[13] and the dotage of the world is fallen to

---

[8] *The Rover; or, The Banished Cavaliers*, by Mrs. Aphra Behn, in two parts (1677 and 1680).

[9] *The Libertine*, by Thomas Shadwell (1675).

[10] *The Old Batchelor*, by William Congreve (1693).

[11] Bellarmine, an Italian Cardinal and staunch defender of the Catholic Church against Protestantism.

[12] *Ipse dixit;* he himself has said it; hence, authority.

[13] The "decay of time" was a prevalent philosophical idea that Nature had been in process of decay ever since the sin of Adam. By this reasoning, the earlier times were nearer the sin, and, hence, less decayed. This was a strong argument for the favorers of the Ancients.

our share. 'Tis a mistake, sir; the world was never more active or youthful, and true downright sense was never more universal than at this very day; 'tis neither confined to one nation in the world nor to one part of a city; 'tis remarkable in England as well as France, and good genuine reason is nourished by the cold of Swedeland as by the warmth of Italy; 'tis neither abdicated the court with the late reigns, nor expelled the city with the playhouse bills; you may find it in the Grand Jury at Hick's Hall, and upon the bench sometimes among the justices: then why should we be hampered so in our opinions, as if all the ruins of Antiquity lay so heavily on the bones of us that we could not stir hand nor foot! No, no, sir, *ipse dixit* is removed long ago, and all the rubbish of old philosophy, that in a manner buried the judgment of mankind for many centuries, is now carried off; the vast tomes of Aristotle and his commentators are all taken to pieces, and their infallibility is lost with all persons of a free and unprejudiced reason.

Then above all men living, why should the poets be hoodwinked at this rate, and by what authority should Aristotle's Rules of Poetry stand so fixt and immutable? Why, by the authority of two thousand years standing; because through this long revolution of time the world has still continued the same. By the authority of their being received at Athens, a city the very same with London in every particular, their habits the same, their Humours alike, their public, their public transactions and private societies *à la mode France;* in short, so very much the same in every circumstance that Aristotle's criticisms may give rules to Drury Lane, the Areopagus give judgment upon a case in the King's Bench, and old Solon shall give laws to the House of Commons.

But to examine this matter a little farther: all arts and professions are compounded of these two parts, a speculative knowledge, and a practical use; and from an excellency in both these, any person is raised to eminence and authority in his calling. The lawyer has his years of student in the speculative part of his business; and when promoted to the bar, he falls upon the practic, which is the trial of his ability. Without all dispute, the great Cook has had many a tug at the bar before he could raise himself to the bench, and had made sufficiently evident his knowledge of the laws in his pleadings before he was admitted to the authority of giving judgment upon the case.

The physician, to gain credit to his prescriptions, must labor for a reputation in the cure of such and such distempers; and, before he sets up for a Galen or Hippocrates, must make many experiments upon his patients. Philosophy itself, which is a science the most abstract from practice, has its public acts and disputations; it is raised gradually, and its professor commences doctor by degrees; he has the labor of maintaining theses, methodizing his arguments, and clearing objections; his memory and understanding is often puzzled by oppositions couched in fallacies and sophisms, in solving all which he must make himself remarkable before he pretends to impose his own systems upon the world. Now, if the case be thus in philosophy, or in any branch thereof, as in ethics, physics, which are called sciences, what must be done in poetry that is denominated an art, and consequently implies a practice in its perfection?

Is it reasonable that any person that has never writ a distich of verses in his life should set up for a dictator in poetry, and without the least practice in his own performance must give Laws and Rules to that of others? Upon what foundation is poetry made so very cheap and so easy a task by these gentlemen? An excellent poet is the single production of an age, when we have crowds of philosophers, physicians, lawyers, divines, every day, and all of them competently famous in their callings. In the two learned commonwealths of Rome and Athens, there was but one Virgil and one Homer, yet have we above a hundred philosophers in each, and most part of 'em, forsooth, must have a touch at poetry, drawing it into Divisions, Subdivisions, &c., when the wit of 'em all set together would not amount to one of Martial's *Epigrams*.

Of all these I shall mention only Aristotle, the first and great lawgiver in this respect, and upon whom all that followed him are only commentators. Among all the vast tracts of this voluminous author we don't find any fragment of an epic poem, or the least scene of a play to authorize his skill and excellence in that art. Let it not be alleged that for aught we know he was an excellent poet, but his more serious studies would not let him enter upon affairs of this nature; for everybody knows that Aristotle was no cynic, but lived in the splendor and air of the court; that he loved riches as much of others of that station, and being sufficiently acquainted with his pupils' affection to poetry, and his complaint that he wanted an Homer to aggrandize his actions, he would never have slipt such an opportunity of further ingratiating himself in the king's favor, had he been conscious of any abilities in himself for such an undertaking; and having a more noble and copious theme in the exploits of Alexander than what inspired the blind bard in his hero Achilles. If his epistles to Alexander were always answered with a considerable present, what might he have expected from a work like Homer's upon so great a subject, dedicated to so mighty a prince, whose greatest fault was his vainglory, and that took such pains to be deified among men?

It may be objected that all the works of Aristotle are not recovered; and among those that are lost some essays of this kind might have perished. This supposition is too weakly founded; for although the works themselves might have 'scaped us, 'tis more probable that some hint or other, either in the life of the conqueror or philosopher, might appear to convince us of such a production. Besides, as 'tis believed he writ philosophy because we have his books, so I dare swear he writ no poetry, because none is extant, nor any mention made thereof that ever I could hear of.

But, stay—without any farther inquiry into the poetry of Aristotle, his ability that way is sufficiently apparent by that excellent piece he left behind him upon that subject. By your favor, sir, this is *Petitio Principii*,[14] or, in plain English, give me the sword in my own hand, and I'll fight with you. Have but a little patience till I make a flourish or two, and then, if you are pleased to demand it, I'll grant you that and everything else.

How easy were it for me to take one of Doctor Tillotson's[15] sermons, and, out of the Economy of one of these discourses, trump you up a pamphlet and call it, *The Art of Preaching!* In the first place I must take a *Text*, and here I must be very learned upon the etymology of this word *text;* then this text must be divided into such and such *Partitions,* which partitions must have their hard names and derivations; then these must be spun into *Subdivisions,* and these backed by proofs of Scripture, *Ratiocinatio Oratoris, Ornamenta Figurarum Rhetoricarum,* and *Authoritas Patrum Ecclesiae,* with some rules and directions how these ought to be managed and applied. And closing up this difficult pedantry with the *Dimensions of Time* for such an

14 *Petitio Principii:* begging the question.
15 Doctor John Tillotson (1630–94), Archbishop of Canterbury. His sermons were noted for their lucidity of style. Dryden approved him, and so, apparently, did Farquhar.

occasion, you will pay me the compliment of an excellent preacher, and affirm that any sermon whatsoever, either by a Presbyter at Geneva, or Jesuit in Spain, that deviates from these Rules deserves to be hissed, and the priest kicked out of his pulpit. I must doubt your complaisance in this point, sir; for you know the forms of eloquence are divers, and ought to be suited to the different Humour and capacities of an audience. You are sensible, sir, that the fiery, choleric Humour of one nation must be entertained and moved by other means than the heavy, phlegmatic complexion of another; and I have observed in my little travels that a sermon of three-quarters of an hour that might please the congregation at St. James's would never satisfy the meeting house in the City, where people expect more for their money; and, having more temptations of roguery, must have a larger portion of instruction.

Be pleased to hear another instance of a different kind, though to the same purpose. I go down to Woolwich, and there upon a piece of paper I take the demensions of the *Royal Sovereign,* and from hence I frame a model of a man of war. I divide the ship into three principal parts, the keel, the hull, and the rigging; I subdivide these into their proper denominations, and by the help of a sailor, give you all the terms belonging to every rope and every office in the whole ship. Will you from hence infer that I am an excellent shipwright, and that this model is proper for a trading junk upon the Volga, or a Venetian galley in the Adriatic Sea?

But you'll object, perhaps, that this is no parallel case, because that Aristotle's *Ars Poetica* was never drawn from such slight observations, but was the pure effect of his immense reason, through a nice inspection into the very bottom and foundation of Nature.

To this I answer that verity is eternal, as that the truth of two and two making four was as certain in the days of Adam as it is now; and that, according to his own position, Nature is the same *apud omnes gentes.* Now if his Rules of Poetry were drawn from certain and immutable principles and fixed on the basis of Nature, why should not his *Ars Poetica* be as efficacious now as it was two thousand years ago? And why should not a single plot, with perfect Unity of Time and Place, do as well at Lincoln's Inn Fields as at the playhouse in Athens? No, no, sir, I am apt to believe that the philosopher took no such pains in poetry as you imagine; the Greek was his mother tongue, and

Homer was read with as much veneration among the schoolboys as we learn our Catechism. Then where was the great business for a person so expert in mood and figure as Aristotle was to range into some order a parcel of terms of art, drawn from his observation upon the *Iliads,* and these to call the model of an epic poem? Here, sir, you imagine that I am caught, and have all this while been spinning a thread to strangle myself. One of my main objections against Aristotle's criticisms is drawn from his non-performance in poetry; and now I affirm that his Rules are extracted from the greatest poet that ever lived, which gives the utmost validity to the precept, and that is all we contend for.

Look ye, sir, I lay it down only for a supposition that Aristotle's Rules for an epic poem were extracted from Homer's *Iliads,* and if a supposition has weighed me down, I have two or three more of an equal balance to turn the scale.

The great esteem of Alexander the Great for the works of old Homer is sufficiently testified by antiquity, insomuch that he always slept with the *Iliads* under his pillow: of this [the] Stagirite, to be sure, was not ignorant; and what more proper way of making his court could a man of letters devise than by saying something in commendation of the king's favorite? A copy of commendatory verses was too mean, and perhaps out of his element. Then something he would do in his own way; a book must be made of the art of poetry, wherein Homer is proved a poet by mood and figure [16] and his perfection transmitted to posterity. And if *Prince Arthur* had been in the place of the *Iliads,* we should have had other Rules for epic poetry, and Doctor B——re [17] had carried the bays from Homer, in spite of all the critics in Christendom. But whether Aristotle writ those Rules to compliment his pupil, or, whether he would make a stoop at poetry to show that there was no knowledge beyond the flight of his genius, there is no reason to allow that Homer compiled his heroic poem by those very Rules which Aristotle has laid down. For, granting that Aristotle might pick such and such observations from this piece, they might be mere accidents resulting casually from the composition of the work and not any of the essential principles of the poem. How usual is it for critics to find out faults and create beauties which the

[16] Two forms of syllogism; hence, by strict rules of logic.
[17] Sir Richard Blackmore (1650?–1729), author of a dull epic, *Prince Arthur* (1695).

authors never intended for such; and how frequently do we find authors run down in those very parts which they designed for the greatest ornament! How natural is it for aspiring, ambitious school-men to attempt matters of the highest reach; the wonderful creation of the world (which nothing but the Almighty Power that ordered it can describe) is brought into mood and figure by the arrogance of philosophy. But till I can believe that the vertigos of Cartesius of the atoms of Epicurus can determine the almighty *Fiat,* they must give me leave to question the infallibility of their Rules in respect of poetry.

Had Homer himself, by the same inspiration that he writ his poem, left us any Rules for such a performance, all the world must have owned it for authentic. But he was too much a poet to give Rules to that whose excellence he knew consisted in a free and unlimited flight of imagination; and to describe the spirit of poetry, which alone is the *true* Art of Poetry, he knew to be as impossible as for human reason to teach the gift of prophecy by a definition.

Neither is Aristotle to be allowed any farther knowledge in dramatic than in epic poetry. Euripides, whom he seems to compliment by Rules adapted to the model of his plays, was either his contemporary or lived but a little before him; he was not insensible how much this author was the darling of the city, as appeared by the prodigious expense disbursed by the public for the ornament of his plays; and, 'tis probable, he might take this opportunity of improving his interest with the people indulging their inclination by refining upon the beauty of what they admired. And besides all this, the severity of dramatic rage was so fresh in his memory in the hard usage that his brother soph [18] not long before met with upon the stage, that it was convenient to humor the reigning wit, lest a second Aristophanes should take him to task with as little mercy as poor Socrates found at the hands of the first.

I have talked so long to lay a foundation for these following conclusions: Aristotle was no poet, and consequently not capable of giving instructions in the art of poetry; his *Ars Poetica* are only some observations drawn from the works of Homer and Euripides, which may be mere accidents resulting casually from the composition of

[18] Not *Soph*ocles, but Socrates, a *soph*ister, or *soph*ist, which here means a teacher of philosophy.

the works, and not any of the essential principles on which they are compiled; that without giving himself the trouble of searching into the nature of poetry, he has only complimented the heroes of wit and valor of his age, by joining with them in their approbation; with this difference, that their applause was plain, and his more scholastic.

But to leave these only as suppositions to be relished by every man at his pleasure, I shall without complimenting any author, either ancient or modern, inquire into the first invention of comedy; what were the true designs and honest intentions of that art; and from a knowledge of the *end,* seek out the *means,* without one quotation of Aristotle or authority of Euripides.

In all productions either divine or human, the final cause is the .first mover, because the end or intention of any rational action must first be considered before the material or efficient causes are put in execution. Now, to determine the final cause of comedy, we must run back beyond the material and formal agents and take it in its very infancy, or rather in the very first act of its generation, when its primary parent, by proposing such or such an end of his labor, laid down the first sketches or shadows of the piece. Now, as all arts and sciences have their first rise from a final cause, so 'tis certain that they have grown from very small beginnings, and that the current of time has swelled 'em to such a bulk that nobody can find the fountain by any proportion between the head and the body; this, with the corruption of time, which has debauched things from their primitive innocence to selfish designs and purposes, renders it difficult to find the origin of any offspring so very unlike its parent.

This is not only the case of comedy, as it stands at present, but the condition also of the ancient theatres, when great men made shows of this nature a rising step to their ambition, mixing many lewd and lascivious representations to gain the favor of the populace, to whose taste and entertainment the plays were chiefly adopted. We must therefore go higher than either Aristophanes or Menander to discover comedy in its primitive institution if we would draw any moral design of its invention to warrant and authorize its continuance.

I have already mentioned the difficulty of discovering the invention of any art in the different figure it makes by succession of improvements; but there is something in the nature of comedy, even in its present circumstances, that bears so great a resemblance to the philosophical mythology of the Ancients, that old Æsop must wear the bays as the first and original author; and whatever alterations or improvements farther application may have subjoined, his *Fables* gave the first rise and occasion.

Comedy is no more at present than a *well-framed tale handsomely told as an agreeable vehicle for counsel or reproof.* This is all we can say for the credit of its institution, and is the stress of its charter for liberty and toleration. Then where should we seek for a foundation but in Æsop's symbolical way of moralizing upon tales and fables? with this difference: that his stories were shorter than ours. He had his tyrant Lion, his statesman Fox, his beau Magpie, his coward Hare, his brave Ass, and his buffoon Ape, with all the characters that crowd our stages every day; with this distinction, nevertheless, that Æsop made his beasts speak good Greek, and our heroes sometimes can't talk English.

But whatever difference time has produced in the form, we must in our own defense stick to the end and intention of his fables. *Utile Dulci* [19] was his motto, and must be our business; we have no other defense against the presentment of the grand jury, and, for aught I know, it might prove a good means to mollify the rigor of that persecution, to inform the inquisitors that the great Æsop was the first inventor of these poor comedies that they are prosecuting with so much eagerness and fury, that the first laureate was as ugly as any of themselves; and that the beasts which are lugged upon the stage by the horns are not caught in the city, as they suppose, but brought out of Æsop's own forest. We should inform them, besides, that those very tales and fables which they apprehend as obstacles to reformation were the main instruments and machines used by the wise Æsop for its propagation; and, as he would improve men by the policy of beasts, so we endeavor to reform brutes with the examples of men. Fondlewife [20] and his young spouse are no more than the eagle and cockle; he wanted teeth to break the shell himself; so somebody else run away with the meat. The fox in the play [21] is the same with the fox in the fable, who stuft his guts so full that he could not get out at the same hole he came in; so both Reynards, being delinquents

---

[19] *Utile Dulci:* from Horace's *De arte poetica,* l. 343.
[20] Fondlewife is a character in Congreve's *The Old Batchelor.*
[21] Jonson's *Volpone; or, The Fox* (1606).

alike, came to be trussed up together. Here are precepts, admonitions, and salutary innuendos for the ordering of our lives and conversations couched in these allegories and allusions. The wisdom of the Ancients was wrapt up in veils and figures; the Egyptian hieroglyphics and the history of the heathen gods are nothing else. But if these pagan authorities give offense to their scrupulous consciences, let them but consult the tales and parables of our Saviour in Holy Writ, and they may find this way of instruction to be much more Christian than they imagine. Nathan's fable of the poor man's lamb had more influence on the conscience of David than any force of downright admonition.[22] So that by ancient practice and modern example, by the authority of Pagans, Jews, and Christians, the world is furnished with this so sure, so pleasant, and expedient an art of schooling mankind into better manners. Now here is the primary design of comedy illustrated from its first institution; and the same end is equally alleged for its daily practice and continuance. Then without all dispute, whatever means are most proper and expedient for compassing this end and intention, they must be the *just Rules of comedy,* and the *true art of the stage.*

We must consider, then in the first place, that our business lies not with a French or a Spanish audience; that our design is not to hold forth to ancient Greece, nor to moralize upon the vices and defaults of the Roman Commonwealth. No, no; an English play is intended for the use and instruction of an English audience, a people not only separated from the rest of the world by situation, but different also from other nations as well in the complexion of our body politic. As we are a mixture of many nations, so we have the most unaccountable medley of Humours among us of any people upon earth; these Humours produce variety of follies, some of 'em unknown to former ages; these new distempers must have new remedies, which are nothing but new counsels and instructions.

Now, sir, if our *Utile,* which is the end, be different from the Ancients, pray let our *Dulce,* which is the means, be so too; for you know that to different towns there are different ways; or, if you would have it more scholastically, *ad diversos fines non idem conducit medium;* or, mathematically, one and the same line cannot terminate in two centers. But waving this manner of concluding by induction,

---

[22] Nathan rebuked David for taking Bathsheba and arranging the death of her husband, Uriah. Cf. II Samuel 12.

I shall gain my point a nearer way, and draw it immediately from the first principle I set down; *That we have the most unaccountable medley of Humours among us of any nation upon the earth;* and this is demonstrable from common experience. We shall find a Wildair in one corner, and a Morose in another; nay, the space of an hour or two shall create such vicissitudes of temper in the same person that he can hardly be taken for the same man. We shall have a fellow bestir his stumps from chocolate to coffee-house with all the joy and gaiety imaginable though he want a shilling to pay for a hack; whilst another, drawn about in a coach and six, is eaten up with the spleen, and shall loll in state with as much melancholy, vexation, and discontent as if he were making the Tour of Tyburn.[23] Then what sort of a *Dulce,* (which I take for the pleasantry of the tale, or the plot of the play) must a man make use of to engage the attention of so many different Humours and inclinations? Will a single plot satisfy everybody? Will the turns and surprises that may result naturally from the ancient limits of time be sufficient to rip open the spleen of some and physic the melancholy of others, screw up the attention of a rover and fix him to the stage in spite of his volatile temper and the temptation of a mask? To make the moral instructive, you must make the story diverting. The splenetic wit, the beau courtier, the heavy citizen, the fine lady, and her fine footman come all to be instructed, and therefore must all be diverted; and he that can do this best, and with most applause, writes the best comedy; let him do it by what rules he pleases, so they be not offensive to religion and good manners.

But *hic labor, hic opus:* how must this secret of pleasing so many different tastes be discovered? Not by tumbling over volumes of the Ancients, but by studying the Humour of the Moderns. The rules of English comedy don't lie in the compass of Aristotle or his followers, but in the pit, box, and galleries. And to examine into the Humour of an English audience, let us see by what means our own English poets have succeeded in this point. To determine a suit at law we don't look into the archives of Greece or Rome, but inspect the reports of our own lawyers, and the acts and statutes of our Parliaments; and by the same rule we have nothing to do with the models of Menander or Plautus, but must consult Shakespeare, Jonson, Fletcher, and others, who, by methods much different from the Ancients, have sup-

[23] The "Tour of Tyburn" was a trip to the gallows.

ported the English stage and made themselves famous to posterity. We shall find that these gentlemen have fairly dispensed with the greatest part of critical formalities; the Decorums of Time and Place, so much cried up of late, had no force of Decorum with them; the economy of their plays was *ad libitum,* and the extent of their plots only limited by the convenience of action. I would willingly understand the irregularities of *Hamlet, Macbeth, Harry the Fourth,* and of Fletcher's plays; and yet these have long been the darlings of the English audience, and are like to continue with the same applause, in defiance of all the criticisms that ever were published in Greek and Latin.

But are there no Rules, no Decorums, to be observed in comedy? Must we make the condition of the English stage a state of anarchy? No, sir—for there are extremes in irregularity as dangerous to an author as too scrupulous a deference to criticism; and as I have given you an instance of one, so I shall present you an example of t'other.

There are a sort of gentlemen that have had the jaunty education of dancing, French, and a fiddle, who, coming to age before they arrive at years of discretion, make a shift to spend a handsome patrimony of two or three thousand pound by soaking in the tavern all night, lolling a-bed all the morning, and sauntering away all the evening between the two playhouses with their hands in their pockets; you shall have a gentleman of this size, upon his knowledge of Covent Garden and a knack of witticizing in his cups, set up immediately for a playwright. But besides the gentleman's wit and experience, here is another motive: there are a parcel of saucy, impudent fellows about the playhouse called doorkeepers that can't let a gentleman see a play in peace without jogging and nudging him every minute. "Sir, will you please to pay? Sir, the act's done, will you please to pay, sir?" [24] I have broke their heads all round two or three times, yet the puppies will still be troublesome. Before gad, I'll be plagued with 'em no longer; I'll e'en write a play myself; by which means my character of wit shall be established, I shall enjoy the freedom of the house, and to pin up the basket, pretty Miss —— shall have the profits of my third night for her maidenhead.[25] Thus we see what a great blessing is a coming girl to a playhouse. Here is a poet sprung from the tail of

[24] A person could see one act before he had to pay.
[25] The playwright received the profits of the third night in payment for his play.

an actress, like Minerva from Jupiter's head. But my spark proceeds: My own intrigues are sufficient to found the plot, and the devil's in't if I can't make my character talk as wittily as those in the *Trip to the Jubilee*. But stay, What shall I call it, first? Let me see—*The Rival Theatres*—very good, by gad, because I reckon the two houses will have a contest about this very play. Thus having found a name for his play, in the next place he makes a play to his name, and thus he begins.

ACT I. Scene *Covent Garden*. *Enter* Portico, Piaza, *and* Turnstile.

Here you must note that Portico, being a compound of practical rake and speculative gentleman, is ten to one the author's own character, and the leading card in the pack. Piaza is his mistress, who lives in the square, and his daughter to old Pillariso, an odd, out-o'-the-way gentleman, something between the character of Alexander the Great and Solon, which must please because it is new.

Turnstile is maid and confidante to Piaza, who for a bribe of ten pieces, lets Portico in at the back door; so the first act concludes.

In the second, enter Spigotoso, who was butler, perhaps, to the Czar of Muscovy, and Fossetana, his wife. After these characters are run dry, he brings you in at the third act Whinewell and Charmarillis for a scene of love to please the ladies, and so he goes on without fear or wit till he comes to a marriage or two, and then he writes—*Finis*.

'Tis then whispered among his friends and Will's and Hippolito's, that Mr. Such-a-One has writ a very pretty comedy; and some of 'em, to encourage the young author, equip him presently with prologue and epilogue. Then the play is sent to Mr. Rich or Mr. Betterton in a fair, legible hand, with the recommendation of some gentleman that passes for a man of parts and a critic. In short, the gentleman's interest has the play acted, and the gentleman's interest makes a present to pretty Miss ——; she's made his whore, and the stage his cully, that for the loss of a month in rehearsing, and a hundred pound in dressing a confounded play, must give the liberty of the house to him and his friends forever after.

Now, such a play may be written with all the exactness imaginable, in respect of Unity in Time and Place; but if you inquire its character of any person, though of the meanest understanding of the whole audience, he will tell you 'tis intolerable stuff; and upon your demanding his reasons, his answer is, "I don't like it." His Humour is the only Rule that he can judge a comedy by, but you find that mere Nature is offended with some irregularities; and, though he be not so learned in the drama, to give you an inventory of the faults, yet I can tell you that one part of the plot had no dependence upon another, which made this simple man drop his attention and concern for the event; and so, disengaging his thoughts from the business of the action, he sat there very uneasy, thought the time very tedious, because he had nothing to do. The characters were so uncoherent in themselves, and composed of such variety of absurdities that in his knowledge of Nature he could find no original for such a copy; and being therefore unacquainted with any folly they reproved, or any virtue that they recommended, their business was as flat and tiresome to him as if the actors had talked Arabic.

Now, these are the material irregularities of a play, and these are the faults which downright mother-sense can censure and be offended at, as much as the most learned critic in the pit. And although the one cannot give me the reasons of his approbation or dislike, yet I will take his word for the credit or disrepute of a comedy sooner perhaps than the opinion of some virtuosos; for there are some gentlemen that have fortified their spleen so impregnably with criticism and hold out so stiffly against all attacks of pleasantry, that the most powerful efforts of Wit and Humour cannot make the least impression. What a misfortune is it to these gentlemen to be natives of such an ignorant, self-willed, impertinent island, where let a critic and a scholar find never so many irregularities in a play, yet five hundred saucy people will give him the lie to his face, and come to see this wicked play forty or fifty times in a year. But this *Vox Populi* is the devil, though, in a place of more authority than Aristotle, it is called *Vox Dei.*[26] Here is a play with a vengeance (says a critic) to bring the transaction of a year's time into the compass of three hours; to carry the whole audience with him from one kingdom to another by the changing of a scene; where's the probability, nay, the possibility of all this? The devil's in the poet, sure; he don't think to put contradictions upon us?

Lookee, sir, don't be in a passion. The poet does not impose con-

[26] The proverb *Vox Populi, Vox Dei,* Farquhar supposes, apparently, to be of scriptural origin.

tradictions upon you, because he has told you no lie; for that only is a lie which is related with some fallacious intention that you should believe it for a truth. Now, the poet expects no more that you should believe the plot of his play than old Æsop designed the world should think his eagle and lion talked like you and I; which, I think, was every jot as improbable as what you quarrel with; and yet the fables took, and I'll be hanged if you yourself don't like 'em. But besides, sir, if you are so inveterate against improbabilities, you must never come near the playhouse at all; for there are several improbabilities, nay impossibilities, that all the criticisms in Nature cannot correct: as, for instance, in the part of Alexander the Great,[27] to be affected with the transactions of the play, we must suppose that we see that great conquerer, after all his triumphs, shunned by the woman he loves and importuned by her he hates, crossed in his cups and jollity by his own subjects, and at last miserably ending his life in a raging madness. We must suppose that we see the very Alexander, the son of Philip, in all these unhappy circumstances, else we are not touched by the moral, which represents to us the uneasiness of human life in the greatest state, and the instability of fortune in respect of worldly pomp. Yet the whole audience at the same time knows that this is Mr. Betterton who is strutting upon the stage and tearing his lungs for a livelihood. And that the same person should be Mr. Betterton and Alexander the Great at the same time is somewhat like an impossibility in my mind. Yet you must grant this impossibility in spite of your teeth, if you han't power to raise the old hero from the grave to act his own part.

Now for another impossibility: the less rigid critics allow to a comedy the space of an artificial day, or twenty-four hours; but those of the thorough reformation will confine it to the natural, or solar, day, which is but half the time. Now, admitting this for a Decorum absolutely requisite—this play begins when it is exactly six by your watch, and ends precisely at nine, which is the usual time of the representation. Now, is it feasible in *rerum natura* that the same space or extent of time can be three hours by your watch and twelve hours upon the stage, admitting the same number of minutes or the same measure of sand to both? I'm afraid, sir, you must allow this for an impossibility too; and you may with as much reason allow the play

[27] This is a reference to Lee's *The Rival Queens; or, Alexander the Great* (1677).

the extent of a whole year; and if you grant me a year, you may give
me seven, and so to a thousand. For that a thousand years should come
within the compass of three hours is no more an impossibility than
that two minutes should be contained in one; *Nullum minus continet
in se majus* is equally applicable to both.

So much for the Decorum of Time: now for the Regularity of
Place. I might make the one a consequence of t'other and allege that
by allowing me any extent of time, you must grant me any change
of place, for the one depends upon t'other; and having five or six
years for the action of a play, I may travel from Constantinople to
Denmark, so to France, and home to England, and rest long enough in
each country besides. But you'll say: "How can you carry us along
with you?" Very easily, sir, if you be willing to go. As for example:
here is a new play; the house is thronged, the prologue's spoken, and
the curtain drawn represents you the scene of Grand Cairo. Where-
abouts are you now, sir? Were not you the very minute before in
the pit in the English playhouse talking to a wench, and now, *presto
pass*, you are spirited away to the banks of the River Nile. Surely,
sir, this is a most intolerable improbability; yet this you must allow
me, or else you destroy the very constitution of representation. Then,
in the second act, with a flourish of the fiddles, I change the scene to
Astrachan. "O, this is intolerable!" Lookee, sir, 'tis not a jot more
intolerable than the other; for you'll find that 'tis as much about the
same distance between Egypt and Astrachan as it is between Drury
Lane and Grand Cairo; and if you please to let your fancy take post, it
will perform the journey in the same moment of time, without any
disturbance in the world to your person. You can follow Quintus
Curtius all over Asia in the train of Alexander, and trudge after Han-
nibal, like a cadet, through all Italy, Spain, and Afric', in the space
of four or five hours; yet the devil a one of you will stir a step over
the threshold for the best poet in Christendom, though he make it
his business to make heroes more amiable, and to surprise you with
more wonderful accidents and events.

I am as little a friend to those rambling plays as anybody, nor have
I ever espoused their party by my own practice; yet I could not forbear saying something in vindication of the great Shakespeare, whom
every little fellow that can form an *A[o]ristus primus* will presume
to condemn for indecorums and absurdities; sparks that are so spruce

upon their Greek and Latin, that, like our fops in travel, they can relish nothing but what is foreign, to let the world know they have been abroad, forsooth; but it must be so, because Aristotle said it; now, I say that it must be otherwise because Shakespeare said it, and I'm sure that Shakespeare was the greater poet of the two. But you'll say that Aristotle was the greater critic. That's a mistake, sir; for criticism in poetry is no more than judgment in poetry; which you will find in your lexicon. Now if Shakespeare was the better poet, he must have the most judgment in his art; for everybody knows that judgment is an essential part of poetry, and without it no writer is worth a farthing. But to stoop to the authority of either, without consulting the reason or the consequence, is an abuse to a man's understanding; and neither the precept of the philosopher nor the example of the poet should go down with me without exam[in]ing the weight of their assertions. We can expect no more Decorum or Regularity in any business than the nature of the thing will bear; now, if the stage cannot subsist without the strength of supposition and force of fancy in the audience, why should a poet fetter the business of his plot and starve his action for the nicety of an hour or the change of a scene; since the thought of man can fly over a thousand years with the same ease, and in the same instant of time, that your eye glances from the figure six to seven on the dial-plate, and can glide from the Cape of Good Hope to the Bay of St. Nicholas, which is quite cross the world, with the same quickness and activity as between Covent Garden Church and Will's Coffee House. Then I must beg of these gentlemen to let our old English authors alone. If they have left vice unpunished, virtue unrewarded, folly unexposed, or prudence unsuccessful, the contrary of which is the *Utile* of comedy, let them be lashed to some purpose; if any part of their plots have been independent of the rest, or any of their characters forced or unnatural, which destroys the *Dulce* of plays, let them be hissed off the stage. But if by a true Decorum in these material points, they have writ successfully and answered the end of dramatic poetry in every respect, let them rest in peace, and their memories enjoy the encomiums due to their merit without any reflection for waiving those niceties, which are neither instructive to the world nor diverting to mankind, but are, like all the rest of critical learning, fit only to set people together by the ears in ridiculous controversies that are not one jot material to the good of the public, whether they be true or false.

And thus you see, sir, I have concluded a very unnecessary piece of work, which is much too long if you don't like it. But let it happen anyway; be assured that I intended to please you, which should partly excuse,

SIR,

Your most humble Servant

Sir Richard Steele

1672-1729

SIR RICHARD STEELE, periodical essayist and important writer of sentimental comedies, was born and raised in Ireland. He was an intimate of
Addison at Oxford, which he left without receiving a degree, and had been
a captain in the army before he wrote his first literary piece, *The Christian
Hero,* in 1701. *The Christian Hero* was one of a series of writings in his
time designed to reconcile once more morality and polite behavior, a
movement that was to be capped in the period between 1709 and 1714 by
the *Tatler* and *Spectator* papers, the conception of which was Steele's
even though his collaborator, Joseph Addison, wrote a larger share of the
significant essays.

Steele's significance for dramatic theory and criticism resides in incidental remarks in some of his *Tatler* papers, which contain clear explorations
of sentimentalism with the notion that the viewing the distresses of others
"makes the heart better" and is productive of virtue, and in critical remarks
in connection with his plays.

Together with Colley Cibber, in the first decade of the eighteenth century, Steele worked on a kind of comedy that differed sharply from the
"hard-shelled" Restoration comedy. Not, however, until after a long absence from the theatre did Steele produce the sentimental comedy that is
the outstanding example in England of the type, *The Conscious Lovers*
(1723). The essence of this kind of comedy is to subject a virtuous character to momentary difficulties in order to arouse the tender sympathies of
the audience and to reward the good characters with happiness at the
end of the play. This, of course, deviated from the formula followed by
neoclassical comedy in painting the foibles and ridiculous mannerisms of
mankind.

Tatler, No. 82

TUESDAY, OCTOBER 18, 1709

[Excerpt]

AFTER the mind has been employed on contemplations suitable to its greatness, it is unnatural to run into sudden mirth or levity; but we must let the soul subside, as it rose, by proper degrees. My late considerations of the ancient heroes impressed a certain gravity upon my mind, which is much above the little gratification received from starts of humor and fancy, and threw me into a pleasing sadness. In this state of thought I have been looking at the fire and in a pensive manner reflecting upon the great misfortunes and calamities incident to human life, among which there are none that touch so sensibly as those which befall persons who eminently love and meet with fatal interruptions of their happiness when they least expect it. The piety of children to parents and the affection of parents to their children are the effects of instinct, but the affection between lovers and friends is founded on reason and choice, which has always made me think the sorrows of the latter much more to be pitied than those of the former. The contemplation of distresses of this sort softens the mind of man and makes the heart better. It extinguishes the seeds of envy and ill-will towards mankind, corrects the pride of prosperity, and beats down all that fierceness and insolence which are apt to get into the minds of the daring and fortunate.

For this reason the wise Athenians, in their theatrical performances, laid before the eyes of the people the greatest afflictions which could befall human life and insensibly polished their tempers by such representations. Among the Moderns, indeed, there has arisen a chimerical method of disposing the fortunes of the persons represented according to what they call poetical justice, and letting none be unhappy but those who deserve it. In such cases, an intelligent spectator, if he is concerned, knows he ought not to be so and can learn nothing from such a tenderness but that he is a weak creature whose passions cannot follow the dictates of his understanding. . . .

The Conscious Lovers

[1723]

PREFACE

THIS COMEDY has been received with universal acceptance, for it was in every part excellently performed; and there needs no other applause of the actors but that they excelled according to the dignity and difficulty of the character they represented. But this great favor done to the work in acting renders the expectation still the greater from the author, to keep up the spirit in the representation of the closet, or any other circumstance of the reader, whether alone or in company: to which I can only say that it must be remembered a play is to be seen and is made to be represented with the advantage of action, nor can appear but with half the spirit without it. For the greatest effect of a play in reading is to excite the reader to go see it; and when he does so, it is then a play has the effect of example and precept.

The chief design of this was to be an innocent performance, and the audience have abundantly showed how ready they are to support what is visibly intended that way. Nor do I make any difficulty to acknowledge that the whole was writ for the sake of the scene of the fourth act, wherein Mr. Bevil evades the quarrel with his friend, and hope it may have some effect upon the Goths and Vandals that frequent the theatres, or a more polite audience may supply their absence.

But this incident and the case of the father and daughter are esteemed by some people no subjects of comedy; but I cannot be of their mind, for anything that has its foundation in happiness and success must be allowed to be the object of comedy; and sure it must be an improvement of it to introduce a joy too exquisite for laughter, that can have no spring but in delight, which is the case of this young lady. I must, therefore, contend that the tears which were shed on that occasion flowed from reason and good sense, and that men ought not to be laughed at for weeping till we are come to a more clear notion of what is to be imputed to the hardness of the head and the softness of the heart; and I think it was very politely said by Mr.

Wilkes, to one who told him there was a general weeping for Indiana, "I'll warrant he'll fight ne'er the worse for that." To be apt to give way to the impressions of humanity is the excellence of a right disposition and the natural working of a well-turned spirit. But as I have suffered by critics who are got no farther than to enquire whether they ought to be pleased or not, I would willingly find them properer matter for their employment, and revive here a song which was omitted for want of a performer, and designed for the entertainment of Indiana. Signor Carbonelli, instead of it, played on the fiddle, and it is for want of a singer that such advantageous things are said of an instrument which were designed for a voice. The song is the distress of a love-sick maid, and may be a fit entertainment for some small critics to examine whether the passion is just or the distress male or female.

I

From place to place forlorn I go,
    With downcast eyes a silent shade;
Forbidden to declare my woe;
    To speak, till spoken to, afraid.

II

My inward pangs, my secret grief,
    My soft, consenting looks betray.
He loves, but gives me no relief;
    Why speaks not he who may?

It remains to say a word concerning Terence, and I am extremely surprised to find what Mr. Cibber told me prove a truth—that what I valued myself so much upon—the translation of him—should be imputed to me as a reproach. Mr. Cibber's zeal for the work, his care and application in instructing the actors and altering the disposition of the scenes, when I was, through sickness, unable to cultivate such things myself, has been a very obliging favor and friendship to me. For this reason I was very hardly persuaded to throw away Terence's celebrated funeral, and take only the bare authority of the young man's character; and how I have worked it into an Englishman, and made use of the same circumstances of discovering a daughter when we least hoped for one, is humbly submitted to the learned reader.

Joseph Addison
1672-1719

IN SPITE OF the fact that the body of critical material produced by Addison is relatively small in volume and that his reputation as a playwright in the eighteenth century was based upon only one play, his tragedy *Cato* (1713), through precept and example alike he was one of the leaders of literary thought in his century. His influence can be attributed in part to the critical ideas that he expressed and in part to incidental aspects of his work. In his series of essays in the *Spectator* on "The Pleasures of the Imagination" he was a pioneer in study of the principles of aesthetics. Although none of this material is included in this volume, as being too far removed from specific questions of dramatic theory or practice, these essays were fundamental to much of the speculation of Du Bos, Hume, and Burke —to mention only obvious and important instances of Addison's influence. His series of essays on tragedy beginning with *Spectator* No. 39 were significant largely because, in attacking the principle of poetic justice, he provided fuel for the sentimentalists who wanted unhappy endings so that more pity could be aroused. In addition, in this series, Addison penetrated more deeply into the nature of the tragic than did most of his opponents.

The philosophy of Stoicism was widely prevalent in the eighteenth century, and Addison owes some of his reputation to the fact that the main character of his tragedy *Cato* was an ideal Stoic, so that "Cato" became the catchword equivalent of Stoicism. When the play was first produced in 1713, it was given political interpretations that had much to do with its success. We must not forget, however, that it became the prime example of a play written in accordance with the Rules, and, in Voltaire's opinion, the only English tragedy sufficiently proper to be compared to French tragedy.

To the man of the eighteenth century the name of Addison was also associated with the return to morality and the bourgeois virtues, for which the *Spectator* papers were in large part responsible.

The Spectator, No. 39

SATURDAY, APRIL 14
[1711]

As a PERFECT TRAGEDY is the noblest production of human nature, so it is capable of giving the mind one of the most delightful and most improving entertainments. "A virtuous man (says Seneca) struggling with misfortunes is such a spectacle as gods might look upon with pleasure"; and such a pleasure it is which one meets with in the representation of a well-written tragedy. Diversions of this kind wear out of our thoughts everything that is mean and little. They cherish and cultivate that humanity which is the ornament of our nature. They soften insolence, soothe affliction, and subdue the mind to the dispensations of Providence.

It is no wonder, therefore, that in all the polite nations of the world this part of the drama has met with public encouragement.

The modern tragedy excels that of Greece and Rome in the intricacy and disposition of the fable; but, what a Christian writer would be ashamed to own, falls infinitely short of it in the moral part of the performance.

This I may show more at large hereafter; and in the meantime, that I may contribute something towards the improvement of the English tragedy, I shall take notice, in this and in other following papers, of some particular parts in it that seem liable to exception.

Aristotle observes that the *Iambic* verse in the Greek tongue was the most proper for tragedy; because at the same time that it lifted up the discourse from prose, it was that which approached nearer to it than any other kind of verse. "For (says he), we may observe that men in ordinary discourse very often speak Iambics, without taking notice of it." [1] We may make the same observation of our English blank verse, which often enters into our common discourse, though we do not attend to it, and in such a due medium between rhyme and prose that it seems wonderfully adapted to tragedy. I am therefore very much offended when I see a play in rhyme, which is as absurd in English, as a tragedy of hexameters would have been in Greek

[1] Aristotle, *Poetics*, Chap. 22; I. Bywater (ed.), *Aristotle on the Art of Poetry* (Oxford, 1909), p. 71.

or Latin. The solecism is, I think, still greater in those plays that have some scenes in rhyme and some in blank verse, which are to be looked upon as two several languages; or where we see some particular similes dignified with a rhyme, at the same time that everything about them lies in blank verse. I would not, however, debar the poet from concluding his tragedy, or, if he pleases, every act of it, with two or three couplets, which may have the same effect as an air in the Italian opera after a long *recitativo,* and give the actor a graceful exit. Besides that we see a diversity of numbers in some parts of the old tragedy, in order to hinder the ear from being tired with the same continued modulation of voice. For the same reason I do not dislike the speeches in our English tragedy that close with an *hemistic,* or half verse, notwithstanding the person who speaks after it begins a new verse, without filling up the preceding one; nor with abrupt pauses and breakings off in the middle of a verse, when they humor any passion that is expressed by it.

Since I am upon this subject, I must observe, that our English poets have succeeded much better in the style than in the sentiments of their tragedies. Their language is very often noble and sonorous, but the sense either very trifling or very common. On the contrary, in the ancient tragedies, and indeed in those of Corneille and Racine, though the expressions are very great, it is the thought that bears them up and swells them. For my own part, I prefer a noble sentiment that is depressed with homely language, infinitely before a vulgar one that is blown up with all the sound and energy of expression. Whether this defect in our tragedies may rise from want of genius, knowledge, or experience in the writers, or from their compliance with the vicious taste of their readers, who are better judges of the language than of the sentiments, and consequently relish the one more than the other, I cannot determine. But I believe it might rectify the conduct both of the one and of the other, if the writer laid down the whole contexture of his dialogue in plain English before he turned it into blank verse; and if the reader, after the perusal of a scene, would consider the naked thought of every speech in it, when divested of all its tragic ornaments; by this means, without being imposed upon by words, we may judge impartially of the thought and consider whether it be natural or great enough for the person that utters it, whether it deserves to shine in such a blaze of eloquence, or show itself in such a variety of lights as are generally made use of by the writers of our English tragedy.

I must in the next place observe that, when our thoughts are great and just, they are often obscured by the sounding phrases, hard metaphors, and forced expressions in which they are clothed. Shakespeare is often very faulty in this particular. There is a fine observation in Aristotle to this purpose, which I have never seen quoted. "The expression (says he) ought to be very much labored in the unactive parts of the fable, as in descriptions, similitudes, narrations, and the like; in which the opinions, manners, and passions of men are not represented; for these (namely, the opinions, manners, and passions) are apt to be obscured by pompous phrases and elaborate expressions." [2] Horace, who copied most of his criticisms after Aristotle, seems to have had his eye on the foregoing rule, in the following verses:

> Et tragicus plerumque dolet sermone pedestri.
> Telephus et Peleus, cum pauper et exul uterque,
> Projicit ampullas et sesquipedalia verba,
> Si curat cor spectantis tetigisse querela.[3]

> Tragedians too lay by their state, to grieve.
> Peleus and Telephus, exiled and poor,
> Forget their swelling and gigantic words. *Ld. Roscommon.*

Among our modern English poets, there is none who was better turned for tragedy than Lee; [4] if, instead of favoring the impetuosity of his genius, he had restrained it and kept it within its proper bounds. His thoughts are wonderfully suited to tragedy, but frequently lost in such a cloud of words that it is hard to see the beauty of them; there is an infinite fire in his works, but so involved in smoke that it does not appear in half its lustre. He frequently succeeds in the passionate parts of the tragedy, but more particularly where he slackens his efforts and eases the style of those epithets and metaphors in which he so much abounds. What can be more natural, more soft, or more passionate than that line in Statira's speech where she describes the charms of Alexander's conversation?

> Then he would talk:—Good Gods! how he would talk!

[2] *Poetics*, Chap. 24; Bywater, *op. cit.*, p. 79.   [3] Horace, *Ars poetica*, ll. 95–8.
[4] Nathaniel Lee (1653–1692) was a playwright of the Restoration noted for the lack of restraint in his poetic language. He was a friend of Dryden and collaborated with him on two plays. Addison is here discussing Lee's *Rival Queens* (1676/7).

That unexpected break in the line, and turning the description of his manner of talking into an admiration of it, is inexpressibly beautiful, and wonderfully suited to the fond character of the person that speaks it. There is a simplicity in the words that outshines the utmost pride of expression.

Otway [5] has followed Nature in the language of his tragedy and therefore shines in the passionate parts more than any of our English poets. As there is something familiar and domestic in the fable of his tragedy, more than in those of any other poet, he has little pomp, but great force, in his expressions. For which reason, though he has admirably succeeded in the tender and melting part of his tragedies, he sometimes falls into too great a familiarity of phrase in those parts which, by Aristotle's Rule, ought to have been raised and supported by the dignity of expression.

It has been observed by others that this poet has founded his tragedy of *Venice Preserved* on so wrong a plot that the greatest characters in it are those of rebels and traitors. Had the hero of his play discovered the same good qualities in the defence of his country that he showed for its ruin and subversion, the audience could not enough pity and admire him; but as he is now represented, we can only say of him what the Roman historian says of Catiline, that his fall would have been glorious *(si pro patria sic concidisset)* had he so fallen in the service of his country.

The Spectator, No. 40

MONDAY, APRIL 16

[1711]

Ac ne forte putes me, quae facere ipse recusem,
Cum recte tractent alii, laudare maligne;
Ille per extentum funem mihi posse videtur
Ire Poeta, meum qui pectus inaniter angit,
Irritat, mulcet, falsis terroribus implet,
Ut magnus; et modo me Thebis, modo ponit Athenis. Hor.

[5] Thomas Otway (1651–1685) has been generally considered the best of the Restoration writers of tragedy.

THE ENGLISH WRITERS of tragedy are possessed with a notion that when they represent a virtuous or innocent person in distress they ought not to leave him till they have delivered him out of his troubles, or made him triumph over his enemies. This error they have been led into by a ridiculous doctrine in modern criticism, that they are obliged to an equal distribution of rewards and punishments and an impartial execution of poetical justice. Who were the first that established this rule I know not; but I am sure it has no foundation in Nature, in reason, or in the practice of the Ancients. We find that good and evil happen alike to all men on this side the grave; and as the principal design of tragedy is to raise commiseration and terror in the minds of the audience, we shall defeat this great end if we always make virtue and innocence happy and successful. Whatever crosses and disappointments a good man suffers in the body of the tragedy, they will make but small impression on our minds when we know that in the last act he is to arrive at the end of his wishes and desires. When we see him engaged in the depth of his afflictions, we are apt to comfort ourselves, because we are sure he will find his way out of them; and that his grief, how great soever it may be at present, will soon terminate in gladness. For this reason the ancient writers of tragedy treated men in their plays as they are dealt with in the world, by making virtue sometimes happy and sometimes miserable, as they found it in the fable which they made choice of, or as it might affect their audience in the most agreeable manner. Aristotle considers the tragedies that were written in either of these kinds and observes that those which ended unhappily had always pleased the people, and carried away the prize in the public disputes of the stage, from those that ended happily.[6] Terror and commiseration leave a pleasing anguish in the mind and fix the audience in such a serious composure of thought as is much more lasting and delightful than any little transient starts of joy and satisfaction. Accordingly, we find that more of our English tragedies have succeeded in which the favorites of the audience sink under their calamities than those in which they recover themselves out of them. The best plays of

---

[6] Aristotle, *Poetics*, Chap. 13; Bywater, p. 37.

this kind are the *Orphan*,[7] *Venice Preserved*,[8] *Alexander the Great*,[9] *Theodosius*,[10] *All for Love*,[11] *Œdipus*,[12] *Oroonoko*,[13] *Othello*, &c. *King Lear* is an admirable tragedy of the same kind, as Shakespeare wrote it; but as it is reformed according to the chimerical notion of poetical justice,[14] in my humble opinion it has lost half its beauty. At the same time I must allow that there are very noble tragedies which have been framed upon the other plan, and have ended happily; as indeed most of the good tragedies which have been written since the starting of the above-mentioned criticism have taken this turn, as the *Mourning Bride*,[15] *Tamerlane*,[16] *Ulysses*,[17] *Phaedra and Hippolytus*,[18] with most of Mr. Dryden's. I must also allow that many of Shakespeare's, and several of the celebrated tragedies of antiquity, are cast in the same form. I do not therefore dispute against this way of writing tragedies, but against the criticism that would establish this as the only method; and by that means would very much cramp the English tragedy and perhaps give a wrong bent to the genius of our writers.

The tragi-comedy, which is the product of the English theatre, is one of the most monstrous inventions that ever entered into a poet's thoughts. An author might as well think of weaving the adventures of Æneas and Hudibras into one poem, as of writing such a motley piece of mirth and sorrow. But the absurdity of these performances is so very visible that I shall not insist upon it.

The same objections which are made to tragi-comedy may in some measure be applied to all tragedies that have a double plot in them;

[7] *The Orphan, or The Unhappy Marriage*, a tragedy by Thomas Otway, first played in 1680.

[8] *Venice Preserved*, also by Thomas Otway; first played in 1681/2.

[9] *Alexander the Great*: the reference here may be to Racine's *Alexandre le grand* (1665) but more probably is to Nathaniel Lee's *The Rival Queens; or, The Death of Alexander* (1676/7), which came to be known as *Alexander* in later editions.

[10] *Theodosius; or, The Force of Love*, by Nathaniel Lee, first played in 1680.

[11] *All for Love*, by Dryden (1678).

[12] Addison is no doubt referring here to the version of the classic story by John Dryden and Nathaniel Lee (1679).

[13] *Oroonoko*, by Thomas Southerne, first performed in 1695, published in 1696.

[14] The version of *King Lear* generally performed in the 18th century up to the time of Garrick and usually even long afterwards was that of Nahum Tate, *The History of King Lear* (1681), in which the good characters are all rewarded at the end; Lear is pensioned off, and Cordelia marries Edgar.

[15] *The Mourning Bride*, by William Congreve; first performed in 1696, published in 1697.

[16] *Tamerlane*, by Nicholas Rowe, first performed in 1701; published in 1702.

[17] *Ulysses*, by Nicholas Rowe; performed in 1705, published in 1706.

[18] *Phaedra and Hippolitus*, by Eugene Smith, 1707.

which are likewise more frequent upon the English stage than upon any other: for though the grief of the audience in such performances be not changed into another passion, as in tragi-comedies, it is diverted upon another object, which weakens their concern for the principal action and breaks the tide of sorrow by throwing it into different channels. This inconvenience, however, may in a great measure be cured, if not wholly removed, by the skillful choice of an under-plot, which may bear such a near relation to the principal design as to contribute towards the completion of it and be concluded by the same catastrophe.

There is also another particular which may be reckoned among the blemishes, or rather the false beauties, of our English tragedy: I mean those particular speeches which are commonly known by the name of *rants*. The warm and passionate parts of a tragedy are always the most taking with the audience; for which reason we often see the players pronouncing, in all the violence of action, several parts of the tragedy which the author writ with great temper and designed that they should have been so acted. I have seen Powell very often raise himself a loud clap by this artifice.[19] The poets that were acquainted with this secret have given frequent occasion for such emotions in the actor by adding vehemence to words where there was no passion or inflaming a real passion into fustian. This hath filled the mouths of our heroes with bombast and given them such sentiments as proceeded rather from a swelling than a greatness of mind. Unnatural exclamations, curses, vows, blasphemies, a defiance of mankind and an outraging of the gods frequently pass upon the audience for towering thoughts and have accordingly met with infinite applause.

I shall here add a remark which I am afraid our tragic writers may make an ill use of. As our heroes are generally lovers, their swelling and blustering upon the stage very much recommends them to the fair part of their audience. The ladies are wonderfully pleased to see a man insulting kings or affronting the gods in one scene and throwing himself at the feet of his mistress in another. Let him behave himself insolently towards the men and abjectly towards the fair one, and it is ten to one but he proves a favorite of the boxes. Dryden and Lee, in several of their tragedies, have practised this secret with good success.

19 George Powell, a leading actor of the period. Also the author of six plays.

But to show how a *rant* pleases beyond the most just and natural
thought that is not pronounced with vehemence, I would desire the
reader, when he sees the tragedy of *Œdipus,* to observe how quietly
the hero is dismissed at the end of the third act, after having pronounced the following lines, in which the thought is very natural
and apt to move compassion.

> To you, good gods, I make my last appeal;
> Or clear my virtues, or my crimes reveal
> If in the maze of fate I blindly run,
> And backward trod those paths I sought to shun,
> Impute my errors to your own decree:
> My hands are guilty, but my heart is free.

Let us then observe with what thunderclaps of applause he leaves
the stage, after the impieties and execrations at the end of the fourth
act, and you will wonder to see an audience so cursed and so pleased
at the same time.

> Oh that, as oft I have at Athens seen *
> The stage arise, and the big clouds descend;
> So now in very deed I might behold
> This ponderous globe, and all yon marble roof,
> Meet like the hands of Jove, and crush mankind,
> For all the elements, &c.

* Where, by the way, there was no stage till many years after Œdipus.

Antoine Houdar de la Motte
1672-1731

IN THE EARLY eighteenth century there were few defenders of the Moderns against the Ancients more ardent than Houdar de la Motte, although he was able to keep sweet-tempered through many controversies. While he was not a great writer, he was one of the distinctive "wits" of his day and was a versatile composer of odes, light verse, fables, pastorals, ballets, comedies, and tragedies—of which *Inès de Castro* (1723) was the most famous. His chief contribution to dramatic theory was his advocacy of the use of prose in the writing of tragedies.

La Motte's dramatic criticism is to be found principally in his commentaries upon his plays. The present translation is from the ten-volume edition of his works published in 1754.

The Discourse on Tragedy on the Occasion
of OEDIPE
[1730; excerpt]

IF, HOWEVER, against these prejudices and these obstacles, the use of prose in the writing of tragedies could be established, I dare to believe that there would be considerable advantage in the change.

First: the advantage of verisimilitude which is absolutely destroyed by versification. For why when men are made to act are they not made to speak like men? Is it not, let me say, against Nature that a hero or a princess should force all his speech into a set number of syllables, that he should scrupulously measure out pauses by rule, or that he should affect, even in the press of his concerns or in his most impetuous passions, the most exact recurrence of the same sounds, a recurrence that can be only the fruit of a labor as puerile as it is painful? What a strange masquerade of speech this is! And is not the pleasure derived from it a triumph of habit?

If ordinary language were used, would not the characters and their sentiments appear more real, and does it not follow from this that the actions would appear more true to life? Formerly all plays were written in verse; comedy submitted to the same yoke as tragedy in spite of its essential familiarity. Comedies now often are written in prose, and from an author's point of view comedy has frequently acquired more vigor and truth from the use of this form.

Perhaps it will be said that there is a greater distance between prose and the majestic style of tragedy than between prose and the easy style of comedy, but this is a deception: the distance is the same in both cases. It is true that, in order to be consistent with their stations in life, the characters of a tragedy ought to speak with more dignity and elegance than comic characters do, but they should not speak less naturally, and their dignity does not make poets out of them. Furthermore, a wise author will not utilize epic bravado in creating speeches for actors to speak. Break up the measure of the verse of Racine and take away his rhymes, and you will find nothing more in the speech of his characters than a natural elegance that is fitting to the social levels, the concerns, and the passions of the characters. In a word, you will lose nothing but this busywork that takes your attention away from the actor in your admiration of the poet and that appears only as an abuse of words to any man of good sense who had never heard poetry.

It is also evident that with greater liberty in choosing and arranging words there can be also a greater facility in making speech more exact. There would never be a necessity of adopting a wrong word knowingly because it is impossible to adjust the right word to the needs of the moment. One could always give proper gradation and force to a line of thought rather than be constrained by the caprice of rhymes to admit some element that is weak or useless. Never would an author have to sink to a mediocre phrase in order to save an excellent one. Order, precision, and the fitting and proper would no longer be at the mercy of rules that are so tyrannic that even the greatest of geniuses do not always master them. And finally, authors could no longer be permitted, nor would readers pardon, real faults under the shelter of poetic license.

Besides, and here is perhaps the most considerable advantage, correction would become infinitely easy. The most skillful writer can commit great errors in the warmth of composition, and when he comes to correct them after reflection or as a result of the criticism of others, that which he would wish to remove is so closely united with his happiest expressions that he soon renounces all revision as impossible; he will put his mind to the task of justifying the fault when he should be using it to correct the fault. If he were writing in prose, he would have only to erase a word and substitute another for it; but in verse the substitution of the word may cost him a happy turn of phrase, a sublime line, or even a long passage of discourse.

M. Despréaux once told me that he spent twenty years in correcting a false rhyme. I discount what is owing here to exaggeration, but there still remains enough for me to be struck by man's foolishness in inventing an art expressly for the purpose of making himself unable to say exactly what he wants to say; or, what is still worse, of having to sacrifice what could be said well to conditions that his reason would never prescribe. It is true that whoever writes a tragedy in prose must take care not to abuse the facility of the style by contenting himself quickly with his first ideas and by not putting forth enough effort to find the best expressions when the ideas that come to him are reasonably good. I recommend to him that he devote the same amount of time to the choice of his materials that versification would consume. It should always be a great encouragement to him that he can be sure of finding words in his language to express well whatever sublime and pathetic images he can conceive.

Lastly, here is a final benefit of the custom that I wish to establish: it would multiply the number of authors of plays, for it would not require of them a talent that many men of wit do not possess. Do not many writers exist who have sufficient invention to imagine great designs, sufficient genius to arrange them well, sufficient reason and wit to execute them well, but who are not skilled in versification or who because of the waste of time that it involves turned away from it early in life? What a pity that all that ability is lost to the theatre!

If M. Fénelon had not put himself above the prejudice that all poems should be in verse, we would not have *Télémaque*,[1] a work that

---

[1] *Télémaque* (1699) by Antoine Fénelon (1651–1715) is a prose epic in which the son of Ulysses meets adventures while pursuing his education. His experiences give Fénelon opportunities for disquisitions on government.

in spite of its form so glitters with beauties that we call poetic that no one could want it to possess the trappings of verse. Let us think the same of tragedy and perhaps we shall soon have works in this genre of equal perfection.

Jean Baptiste Du Bos
1670-1742

THE IDEAS that the Abbé Du Bos expressed in the opening sections of his *Critical Reflections on Poetry and Painting* provided the theoretical background for one kind of sentimentalism that flourished during the eighteenth century. Of few of these ideas was Du Bos the originator; his indebtedness to Addison was especially heavy; but the very simplicity of his explanations attracted an extensive following who created plays and other kinds of literature that allowed the sort of effects described by Du Bos. The sentimentalism of Du Bos was largely without ethical implications, for he conceived of the functioning of art as the rousing of emotions in order to procure the pleasure that comes from the relief of tedium. Art is a titillater of sensibility, and the sentimentalism that results from the following of his recipes for the creation of literature is sentimentalism in the sense that emotion is cut adrift from more rational meaning and is out of proportion in relation to it. Thus the sentimentalism of Du Bos is far from identical with the sentimentalism of those who had concocted an abstract ethical system that involved doing good by a "moral sense" and that found weeping and the expression of pity signs of a properly adjusted moral sense, exhibits of an emotionality to be treasured for its moral value. The followers of Du Bos were interested in emotion for its own sake, although both groups found the expression of emotionality pleasant. The short excerpt presented here shows that, although Du Bos was not opposed to the concept of a moral sense, that concept played only an unimportant part in his thinking.

The opening passages of the *Critical Reflections* (the passages reprinted here) do not, for the most part, speak directly about the theatre or about dramatic criticism, since Du Bos was laying the foundation for an aesthetic system. But the application to drama, particularly to tragedy, is closer than it might at first appear to be, for the kinds of art that interested him were tragedy and the sort of painting that depicts tragic events. The paintings that he approves have literary subjects and depict violence and catastrophes. The parts of the treatise in which dramatic forms are specifically discussed are in general derivative and of little interest. The introductory ideas, however, had the force of novelty in the eighteenth century. Of particular interest in the evolution of the line of reasoning that began with Du Bos are the ideas of David Hume in his "Essay on Tragedy," of

Richard Hurd in his replies to Hume, and of Nicolai in his part of the published correspondence between Lessing, Nicolai, and Moses Mendelssohn.[1]

First published in 1719, the *Critical Reflections on Poetry and Painting* reached its seventh edition by 1770. It was translated into English by Thomas Nugent in 1748. The translation here is new.

Critical Reflections on Poetry and Painting

[1719; excerpt]

PART I

WE OFTEN experience the palpable pleasures that poetry and painting excite; but the frequency makes no less difficult the explaining the nature of these pleasures, which do indeed often resemble afflictions and sometimes have some of the same symptoms as the most painful sorrows. The arts of poetry and painting are never more applauded than when they have succeeded in causing us pain. . . . Generally speaking, men derive more pleasure from weeping at the theatre than from laughing.

In fact, the more profoundly as the actions portrayed in poetry and painting stir up a painful sympathy in us when we witness them in real life, the more powerfully do their imitations grip us when art presents them to us. Such actions, everyone says, are happy subjects. A secret charm thus attracts us to the imitations provided by poets and painters, even while our nature testifies by an internal shudder that it rebels against its own pleasure.

I dare undertake to resolve this paradox, and to explain the origin of the pleasure that we derive from verse and pictures. Far less hardy undertakings may pass for bold, since I wish to give an account of what pleases every man and what disgusts him; it is my wish to show my fellows how their sentiments come into being. In doing this I cannot hope to be approved if I do not succeed in my book in making

[1] For a full treatment of the influence of the Abbé Du Bos upon literary criticism in the eighteenth century see Marcel Braunschvig, *L'Abbé Du Bos, Rénovateur de la critique au XVIIIe siècle*, Toulouse, 1904; and A. Lombard, *L'Abbé Du Bos, un initiateur de la pensée moderne*, Paris, 1913.

recognizable to the reader what takes place within himself—in a word, the most intimate movements of his heart. We do not hesitate to reject a mirror as unfaithful if we cannot recognize ourselves in it. . . .

SECTION I

OF THE NECESSITY OF BEING OCCUPIED IN ORDER TO FLEE ENNUI, AND OF THE ATTRACTION THAT THE MOVEMENT OF PASSION HAS FOR MEN

WE HAVE NO natural pleasure that is not the fruit of need; this is perhaps what Plato meant when he said in his allegorical style that love was born of the marriage of need and abundance. Let those whose task it is to create courses of philosophy expose to us the wisdom of the precautions that Providence has willed to take and what means It has chosen to force us, by means of the attraction of pleasure, to take care of our own well-being. This truth is so clearly beyond debate that I feel confident in basing my reasoning upon it.

When need is great, it is easy to feel the pleasure that comes from the satisfying of it. When we bring an ordinary appetite to a fine feast, we do not feel as strong a pleasure as when we appease a real hunger with a humble meal. Art is a poor substitute for Nature, and all the refinements cannot pave the way, so to speak, for pleasure as need can.

The mind has its needs as well as the body, and one of the greatest needs of man is to have his mind occupied. The boredom that follows the mind's inaction is an evil so oppressive for man that he often undertakes the most irksome of tasks in order to spare himself the pain of being tormented by it.

It is easy to see how physical labor, even when it seems to demand slight effort, keeps the mind occupied. But, other than by this means, the mind can occupy itself in only two ways: either it delivers itself to the impressions that external objects make on it—and this is what is termed feeling—or it concerns itself with speculations on various matters—and this is what is termed reflecting or meditating.

The mind finds this second manner of busying itself irksome, and at times even impracticable, especially when the subject of reflection is not a present or recent feeling. Under those conditions it is necessary for the mind to make continual efforts to follow the object of its attention; and these efforts, often rendered unfruitful by the disposition of the organs of the brain at the time, end only in a vain and sterile contention. Either a feverish imagination no longer presents any object distinctly and an infinite number of disconnected and irrelevant ideas succeed one another tumultuously in the mind, or the mentality that is weary of exerting itself relaxes, and a dismal and languishing reverie, during which the mind plays with no object precisely, is the only reward of the efforts it makes in order to keep itself busy. Everyone has experienced the boredom of that condition, in which one does not have the strength to think of anything, and the painfulness of the other condition in which, in spite of himself, he thinks of a great many things without being able to fix his choice on any one in particular. Few people are fortunate enough, and they but rarely, to experience one of these two conditions, and to be good company for themselves ordinarily. Only a small number can learn this art, which, to use an expression of Horace, makes them live in friendship with themselves: *Quod te tibi reddat amicum.* To be capable of it, one must have a certain temperament of Humours, which makes those who were given it at birth under as great obligation to Providence as the eldest sons of sovereigns; one must also apply one's mind from childhood on to studies and occupations whose tasks demand much meditation; one must also have a mind that has contracted the habit of putting its ideas in order and thinking about what it reads, for the reading in which the mind is not active and does not concern itself with reflecting on the subject matter soon becomes subject to ennui. But by force of exercising imagination, one comes to govern it, and when this faculty is once made docile, it does what one demands of it. By meditating one can acquire the habit of transferring his thought at will from one object to another or of fixing it upon another object.

This ability to converse with oneself gives whoever has the skill shelter against the state of languor and misery of which we have just spoken. But, as I have said, the mortals whom a blood without acidity and Humours without acidity have predestined to so pleasant an internal life are indeed rare. The condition of their minds is even incomprehensible to most men, who, judging how much others suffer from being alone by what they suffer themselves, think that solitude is an evil that oppresses everyone.

Of the ways of busying ourselves, the first that we mentioned, the giving ourselves up to the impressions that strange things make on us, is much the easiest. It is the only resource of most men against ennui, and even those who know how to occupy themselves in other ways lend themselves to the employments and to the pleasures of the generality of men in order not to fall into the languor which follows the continuation of the same occupation. The alternation of work and pleasure agitates a mind that is beginning to grow sluggish and this change seems to give the burdened imagination a new pleasure.

That is why we see men engaging in so many frivolous occupations and useless activities. That is what makes them run so feverishly after what they call their pleasure, even to delivering themselves up to passions whose consequences they know to be distressing even from their own experience. Neither the disturbance that activity causes nor the stir that it demands can please men in themselves. The passions that give them the most exquisite joys also cause them, lasting and regrettable pains, but they fear the boredom that follows inaction even more and find in the stir of affairs and the dizzy whirl of passions an emotion that keeps them occupied. The agitations that excite them can be revived during periods of solitude; they prevent us from coming face to face with ourselves with nothing to do—that is to say, of finding ourselves in trouble or boredom.

When those who are disgusted with what they call "the world" take the resolution to renounce it, they can seldom carry out their resolves. When they have once experienced inaction and have had a chance to compare with the indolence of ennui what they once suffered from too much activity and from the disturbances of passion, they come to look back longingly at the tumult with which they were once so disgusted. We often accuse them wrongly of parading a pretended moderation when they argue the side of retirement. At those times they are of good faith, but just as excessive turbulence makes them desire a complete tranquility, a too great leisure makes them sigh for the times when they were always occupied. Man is more volatile than he is hypocritical, and often he is guilty only of inconstancy on the occasions when we accuse him of artifice.

Truly, the agitation in which our passions keep us, even in times of solitude, is so strong that all other states of mind seem languorous after it. And so instinctively we run after the objects that can support our passions, even though they make impressions on us that cost us disturbed nights and dolorous days; but, in general, we suffer even more from living without passions than passions make us suffer.

SECTION II

CONCERNING THE ATTRACTION OF SPECTACLES THAT ARE CAPABLE OF EXCITING STRONG PASSION IN US. CONCERNING GLADIATORS

THAT NATURAL emotion which is excited in us mechanically when we see people like ourselves in danger or misfortune attracts us only by being a passion whose movements agitate our minds and keep us occupied. However, this emotion has charms sufficient to make us seek it, in spite of the sad and importunate ideas that accompany and follow it. A feeling of attraction that reason can never repress makes many people pursue objects capable of breaking their hearts. They go in crowds to see one of the most frightful spectacles a man can face —I mean the punishment of a fellow man who must endure the rigors of the law on a scaffold and who is put to death with frightful torments. They are impelled to the sight even though they know beforehand from past experience that the circumstances of the punishment and the groans of a fellow mortal will, in spite of themselves, make on them a lasting impression, one that will torment them for a long time before it is effaced. But the pull of the emotion is stronger for many people than reflection and the counsel of experience. Everybody everywhere goes in crowds to see the horrible spectacles of which I have just spoken.

It is the same attraction that makes us love the disturbances and the alarms caused by witnessing the perils of others when we are not involved in their dangers. We are affected, says Lucretius, when from the shore we can watch a vessel struggling with waves that threaten to engulf it,* or watch a battle from a height from which we look down upon the melee in safety.

> Suave mari magno, turbantibus aequora ventis,
> E terra alterius magnum spectare laborem:
>
> . . .
>
> Suave etiam belli certamina magna tueri
> Per campos instructa, tui sine parte pericli.

* De Nat. Rer. lib. 2.

The more dangerous the tricks performed by an acrobat on a tightrope, the more attentive most spectators become. Whenever, while he is making a jump between two swords that can wound him, his body deviates in the haste of his movement from the arc it should describe, he becomes an object worthy of all our attention. Let him substitute two sticks for the swords or stretch his rope two feet above the ground, and the same jumps and the same tricks will have no effect on us; we no longer deign to watch them. The attention of the spectator ceases with the danger.

Whence came the extreme pleasure that the Romans derived from spectacles in the amphitheatre? Living men were there torn to pieces by ferocious beasts. Gladiators cut one another's throats wholesale in the arena. They even refined upon the murderous instruments that these unfortunates used in slaying one another. Not by chance was the retiary [2] armed in one fashion and the mirmillon [3] in another; a search must have been conducted for the proportion between offensive and defensive weapons for the quadrille [4] which would make the combats longer and fuller of events. The aim was to make death come slowly and frightfully. Other quadrilles fought with different arms. It was the intention to diversify the kinds of death imposed upon these otherwise innocent men. They were usually fed pastries and other foods that would keep them fat so that their blood would flow slowly from their wounds so that the spectator could enjoy for a longer time the horrors of their agony. The profession of instructing gladiators became an art: the taste the Romans had for such combats forced them to hunt out subtleties and introduce diversions into the spectacle that today we can scarce imagine without horror. The fencing masters [*] who instructed the gladiators had to teach them not only to use their arms well but also the attitudes to strike in falling and the position to maintain while they bled to death. These masters taught them, in other words, to die gracefully.

[*] Lanistae.

---

[2] *Retiarius:* A gladiator armed with a net and trident. He was usually matched with a Secutor, who was fully armed.

[3] *Mirmillon:* A gladiator armed with helmet, sword, and shield. Mirmillones were generally pitted against Thraces, who carried a round buckler and a dagger shaped like a scythe.

[4] *Quadrilles:* Combat exhibitions of teams of four.

This kind of spectacle found little favor with the grossness of the first five centuries that rolled by after the founding of Rome. When the two Brutuses gave the Romans the first gladiatorial combat to be seen in their city, the Romans were already civilized. But the humaneness of the Romans of the following centuries, far from making them turn with disgust from barbaric spectacles in their amphitheatres, made them more eager to have them. The Vestal Virgins had their reserved boxes in the first row of the amphitheatre during the period of greatest refinement among the Romans; yet among these pagan peoples "a slave was branded with a hot iron for stealing table linen," * a crime for which the laws of most Christian countries condemn to death domestics who are free men. But the Romans felt an emotion in the amphitheatre that they did not find at circus or theatre. The gladiatorial combats did not cease until after the Christian religion became dominant and until they were expressly forbidden by law by Constantine the Great. After the Romans had implicitly condemned their taste for spectacles by prohibiting the making of a human sacrifice by any subject of the Republic, five centuries passed before the combats of which I speak were abolished. . . .

. . .

Bullfights often cost the lives of the bullfighters. A grenadier is no more exposed in an attack on a fortified position than are the champions who fight these angry animals. However, Spaniards of all classes show as much eagerness for these dangerous spectacles as the Romans did for gladiatorial contests. In spite of the efforts of the popes to discourage bullfights, they still exist; and the Spanish nation, which prides itself on at least appearing to obey the popes submissively, has exhibited scanty deference in this case to their remonstrances and orders. The attraction of emotion makes the most enlightened nations forget the first principles of humanity and hides from the best of Christians the most evident maxims of their religion.

Many people every day put a considerable part of their wealth at the mercy of cards and dice, even though they are not unaware of the disastrous consequences of playing for high stakes. The men who are enriched by gambling are known throughout the length of Europe, like those to whom something rare and singular happens.

* Juvenal, *Sat.* 14, v. 22.

The number of rich men ruined by play exceeds the number of the robust whom the doctors have made infirm. Only fools and knaves play from any motive of avarice and with a view of augmenting their wealth by continual gains. It is thus not avarice but an attraction for gambling that makes so many people ruin themselves at it. In fact, a skillful gambler endowed with a talent of easily combining an infinity of circumstances and of drawing the right answers from them quickly—such a gambler, I say, could make a certain gain each day by risking his money only on games where success depends more upon skill than upon the chances with cards and dice; however, he will prefer by choice the games in which gain depends entirely upon the caprice of the dice and cards and those in which his talent does not give him any superiority over the other players. The reason for a predilection so opposed to his interests is that games which leave a large part of the outcome to the skill of the player demand a consistent concentration of mind, and that they do not keep emotions perpetually aroused, as do Landsquenets,[5] Basset,[6] and other games in which the outcome depends entirely on chance; in the latter, all plays are decisive and each trick brings some loss or gain. For that reason, they keep the mind in a sort of ecstasy, without the necessity of contributing to one's own pleasure by paying serious attention, with which our natural laziness seeks always to dispense. Laziness is a vice which men sometimes overcome but never completely extinguish. Perhaps it is a good thing for society that this vice can never be completely wiped out, for many believe that it prevents more wicked deeds than all the virtues do.

Those who drink too much or who deliver themselves up to other passions know the evil consequences of their actions better than do those who remonstrate with them, but the natural instinct of the mind is to give itself over to whatever will occupy it, so long as the activity does not demand the pain of concentration. That is why most men are subject to tastes and inclinations which give them frequent occasion of being agreeably occupied by lively and satisfying sensations. *Trahit sua quemque voluptas.* In that men all have the same end, but as they are not all made the same, they do not all seek the same pleasures.

5 *Lansquenet:* A foot soldier; also the game of chance played by such soldiers.
6 *Basset:* A card game resembling faro.

THAT THE PRINCIPAL MERIT OF POEMS AND PICTURES CONSISTS IN IMI-
TATING THE OBJECTS WHICH CAN EXCITE REAL PASSIONS IN US. THE PAS-
SIONS THAT THESE IMITATIONS GIVE BIRTH TO ONLY SUPERFICIAL

WHEN REAL and veritable passions which procure lively sensations to
the mind have costly returns because the happy moments they give
us are followed by dismal days, does art have no means at its disposal
of separating the disagreeable consequences of the greater part of the
passions from what is agreeable in them? Can art create, so to speak,
beings of a new kind? Can it not produce objects that can excite in
us artificial passions capable of occupying us while we feel them, but
incapable of causing real pain and actual affliction as a consequence?

Poetry and painting can attain that end. I do not pretend to think
that famous painters or poets or masters of similar arts actually carry
their intentions this far or propose to themselves any such far-fetched
goal when they set to work. The first inventors of the bath did not
dream that it would be a remedy for curing certain diseases, but made
use of it only as an agreeable refreshment during hot spells, later discovering it to be useful in regaining health from certain maladies;
similarly great poets and painters have probably intended only to
flatter our senses and our imagination, and by working toward that
end have found the means of exciting artificial passions in our hearts.
The inventions that have been most useful to society were discovered
by chance. However it may be, the phantoms of passion excited by
poetry and painting satisfy our need of being occupied when these
arts move us through the imitations which they present to us.

Painters and poets excite artificial passions by presenting imitations
of objects that are capable of exciting real ones. Since the impression
that these imitations make upon us is of the same kind as the impression made upon us by the object that poet or painter has imitated,
differing from it only in that it is weaker, it should excite in our
minds a passion which resembles that which the imitated object
would have excited. That is to say that a copy of an object should excite in us a copy of the passion which the object would have excited.
But since the impression that the imitation makes is not as profound
as the impression that the object itself would make—since the impression made by the imitation is not serious . . . —and finally since

the impression made by the imitation vividly affects only the sense-part of the mind, it is soon effaced. This superficial impression made by an imitation disappears without having the lasting consequences that the impression made by the object imitated by poet or painter would have had.

We can easily understand why a difference can be found between the impression made by the object itself and the impression made by the imitation. The most perfect imitation has only an artificial existence, only a borrowed life, and not the force and activity of nature to be found in the object imitated. It is by virtue of the power that it possesses from nature itself that the real object acts on us. *Namque iis, quae in exemplum assumimus, subest natura et vera vis: contra omnis imitatio ficta est*, says Quintillian.*

From thence proceeds the pleasure that poetry and painting provide for all men. That is why we regard with approbation pictures whose merit consists in placing before our eyes adventures that are so dreadful that we would feel only horror from them if we saw them in real life; for, as Aristotle puts the matter in his *Poetics*,† *Monsters and dead or dying men which we would not dare to look at or which we would see only with horror we can look at with pleasure when they are imitated in the works of painters.* The better imitated they are, the more eagerly we look at them. It is the same with the imitations that poetry makes.

The pleasure we feel on seeing the poet's or painter's imitation of objects which, if real, would excite troublesome passions in us, is a pure pleasure. It is not accompanied by the disturbing effects of the serious emotions roused by the object itself.

Some examples may clarify better than arguments this opinion which I am afraid I can never distinctly express. A massacre of innocents ought to leave horrible images in the minds of those who really saw ungovernable soldiers slitting the throats of children at the bloody breasts of their mothers. The picture by Le Brun in which we see the imitation of this tragic happening moves and softens us but leaves no importunate idea in our minds; it excites our compassion without really afflicting us. A death such as that of Phaedra, a young princess expiring with frightful convulsions while accusing herself of atrocious crimes for which she is punished by the poison, would be an object

* *Instit. lib.* 10 *cap.* 2.   † Chap. 4.

to flee from. It would take several days for us to rid our minds of the dark and depressing ideas that such a spectacle would inevitably impress upon our imaginations. The tragedy by Racine [7] that presents us with the imitations of this scene moves and touches us without sowing in us the seed of a lasting sadness. We enjoy our emotion without being alarmed by the fear that it will last for too long a time. Without really saddening us, Racine's play brings tears to our eyes; the affliction, that is to say, is only on the surface of our hearts, and we feel certain that the tears will end with the representation of the ingenious fiction that makes them roll.

We listen, then, with pleasure to most unhappy men when they tell us of their misfortunes by way of the painter's brush or in the verse of a poet, but, as Diogenes Laertius remarks, we listen to them only with repugnance when they bewail their misfortunes to us in person. *Itaque eos qui lamentationes imitantur libenter, hos sine voluptate audimus,* says the Latin version.* Painter and poet trouble us only as we wish them to do so: where on the one hand we are not the masters of the extent of our emotions, on the other we are masters neither of their strength nor of their duration, when we are faced by the real objects that these noble artisans have imitated.

It is true that young people who give themselves up to the reading of romances whose attractions lie in poetical imitations are subject to being tormented by afflictions and too real desires; but these evils are not the necessary consequence of the artificial emotion caused by the portrayal of Cyrus and Mandane.[8] This artificial emotion is only the occasion for them. In the bosom of a young girl who is too avid a reader of romances, it foments the basic natural passions already present, encouraging her the more easily to conceive impassioned and profound feelings for someone who is on the verge of inspiring her with them; Cyrus and Mandane are not the cause of these agitations.

It has indeed been said that men have been seen to deliver themselves so much to impressions from poetical imitations that reason could not regain its proper ascendancy over their distracted imaginations. We know the incident of the inhabitants of Abdera, upon whom

* In *Aristippo.*

---

[7] Racine's *Phèdre* (1677).
[8] The reference is to Madelaine de Scudéry's *Artamène; ou Le Grand Cyrus* (10 vols., 1649–53).

the tragic figures in the *Andromeda* of Euripides made so deep an impression that the effect of the imitation on them was as strong —and of the same kind—as the effect of the actual events would have been: on account of it they lost their senses for a time, just as one might lose his senses at the sight of exceedingly tragic events. We can cite also a wit of the last century who, too much moved by the portrayals of *Astrée*,[9] believed himself the successor of those courtly shepherds who have never had other habitation than prints and tapestries. His unbalanced imagination made him do extravagant things similar to the actions Cervantes created for a fool of the same genus, but of another species, in his *Don Quixote*, on the assumption that the reading of the brave deeds of knight-errantry had turned the good gentleman's head.

It is very rare to find men who have at once a heart so sensitive and a head so feeble as this. But suppose there actually were such cases— their small number would not merit our making an exception to this general rule: that our mind remains always the mistress of the superficial emotions that verse and pictures excite in it.

One can even think that the visionary shepherd I had just mentioned would never have taken either shepherd's pouch or crook unless he had seen some shepherdess every day; it is true only that his passion would not have produced such bizarre effects if, to make use of the expression, it had not been grafted onto the chimeras with which the reading of *Astrée* had filled his imagination. As for the incident at Abdera, the fact, as it always happens, is much less marvelous in the original author than in the telling of those who got it at second or third hand. Lucian tells only * that after the people of Abdera had seen the performance of the *Andromeda* of Euripides during the hottest part of the summer, several fell sick shortly afterwards and recited verses from this tragedy during delirium from the fever; it was the last thing that had made an impression on them. Lucian adds that the cold of winter, whose property is to extinguish the epidemic maladies heightened by the intemperate climate of summer, brought to an end both malady and declamation.

* In *How to Write History*.

---

9 D'Urfee's *Astrée* (1610–27). In this work Platonic love forms the basis for extended arguments among idyllic shepherds.

Francis Hutcheson
1694-1746

ALTHOUGH Francis Hutcheson was primarily a moral philosopher with relatively little to say about plays or the theatre, there is no necessity to apologize for the inclusion of some of his more pertinent comments within a book of dramatic criticism and theory; for Hutcheson was the outstanding theorizer of sentimentalism, and the full treatment of sentimental principles merely implied elsewhere or casually accepted are to be found in his works. It is true that Hutcheson, in turn, was merely a disciple of Anthony Ashley Cooper, the third Earl of Shaftesbury. Both set up an analogy between beauty and virtue, both founded the functioning of moral behavior in a "moral sense," by which we automatically distinguish right from wrong and which in its operations gives us distinct pleasures; both tended to identify morality with benevolence and the good of the greatest number, and hence both were early utilitarians. Hutcheson manufactured a number of other senses to complement the moral sense described by Shaftesbury, and he reduced to a more distinct system the somewhat random ideas of his predecessor. Hutcheson's two most important books (*An Inquiry into the Original of Our Ideas of Beauty and Virtue*, 1725, and *An Essay on the Nature and Conduct of the Passions and Affections*, 1728) were written while he was operating a private academy in Dublin. In 1729 he became professor of moral philosophy in the University of Glasgow, with which position he is usually identified.

An Inquiry into the Original of Our Ideas of Beauty and Virtue
[1725; excerpts]
AN INQUIRY CONCERNING MORAL GOOD AND EVIL
SECTION I, ARTICLE II

IN OUR SENTIMENTS of actions which affect ourselves, there is indeed a mixture of the ideas of natural and moral good, which require some attention to separate them. But when we reflect upon the actions which affect other persons only, we may observe the moral ideas unmixed with those of natural good or evil. For let it be here observed that those senses by which we perceive pleasure in natural objects whence they are constituted advantageous could never raise in us any desire of public Good, but only of what was good to ourselves in particular. Nor could they ever make us approve an action merely because of its promoting the happiness of others. And yet, as soon as any action is represented to us as flowing from love, humanity, gratitude, compassion, a study of the good of others and an ultimate desire of their happiness, although it were in the most distant part of the world or in some past age, we feel joy within us, admire the lovely action, and praise its author. And on the contrary, every action represented as flowing from ill-will, desire of the misery of others without view to any prevalent good to the public, or ingratitude, raises abhorrence and aversion.

It is true indeed that the actions we approve in others are generally imagined to tend to the natural good of mankind or of some parts of it. But whence this secret chain between each person and mankind? How is my interest connected with the most distant parts of it? And yet I must admire actions which show good will toward them and love the author. Whence this love, compassion, indignation, and hatred toward even feigned characters, in the most distant ages and nations, according as they appear kind, faithful, compassionate, or of the opposite dispositions toward their imaginary contemporaries? If there is no Moral Sense which makes benevolent actions appear beautiful, if all approbation be from the interest of the approver,

What's Hecuba to us, or we to Hecuba?

ARTICLE III

SOME REFINED explainers of self-love may tell us that we approve or condemn characters according as we apprehend we should have been supported or injured by them had we lived in their days. But how obvious is the answer if we only observe that, had we no sense of moral good in humanity, mercy, faithfulness, why should not self-love and our sense of natural good engage us always to the victorious side and make us admire and love the successful tyrant or traitor. Why do we not love Sinon or Pyrrhus in the *Aeneid?* For had we been Greeks, these two would have been very advantageous characters. Why are we affected with the fortunes of Priamus, Polites, Choroebus, or Aeneas? Would not the parsimony of a miser be as advantageous to his heir as the generosity of a worthy man is to his friend? And cannot we as easily imagine ourselves heirs to misers as the favorites of heroes? Why don't we then approve both alike? It is plain that we have some secret sense which determines our approbation without regard to self-interest; otherwise we should always favor the fortunate side without regard to virtue and suppose ourselves engaged with that party.

SECTION V, ARTICLE VIII

LET US NEXT consider another determination of our mind, which strongly proves benevolence to be natural to us, and that is compassion, by which we are disposed to study the interests of others without any views of private advantage. This needs little illustration. Every mortal is made uneasy by any grievous misery he sees another involved in, unless the person be imagined morally evil. Nay, it is almost impossible for us to be unmoved even in that case. Advantage may make us do a cruel action or may overcome pity, but it scarce ever extinguishes it. A sudden passion of hatred or anger may represent a person as absolutely evil and so extinguish pity; but when the passion is over, it often returns. Another disinterested view may even in cold blood overcome pity, such as love to our country or zeal for religion. Persecution is generally occasioned by love of virtue and a desire of the eternal happiness of mankind, although our folly makes us choose absurd means to promote it; and is often accompanied with pity enough to make the persecutor uneasy in what, for prepollent reasons, he chooses, unless his opinion leads him to look upon the heretic as absolutely and entirely evil.

We may here observe how wonderfully the constitution of human nature is adapted to move compassion. Our misery or distress immediately appears in our countenance if we do not study to prevent it and propagates some pain to all spectators, who, from observation, universally understand the meaning of those dismal airs. We mechanically send forth shrieks and groans upon any surprising apprehension of evil, so that no regard to decency can sometimes restrain them. This is the voice of Nature, understood by all nations, by which all who are present are roused to our assistance, and sometimes our injurious enemy is made to relent.

We observed above that we are not immediately excited by compassion to desire the removal of our own pain. We think it just to be affected upon the occasion and dislike those who are not so. But we are excited directly to desire the relief of the miserable without any imagination that this relief is a private good to ourselves. And if we see this impossible, we may by reflection discern it to be vain for us to indulge our compassion any farther; and then self-love prompts us to retire from the object which occasions our pain and to endeavor to divert our thoughts. But where there is no such reflection, people are hurried by a natural kind instinct to see objects of compassion and expose themselves to this pain when they can give no reason for it, as in the instance of public executions.

This same principle leads men to tragedies; only we are to observe that another strong reason of this is the moral beauty of the characters and actions, which we love to behold. For I doubt whether any audience would be pleased to see fictitious scenes of misery if they were kept strangers to the moral qualities of the sufferers or their characters and actions. As in such a case there would be no beauty to raise desire of seeing such representations, I fancy we would not expose ourselves to pain alone, from misery which we knew to be fictitious. . . .

SECTION VI, ARTICLE I

. . . Labor, hunger, thirst, poverty, pain, danger have nothing so detestable in them that our self-love cannot allow us to be so often exposed to them. On the contrary, the virtues which these give us occasions of displaying are so amiable and excellent that scarce ever is any imaginary hero in romance or epic brought to his highest pitch of happiness without going through them all. Where there is no virtue, there is nothing worth desire or contemplation; the romance or epos must end. Nay, the difficulty, or natural evil, does so much increase the virtue of the good action that it accompanies that we cannot easily sustain these works after the distress is over, and if we continue the work, it must be by presenting a new scene of benevolence in a prosperous fortune. A scene of external prosperity or natural good without anything moral or virtuous cannot entertain a person of the dullest imagination, had he ever so much interested himself in the fortunes of his hero; for where virtue ceases there remains nothing worth wishing to our favorite, or which we can be delighted to view his possession of, when we are most studious of his happiness.

THIS POWERFUL determination even to a limited benevolence and other moral sentiments is observed to give a strong bias to our minds toward a universal goodness, tenderness, humanity, generosity, and contempt of private good in our whole conduct, besides the obvious improvement it occasions in our external deportment and in our relish of beauty, order, and harmony. As soon as a heart, before hard and obdurate, is softened in this flame, we shall observe arising along with it a love of poetry, music, the beauty of Nature in rural scenes, a contempt of other selfish pleasures of the external senses, a neat dress, a humane deportment, a delight in and emulation of everything which is gallant, generous, and friendly.

WE SHALL FIND this [moral] sense to be the foundation also of the chief pleasures of poetry. We hinted in the former treatise at the foundation of delight in the numbers, measures, mataphors, similitudes. But as the contemplation of moral objects, either of vice or virtue, affects us more strongly and moves our passions in a quite different and a more powerful manner than natural beauty or what we commonly call deformity, so the most moving beauties bear a relation to our moral sense and affect us more vehemently than the representations of natural objects in the liveliest descriptions. Dramatic and epic poetry are entirely addressed to this sense and raise our passions by the fortunes of characters distinctly represented as morally good or evil, as might be seen more fully were we to consider the passions separately.

Where we are studying to raise any desire or admiration of an object really beautiful, we are not content with a bare narration but endeavor if we can to present the object itself or the most lively image of it. And hence the epic poem or tragedy gives a far greater pleasure than the writings of philosophers, though both aim at recommending virtue. The representing the actions themselves, if the representation be judicious, natural, and lively, will make us admire the good and detest the vicious, the inhuman, the treacherous and cruel by means of our moral sense without any reflections of the poet to guide our sentiments.

George Lillo
1693-1739

GEORGE LILLO is often considered the father of domestic tragedy, tragedy which has as its subject common men rather than kings and princes and great leaders. The idea of domestic tragedy was a contradiction in terms to most critics, who believed that tragedies dealt only with people of high estate and that comedy was the only form which could depict ordinary people. Their arguments were based on an overstrict reading of Aristotle.[1]

Lillo did not invent the form, but it can be said with some degree of justice that since his time domestic tragedy has been written fairly consistently in Europe if not always in England, and its basic idea is taken for granted in our modern tragedies and social problem plays. Before Lillo's time, especially in Elizabethan England, many examples of the genre had appeared, among them *Arden of Feversham, A Woman Killed with Kindness,* and *A Yorkshire Tragedy;* but it died out before the closing of the theatres, and although around the beginning of the eighteenth century such men as Otway and Rowe were groping in that direction, it remained for Lillo to establish the form permanently.

The importance of Lillo is less as an artist than as an influence, for his two original domestic tragedies, *George Barnwell; or, The London Merchant* (1731), and *The Fatal Curiosity* (1736), and his adaptation of *Arden of Feversham* (left unfinished and not produced until 1759) have little artistic merit. While England pretty much neglected his example, on the Continent he was enormously influential, and we can trace a chain of imitation through Diderot, Lessing, and Hebbel to Ibsen, from whom we get the social problem play of our own time.

[1] For a further treatment of this subject, see Henry Hitch Adams, *English Domestic or Homiletic Tragedy, 1575–1642* (New York, 1943), Chap. I.

The London Merchant
[1731; excerpt]

DEDICATION

IF TRAGIC POETRY be, as Mr. Dryden has somewhere said,[2] the most excellent and most useful kind of writing, the more extensively useful the moral of any tragedy is, the more excellent that piece must be of its kind.

I hope I shall not be thought to insinuate that this, to which I have presumed to prefix your name, is such; that depends on its fitness to answer the end of tragedy, the exciting of the passions in order to the correcting such of them as are criminal, either in their nature, or through their excess. Whether the following scenes do this in any tolerable degree, is, with the deference that becomes one who would not be thought vain, submitted to your candid and impartial judgment.

What I would infer is this, I think, evident truth: that tragedy is so far from losing its dignity by being accommodated to the circumstances of the generality of mankind that it is more truly august in proportion to the extent of its influence, and the numbers that are properly affected by it. As it is more truly great to be the instrument of good to many, who stand in need of our assistance, than to a very small part of that number.

If princes, &c., were alone liable to misfortunes arising from vice or weakness in themselves or others, there would be good reason for confining the characters in tragedy to those of superior rank; but, since the contrary is evident, nothing can be more reasonable than to proportion the remedy to the disease.

I am far from denying that tragedies founded on any instructive and extraordinary events in history or a well-invented fable where the persons introduced are of the highest rank are without their use, even to the bulk of the audience. The strong contrast between a Tamerlane and a Bajazet,[3] may have its weight with an unsteady

2 This exact statement has not been found in Dryden's works.

3 The reference is not to Marlowe's *Tamburlaine*, but to Nicholas Rowe's *Tamerlane* (1701/2). In this play, Bajazet is a tyrant and Tamerlane a benevolent monarch.

people and contribute to the fixing of them in the interest of a prince of the character of the former, when, thro' their own levity or the arts of designing men, they are rendered factious and uneasy though they have the highest reason to be satisfied. The sentiments and example of a Cato [4] may inspire his spectators with a just sense of the value of liberty when they see that honest patriot prefer death to an obligation from a tyrant who would sacrifice the constitution of his country and the liberties of mankind to his ambition or revenge. I have attempted, indeed, to enlarge the province of the graver kind of poetry and should be glad to see it carried on by some abler hand. Plays founded on moral tales in private life may be of admirable use by carrying conviction to the mind with such irresistible force as to engage all the faculties and powers of the soul in the cause of virtue by stifling vice in its first principles. They who imagine this to be too much to be attributed to tragedy must be strangers to the energy of that noble species of poetry. Shakespeare, who has given such amazing proofs of his genius in that as well as in comedy, in his *Hamlet,* has the following lines:

> Had he the motive and the cause for passion
> That I have, he would drown the stage with tears
> And cleave the general ear with horrid speech;
> Make mad the guilty, and appall the free,
> Confound the ignorant, and amaze indeed
> The very faculty of eyes and ears.[5]

And farther, in the same speech,

> I've heard that guilty creatures at a play,
> Have, by the very cunning of the scene,
> Been so struck to the soul that presently
> They have proclaim'd their malefactions.[6]

Prodigious! yet strictly just. But I shan't take up your valuable time with my remarks; only give me leave just to observe that he seems so

[4] Addison's *Cato* (1713).

[5] *Hamlet,* II, ii, 587–92. Shakespeare has "cue" instead of "cause" in the first line, and "faculties" instead of "faculty" in the last.

[6] *Hamlet,* II, ii, 618–21. Inaccurately quoted. Cf. Shakespeare.

> . . . I have heard
> That guilty creatures sitting at a play
> Have by the very cunning of the scene
> Been struck so to the soul that presently
> They have proclaim'd their malefactions.

firmly persuaded of the power of a well wrote piece to produce the effect here ascribed to it as to make Hamlet venture his soul on the event and rather trust that than a messenger from the other world, tho' it assumed, as he expresses it, his noble father's form and assured him that it was his spirit. I'll have, says Hamlet, "grounds more relative."

> . . . The Play's the thing
> Wherein I'll catch the conscience of the king.[7]

Such plays are the best answers to them who deny the lawfulness of the stage.

Considering the novelty of this attempt, I thought it would be expected from me to say something in its excuse; and I was unwilling to lose the opportunity of saying something of the usefulness of tragedy in general and what may be reasonably expected from the farther improvement of this excellent kind of poetry.[8] . . .

[7] *Hamlet*, II, ii, 632–34.
[8] The paragraphs omitted contain merely Lillo's compliments to his patron.

Colley Cibber
1671-1757

COLLEY CIBBER had a long career in the theatre as actor, author, and manager. Of an engaging personality, he achieved his success by endeavor and by his good nature. His first play, *Love's Last Shift* (1696), has the distinction of being the first sentimental comedy. In the same year Vanbrugh wrote an unsentimental sequel to it, *The Relapse,* in which the reformed rake returns to his earlier pursuits. Cibber was so far from malice at this demolishment of his view of life that he acted a leading part in Vanbrugh's play.

An Apology for the Life of Mr. Colley Cibber, Comedian, is an informal autobiography. It first appeared in 1740 and is one of the most readable accounts of the stage for its period.

An Apology for the Life of Mr. Colley Cibber, *Comedian*
[1740]

THERE IS another point relating to the hard condition of those who write for the stage which I would recommend to the consideration of their hearers, which is that the extreme severity with which they damn a bad play seems too terrible a warning to those whose untried genius might hereafter give them a good one. Whereas, it might be a temptation to a latent author to make the experiment, could he be sure that, though not approved, his Muse might, at least, be dismissed with decency. But the vivacity of our modern critics is of late grown so riotous that an unsuccessful author has no more mercy shewn him than a notorious cheat in a pillory; every fool, the lowest member of the mob, becomes a wit and will have a fling at him. They come now to a new play like hounds to a carcass and are all in a full cry, sometimes for an hour together, before the curtain rises to throw it amongst them. Sure, those gentlemen cannot but allow that a play condemned after a fair hearing falls with thrice the ignominy as when it is refused that common justice.

But when their critical interruptions grow so loud and of so long a continuance that the attention of quiet people (though not so complete critics) is terrified and the skill of the actors quite disconcerted by the tumult, the play then seems rather to fall by assassins than by a lawful sentence. Is it possible that such auditors can receive delight or think it any praise to them to prosecute so injurious, so unmanly a treatment? And though perhaps the compassionate, on the other side, who know they have as good a right to clap and support as others have to catcall, damn, and destroy, may oppose this oppression, their good nature, alas! contributes little to the redress; for in this sort of civil war, the unhappy author, like a good prince while his subjects are at mortal variance, is sure to be a loser by a victory on either side; for still the commonwealth, his play, is, during the conflict, torn to pieces. While this is the case, while the theatre is so turbulent a sea and so infested with pirates, what poetical merchant of any substance will venture to trade in it? If these valiant gentlemen pretend to be lovers of plays, why will they deter gentlemen from giving them such as are fit for gentlemen to see? In a word, this new race of critics seem to me like the lion whelps in the Tower who are so boisterously gamesome at their meals that they dash down the bowls of milk brought for their own breakfast.

As a good play is certainly the most rational and the highest entertainment that human invention can produce, let that be my apology (if I need any) for having thus freely delivered my mind in behalf of those gentlemen who, under such calamitous hazards, may hereafter be reduced to write for the stage; whose case I shall compassionate from the same motive that prevailed on Dido to assist the Trojans in distress.

Non ignora mali miseria succurrere disce.—Virg.

Or, as Dryden has it:

I learn to pity woes so like my own.

.   .   .

Sir John Vanbrugh's pen is not to be a little admired for its spirit, ease, and readiness in producing plays so fast upon the neck of one another; for, notwithstanding this quick dispatch, there is a clear and lively simplicity in his wit that neither wants the ornament of learning nor has the least smell of the lamp in it. As the face of a fine woman with only her locks loose about her may be then in its greatest beauty, such were his productions, only adorned by Nature. There is something so catching to the ear, so easy to the memory, in all he writ that it has been observed by all the actors of my time that the style of no author whatsoever gave their memory less trouble than that of Sir John Vanbrugh; which I myself, who have been charged with several of his strongest characters, can confirm by a pleasing experience. And indeed his wit and humor was so little labored that his most entertaining scenes seemed to be no more than his common conversation committed to paper. Here, I confess my judgment at a loss, whether in this I give him more or less than his due praise? For may it not be more laudable to raise an estate (whether in wealth or fame) by pains and honest industry than to be born to it? Yet, if his scenes really were, as to me they always seemed, delightful, are they not, thus expeditiously written, the more surprising? Let the wit and merit of them, then, be weighed by wiser critics than I pretend to be. But no wonder, while his conceptions were so full of life and humor, his Muse should be sometimes too warm to wait the slow pace of judgment or to endure the drudgery of forming a regular fable to them. Yet we see the *Relapse,* however imperfect in the conduct, by the mere force of its agreeable wit ran away with the hearts of its hearers; while *Love's Last Shift,* which (as Mr. Congreve justly said of it) had only in it a great many things that were *like* wit that in reality were *not* wit. And, what is still less pardonable (as I say of it myself), has a great deal of puerility and frothy state language in it, yet by the mere moral delight received from its fable it has been, with the other, in a continued and equal possession of the stage for more than forty years.

·   ·   ·

It may be observable, too, that my Muse and my spouse were equally prolific, that the one was seldom the mother of a child but, in the same year, the other made me the father of a play; I think we had about a dozen of each sort between us; of both which kinds some died in their infancy and near an equal number of each were alive when I quitted the theatre. But it is no wonder, when a Muse is only called upon by family duty, she should not always rejoice in the fruit of her labor. To this necessity of writing, then, I attribute the defects of my second play, which coming out too hastily the year after my first, turned to very little account. But having got as much by my first as I ought to have expected from the success of them both, I had no great reason to complain. Not but, I confess, so bad was my second that I do not choose to tell you the name of it; [1] and, that it might be peaceably forgotten, I have not given it a place in the two volumes of those I published in quarto in the year 1721. And whenever I took upon me to make some dormant play of an old author to the best of my judgment fitter for the stage, it was, honestly, not to be idle that set me to work, as a good housewife will mend old linen when she has not better employment. But when I was more warmly engaged by a subject entirely new, I only thought it a good subject when it seemed worthy of an abler pen than my own, and might prove as useful to the hearer as profitable to myself. Therefore, whatever any of my productions might want of skill, learning, wit, or humor, or however unqualified I might be to instruct others, who so ill-governed myself, yet such plays (entirely my own) were not wanting, at least, in what our most admired writers seemed to neglect, and without which I cannot allow the most taking play to be intrinsically good or to be a work upon which a man of sense and probity should value himself; I mean, when they do not as well *prodesse* as *delectare,* give profit with delight. The *Utile dulci* was, of old, equally the point and has always been my aim, however wide of the mark I may have shot my arrow. It has often given me amazement that our best authors of that time could think the wit and spirit of their scenes could be an excuse for making the looseness of them public. The many instances of their talents so abused are too glaring to need a closer comment, and are sometimes too gross to be recited. If, then, to have avoided this imputation, or rather to have had the interest and honor of virtue always in view, can give merit to a play, I am contented that my readers should think such merit the all that mine have to boast of. Libertines of mere wit and pleasure may laugh at these grave laws that would limit a lively genius, but every sensible honest man, conscious of their truth and use, will give these railers smile for smile and shew a due contempt for their merriment.

1 *The Woman's Wit; or, The Lady in Fashion,* 1697.

But while our authors took these extraordinary liberties with their wit, I remember the ladies were then observed to be decently afraid of venturing bare-faced to a new comedy till they had been assured they might do it without the risk of an insult to their modesty; or, if their curiosity were too strong for their patience, they took care, at least, to save appearances, and rarely came upon the first days of acting but in masks (then daily worn and admitted in the pit, the side boxes, and gallery), which custom, however, had so many ill consequences attending it [2] that it has been abolished these many years.

These immoralities of the stage had, by an avowed indulgence, been creeping into it ever since King Charles his time. Nothing that was loose could then be too low for it. *The London Cuckolds*,[3] the most rank play that ever succeeded, was then in the highest court favor. In this almost general corruption, Dryden, whose plays were more famed for their wit than their chastity, led the way, which he fairly confesses and endeavors to excuse in his Epilogue to the *Pilgrim*, revived in 1700 for his benefit in his declining age and fortune.[4] The following lines of it will make good my observation.

> Perhaps the parson stretch'd a point too far,
> When with our theatres he waged a war.
> He tells you that this very moral age
> Received the first infection from the stage.
> But sure, a banished court, with lewdness fraught,
> The seeds of open vice returning brought.
> Thus lodged (as vice by great example thrives)
> It first debauched the daughters, and the wives.
> London, a fruitful soil, yet never bore
> So plentiful a crop of horns before.
> The poets, who must live by courts or starve,
> Were proud, so good a Government to serve;
> And mixing with buffoons and pimps profane
> Tainted the stage for some small snip of gain;
> For they, like harlots under bawds professed
> Took all th'ungodly pains, and got the least.
> Thus did the thriving malady prevail,
> The court, its head, the poets but the tail.
> The sin was of our native growth, 'tis true,

[2] During the reign of Charles II a mask became the mark of a prostitute.

[3] *The London Cuckolds,* by Edward Ravenscroft, 1681.

[4] A play by Fletcher, produced for Dryden's benefit a week before his death. Dryden wrote a prologue, an epilogue, and a "Secular Masque" for it.

The scandal of the sin was wholly new.
Misses there were but modestly concealed;
Whitehall the naked Venus first revealed.
Where standing, as at Cyprus, in her shrine
The strumpet was adored with rites divine, &c.

. . .

Our theatrical writers were not only accused of immorality but profaneness, many flagrant instances of which were collected and published by a nonjuring clergyman, Jeremy Collier, in his *View of the Stage*, &c., about the year 1697.[5] However just his charge against the authors that then wrote for it might be, I cannot but think his sentence against the stage itself is unequal; reformation he thinks too mild a treatment for it, and is therefore laying his axe to the root of it. If this were to be a Rule of Judgment for offences of the same nature, what might become of the pulpit, where many a seditious and corrupted teacher has been known to cover the most pernicious doctrine with the mask of religion? This puts me in mind of what the noted Jo. Haines, the comedian, a fellow of a wicked wit, said upon this occasion, who being asked what could transport Mr. Collier into so blind a zeal for a general suppression of the stage when only some particular authors had abused it, whereas the stage, he could not but know, was generally allowed, when rightly conducted, to be a delightful method of mending our morals? "For that reason" replied Haines, "Collier is, by profession, a moral-mender himself, and two of trade, you know, can never agree."

The authors of the *Old Batchelor* [6] and of the *Relapse* [7] were those whom Collier most labored to convict of immorality; to which they severally published their reply. The first seemed too much hurt to be able to defend himself; and the other felt him so little that his wit only laughed at his lashes.

My first play, of the *Fool in Fashion*,[8] too being then in a course of success, perhaps for that reason only this severe author thought himself obliged to attack it; in which, I hope, he has shewn more zeal than justice. His greatest charge against it is that it sometimes uses the word *Faith!* as an oath in the dialogue; but if *Faith* may as well signify our given word or credit as our religious belief, why might not his

[5] Actually published in 1698.   [6] Congreve.
[7] Vanbrugh.   [8] *Love's Last Shift*, 1696.

charity have taken it in the less criminal sense? Nevertheless, Mr. Collier's book was, upon the whole, thought so laudable a work that King William, soon after it was published, granted him a *Nole Prosequi* when he stood answerable to the law for his having absolved two criminals just before they were executed for high treason. And it must be farther granted that his calling our dramatic writers to this strict account had a very wholesome effect upon those who writ after this time. They were now a great deal more upon their guard; indecencies were no longer wit; and, by degrees, the fair sex came again to fill the boxes on the first day of a new comedy, without fear or censure.

Bernard le Bovier
de Fontenelle
1657-1757

Partly because of his nature and partly because of the length of his life, Fontenelle, who in his youth had been an innovator, lived to be one of the last defenders of the seventeenth century spirit in drama, or, to be more precise, of the spirit of Corneille against that of Racine. Fontenelle was a nephew of Corneille and spent much of the space he devoted to dramatic criticism to explanation and defence of his uncle. He was typical of several of the French writers of his time in trying his hand at almost every form of literary production. His mind was clear, unemotional. Like Houdar de la Motte, he was usually on the side of the Moderns. His comments on drama are marked by an ability to analyze the ideas that were coming into being in his day even though he himself had little sympathy for them.

Reflections on the Poetic Art, although not published until 1742, was, it is generally believed, written early in the century.

Reflections on the Poetic Art
[1742; excerpts]

I

It sometimes happens that the irregularity of some plays, such as *Le Cid*,[1] does not keep them from being extremely pleasing; as a result, everyone begins to scorn the Rules. All that, they say, is bothersome and useless pedantry, and there is a certain art of pleasing that is above all Rules. What, then, is this art of pleasing? It cannot be defined; it is caught by chance; one can never with certainty come upon it twice; in short, it is a kind of magic that is wholly unknown.

1 An heroic drama by Pierre Corneille (1636).

282 Fontenelle

Perhaps all this is not true. It frequently seems that when irregular pieces please it is not because of their irregularity; and it is certain that, in some ways, no other dramatic piece is as regular as *Le Cid*. But it could well be that it is impossible to reduce everything in the theatre to Rules, or at least to well-known Rules. The Rules that have never been discovered or that are not known to everybody—in these the art of pleasing is to be found; that is where the magic lies.

I I

To FIND the Rules of drama, it is necessary to go back to the first sources of the beautiful, to discover what the things are that men are pleased to see—that is to say, the things that occupy their minds or move their hearts agreeably; and that is in itself a vast undertaking requiring close discussion. After having ascertained the actions that by their nature are suitable for pleasing, it is necessary to examine what changes dramatic form would impose upon them, either by necessity or merely by consent. And these researches having been made with all the necessary exactitude and discrimination, then one would not only have found the Rules of the theatre but also could be sure that he had found all of them; and if in descending to detail one of them were overlooked, it could easily be traced back to the principles that had been established.

I I I

To HAVE FOUND all the Rules of the theatre would still not constitute the whole poetic; it would be necessary to make comparisons among the different Rules and to judge their relative importance. It is almost always in the nature of things that not every sort of beauty can be utilized; it is necessary to make a choice and to sacrifice some to others. Thus, it would be very useful to have a scale in which one could, so to say, weigh the Rules. It would be seen that they do not all merit equal authority. Some must be observed rigorously, others may be slighted; and, so to speak, some demand sincere submission, while others are content with apparent submission. When the different sources which produce them have been found, it should not be difficult to give to each its true value.

IV

THE MIND loves to see or to act, which for it is the same thing, but it wishes to see and act painlessly; and what is worthy of remark is that so long as it is restrained within the limits of what it can do effortlessly, the more that action is demanded of it, the more pleasure it derives. The mind is active up to a certain point, beyond that very lazy. From another side, it loves a change of objects and actions. Thus, it is necessary at the same time to excite its curiosity, husband its laziness, prevent its inconstancy.

VI

WHATEVER is important, novel, singular, rare of its kind, or of uncertain outcome pricks the curiosity of the mind; whatever is unified and simple accommodates its laziness; whatever is diversified is suited to its inconstancy. From all this it is easy to conclude that the object presented to it must have all of these qualities together to please it perfectly.

VII

THE IMPORTANCE of the action of a tragedy is derived from the dignity of the characters and from the greatness of their concerns. When the actions are of such nature that they can, without losing any of their beauty, take place among people of little consequence, the names of princes and kings are only an extraneous ornament given to the subjects; but this ornamentation, extraneous as it is, is necessary. . . .

VIII

GREAT CONCERNS may be defined as the peril of losing life or honor, or liberty or a throne, or a friend or a mistress. It is frequently asked whether the death of some one of the characters is necessary in tragedy. A death is, truly, an important event, but often it is more useful in bringing about the denouement than to the importance of the action, and the peril of death has no usefulness there. What is it that renders Rodrigue so worthy of attention? Is it the peril that he courts in fighting the Count, the Moors or Don Sanche? [2] Hardly. It is the dilemma in which he may lose his honor or his mistress; it is the difficulty of

[2] *Le Cid* by Corneille.

obtaining forgiveness from Chimène, whose father he has killed. The great concerns are those that move men strongly, and there are moments when life is not man's greatest passion.

I X

IT SEEMS that the great concerns can be divided into two kinds: those that are more noble, such as the acquisition or the conservation of a throne, an indispensable duty, an act of vengeance, etc.; the other kind, the more touching, such as friendship or love. The one or the other of these two kinds of concern gives its character to the tragedies in which it is dominant. Naturally, the noble ought to prevail over the touching, and *Nicomède*,[3] which is all noble, is of a superior order to *Bérénice*,[4] which is all touching. But what is incontestably above all the rest is the union of the noble and the touching. The only secret for this is to put love in opposition to duty, ambition, or glory, so that it combats them forcefully and is in the end overcome by them. These actions are then important from the greatness of their opposed concerns. These pieces are at the same time touching on account of the combats of love, and noble on account of its defeat. Such are *Le Cid, Cinna,* and *Polyeucte*.[5]

X

THE ANCIENTS almost never put love in their pieces, and some there are who praise them for not having debased their theatre with such slight sentiments. On my part, I am afraid they did not know what love could produce. I do not see very well wherein would lie the shrewdness of not treating subjects like those of *Cinna* or *Le Cid*. The whole question is one of putting love in its place; that is to say, subordinate to some nobler passion, against which it revolts with violence, but uselessly. This rule is necessary only for pieces of the highest order, and has hardly been practiced except by Corneille.

X I

THE NOVEL and the singular ought to be found in the action of a piece and in its characters, but these will be treated more closely elsewhere. Here we shall speak only of the novel and the singular

---

[3] A tragedy by Corneille (1651).　　　[4] A tragedy by Racine (1670).
[5] Tragedies by Corneille (1636, 1639, and 1640).

as they are to be found in the passions. The simple truth is not enough to attract the attention of a mind; for that, a less common truth is necessary. Everyone knows the passions of men up to a certain point; for most people, beyond that point is country that is unknown, but country in which they are willing to make discoveries. How often do the passions have delicate and subtle effects which appear only rarely or which, when they appear, fail to find such skillful observers? To be novel they must also be extreme. We rarely see them except in ordinary form. Where do we find men wholly amorous, or ambitious, or miserly? We are perfect in nothing, not even in our vices.

XII

SUPPOSE a lover, at odds with his mistress, gets to the point of saying that he does not lose much in losing her for she is not very beautiful; and suppose a friend to whom the lover speaks agrees that the woman does not have much beauty, that, for example, her eyes are too small; suppose too that the lover answers that her eyes are not at fault for he finds them pleasing; suppose the friend then attacks her mouth and the lover again comes to her defense. The same play on her complexion, on her height. All that is a play of passion that is uncommon, subtle, delicate, and very agreeable to consider. This example, although comic and drawn from the *Bourgeois gentilhomme*,[6] has seemed to me so proper to explain my thought that I have not been able to bring myself to search for a more serious one. We do not often realize to what an extent the romances of our century are rich in this sort of trait, and to what point they have pushed the science of the heart.

XIII

THE SUBTLETY, the delicacy, and finally the pleasantness of these portraits of passion consist rather ordinarily in a kind of contradiction that is found in them. One does what he does not believe in doing, or says the contrary of what he wishes to say, or is dominated by an emotion which he thinks he has conquered, or lets others see what he has taken great pains to hide. Of all the passions the one that furnishes the most scenes of these kinds, and perhaps the only one that pro-

6 A comedy by Molière (1670).

vides them, is love. The obligation by which women must conquer or hide it and the delicacy of reputation which makes them pretend even to themselves about it are very fecund sources of these pleasant contradictions. Men are rarely, in this respect, in the same situation as women; also love does not make them so attractive as it does women. Ambition and vengeance are not in themselves contrasting effects; and whoever has the kind of character to feel these passions strongly will give himself up to them without combatting them and without disguising them.

XIV

NOT OFTEN are men who aspire either to elevate themselves or to avenge themselves subtle in the means by which they gain their ends; but lovers are subtle in devising means of arriving at the possession of their loved ones. The hope of being loved, or the fear of not being loved, hang on a glance, a sigh, or a word—in short, on almost imperceptible things of doubtful interpretation. On the other hand, the hopes and fears which accompany ambition and vengeance have motives more distinct, more discernible and palpable. Even those who are loved can doubt that they really are, or can be afraid from moment to moment of being loved no longer, or can afflict themselves with not being loved enough. When one is avenged or has arrived at the goal of his ambition, all is finished. Finally, love produces more effects that are novel and pleasant to consider because its objects are more refined, more uncertain, and more changeable. I know that the parallel between love and the other passions can be pushed further and that love will always show up to advantage. But I believe I have said enough to show that in comparison no other passion can provide as much pleasure on the stage. To the effects of love the dispositions of the spectators can add still more. Is there not more love in the world than ambition and vengeance?

XV

THE SINGULARITY or the bizarre qualities in the effects of a passion can make a spectacle more pleasing than its violence alone, because it occasions a greater discovery. It is true that these two beauties can be united, and a passion that is forceful can be at the same time singular. From that it follows further that love has more to furnish the theatre than vengeance or ambition, which can please only through their violence and which are deprived of an infinity of refinements and subleties which love alone shares. . . .

X V I

WHATEVER is rare and perfect of its kind cannot fail to attract attention. Thus it is always necessary to paint characters elevated a degree; nothing mediocre, neither virtues nor vices. It is the great obstacles that characters surmount that make great virtues. . . .

X V I I

VICES also have their perfection. A demi-tyrant is scarcely worthy of regard, but ambition, cruelty, perfidy, pushed to their highest point, become great objects. As much as possible tragedy must be filled with objects of beauty. There is an art of embellishing vices and giving them an air of nobility and elevation. Ambition is noble when it proposes for itself nothing short of thrones; cruelty is noble in another way when it is sustained by great firmness of mind; even perfidy is noble when it is accompanied by great cleverness. . . . The theatre is not the enemy of the vicious but of whatever is low or little. . . .

X I X

WHEN one tries to justify authors who have portrayed scarcely anything but low characters and have done that with little art, or who have depicted characters who are common or feeble examples of their species, one says, "It's Nature," and believes he has said all. That is Nature, it is true; but is there not something else that is more perfect, rarer of its kind, more noble, which is also Nature? That is what one wishes to see. What should be said of a painter who represented men only as they are commonly made, small, badly shaped and proportioned, and of insignificant appearance? That would be Nature too.

X X

ONE of the big secrets for pricking curiosity is to keep the outcome uncertain. For this purpose the knot must be such that the untying of it can be foreseen only with difficulty; that the denouement remain in doubt until the end—if possible, up to the last scene. . . .

X X I

ONCE EXCITED, curiosity must not be allowed to languish; it is necessary to keep promising it satisfaction, all the while leading it along, unappeased, right up to the goal that has been proposed. The spectator must be brought steadily closer to the conclusion even while the conclusion is hid from him always, so that if possible, he will not know where he is going, but so that he knows that he is advancing. The subject ought to move along quickly. A scene that does not move forward toward the end is pernicious. On the stage all must be action, and even the most beautiful discourse will be insupportable if it is only discourse. . . .

X X V I I I

SIMPLICITY is not pleasing in itself; it merely spares the mind trouble. Diversity, on the contrary, is pleasing in itself, since the mind loves change in actions and objects. Nothing pleases precisely for being simple; it is not proportionately more pleasing in that it is more simple, but in being diversified without ceasing to be simple. The more it is diversified without ceasing to be simple the more it pleases. . . .

X X I X

DIVERSITY of action, if it can be called that, is then scarcely less important than unity and simplicity. The Spaniards ordinarily diversify their pieces by putting in too many intrigues and incidents. Princes in disguise or unknown to one another; equivocal letters or letters that fall into the hands of persons to whom they are not addressed, lost pictures, mistakes that happen in the night, surprising and unexpected meetings: with plays and confusions like these they never get enough. On our part, we liked them for some time, and then our taste changed. Perhaps the Spaniards, who because of the constraint in which their women live are more accustomed to adventures than we, have more occasion than we to be fond of the representation of them. Perhaps their vivacity makes them consider simple and easy what is too overloaded and tiring for us. Perhaps, finally, and this is the most likely, they are pleased by plays of intrigue only for lack of knowing better. . . .

XXXV

UP TO NOW we have considered only those aspects of an action that can please the mind. That is not enough; we must also consider the heart. With all of the qualities of which we have spoken a play may be engaging, but there is still something beyond that; the playwright must, if he can, make it touching. We wish to be moved, agitated; we wish to shed tears. This pleasure that we take in weeping is so strange that I cannot refrain from making some reflection on it. Would we be pleased to see someone we loved in a situation as unhappy as that of the Cid after he has killed the father of his mistress? No, surely not. However, the extreme despair of the Cid, the danger that he will lose all that is most dear to him, pleases for this same reason that the Cid is loved by the spectator. How does it happen that we are pleased by the representation of a thing which would afflict us if it were real?

XXXVI

PLEASURE and sorrow, which are two such different sentiments, do not differ much in their cause. It will appear by the example of tickling that the movement of pleasure pushed a little too far becomes pain, and that the movement of pain a little moderated becomes pleasure. From thence it follows in addition that there is a soft and agreeable sadness; it is a pain that is weakened and diminished. It is the nature of the heart to love to be moved; thus sad objects please it, even painful objects, provided that something softens them. It is certain that the representation in the theatre gives almost the effect of reality, but it does not do so entirely. However entranced one may be by the force of the spectacle, whatever empire the senses and imagination achieve over reason, there remains always at the back of the mind I do not know what idea of falseness in what one sees. This idea, although feeble and hidden, is enough to diminish the pain of seeing some loved one suffer, and to reduce this pain to the point where it is changed to pleasure. We weep for the misfortunes of a hero whom we love and in the same moment console ourselves because we know it is only a fiction, and it is exactly this mixture of sentiments compounding a pleasing sorrow and tears that provides pleasure. Furthermore, since the grief inflicted by perceptible exterior objects is stronger than the consolation which comes only from inner reflection, the effects and marks of sorrow ought to dominate in the composition of sentiments of this kind.

XXXVII

THE CHARACTERS who draw tears from our eyes ought to be interesting and amiable, but how should they be made so? Is it enough that they are unhappy? The act of falling into great misfortunes is meritorious in the eyes of all feeling persons, and such characters naturally attract affection provided that nothing repulses it. The hero and heroine of the piece find the spectator in a favorable mood, and to engage him in pitying their woes need only not to displease him in some other way. . . .

XLIII

VIRTUOUS and amiable characters can be divided into two kinds: those that are gentle, tender, full of innocence, and those that are noble, elevated, courageous, proud. Both kinds are put into painful situations on the stage, and those of the one kind who are more sensitive to their woes and who spend more words in pitying themselves easily soften the spectator and give rise to pity. The others, who have as much courage as sensibility in their misfortunes and who disdain to complain, cause either admiration or a pity mixed with admiration, a pity that is without tears and that can be felt in the greatest hearts. We feel compassion toward the first kind, and when we apply their woes to ourselves, we tremble with fear. We admire the latter to such a point that we would almost wish to have their misfortunes with their feelings. . . .

XLV

HERE is a natural place for some reflections on the utility of tragedy. I have never understood the purgation of the passions by means of the passions themselves, so I will not say anything about it. If anyone is purged in this way, well and good; indeed, I do not see well in what way it would be good to be cured of pity. But it seems to me that the greatest utility of the theatre is to render virtue amiable to men, to accustom them to interest themselves in virtue, to touch their hearts, to put before them great examples of resoluteness and courage in their misfortunes, and by that means to fortify and elevate their sentiments. From that it follows that not only must characters be virtuous but also that they must be virtuous in the proud and elevated manner of Corneille, so that they will strengthen the heart and give lessons in courage. Some other characters, likewise virtuous but conforming more to ordinary Nature, will soften the mind and induce in the spectator a habit of weakness and despondency. As for love, since it is a necessary evil, it is to be wished that the plays of Corneille would inspire in the spectators only such kinds of it as they represent.

X L V I

WE HAVE SEEN that what makes characters interesting is either their misfortunes or their virtue, and that they are still more interesting when they exhibit together both great misfortunes and much virtue. But what would we have if the virtue itself produced the misfortunes? Without doubt the love of the spectator would increase even more. A misfortune is that much more touching to the extent that the man who falls into it is undeserving of it. . . .

X L V I I

NEXT TO the misfortunes which befall a character through his own virtue, the most touching are those into which he falls through the crime or the injustice of another. Oppressed innocence is always appealing, and love for it is redoubled by the hate for the persecutor. In such cases, tyrants cannot be painted in colors too black, since the horror felt toward them turns to the profit of the hero. Cléopâtre [7] and Néron [8] make Rodogune and Britannicus beloved. The love of virtue and the hate of vice is the same feeling in two different forms and, for the sake of variety and contrast in the theatre, it is good that both kinds be present.

X L V I I I

PITY-EVOKING misfortunes of still another kind are those into which the hero falls on account of a pardonable weakness, and the only one that we will pardon a hero for, as we have said, is love. Those whom love makes unfortunate are pitied almost as much as those who are unfortunate through virtue; witness Ariane [9] and Bérénice.[10] It must

[7] A character in Corneille's Rodogune (1644).
[8] A character in Racine's Britannicus (1669).
[9] A character in Corneille's Ariane (1672).
[10] The heroine in Racine's Bérénice (1670).

be remembered, however, that these same spectators so favorable to love would be wounded if love triumphed over some more noble sentiment. Love is permitted to draw the hero into misfortune but not into shame.

XLIX

FINALLY, catastrophes into which a character falls neither through his virtue, the crime of another, nor a pardonable weakness, but by a pure fatality, as the misfortune of Oedipus, would appear the least touching, not so much because they cause a certain amount of horror, but because they do not build up interest in characters. What impressions do these two happenings have on you? Let somebody tell you the story of a man who has poisoned a benefactor who has made the poisoner his heir, and who expresses tender love to his murderer while he is dying, or the story of a man wiped out by a bolt of lightning. It is true that in the one case the blackness of ingratitude, and on the other the thunderbolt, makes you shudder, but the frightful ingratitude makes you take the part of the one who suffers from it; you pity him tenderly, while the thunderbolt leaves you rather indifferent about the one who has been killed by it; his character does not become any dearer to you. You hate, you detest the poisoner, but you do not hate, nor ought you to hate, the one who has sent the thunderbolt. Finally, the latter event presents a frightful idea from which the imagination turns away as fast as it can, whereas the other gives birth to a pity with which one converses with some sort of complacency; and what is especially notable, all the circumstances of the death of the poisoned man are sought out, and all provide a kind of pleasure. It is easy to see that the misfortune of Oedipus is the same kind of thing as a thunderbolt and that it would only produce the same effect. One brings away from *Oedipus*, and from other plays that resemble it, only a disagreeable and useless conviction of the miseries of the human lot.

L

ONCE the characters have been made pleasing to us, either by their virtue or their misfortunes, once our hearts have been reached, all that happens to the characters affects us; their joys and their sorrows are ours. But whatsoever tenderness we may feel for them, we would rather not see their joy prolonged; yet we are willing to watch them suffer throughout the play. What is this strange thing? It comes apparently because all men feel sorrow more deeply than joy; and since the theatre diminishes all feelings in the way that has been explained, these two being equally diminished, there still remains in the sorrow enough force to move us, but there does not remain enough of the joy. Thus a scene of happy lovers should pass very quickly, and a scene of unhappy lovers who make much of all their woes may be prolonged without boring us. There is still another reason, but taken from the side of intellect. With happy people, curiosity has nothing further to occupy itself; it abandons them unless there is reason to anticipate that they will soon relapse into unhappiness, and it is anxious for this change. In this case the contrast agreeably diversifies the picture offered to the intellect and the passions which move the heart.

L I

It is necessary, if possible, that our emotion toward the hero should steadily increase; at the very least it would be insupportable for it to diminish gradually. A weakness, however slight, in a character who up to that time had appeared exalted, a lesser peril or a lesser misfortune after a greater one—all these can only displease. Once accustomed to a lively and pleasing agitation, the heart will not adjust itself either to repose or to a lesser agitation.

L I I

The more a hero is loved, the more fitting it is to make him happy at the end. It is not necessary to send a spectator away with the pain of pitying the destiny of a virtuous man. It is certain that, after having long trembled for the hero, one is relieved at his release from peril; and although this feeling may be saved for the last scene, if possible, and although the spectator is touched by it only for a moment, this moment is of great importance. It seems that its effect is a turning back upon the rest of the play, although already past, and a heightening of what has been seen. There is a law which demands that virtue be happy, and the play that has disregarded it should provide satisfaction in this respect in the ending. The most beautiful lesson that tragedy can give to man is to teach him that virtue, although long crossed and persecuted, remains in the end victorious.

L I I I

A VOLUNTARY death chosen by a hero to escape even greater misfortune —a death like that of Cato,[11] Sophonisba,[12] or Camma [13]—ought not to be counted among these unhappy endings which send the spectator away discontented. The hero dies, it is true, but he dies nobly. He makes his own destiny; he is to be admired as much as pitied; and although he sets a very bad example for us, it is a bad example that is not dangerous. The disagreeable endings are those in which the hero dies under oppression, or where crime triumphs over virtue.

L I V – L X X I

[THIS PASSAGE contains a long discussion of the principles of probability. Why cannot a theatrical action be resolved by use of a force from the outside? Why cannot characters exhibit sudden conversions? Why do we have Rules concerning the Unities of Time and Place? The answer to all these questions, Fontenelle says, is in the difference between Nature and art. Since a play is merely a representation of reality, there is no reality in it and the appearance of reality must be given it. The truth in Nature is whatever is; the semblance of truth in a play is whatever we judge can exist, drawing from our ordinary experiences. Truth in Nature needs no proof; in art it does. Characters in a play must be consistent. Singularly of character is not incompatible with probability, but singularity of action is. The Unities of Time and Place must be maintained even though they are not necessary in the account of a real-life action because the playwright must avail himself of everything that will give his work of art probability. Fontenelle allows some leeway, but is in general a defender of these Unities. LXX and LXXI contain discussion of rhyme and metre.]

L X X I I

ALL THIS may easily be applied to tragedy. Even though an action in itself is gripping and interesting and even though its representation has all possible probability, it is still not enough. Art imposes on it other, new laws. Of these laws, some are purely arbitrary, like the use of rhyme in verse. Others are more fundamental. That every action should be divided into five parts, all approximately equal—assuredly

---

[11] Cato was a frequently discussed character of history in connection with the comment on Stoicism frequent during the seventeenth century. Cf. Addison's *Cato* (1713).

[12] Heroine of Corneille's *Sophonisbe* (1663).

[13] Character in Thomas Corneille's *Camma* (1661). Thomas Corneille was the nephew of Pierre Corneille, the famous dramatist.

that is not to be found in the nature of the thing, but is pure fantasy of art. But other principles are better founded. It is equally natural whether an action is resolved by some accident that comes from the outside (that is, by something alien to the action) or by an event whose causes are within the action itself. . . . But between these two conclusions, both of them natural and probable, art chooses the second because it is the consequence of all that the play contains, and absolutely excludes the former because it comes from outside the play., From that can be formed a Rule that is general and without exceptions. In effect, it is pleasant to see an action that contains in itself the seeds of its denouement, if these are imperceptible and hidden from the eyes, and which, developing step by step and without outside aid, comes finally to bring the denouement to light. For the same reason, more or less, art has determined that all the seeds of denouement should be contained in the first act, that all the characters should appear there or should be announced there. It is clear that in a natural chain of events there could be found at the end of an action the introduction of characters who had no part in the beginning, but through the use of this principle of art, the play forms a whole that is more pleasing to contemplate because it has more symmetry, is more self-contained and better rounded.

LXXIII

STILL ANOTHER reason, but more general. If plays are brought to conclusion either by something from the outside, or by characters who were unknown at first, the need of the poet to find a denouement and the difficulty of finding one are too strongly felt. From this same source come still other Rules, or usages which amount to Rules. Why should an actor, detached from the play, come before us to tell us the subject matter from antiquity? Why—and this is incomparably less gross—should a poet introduce in the first act some character who does not know the story chosen as subject matter, who in learning about it himself instructs the spectators at the same time, as in *Rodogune?* All this has too much the appearance of being affected by the poet for his own convenience. If it is possible, the poet should not give the impression that he has had to think about how to construct his play. He ought, like a skillful politician, who adroitly covers his own design by appearing to act only for the public interest, to convince the spectator that nothing has been artificially contrived.

LXXIV

THERE, approximately, are the principal sources of all the Rules of tragedy. They are drawn from actions that can be considered either in themselves or on the stage. Considered in itself, an action pertains to the mind and the heart. If it is considered as being put on a stage, it is a representation and a work of art. From this difference in aspects comes a difference of views and Rules. It should now be our intention to consider all these Rules as a group with the view of determining which are the most important, which of them in the necessity of choice ought to be preferred; in making this comparison it should be of great aid to have discovered their true sources. But I say now that strength and courage fail me in mid-course; others can happily finish the work if indeed this road that I have opened up deserves to be followed. Speculation of this kind cannot give genius to anyone who lacks it; nor does it much help those who have it, and most often even men of genius are incapable of being aided by speculations. For what then are they good? The answer: to aid in restoring the fundamental ideas of beauty to those people who love reasoning and who content themselves with bringing under the empire of philosophy the things that appear most independent of it and that commonly appear abandoned to the peculiarities of taste.

Louis Jean Levesque de Pouilly

1691-1750

DISCIPLE of Newton, mathematician in his early years, devotee of scientific learning, member of the *Académie des inscriptions et belles lettres,* and traveller, Levesque de Pouilly was one of a class of men common in the eighteenth century who were known widely for their learning and were received royally wherever they went but whose actual accomplishment was little. Levesque de Pouilly's chief claim to fame is the rather slim *Theory of Agreeable Sensations.* Originally, this was merely a long letter to Bolingbroke, who had it published in 1736 without Levesque de Pouilly's knowledge. An authorized edition in 1747 contained emendations and additions by the author. The work is important to dramatic criticism because it attempts to find a scientific basis for our aesthetic responses, and because it represents one important aspect of sentimentalism. The sentimentalist was often, we are likely to forget, an analyst of emotional reactions. Sentimentalism thus becomes a part of the Enlightenment. The moral doctrines of the Shaftesburys and Hutchesons are taken over entire and are given psychological elaboration. The parallel between Levesque de Pouilly and Sulzer in Germany is close.

Bolingbroke once wrote to Levesque de Pouilly, "I have only met three men who have seemed to me worthy of being trusted with the government of nations. . . . These three are you, Pòpe, and myself."

The excerpt presented here is from the anonymous English translation published in Edinburgh in 1766 with an explanatory Preface by Jacob Vernet.

The Theory of Agreeable Sensations
[1736; excerpt]

CHAPTER IV

ALL OTHER motions of the heart besides those of fear and hatred are agreeable. Whatever we feel of compassion, friendship, gratitude, generosity, or benevolence affords us a pleasing sensation. "How unhappy are the damned," said St. Catherine of Genes, "because they are no longer capable of loving, whilst every person of a benevolent soul has a natural mirth and gaiety, in his temper. . . ."

If there have been divines who have imagined the soul to be capable of being wholly disinterested with regard to pleasure, as a balance to them there have been philosophers who have believed her unable to be swayed by any motives but those which took their rise from the prospect of self-interest. But in order to confirm this notion, let us but for a moment take a view of our public theatres. The shows exhibited there, though they are often calculated to debauch the mind, yet are sufficient to convince us that she is formed for virtue. What means our tears for unfortunate heroes! With what joy would we rescue them from their impending ruin! Whence comes this attachment? Does it proceed from the ties of blood or friendship? No, it does not; but they are men who appear to be virtuous. We have implanted in us the seeds of benevolence, which are always ready to spring up in favor of virtue and incline us to humanity when their growth is not obstructed by contrary passions. History furnishes us with the story of a Grecian tyrant, who being present at the representation of Euripides's *Hecuba,* went out at the end of the first act filled with a conscious shame when he found himself, in spite of himself, all in tears, by this means showing a tender feeling for the manes of the Trojans, which he had never felt for his own countrymen. Cruel when in the pursuit of what seemed to be his interest, yet by nature formed for humanity, which he could not withhold from those illustrious but unfortunate men from whom he had nothing to fear, he paid to them the tribute of benevolence which was their due.

Since the motions of the heart are agreeable where benevolence reigns and only become painful when hatred prevails, for this reason we are of opinion that the Ancients ought to have accounted those tragedies only to be defective which raised the misfortunes of virtuous persons to such a degree as to kindle our indignation but not those wherein our solicitude for their fate is worked up to the catastrophe and at last gives place to the joy of seeing them completely happy.

However, we must so far agree with Aristotle and his commentators that a strong regard for our own preservation makes us more ready to receive the impression of sorrow than pleasure, so that the soul more deeply interests herself with the misfortunes of a virtuous hero than with his prosperity. His happiness, no doubt, would have given us joy, but by a certain magic power of tragedy his very misfortunes affect us with a sort of pleasing sorrow more agreeable than joy itself because it affords a more lively exercise to our benevolence and humanity, the hidden charms of which are so powerful as to be able to convert grief into pleasure and render tears more agreeable than smiles.

But by what miracle is it brought about that we should be so agreeably entertained with certain representations on the stage while, at the same time, had they been really performed before us, we should have been shocked with inward horror? 'Tis owing to the different position of the object that we feel such different impressions. The more likely the misfortunes of others are to reach us, so much the more we dread their becoming personal; whereas those which tragedy presents us with are seen at a remote view; they do not alarm the love we bear to ourselves; they only excite that benevolent love which prevails within us in favor of virtuous persons.

Henry Fielding

1707-1754

Readers who know Henry Fielding only through his novels are sometimes surprised to learn that he was also a very active playwright, and, as the selection shows, widely conversant with the critical problems of his day. Fielding's first literary activity was in the theatre, to which he contributed farces, comedies, and some adaptations from Molière. His burlesque, *The Tragedy of Tragedies; or, The Life and Death of Tom Thumb the Great* (1731) is much in the same vein as *The Rehearsal* of Buckingham (1671) which, with revisions, was still being produced occasionally at the time of Fielding's work. In the printed version of *Tom Thumb*, which was lengthened from two to three acts, Fielding supplied the Preface reproduced here and a series of footnotes in which he identifies the people, plays, and ideas burlesqued and mocks the critics as cleverly as he did the playwrights in the play itself. Unlike *The Rehearsal*, which primarily attacks Dryden, this play does not attack one man, but ridicules many of the absurdities of dramatic theory and practice of the time. *Tom Thumb* remained popular until Sheridan's *The Critic* (1779) replaced it.

The Tragedy of Tragedies; or, The Life and Death of Tom Thumb the Great

[1731]

H. Scriblerus Secundus,[1] His Preface

The town hath seldom been more divided in its opinion than concerning the merit of the following scenes. Whilst some publicity affirmed that no author could produce so fine a piece but Mr. P——,[2] others have with as much vehemence insisted that no one could write anything so bad but Mr. F——.[3]

[1] Fielding takes this name in honor of Pope who was the first Scriblerus.
[2] Pope.   [3] Fielding.

Tom Thumb the Great 301

Nor can we wonder at this dissension about its merit, when the learned world have not unanimously decided even the very nature of this tragedy. For though most of the universities in Europe have honored it with the name of *egregium et maximi pretii opus, tragoediis tam antiquis quam novis longe anteponedum;* nay, Dr. B—— [4] hath pronounced, *Citius Maevii, Æneadem quam Scribleri istius tragaediam hanc crediderim, cujus auctorem Senecam ipsum tradidisse haud dubitarim;* and the great Professor Burman [5] hath styled *Tom Thumb, Heroum omnium tragicorum facile principem.* Nay, though it hath, among other languages, been translated into Dutch and celebrated with great applause at Amsterdam (where burlesque never came) by the title of *Mynheer Vander Thumb,* the burgomasters receiving it with that reverent and silent attention which becometh an audience at a deep tragedy, notwithstanding all this, there have not been wanting some who have represented these scenes in a ludicrous light, and Mr. D—— [6] hath been heard to say, with some concern, that he wondered a tragical and Christian nation would permit a representation on its theatre so visibly designed to ridicule and extirpate everything that is great and solemn among us.

This learned critic and his followers were led into so great an error by that surreptitious and piratical copy which stole last year into the world—with what injustice and prejudice to our author, I hope will be acknowledged by everyone who shall happily peruse this genuine and original copy. Nor can I help remarking, to the great praise of our author, that, however imperfect the former was, still did even that faint resemblance of the true *Tom Thumb* contain sufficient beauties to give it a run of upwards of forty nights, to the politest audiences. But, notwithstanding that applause which it received from all the best judges, it was as severely censured by some few bad ones and, I believe, rather maliciously than ignorantly reported to have been intended a burlesque on the loftiest parts of tragedy and designed to banish what we generally call *fine things* from the stage.

Now, if I can set my country right in an affair of this importance, I shall lightly esteem any labor which it may cost. And this I the rather undertake; first, as it is indeed in some measure incumbent on me to vindicate myself from that surreptitious copy before mentioned, pub-

4 Bentley, a leading English classical scholar. 5 A Latin scholar of Amsterdam.
6 Dennis.

lished by some ill-meaning people under my name; secondly, as knowing myself more capable of doing justice to our author than any other man, as I have given myself more pains to arrive at a thorough understanding of this little piece, having for ten years together read nothing else; in which time I think I may modestly presume, with the help of my English dictionary, to comprehend all the meanings in every word in it.

But should any error of my pen awaken Clariss: Bentheium to enlighten the world with his annotations on our author, I shall not think that the least reward or happiness arising to me from these my endeavors.

I shall waive at present what hath caused such feuds in the learned world, whether this piece was originally written by Shakespeare, though certainly that, were it true, must add a considerable share to its merit, especially with such as are so generous as to buy and to commend what they never read, from an implicit faith in the author only —a faith which our age abounds in as much as it can be called deficient in any other.

Let it suffice that the *Tragedy of Tragedies; or, The Life and Death of Tom Thumb,* was written in the reign of Queen Elizabeth.[7] Nor can the objection made by Mr. D——,[8] that the tragedy must then have been antecedent to the history, have any weight when we consider that though the *History of Tom Thumb,* printed by and for Edward M——r [9] at the Looking-Glass on London Bridge, be of a later date; still must we suppose the writer thereof to be inspired, a gift very faintly contended for by the writers of our age. As to this history's not bearing the stamp of second, third, or fourth edition, I see but little in that objection, editions being very uncertain lights to judge of books by; and perhaps Mr. M——r may have joined twenty editions in one, as Mr. C——l [10] hath ere now divided one into twenty.

Nor doth the other argument, drawn from the little care our author hath taken to keep up to the letter of the history, carry any greater force. Are there not instances of plays wherein the history is so perverted that we can know the heroes whom they celebrate by

[7] Actually written in 1730 and revised in 1731.
[8] Dennis.
[9] Midwinter, a leading London printer and publisher.
[10] Curll, another famous London printer and publisher.

no other marks than their names? Nay, do we not find the same character placed by different poets in such different lights that we can
discover not the least sameness or even likeness in the features? The
Sophonisba of Mairet [11] and of Lee [12] is a tender, passionate, amorous
mistress of Massinissa. Corneille [13] and Mr. Thomson [14] give her no
other passion but the love of her country, and make her as cool in her
affection to Massinissa as to Syphax. In the two latter she resembles
the character of Queen Elizabeth; in the two former, she is the picture of Mary, Queen of Scotland. In short, the one Sophonisba is as
different from the other as the Brutus of Voltaire [15] is from the Marius,
Jun. of Otway,[16] or as the Minerva is from the Venus of the Ancients.

Let us now proceed to a regular examination of the tragedy before
us, in which I shall treat separately of the fable, the moral, the characters, the sentiments, and the diction. And first of the *fable,* which
I take to be the most simple imaginable, and, to use the words of
an eminent author, "One, regular, and uniform, not charged with a
multiplicity of incidents, and yet affording several revolutions of fortune; by which the passions may be excited, varied, and driven to
their full tumult of emotion." [17] Nor is the action of this tragedy less
great than uniform. The spring of all is the love of Tom Thumb for
Huncamunca, which causeth the quarrel between their majesties in
the first act; the passion of Lord Grizzle in the second; the rebellion,
fall of Lord Grizzle and Glumdalca, devouring of Tom Thumb by
the cow, and that bloody catastrophe, in the third.

Nor is the *moral* of this excellent tragedy less noble than the
fable: it teaches these two instructive lessons, *viz.:* that human happiness is exceeding transient and that death is the certain end of all
men; the former whereof is inculcated by the fatal end of Tom
Thumb, the latter by that of all the other personages.

The *characters* are, I think, sufficiently described in the *Dramatis
Personae,* and I believe we shall find few plays where greater care is
taken to maintain them throughout and to preserve in every speech
that characteristic mark which distinguishes them from each other.
"But," says Mr. D——, "how well does the character of Tom Thumb,

[11] Mairet's *Sophonisbe* (1634).   [12] Lee's *Sophonisba* (1675).
[13] Corneille's *Sophonisbe* (1663).
[14] Thomson's *The Tragedy of Sophonisba* (1730).
[15] Voltaire's *Brutus* (1730).   [16] Otway's *Caius Marius* (1679).
[17] James Thomson, Preface to *The Tragedy of Sophonisba.*

whom we must call the hero of this tragedy—if it hath any hero—agree with the precepts of Aristotle, who defineth tragedy to be the imitation of a short but perfect action containing a just greatness in itself, etc.? What greatness can be in a fellow whom history relateth to have been no higher than a span?" This gentleman seemeth to think, with Sergeant Kite,[18] that the greatness of a man's soul is in proportion to that of his body, the contrary of which is affirmed by our English physiognomical writers. Besides, if I understand Aristotle right, he speaketh only of the greatness of the action, and not of the person.

As for the *sentiments* and *diction*, which now only remain to be spoken to: I thought I could afford them no stronger justification than by producing parallel passages out of the best of our English writers. Whether this sameness of thought and expression which I have quoted from them proceeded from an agreement in their way of thinking, or whether they have borrowed from our author, I leave the reader to determine. I shall adventure to affirm this of the sentiments of our author, that they are generally the most familiar which I have ever met with and at the same time delivered with the highest dignity of phrase; which brings me to speak of his *diction*. Here I shall only beg one postulatum, *viz.:* that the greatest perfection of the language of a tragedy is that it is not to be understood; which granted (as I think it must be), it will necessarily follow that the only way to avoid this is by being too high or too low for the understanding, which will comprehend everything within its reach. These two extremities of style Mr. Dryden illustrates by the familiar image of two inns, which I shall term the aërial and the subterrestrial.[19]

Horace goes farther, and showeth when it is proper to call at one of these inns, and when at the other:

> *Telephus et Peleus, cum pauper et exsul uterque,*
> *Projicit ampullas et sesquipedalia verba.*

That he approveth of the *sesquipedalia verba* is plain; for had not Telephus and Peleus used this sort of diction in prosperity, they could not have dropped it in adversity. The aërial inn, therefore, says Horace, is proper only to be frequented by princes and other great men in the highest affluence of fortune: the subterrestrial is

---

18 In Farquhar's *The Recruiting Officer* (1706).
19 Taken from *Of Heroic Plays*, prefixed to *The Conquest of Granada*. (1670)

appointed for the entertainment of the poorer sort of people only, whom Horace advises *dolere sermone pedestri;* the true meaning of both which citations is that bombast is the proper language for joy and doggerel for grief, the latter of which is literally implied in the *sermo pedestris* as the former is in the *sesquipedalia verba.*

Cicero recommendeth the former of these. *Quid est tam furiosum vel tragicum qual verborum sonitus inanis, nulla subjecta sententia neque scientia.* What can be so proper for tragedy as a set of big-sounding words, so contrived together as to convey no meaning?—which I shall one day or other prove to be the sublime of Longinus. Ovid declareth absolutely for the latter inn: *Omne genus scripti gravi-tate tragaedia vincit.* Tragedy hath of all writings the greatest share in the bathos, which is the profound of Scriblerus.

I shall not presume to determine which of these two styles be prop-erer for tragedy. It sufficeth that our author excelleth in both. He is very rarely within sight through the whole play, either rising higher than the eye of your understanding can soar or sinking lower than it careth to stoop. But here it may perhaps be observed that I have given more frequent instances of authors who have imitated him in the sublime than in the contrary. To which I answer: First, bombast being properly a redundancy of genius, instances of this nature occur in poets whose names do no more honor to our author than the writ-ers in the doggerel which proceeds from a cool, calm, weighty way of thinking—instances whereof are most frequently to be found in authors of a lower class; secondly, that the works of such authors are difficultly found at all; thirdly, that it is a very hard task to read them, in order to extract these flowers from them; and lastly, it is very often difficult to transplant them at all, they being like some flowers of a very nice nature which will flourish in no soil but their own. For it is easy to transcribe a thought, but not the want of one. The *Earl of Essex,*[20] for instance, is a little garden of choice rarities whence you can scarce transplant one line so as to preserve its original beauty. This must account to the reader for his missing the names of several of his acquaintance, which he had certainly found there had I ever read their works; for which, if I have not a just esteem, I can at least say with Cicero, *Quae non contemno, quippe quae nunquam legerim.* However, that the reader may meet with due satisfaction in

20 John Banks's *The Unhappy Favourite, or The Earl of Essex* (1681).

this point, I have a young commentator from the University who is
reading over all the modern tragedies at five shillings a dozen, and
collecting all that they have stole from our author, which shall shortly
be added as an appendix to this work.

Voltaire

1694-1778

Fʀᴀɴçᴏɪs Mᴀʀɪᴇ Aʀᴏᴜᴇᴛ, known to the world by his adopted name, Voltaire, was the best-known—even though it might be argued that he was not the best—European playwright of the first three-quarters of the eighteenth century. That fact is sometimes obscured by the attention given his long struggles against church and state as he found them in the France of his day, by his agitation for the kind of freedom of thought and action that he found in England during his stay there [1726–1729], by the popularity of such philosophical tales as *Candide* and *Zadig*, and by the identification of his name with the *Encyclopédie* group. But throughout his long and stormy career the theatre of Paris was brightened by the steady presentation of his plays—some of them the highlight of Parisian seasons when Voltaire himself was in political exile in Switzerland or elsewhere.

Voltaire's plays present a curious mixture of an outdated heroic drama and newer influences from his own day. The mark of his own personality upon the forms he used is to be noted most clearly in the "reasoning" that is to be found in them, the constant propaganda for one kind or another of tolerance and enlightenment. Sentimentalism he embraced intellectually but commonly ignored in practice. His artistic tastes were at one with Corneille, not with the "touching" Racine nor with the "sensationalistic" Crébillon.

In prefaces to his own plays and in his commentaries upon Corneille, Voltaire's body of dramatic criticism is considerable. There is little depth to most of his comments, and the force of his ideas on purely literary matters is usually reactionary. Nevertheless, he was partly responsible for introducing Shakespeare into France and for freeing the French stage of some of its more cramping Rules. His plays, in turn, set the tone of much of the English dramatic production of the mid-eighteenth century, and they were often adapted to the London stage. He was a force to be reckoned with, rather than a body of ideas.

Voltaire's *Oedipe* was first produced in 1718, but the Preface was not written until 1730. In the following year, 1731, he wrote his *Discourse on Tragedy* to Lord Bolingbroke, with whom he had been on intimate terms during his stay in England. The translation of text, and of notes by former editors, is from the fifty-two volume edition of Voltaire's *Oeuvres complètes* edited by Louis Moland and published in Paris in 1877–1883.

Oedipe (*Edition of 1730*)
[Excerpt]

PREFACE

O*edipe*, of which this is a new edition, was presented for the first time at the end of the year 1718. The public received it with much indulgence. Since then this tragedy has been maintained on the stage, and it can still be seen with some pleasure in spite of its faults. This I attribute in part to the advantage it has always had of being very well acted, and in part to the pomp and the pathos of the play itself.

Father Folard, Jesuit, and M. de la Motte, of the French Academy, have since then both treated the same subject,* and both avoided the errors into which I fell. It is not for me to speak of their plays. My criticisms and my praises would be equally suspect.

I am equally far from pretending to write a poetic on the occasion of this tragedy. I am persuaded that all the delicate theorizing by which we have been overwhelmed for several years is not worth a scene of genius, and that much more can be learned from *Polyeucte* and *Cinna* [1] than from all the precepts of the Abbé d'Aubignac; [2] Sévère and Pauline [3] are the true teachers of the art. The large number of books written on painting by the connoisseurs do not teach a student as much as a single view of a head by Raphael.

The principles of all the arts which depend on imagination are all simple and easy, are all founded in Nature and in Reason. The Pradons and the Boyers [4] have known them as well as the Corneilles and the Racines. The difference has been and will always be in their application. The composers of *Armide* and *Issé* † and the worst com-

---

* The *Oedipe* of Father Folard was first presented by the students of the College of Lyon. The edition bears the date of 1722, but perhaps the performance was at the end of 1721. [Beuchot's note.]

M. de La Motte wrote two *Oedipes* in 1726, one in rhyme, the other in unrhymed prose. The *Oedipe* in rhyme was presented four times; the other has never been played. [Voltaire's note.]

† *Armide*, by Quinault, music by Lully; *Issé* by La Motte, music by Destouches.

---

[1] Tragedies by Pierre Corneille: *Polyeucte* (1640); *Cinna* (1639).
[2] François Hedelin, the Abbé D'Aubignac, published his *Practique du théâtre* in 1657.
[3] Characters in *Polyeucte*.
[4] Nicolas Pradon was an incompetent writer who won some acclaim because of the support of a *cabale* that was anti-Racine. The Abbé Claude Boyer (1618–1698) was a second-rate playwright.

posers have known the same rules of music. Poussin has worked on the same principles as Vignon.[5] It would seem then as useless to speak of Rules at the beginning of a tragedy as it would be for a painter to ward off his public by dissertations on his pictures, or for a musician to wish to demonstrate that his music ought to please.

But since M. de la Motte wishes to establish Rules that are entirely contrary to those that have guided our great masters, it is fitting to defend the ancient laws, not because they are ancient but because they are good and necessary and because they have in a man of his merit a redoubtable adversary.

First, M. de la Motte wishes to do away with the Unities of Action, Place, and Time.

The French were the first among modern nations to revive these wise Rules of the stage; other peoples have for a long time remained unwilling to receive a yoke which appears so severe, but since the yoke was a fitting one and reason overcomes everything, in time they submitted to it. Today, even in England, authors remark in the prologues of their plays that the duration of the action is the same as the duration of the representation; and they go further than we do who have been their masters in that respect. All nations are beginning to regard as barbarous the time when this practice was ignored by the greatest geniuses, such as Don Lope de Vega and Shakespeare; they even admit their indebtedness to us for having removed them from that barbarism. Is it necessary that a Frenchman should exert all his energies to lead us back into it?

If I had nothing else to say to M. de la Motte except that MM. Corneille, Racine, Molière, Addison, Congreve, and Maffei have all observed the laws of the stage, that should be enough to give pause to anyone who wished to violate them; but M. de la Motte deserves to be opposed by reasons rather than by authorities.

What is a stage play? The representation of an action. Why of one and not of two or three? Because the human mind cannot embrace several objects at once; because interest that is divided soon vanishes; because we are disturbed to see two happenings, even in a picture; finally because Nature itself suggests this precept to us; which ought to be as invariable as Nature itself.

---

[5] Nicolas Poussin (1594–1665) was a celebrated painter. Claude Vignon (1593–1670) was a painter and engraver.

For the same reason, Unity of Place is essential, for a single action cannot take place in several places at once. If the actors whom I see are in Athens in the first act, how can they be found in Persia in the second? Has M. Le Brun painted Alexander at Arbella and in India on the same canvas? [6] "I would not be surprised," M. de la Motte says adroitly, "should a nation that is enlightened but less friendly to the Rules become accustomed to see Coriolanus condemned at Rome in the first act, received by the Volscians in the third, and lay siege to Rome in the fourth, etc." In the first place, I do not believe that an enlightened and informed people would not be a friend of Rules that are entirely founded in good sense and formed entirely for their pleasure. Secondly, who does not feel that here would then be three tragedies, and that a project like this, even were it executed in splendid verse, would ever be anything but a play by Jodelle [7] or Hardy [8] versified by a skillful modern?

The Unity of Time is joined naturally to the first two. For this there is, I believe, a very tangible proof. Suppose I am a spectator at a tragedy; that is to say, at the representation of an action. The subject is the accomplishment of this unique action. There is a conspiracy against Augustus in Rome; I wish to know what is going to happen to Augustus and to the plotters. If the poet makes the action last fifteen days, he ought to give me an account of what happens during those fifteen days, for I am there to be informed about what is going on, and nothing ought to happen that is useless. However, if he puts the events of fifteen days in front of my eyes, there would be at least fifteen different actions, however little each might be. The play no longer would have to proceed rapidly only to the completion of the conspiracy; it is now a long story which will no longer be interesting because it will no longer be vivid, because all events will not be leading toward the moment of decision, which is the sole moment that I await. I have not come to the play to hear the history of a hero but to see a single event in his life. Furthermore, the spectator spends only three hours at the play; it is then not necessary that the action cover more than three hours. *Cinna* [9] *Andromaque*,[10] *Bajazet*,[11] *Oedipe*,

[6] Charles Le Brun (1619–1690) was a noted French painter.
[7] Étienne Jodelle (1532–1573) was an early French playwright; his best known play was *Cléopâtre captive* (1552).
[8] Alexandre Hardy (1560–1631) is often considered the originator of classical drama in France.   [9] Corneille, *Cinna* (1639).
[10] Racine. *Andromaque* (1668).   [11] Racine, *Bajazet* (1672).

whether it be the *Oedipe* of the great Corneille or of M. de la Motte, or even of my own, if I dare to speak of it, do not cover a longer time. If some other plays demand more time, it is a license which is pardonable only in favor of the beauties of the work; and the greater this license, the more the play is faulty.

We often extend the Unity of Time up to twenty-four hours and the Unity of Place to the area of a whole palace. More severity will sometimes render several good subjects impracticable, and too much indulgence would open the profession to too much abuse. For if it were once established that a theatrical action could occupy the space of two days, soon some author would use up two weeks and another two years; and if the place of an action were not reduced to a limited space, we would in a short time see plays like the old *Julius Caesar* of the English, in which Cassius and Brutus are at Rome in the first act and in Thessaly in the fifth.

The observance of these Rules not only helps to avoid faults but also paves the way to real beauties, just as the rules of fine architecture, exactly followed, necessarily bring into being a building that is pleasing to the view. It can be seen that with the Unities of Time, Action, and Place, it is difficult for a play not to be simple: that is the merit of all of Racine's plays and what Aristotle demanded. M. de la Motte, in defending a tragedy of his own composition, prefers a multiplicity of events to this noble simplicity. He considers his belief authorized by the scant esteem paid to *Bérénice* [12] and the considerable esteem still paid to *Le Cid*.[13] But *Bérénice* is at fault only because it is an elegy rather than a simple tragedy; and *Le Cid*, whose action is truly tragic, does not owe its success to the multiplicity of events, but it pleases in spite of this multiplicity, as it touches in spite of the Infanta and not because of the Infanta.

M. de la Motte believes that an author can put himself above all these Rules in maintaining a Unity of Interest, which he claims to have invented and which he calls a paradox; but this Unity of Interest does not seem to me to be anything but Unity of Action. "If several actors," he says, "are differently interested in the same event, and if they are all worthy that I enter into their passions, there is then Unity of Action and not Unity of Interest."

After having taken the liberty of disputing with M. de la Motte on this small question, I have re-read the great Corneille on the Three

[12] Racine, *Bérénice* (1670).   [13] Corneille, *Le Cid* (1636).

Unities; it is more profitable to consult this great master than me. Here is how he expresses himself: "I believe, as I have already said, that the Unity of Action consists in the Unity of Intrigue and in the Unity of Peril." Let the reader read this passage in Corneille and he will quickly decide between M. de la Motte and me; and if the authority of this great man is not strong enough, have I not a still more convincing reason: It is experience. Whoever reads our best French tragedies will always find the principal characters diversely interested, but these different interests pertain to the interest of the principal character, and then there is Unity of Action. If, on the contrary, all these different interests do not pertain to the principal character, if they are not lined up to end in a common center, the interest is double, and what is called action in the theatre is double also. Let us confine ourselves then, like the great Corneille, to the Three Unities, within which the other Rules—that is to say the other beauties—are contained.

M. de la Motte calls them the principles of fantasy, and pretends that we can do without them in our tragedies because they are neglected in our operas; which is, it seems to me, to wish to reform a regular government on the example of an anarchy.

The opera is a spectacle as bizarre as magnificent, where the eyes and ears are more satisfied than the mind, where the subordination of everything to the music makes necessary the most ridiculous faults, where it is necessary to sing little arias during the destruction of a city and dance around a tomb, where there are to be seen the palaces of Pluto and of the sun, gods, demons, magicians, wonders, monsters, palaces formed and destroyed in the blink of an eye. These extravagances can be tolerated, or even loved, because it is all in fairyland, and, provided that there is enough spectacle, splendid dances, beautiful music, and some interesting scenes, the spectator is content. It would be as ridiculous to demand the Unities of Action, Place, and Time in *Alceste* [14] as to wish to introduce dances and demons into *Cinna* and *Rodogune*.[15]

However, although operas have dispensed with these three Rules, the best are still those that have violated them the least. They are even observed in several, if I do not deceive myself, as much as they

[14] A classical ballet (1674), libretto by Quinault, music by Lully.
[15] *Cinna* (1639) and *Rodogune* (1646) were tragedies by Corneille.

are necessary and natural and as much as they serve to interest the spectator. How then can M. de la Motte reproach our nation with the fickleness of condemning in one kind of spectacle what we approve in another? There is no one who could not respond to M. de la Motte, "I reasonably demand much more perfection from a tragedy than from an opera, since in a tragedy my attention is not shared, since my pleasure depends neither upon a sarabande nor on a two-step, and since it is my mind alone that must be pleased. It is an object of admiration for me that a man can arrange and dispose a single action in a single place and in a single day so that my mind can conceive it without fatigue and my heart can become interested by degrees. And the more I understand how difficult is this simplicity, the more it charms me, and if I wish further to add reason to my pleasure, I find that I am of the opinion of M. Despréaux, who says (*Art poétique*, III, 45):

> *Qu'en un lieu, qu'en un jour, un seul fait accompli*
> *Tienne jusqu'à la fin le théâtre rempli.*

"I have on my side," he could say, "the authority of the great Corneille. I have more; I have his example and the pleasure that his works give me in proportion as they more or less obey this rule."

M. de la Motte is not content with wishing to deprive the theatre of its principal Rules; he wishes also to take away its poetry and give us tragedies in prose.

This ingenious and fecund author, who has made only verses in his whole life or works of prose on the occasion of his verses, writes against his own art and treats it with the same scorn that he treated Homer, whom however he has translated. Never did Virgil or Tasso or M. Despréaux or M. Racine or M. Pope think of writing against the harmony of verse, nor M. de Lully against music, nor M. Newton against mathematics. There are men who have at times had the weakness to believe themselves superior to their profession, which is the sure way of being below it, but we have not yet seen any of these who would wish to revile it. There are too many people who are scornful of poetry only because they do not understand it. Paris is full of people of good sense born with organs insensible to all harmony, for whom music is only noise and to whom poetry seems to be only an ingenious folly. If these people learn that a man of merit who has written five or six volumes of verse is of their opinion, will they not believe themselves in the right in regarding all other poets as fools, and that one poet as the sole one to whom reason has returned? Thus it is necessary to make answer to him for the honor of the art and, I dare say, for the honor of a country which is indebted for part of its glory among strangers to the perfection of this same art.

M. de la Motte argues that rhyme is a barbarous usage that was invented a short time ago.

However, all the peoples of the earth, except the ancient Romans and Greeks, have rhymed and still rhyme. The repetition of the same sounds is so natural to man that rhyme can be found established among savages, just as it is at Rome, Paris, London, and Madrid. There is in Montaigne a rhymed American song translated into French; to be found in one of the *Spectators* of M. Addison is a translation of a rhymed Laplander ode which is full of sentiment.

The Greeks, *quibus dedit ore rotondo Musa loqui,** born under a happier sky and favored by a nature of more delicate organs than those of other countries, formed a language all of the syllables of which could, by their length or brevity, express the slow or impetuous emotions of the mind. From this variety of syllables and intonations there resulted in the verse, and even in their prose, a harmony that the ancient Italians felt and imitated and that no other nation has been able to grasp since then. But poetry, whether it be rhymed or cadenced syllables, against which M. de la Motte revolts, has been and always will be cultivated by all peoples.

Before Herodotus, even history was written in verse by the Greeks, who had borrowed this custom from the ancient Egyptians, the wisest, most civilized and learned people of the earth. This custom was entirely reasonable, for the end of history was to conserve for posterity the memory of the small number of great men who could be useful to it as examples. It had not yet occurred to them to write the history of a convent or of a small town in several folio volumes; they wrote about only what was worthy of the writing, that which men should learn by heart. For that reason they used verse as an aid to memory. It is for that reason that the first philosophers, legislators, founders of religions, and historians were all poets.

It seems that poetry ought to lack generally, in such subjects,

* Graiis ingenium, Graiis dedit ore rotundo Musa loqui. Hor. *Art. poet.*, 323-24.

either precision or harmony; but since Virgil and Horace combined
these two great values that seem so incompatible, since MM. Despréaux
and Racine have written like Virgil and Horace, can a man who has
read them and who knows that they have been translated into almost
all of the languages of Europe revile at this point a talent that has
brought so much honor to himself? I will place our Despréauxs and
our Racines by the side of Virgil in skill of versification; because if
the author of the Æneid had been born in Paris, he would have rhymed
like them; and if these two Frenchmen had lived at the time of Augustus, they would have followed the usage of Virgil in Latin verse measures. When, then, M. de la Motte calls versification "a mechanical
and ridiculous labor," he is charging with the ridiculous not only
our great poets but also all those of antiquity.

Virgil and Horace submitted themselves to a task that was as
mechanical as that of our authors: a happy arrangement of spondees
and dactyls was as painful as our rhymes and hemistiches. The work
must indeed have been laborious, since the Æneid after twelve years
was still not in a state of perfection.

M. de la Motte pretends that at least a scene of tragedy put into
prose loses none of its grace or force. To prove his point, he turns
into prose the first scene of Mithridate,[16] and no one can read it. He
does not realise that the great merit of verses is that they may be as
correct as prose. It is the surmounting of this extreme difficulty that
charms lovers of poetry. If you reduce verse to prose, there is no longer
any merit or pleasure.

"But," says he, "our neighbors do not rhyme in their tragedies."
That is true, but their plays are in verse, because harmony is necessary to all peoples of the earth. There is no further question then
than to ask whether our verse ought to be rhymed or not. MM. Corneille and Racine employed rhyme; let us be afraid that if we want
to open a new road it is rather because of inability to walk in that
of these great men than because of a desire for novelty. The Italians
and the English can do without rhymes because their languages
allow inversions and their poetry a thousand liberties that we lack.
Each language has its own genius, determined by the nature of the
construction of its phrases, by the frequency of its vowels or con-
sonants, its inversions, its auxiliary words, etc. The genius of our

16 Racine, Mithradate (1673).

language is clarity and elegance. We do not permit any license in our poetry, which ought to move, like our prose, in the precise order of our ideas. Thus we have a need for the return of the same sounds so that our poetry may not be confounded with prose. . . .

M. de la Motte compares our poets—that is to say, our Corneilles, our Racines and our Despréauxs—to makers of acrostics, and to the charlatan who makes grains of millet pass through the eye of a needle; he adds that all these puerilities have no merit other than the surmounted difficulty. I avow that this is more or less the case with bad verses; they differ from bad prose only in their rhyme; rhyme alone does not show the worth of a poet or provide the pleasure of the reader. It is not only spondees and dactyls that please in Homer and Virgil; it is the charming harmony to which this measure gives birth that enchants the whole world. Whoever constrains himself to conquer a difficulty for the sole value of conquering the difficulty is a fool; but whoever draws from the essence of these same difficulties beauties that please everybody is a very wise and unique man. It is very difficult to make beautiful pictures, fine statues, good music, and good verse; also the names of the superior beings who conquer these obstacles will endure longer perhaps than the kingdoms in which they have been born.

I could take further liberty of disputing with M. de la Motte on some other points, but that would make it appear that I am attacking him personally and give a suspicion of a malignity that is as alien to me as to his sentiments. I would much rather profit from the judicious and fine reflections that he has treated in his book than to engage myself in refuting some of them that seem to me less true than the others. It is enough for me to have tried to defend an art that I love, and that he ought to have defended himself. . . .

Discourse on Tragedy

[1731; excerpts]

To Lord Bolingbroke

. . . BEING UNABLE, milord, to hazard unrhymed verses on the French stage, such as are to be found in Italy and England, I would at least have wished to transport to our stage some of the beauties of yours. It is true, and I acknowledge it, that the English stage is very defective. I have heard from your own mouth that you do not have a good tragedy; but in recompense you have some admirable scenes in plays that are monstrous. Up to the present almost all of the tragic poets of your nation have lacked that purity, the regular conduct, the propriety of action and style, the elegance, and all the artistic finesse which have established the reputation of the French stage from the time of Corneille. But your irregular plays have great worth. It is that of action.

In France we have some esteemed tragedies that are more conversations than they are representations of an action. An Italian author once wrote me in a letter on the stage, "A critic of our *Pastor Fido* says that this composition is a collection of admirable madrigals; I think it can be said of French tragedy that it is also a collection of beautiful elegies and pompous epithalamia." I am much afraid that this Italian was only too right. Our excessive delicacy sometimes forces us to put into narration what we would like to expose on the stage. We are afraid to risk on the stage new spectacles before a nation that is accustomed to ridicule anything that is not traditional.

The kind of theatre in which our plays are performed and the abuses that have slipped in there are also a cause of the dryness with which we are reproached in some of our plays. The benches on the stage allotted to spectators shrink the acting space and make all action practically impossible. It is for this reason that the decorations so much recommended by the Ancients are rarely suitable to our plays. It especially prevents the movement of actors from one room to another before the eyes of the spectators, as the Greeks and Romans wisely managed it, to conserve at the same time verisimilitude and the Unity of Place.

For example, how could we dare to have appear on our stage the shade of Pompey or the ghost of Brutus in the midst of so many young people who never consider the most serious subjects as anything but an opportunity to make a clever remark. How is it possible to bring into the midst of them on the stage the body of Marcus before his father, Cato, who speaks, "Happy young man, you have died for your country. O my friends, let me count these glorious wounds. Who would not wish to die for his country? Why are we given only one life to sacrifice for her? My friends, do not bewail my loss; do not mourn for my son. Weep for Rome; the mistress of the world is no more. O liberty! O my country! O virtue! etc." [17] The late M. Addison was not afraid to put that scene on the stage in London, and it was played in that way, translated into Italian, in more than one city of Italy. But if we hazarded a scene like that in Paris, cannot you hear the pit jeering and see the women turning their heads?

You cannot imagine to what degree this delicacy of ours is carried. The author of our tragedy of *Manlius* took his subject from the English piece of M. Otway entitled *Venice Preserved*. The subject is taken from the history of the conspiracy of the Marquis of Bedmar written by the Abbé de Saint-Réal; permit me to say in passing that this piece of historical writing, equal perhaps to Sallust, is much superior to Otway's play and to our *Manlius*. First, you will notice the prejudice that forced the French author to disguise a known story by the use of Roman names, which the English version has treated naturally under the real names. On the stage at London no one found it ridiculous that a Spanish ambassador should be called Bedamar and that the conspirators should have the names of Jaffeir, Jacque-Pierre, and Eliot; that alone in France would have made the play fail.

But you see that Otway is not afraid of bringing together all the conspirators. Renault hears their oaths, assigns to each his post, determines the hour of the slaughter, and casts from time to time disturbed and suspicious glances at Jaffeir, whom he distrusts. Before them all he speaks this pathetic speech, translated word for word from the Abbé de Saint-Réal;

> Never did so profound repose forerun
> Calamity so great! Nay, our good fortune
> Has blinded the most piercing of mankind,
> Strengthened the fearfullest, charmed the most suspectful,
> Confounded the most subtle; for we live,
> We live, my friends, and quickly shall our life
> Prove fatal to these tyrants. etc.[18]

What has the French author done? He was afraid to hazard so many actors on the stage; he had to content himself with having Renault, under the name of Rutile, describe a small part of this same speech which he had just obtained, he said, from the conspirators. Do you not

[17] Loosely paraphrased from Addison's *Cato* (1713) IV, iv.
[18] Otway, *Venice Preserved* (1682) III, ii.

feel from this single example the superiority of the English version of this scene to the French, however monstrous otherwise the play of Otway may have been?

With what pleasure did I see in London your tragedy of *Julius Caesar*, which after a hundred and fifty years still gives delight to your nation. I assuredly do not pretend to approve the barbarous irregularities with which it is filled; the surprising thing is that there are not more of them in a work composed in a century of ignorance by a man who did not even know Latin and who had no master but his own genius. But in the midst of so many gross faults, with what pleasure did I not see Brutus, holding still a dagger stained with the blood of Caesar, assemble the Roman people and speak to them thus from the height of the rostrum: "Romans, countrymen, lovers . . ."

After this scene, Anthony comes to move with pity these same Romans into whom Brutus had breathed his rigor and his savageness. Anthony, by an artificial discourse, insensibly quiets these excited spirits, and when he sees them softened, then he shows them the body of Caesar and, utilizing the most pathetic figures, excites them to riot and to vengeance. The French would probably not allow a chorus composed of artisans and plebian Romans to appear on their stages or the bloody corpse of Caesar to be exposed to the eyes of the people, or have the people excited to vengeance from the height of the rostrum. It is for custom, the queen of this world, to change the taste of nations and to convert to pleasure the objects of our aversion.

The Greeks chanced spectacles that are not less revolting to us. Hippolytus, broken by his fall, appears to count his wounds and utter his dolorous cries. Philoctetes falls into his fit of agony; black blood runs from his wound. Oedipus, covered with blood which still drips from the remnants of his eyes which he has just snatched out, complains of gods and men. One can hear the cries of Clytemnestra as her own son kills her, and Electra cries on the stage, "Strike! Do not spare her; she did not spare our father!" Prometheus is attached to a rock with nails driven through his stomach and arms. The Furies respond to the bloody shade of Clytemnestra with shrieks without any articulation. In a word, many Greek tragedies are filled with a terror that is carried to excess.

I know indeed that the Greek tragic poets, otherwise superior to the English, erred often in mistaking horror for terror and the disgusting and the unbelievable for the tragic and the marvelous. The art was in its infancy at the time of Æschylus, as at London in the time of Shakespeare; but among the great faults of the Greek poets and even of ours there are to be found singular beauties and a true pathos; and if some Frenchmen who know the tragedies and manners of other countries only in translation and by hearsay should condemn them with no reservations, they are, it seems to me, like the blind men who might assure you that a rose cannot have vivid colors, because by groping they have counted the thorns. But if you and the Greeks go beyond the limits of decorum and if the English especially present frightful spectacles while wishing to present the terrible, we Frenchmen, as scrupulous as you are bold, hold ourselves in too tightly for fear of losing ourselves, and sometimes we do not reach the tragic for fear of going beyond the limits of it.

I am far from proposing that the stage become a slaughterhouse as it is in Shakespeare and in his successors, who, not having his genius, imitated only his faults, but I dare to believe that there are some situations that appear merely disgusting and horrible to the French and that, well-managed, represented with art, and especially softened by the charm of beautiful verse, could give us a sort of pleasure which we could not doubt.

> Il n'est point de serpent, ni de monstre odieux
> Qui, par l'art imité, ne puisse plaire aux yeux.
> Boileau, *Art. Poet.*, III, 1–2.

At least, will someone tell me why our heroes and heroines of the stage are permited to kill themselves but are not allowed to kill anyone else? Would the stage be any less bloodied by the death of Atalide,[19] who stabs herself for her lover, than it would be by the murder of Caesar; and if the sight of the son of Cato who appears dead before the eyes of his father is the occasion of an admirable speech from that old Roman, if this play has been applauded in England and Italy by those who are the firmest partisans of French decorum, if the most delicate women have not been shocked by it, why cannot the French accustom themselves to it? Is not Nature the same in all men?

All these laws—of not bloodying the stage, of not making more than

[19] A character in Racine's *Bajazet* (1672).

three actors speak, etc.—are laws in regard to which we could make some exceptions, as the Greeks did. For these there are no Rules of decorum, always a little arbitrary as they are, as with the fundamental Rules of the stage, the Three Unities. There is weakness and sterility in stretching an action beyond the proper space of time and place. Ask anyone who has inserted too many events into a play the reason for this fault, and, if he is of good faith, he will tell you that he did not have enough genius to fill his play with a single action; and if he takes two days and two cities for his action, you may believe that it is for the reason that he has not had enough skill to condense it into the space of three hours and within the precincts of a palace as probability demands. The case is different with the one who dares to bring a horrible spectacle onto the stage: he will not violate probability; and this audacity, far from implying weakness in the author, will require on the contrary a great genius to catch in his verse the true grandeur in an action which without a sublime style would be only atrocious and disgusting.

Our great Corneille once tried that in *Rodogune*. He brought on the stage a mother who, in the presence of the court and of an ambassador, wished to kill her son and her daughter-in-law after having killed her other son with her own hand. She presented them with the poisoned cup and, when they refused and became suspicious, she drank it herself and died of the poison that she had destined for them. Scenes as terrible as this must not be used frequently, and it is not for everyone to dare to affect them. These novelties require great circumspection and masterly execution. The English themselves avow, for example, that Shakespeare has been the only one among them who has been able to evoke ghosts and make them talk successfully:

> Within that circle none durst move but he.

The more a theatrical action is majestic or frightful, the more it becomes insipid if it is often repeated, somewhat like the details of battles which, in themselves being very terrible, become cold and tiresome from frequent repetition in history books. The only play in which M. Racine used spectacle was his masterpiece *Athalie*. In that play one could see a child on the throne, his nurse and priests around him, a queen who commanded his soldiers to kill him, and

Levite armies that hastened to defend him. This whole action is pathetic, but if the style were not pathetic also, it would be only puerile.

The more one wishes to stun the eyes of the spectator with brilliant pomp, the more necessary it becomes to say great things; otherwise, one will be a mere decorator and not a tragic poet. Nearly thirty years ago the tragedy of *Montezume* was presented at Paris; the scene opened with a new spectacle; it was a palace decorated in magnificent and barbaric taste. Montezume appeared in strange dress; in the background were slaves armed with arrows; around him were eight grandees of his court prostrated with their faces against the earth. Montezume opened the play by saying to them:

> *Levez-vous; votre roi vous permet aujourd'hui*
> *Et de l'envisager, et de parler à lui.**

That spectacle was charming, but that was the only thing that was good in that tragedy. . . .

The English by relying more on action than we do speak more to the eyes; the French rely more on elegance, on harmony, and on the charm of verse. It is certain that it is more difficult to write well than it is to put assassinations, racks, gallows, magicians, and ghosts on the stage. Thus, the tragedy of *Cato,* which has brought so much honor to M. Addison, your successor in the ministry, the only tragedy well-written from beginning to end in your kingdom, owes its reputation solely to its beautiful poetry: that is to say, to thoughts that are strong and true and expressed in harmonious verse. Beauties of detail are what sustain works in verse and make them last for posterity. Art is often the singular way of saying common things. It is often a matter of embellishing by diction what everyone thinks and feels that makes a poet great. There are neither far-fetched sentiments nor romantic adventures in the fourth book of Virgil. It is all natural and a worthy effort of the human spirit. Racine is superior to others who have said the same things as he only in that he has said them better. Corneille is truly great only when he expresses himself as well as he thinks. Let us remember this precept of Despréaux (*Art poét.,* III, 157–158):

> *Et que tout ce qu'il dit, facile à retenir,*
> *De son ouvrage en nous laisse un long souvenir.†*

* These lines are from the tragedy of *Montezume* by Ferrier, played in 1702. "Arise, your king permits you today to look at him and talk to him."

† And let all that he says be easy to retain and leave a long memory of his work in us.

That is what so many dramatic works that the art of an actor and the figure and voice of an actress have made succeed in our theaters do not have. How many badly written plays have had longer runs than *Cinna* and *Britannicus*.[20] But not even two lines from these weak poems are remembered while everyone knows a part of *Britannicus* and *Cinna* by heart. In vain did the *Regulus*[21] of Pradon make the spectators shed tears over some touching situations. That work and all those like it are scorned even while their authors are applauding themselves in their prefaces. . . .

[20] Racine, *Britannicus* (1669).   [21] Nicolas Pradon, *Regulus* (1688).

Samuel Richardson
1689-1761

O F THIS PRINTER who became a famous figure in European literature of the eighteenth century and who is often called the "Father of the novel" little needs to be said here, except that he did not write plays. In the eighteenth century, the literary forms that were given most consideration by critics were tragedy and epic. It is curious to note that of the two men most responsible for originating the novel form, Fielding made his novels conform to the structures and principles of the epic and Richardson modeled his on the principles of tragedy. Richardson's novels shared many features with domestic tragedy. The Postscript to *Clarissa* (1748) indicates that Richardson can hardly be called a thoroughgoing sentimentalist in theory. It is strange that Fielding, who was sufficiently sickened by the prurient sentimentality of *Pamela* to begin his *Joseph Andrews* as a parody of it, was himself the more consistent sentimentalist of the two.

Although in his Postscript Richardson is making an apology for the ending of his novel, the application to plays is made, and the innovations to be found in Richardson's novels were quickly and frequently imitated by playwrights throughout Europe.

Clarissa

[1748; excerpts]

POSTSCRIPT

T HE FOREGOING work having been published at three different periods of time, the author, in the course of its publication, was favored with many anonymous letters, in which the writers differently expressed their wishes with regard to the apprehended catastrophe. Most of those directed to him by the gentler sex turned in favor of what they called a *fortunate ending*. Some of the fair writers, enamored, as they declared, with the character of the heroine, were warmly solicitous to have her made happy; and others likewise of their mind insisted that poetical justice required that it should be so. And when, says one ingenious lady, whose undoubted motive was good-nature and humanity, it must be concluded that it is in an author's power to make his piece end as he pleases, why should he not give pleasure rather than pain to the reader whom he has interested in favor of his principal characters? Others, and some gentlemen, declared against tragedies in general and in favor of comedies almost in the words of Lovelace, who was supported in his taste by all the women at Mrs. Sinclair's and by Sinclair herself. "I have too much feeling," said he.* "There is enough in the world to make our hearts sad without carrying grief into our diversions and making the distresses of others our own."

And how was this happy ending to be brought about? Why, by this very easy and trite expedient; to wit, by reforming Lovelace and marrying him to Clarissa—not, however, abating her one of her trials nor any of her sufferings for the sake of the sport her distresses would give to the *tender-hearted* reader as she went along, the last outrage excepted: that, indeed, partly in compliment to Lovelace himself and partly for delicacy-sake, they were willing to spare her. But whatever were the fate of his work, the author was resolved to take a different method. He always thought that sudden conversions, such especially as were left to the candor of the reader to suppose and make out, had neither art, nor nature, nor even probability in them; and that they were, moreover, of very bad example. To have a Lovelace for a series of years glory in his wickedness and think that he had nothing to do but as an act of grace and favor to hold out his hand to receive that of the best of women whenever he pleased and to have it thought that marriage would be a sufficient amends for all his enormities to others as well as to her—he could not bear that. Nor is reformation, as he has shown in another piece, to be secured by a fine face, by a passion that has sense for its object, nor by the goodness of a wife's heart, nor even example, if the heart of the husband be not graciously touched by the divine finger.

It will be seen by this time that the author had a great end in view. He has lived to see scepticism and infidelity openly avowed and even endeavored to be propagated from the press, the great doctrines of

* Volume III, Letter XX.

the Gospel brought into question, those of self-denial and mortification blotted out of the catalogue of Christian virtues, and a taste even to wantonness for outdoor pleasure and luxury to the general exclusion of domestic as well as public virtue industriously promoted among all ranks and degrees of people. In this general depravity, when even the pulpit has lost great part of its weight and the clergy are considered as a body of interested men, the author thought he should be able to answer it to his own heart, be the success what it would, if he threw in his mite towards introducing a reformation so much wanted; and he imagined that if in an age given up to diversion and entertainment he could steal in, as may be said, and investigate the great doctrines of Christianity under the fashionable guise of an amusement, he should be most likely to serve his purpose, remembering that of the poet:

> A verse may find him who a sermon flies,
> And turn delight into a sacrifice.

He was resolved, therefore, to attempt something that never yet had been done. He considered that the tragic poets have as seldom made their heroes true objects of pity as the comic theirs laudable ones of imitation, and still more rarely have they made them in their deaths look forward to a future hope. And thus when they die they seem totally to perish. Death in such instances must appear terrible. It must be considered as the greatest evil. But why is death set in such shocking lights when it is the universal lot?

He has, indeed, thought fit to paint the death of the wicked as terrible as he could paint it. But he has endeavored to draw that of the good in such an amiable manner that the very Balaams of the world should not forbear to wish that their latter end might be like that of the heroine. And after all, what is the poetical justice so much contended for by some, as the generality of writers have managed it, but another sort of dispensation than that with which God by revelation teaches us. He has thought fit to exercise mankind, whom placing here only in a state of probation, He hath so intermingled good and evil as to necessitate us to look forward for a more equal dispensation of both.

The author of the History (or rather, Dramatic Narrative) of Clarissa is therefore well justified by the Christian system in deferring to extricate suffering virtue to the time in which it will meet with the completion of its reward.

[There follows a long passage of quotations from the *Spectator* No. 40, *Spectator* No. 548, René Rapin's *Reflections on Aristotle's Poetics*, from a contemporary poem, and from the *Psalms*, to support Richardson's position on "poetical justice."]

The more pains have been taken to obviate the objections arising from the notion of poetical justice as the doctrine built upon it had obtained general credence among us, and as it must be confessed to have the appearance of humanity and good nature for its supports. And yet the writer of the *History of Clarissa* is humbly of opinion that he might have been excused referring to them for the vindication of his catastrophe even by those who are advocates for the contrary opinion, since the notion of poetical justice, founded on the modern Rules, has hardly ever been more strictly observed in works of this nature than in the present performance.

For is not Mr. Lovelace, who could persevere in his villainous views against the strongest and most frequent convictions and remorses that ever were sent to awaken and reclaim a wicked man—is not this great, this willful transgressor condignly punished, and his punishment brought on through the intelligence of the very Joseph Leman whom he had corrupted and by means of the very woman whom he had debauched, is not Mr. Belton, who has an uncle's hastened death to answer for, are not the whole Harlowe family—is not the vile Tomlinson, are not the infamous Sinclair and her wretched partners, and even the wicked servants who with their eyes open contributed their parts to the carrying on of the vile schemes of their respective principals—are they not all likewise exemplarily punished?

On the other hand, is not Miss Howe for her noble friendship to the exalted lady in her calamities, is not Mr. Hickman for his unexceptionable morals and integrity of life, is not the repentant and not ungenerous Belford, is not the worthy Norton—made signally happy?

And who that are in earnest in their profession of Christianity but will rather envy than regret the triumphant death of Clarissa, whose piety from her early childhood, whose humility, whose forgiving spirit, whose meekness and resignation Heaven only could reward? . . .

Gotthold Ephraim Lessing

1729-1781

As THE FIRST German dramatist to receive widespread recognition from the rest of Europe, Lessing has had a considerable reputation for the past two centuries. In addition to his plays, he left a substantial body of criticism, much of it important because he was one of the group of German critics responsible for the shift of opinion in Europe that dethroned French drama from its dominant position of authority and substituted Shakespeare in its place.

Although the *Hamburg Dramaturgy* (1767) is usually considered Lessing's most mature work of dramatic criticism, a selection from the earlier *Correspondence with Nicolai and Moses Mendelssohn* is reprinted here because in this work Lessing more clearly shows his connections with the thought of his day. No small part of the excellence of the *Hamburg Dramaturgy* resides in its break with Neoclassic traditions, and the esteem in which it is held may depend in part upon the assumption that breaking with Neoclassic traditions is right. Actually the basic ideas expressed in the *Correspondence* are carried over into the *Hamburg Dramaturgy* but are only implied there. In a book that attempts to present typical eighteenth century thought, the *Correspondence* is a fitting choice. It is more clearly the product of a sentimentalist.

In 1755 Lessing had finished *Miss Sara Sampson*, a domestic tragedy that took Richardson's *Clarissa* as its model. From as far away as Germany, Lillo's work with domestic tragedy, the doctrines of Hutcheson, and the long prose "dramas" of Richardson seemed to be part of one movement. At the time Lessing was full of these sentimental ideas.

The *Correspondence* began with Lessing's criticism of Christoph Freidrich Nicolai's *Abhandlung vom Trauerspiele* and continued with the further arguments back and forth between Lessing, Nicolai, and Moses Mendelssohn, the latter a famous German philosopher of the eighteenth century then at the beginning of his career. Mendelssohn, it must be noted, in his stress on admiration, defended the ideology of heroic drama, even though he is usually credited with being an important forerunner of the Romantics.

Although the letters of the *Correspondence* may be found in editions of Lessing's *Works,* an orderly arrangement of the documents in the three-sided argument was made for the first time in an edition by Robert Petsch,

To Nicolai and Mendelssohn 329

Lessings Briefwechsel mit Mendelssohn und Nicolai über das Trauerspiel, Leipzig, 1910.

Correspondence with Nicolai and Mendelssohn

[1756–1757; excerpts]

LESSING TO NICOLAI, NOVEMBER 13, 1756

... It may be that we are indebted to the principle that tragedy should improve us for many a miserable but well-intentioned play; it *may* be, I say, for your observations sound a little too witty for me to be assured that they are true. However, this I know to be true, that no principle, if it is widely disseminated, can help to beget better tragedies than this: tragedy should rouse passions.

Consider for a moment that the first principle may be just as true as the other; likewise, adequate reasons can be given to show why in practice the former must have the worse and the latter better consequences. But the former leads to bad results not because it is a false principle but because it is less immediate, because it merely provides us with the end and the latter with the means. If I have the means, I have the end also, but not the other way around. You ought, consequently, to have stronger reasons for disagreeing with Aristotle, and I wish you had given me a little more light on that subject; but you may attribute it to this omission that you must here read my ideas, since I believe that the teachings of the ancient philosopher ought to be understood and since I think that tragedy can improve us through its rousing of the passions.

The most important question then is: what passions does tragedy raise? In its characters it brings into play all possible passions that are in keeping with the dignity of the material. But are all these passions likewise aroused in the spectator? Does he become joyful? Enamored? Angry? Revengeful? I do not ask whether the poet brings him to the point where he is conscious of the presence of these passions in the actor, but whether he brings him to the point where he himself feels these passions, and is not merely sensible that someone else feels them?

To be brief, I find no other passion that tragedy raises in the spectator except pity. You will say: does it not arouse terror? does it not arouse admiration also? In my opinion, terror and admiration are not passions? What then? If in your description you have made clear what terror is, *eris mihi magnus Apollo;* and if you have made clear what admiration is, *Phyllida solus habeto.*[1]

Sit here on the judges' bench, Sirs Nicolai and Moses. I will tell you what my conception is of both.

Terror in tragedy is nothing more than the sudden surprising of pity, whether I do or do not know the object of my pity. For example, the priest at last speaks forth: "You, Oedipus, are the murderer of Laius"; I am terrified, for all at once I see the righteous Oedipus unfortunate, and immediately my pity is aroused. Another example: a ghost appears; I am terrified; the thought comes that he would not have appeared if he were not bringing misfortune to someone or other. The shadowy representation of this misfortune, whether I know or not whom it concerns, surprises my pity, and this surprised pity is called terror. Teach me a better idea if I am wrong.

Now for admiration! Admiration! In tragedy—to express myself in oracle-like fashion—admiration is pity that has become transmuted. The hero is unfortunate, but he is so far exalted above his misfortune and is so proud that the terrible part begins to disappear from my thoughts and I may more envy than pity him. The steps are thus these: terror, pity, admiration. The whole ladder, however, is to be called pity; and terror and admiration are only rungs, the beginning and the end of pity. For instance, I hear suddenly: "Cato is about to be killed by Caesar."[2] Terror! But then I become acquainted with the noble character of Cato and after that with his misfortune. Terror is dissipated into pity. But now I hear him say to himself, "The world that serves Caesar is no longer worthy of me." Admiration sets limits to pity. The poet uses terror to bring pity into being and admiration as relief from it. The road to pity would be too long for the spectator if he were not made attentive by the terror that precedes it;

---

[1] From Virgil's *Third Eclogue,* ll. 104–7. Two shepherds in the poem are asking riddles of one another. One tells the other that, if he answers, "You will be my great Apollo." The other answers with another riddle and remarks that if the first answers, "You will have Phyllis for yourself."

[2] The fame of Addison's *Cato* had spread throughout Europe and the reference is quite possibly to that version. However, the story of Cato appeared many times in neo-classical tragedy. Another likely reference is the version by Gottsched.

and pity would wear itself out if it were not transformed into admiration. Therefore, if it is true that the whole art of the tragic poet rests on the certain raising and maintaining of pity alone, I can merely add that the purpose of tragedy is this: it should extend our disposition to feel pity. It should not merely teach us to feel pity in connection with this or that unfortunate man, but it should increase our sympathies to the point that our feelings are aroused for the unfortunate of all times and all places and that we adopt their troubles for our own. And now I call to mind a statement, the truth of which Herr Moses may demonstrate for you if you choose to doubt it in opposition to your own feelings. The best man is the man who pities most, the one who is the most outstanding in all social virtues and most disposed to generosity. Therefore, whoever makes us sympathetic, makes us better and more virtuous; and tragedy, which does that, does this too, or it does that in order to do this. Apologize to Aristotle for this, or show me my error.[3]

I deal with comedy in a similar way. It should increase our disposition to perceive all kinds of ridiculous things easily. Whoever possesses this disposition will seek to avoid all kinds of foolishness in his behavior and will become in that way an excellent man of parts. And in this way is the usefulness of comedy likewise justified.

The usefulness of both, of tragedy as well as comedy, cannot be separated from pleasure, since a full half of pity and laughter is pleasure, and it is a great advantage for the dramatic poet that he can be neither profitable nor pleasant unless he is both.

I am now so taken by this whimsy of mine that if I were to write a dramatic poem I would prefix to it an extensive treatise on pity and laughter. I would compare both with one another. I would show that weeping depends as much on a mixture of sadness and joy as laughter on a mixture of pleasure and displeasure. I would show how laughter can be converted into tears, in which pleasure in joy on one side and on the other displeasure in sadness are allowed to develop together in a continual mixing. I would —— you would hardly believe all I would do.

I will now give you a few further proofs of how easily and happily one can derive from my principles not only the most famous known

---

[3] Lessing is clearly referring to the "catharsis" clause in Aristotle's definition of tragedy in Chapter 6 of the *Poetics*.

Rules but also a flock of new ones where formerly one has had to be content with mere vague feelings.

Tragedy should arouse as much pity as it can; consequently, all characters who are left in misfortunes must have good qualities; it will follow also that the best character will be the most unfortunate, and desert and misfortune will stand in integral relation together. That is, the poet must present no wretches bereft of all good qualities. The hero or the character of most virtue must not, like a god, survey his own virtues calm and undisturbed—a mistake of Canute's,[4] as you have noticed in another connection. Notice well, however, that I am not here speaking about the conclusion of a tragedy, since I consider it within the poet's province to decide whether he would rather have virtue shine out in a happy ending or be more interesting to us in an unhappy one. I ask only that the characters to whom I am most attached should be the most unfortunate during the duration of the play. The conclusion, however, is not part of this duration.

Terror, I have said, is suddenly surprised pity; I will say here a few words in addition in respect to the suddenly surprised and undeveloped pity: for what purpose should it be suddenly surprised if it is not developed? A tragedy full of terror without pity is lightning without thunder. So many flashes, so many thunderclaps if the flashes are not soon to become matters of no concern to us, so that we come to gape at them with only a childish pleasure. Admiration, as I have expressed myself, is pity that has become transmuted. Since, however, pity is the principal object, it must as rarely as possible be transmuted. The poet must not make his hero too much or too continuously an object of mere admiration; and Cato as a Stoic is to my way of thinking a bad tragic hero. The admired hero is the subject of an epic, the pitied hero the subject of a tragedy. Can you remember a single place in Homer, or Virgil, or Tasso, or Klopstock in which the hero arouses pity? or a single place in one of the tragedies of the Ancients in which the hero is more admired than pitied . . . ?

LESSING TO NICOLAI, NOVEMBER 29, 1756

PITY furnishes no more tears as soon as unpleasant emotions gain the ascendency. I distinguish three levels of pity, of which the middle

---

[4] Johann Elias Schlegel wrote *Canut, ein Trauerspiel*. It was first performed in 1746 and published in 1747.

one is the weeping pity, and perhaps I can distinguish the three kinds with the words sensibility, tears, oppression. Pathetic sensibility occurs when I consider neither the virtues nor the misfortunes of the object, clearly, but have only a vague idea of both. For instance, I am touched by the sight of a beggar. He brings tears to my eyes only when he reveals to me more his good qualities than his misfortune, and both of them bound up together, which is the real secret of arousing tears. Unless he makes me acquainted first with his good qualities and afterwards with his troubles, or first with the latter and afterwards with the former, the emotion, though stronger, will not become strong enough to bring forth tears. Suppose, for example, that I ask the beggar about his circumstances and he answers, "I have been out of a job for three years; I have a wife and children; they are either too sick or too small to provide for themselves; I myself have been up from my sickbed only for a few days." That is his misfortune! But who are you then? I ask further. "I am such and such, of whose ability in this or that public office you have probably heard; I clothed my position with the highest trust; I could return to it any day if I would prefer to be the creature of a Minister to an honest man." These are his virtues! No one can weep over a tale like that. But if the unfortunate will have my tears, he must put together both parts. He must say, "I have been removed from my position because I was too honest and made myself hated by the Minister on that account. I am hungry, and with me in hunger is my sick, loving wife, and also hungry are my children who were once promising but are now weakened by poverty, and we will certainly have to be hungry still longer. Yet I would rather be hungry than base; also my wife and children would rather be hungry and receive their bread direct from God, that is, from the hand of a generous man, than to know that their father and husband were wicked." (I do not know whether you understand me. You must fill out my explanation with your own reflections.) For such a tale I always have tears in readiness. Misfortune and desert are always here in balance. But allow the weight to increase in either one scale or the other and watch what happens. Let us first put an addition onto the side of the virtues. The poor man may continue, "But if I and my sick wife once more recover, things will be different. We shall live by the work of our hands; we are not ashamed to do anything; all ways of earning bread are fitting for an honest man—woodcutting or sitting at the helm of State. It is no matter how useful he *is* but how useful he *wants* to be." Now my weeping stops; admiration has stifled it. And in such a way that I hardly recognize that the admiration has had its origin in pity. Let us now make a trial with the other scale. The honest beggar has reason to believe that through some miracle or supernatural rarity his wants are to be taken care of through the generosity of man or straight from the hand of God. But his hopes are dashed with positive insults; on this account his distress is increased, and with it his perplexity. Finally he becomes mad and kills his wife, his children, and himself. Do you weep now? Here the painfulness stifles the tears but not the pity, as admiration did. . . .

LESSING TO MENDELSSOHN, DECEMBER 18, 1756

. . . IN MY FIRST letter to Herr Nicolai concerning this matter, I wrote: "In a tragedy admiration must be only the relief from pity." Have you correctly understood me? Herr Nicolai set up as his second category of tragedies that kind by which admiration is raised by means of terror and pity. In this category, then, admiration becomes the principal emotion; that is, the misfortune that befalls the hero should not so much move us as provide the hero with the opportunity to show off his extraordinary virtues, the intuitive perception of which arouses in us the pleasant feeling which you call admiration.

I say that such a tragedy becomes an epic poem in dialogue and not a tragedy. The admired hero, as I have expressed myself to Herr Nicolai, is material for an epic poem. You would indeed give me credit in that connection of believing that an epic poem (a poem full of admiration) can be a beautiful poem, but I cannot understand how you would attribute so much blame to me as to suppose that I would want to rob admiration of everything that is beautiful or pleasant. It is a pleasant feeling—good, but does it deserve for that reason the foremost place in a tragedy? Tragedy, says Aristotle (Chapter XIV), should not provide us with every kind of pleasure without distinction, but only that kind of pleasure which is characteristic of it.

Why do you want to confuse the art of poetry unnecessarily and let the boundaries of one kind overlap another? Just as in an epic poem admiration is the principal emotion and all other emotions, pity especially, are subordinated to it, so likewise in tragedy pity is the chief emotion, and all other emotions, admiration especially, ought to be subordinated to it; that is, ought to serve only as an aid in arousing pity. The epic poet allows the hero to be unfortunate in order to bring his virtues into the light. The writer of tragedy brings the virtues of his hero into the light in order to make his misfortune all the more painful to us.

A great pity cannot exist unless there are great virtues in the object of the pity, and there cannot be great virtues, well-expressed, without admiration. However, in tragedy these great virtues should never be unaccompanied by great misfortunes; they should at all times be closely associated with them; and should therefore arouse, not admiration alone, but admiration and pain; that is, pity. And that is what I mean to say. Admiration is thus not to be found in tragedy as a separate emotion, but only as a part of pity. And in this view I was also right to explain it not as a separate emotion but only in connection with its relation to pity.

And in this regard I still say it ought to be the relief from pity, namely there where it should be effective for itself alone. Since you bring up the example of Mithridates here for the second time,[5] I am forced to believe that you have understood my words to mean that I want this relief to help allay pity. However, I don't mean that at all, but just the opposite. Now listen to me!

We are not able to remain for a long time in a state of strong emotion; thus we cannot sustain for a long time even a strong pity; it loses its force. Even mediocre poets have noticed this and have saved the strong pity until the end. But I hate the French tragedies which do not cause my tears to be shed before the end of the fifth act. The true poet scatters pity throughout the whole of his tragedy. He introduces situations throughout in which he shows the virtues and the misfortunes of his hero in moving combination; that is, he arouses tears. Since, however, the whole play cannot be a continuous parade of such situations, he mixes situations with them in which the virtues of his character are alone portrayed, and in these places admiration prevails as admiration. What are these places except a kind of relief in which the spectator catches his breath for the new pity? The former pity should not be quenched in this part; that thought

5 Racine, *Mithridate* (1673).

has never come into my mind and would be completely contrary to my system.

. . .

. . . Read the 13th Chapter of Aristotle's *Poetics*. The philosopher says there that the hero of a tragedy must be a middle sort of character; he must neither be too villainous nor too virtuous. If he is too villainous and deserves his misfortunes on account of his crimes, we can feel no pity for him; and should he be entirely virtuous and still encounter misfortune, the pity is turned to horror and aversion.

I would like to know how Herr Nicolai would reconcile this rule with the qualities of his hero that arouse admiration—but that is not what I want to write about now.

I myself am against Aristotle here, who it seems to me founded his idea on a false explanation of pity. And if I am closer to the truth, I have to thank for it your better concept of the act of pitying. Is it true that the misfortune of an entirely virtuous man arouses horror and aversion? If it is true, horror and aversion must be the highest degree of pity, and of course they are not. The pity that would grow in precisely those circumstances in which virtue and misfortune grow would cease for me to be pleasant and would become all the more unpleasant the greater the virtue on one side and the misfortune on the other.

In the meanwhile it is, however, still true that there must be in the hero a certain *hamartia,* a certain flaw, through which he has brought his misfortune upon himself. But why that kind of *hamartia* that Aristotle described? Perhaps because without it he would be perfect and the misfortune of a perfect man would arouse abhorrence? Certainly not. I think I have found the only real reason. It is this: that without the flaw that leads him into misfortune his character and his misfortune would not comprise a unity, that the one would not be based in the other and we would consider the two of them as two plays. An example will make my meaning clear. Canute may be an example of perfect goodness. Then if he is to arouse pity, I must let him, because of his failure to govern his goodness with prudence, by overwhelming Ulfo with kindnesses, whom he should merely pardon, bring a great misfortune upon himself. Ulfo must take him prisoner and murder him. Pity in the highest degree! But suppose I do not let Canute perish because of his abused goodness but be struck by lightning suddenly or be crushed when his palace collapses on him. Horror and aversion without pity! Why? because there is not the least connection between his goodness and the lightning or the collapsing palace, between his virtue and his misfortune. These are two different things which cannot bring about a single common effect such as pity is, but each of them has its own effect. Another example! Think of the old cousin in *The London Merchant*.[6] When Barnwell chokes him, the spectator is horrified without being compassionate because the good character of the old man contains nothing that can provide a basis for this misfortune. But as soon as he is heard praying to God for his murderer and cousin, the horror is converted into a very rapturous pity, and entirely naturally because this generous act proceeds from his misfortune and has its foundation in it. . . .

. . . IN THE very beginning you assign the tragic passions, admiration and pity, to different provinces and want the one to lord it over the territory of the epic poem and the other over the stage. On this occasion you ask, "Why do we wish to confuse the different kinds of poetry needlessly and allow the boundaries of one kind to overlap upon the other?" Here you let a prejudice run away with you, a kind of behavior that I have often heard you yourself condemn. On what are these fancied lines of demarcation based? In observation of the works of Nature, it has been decided in the last century that they have not been divided by their mistress into special and separate classes. Why do we not want to let art be in this respect also an imitator of Nature? If word usage, the authority of the Ancients, the division of the arts into their special kinds, and a thousand other prejudices have allowed only such dramatic plays to be given the name of tragedy which particularly arouse pity, the philologist can content himself with this recipe. However, Reason speaks otherwise. It considers any great and worthy event as the subject matter of tragedy only if it is capable of imitation of an important action through a lively presentation. (See my enclosed ideas on aesthetic illusion.)

---

6 George Lillo, *George Barnwell; or, The London Merchant* (1731), a well-known English domestic tragedy.

Therefore, do not bar any single passion from the theatre. To the extent that the imitated passion can convince the perceiver of the excellence of the imitation, it deserves to be performed on the stage. Even hate and aversion can, in spite of Aristotle and his followers, be pleasing on the stage, because it is sufficient if the imitated passion can convince us that the imitation is like the original. . . .

Let us however come somewhat nearer together. I will concede to you that pity can more easily give us an intuitive illusion than admiration can. I mean that it is easier to convince us by means of an imitated pity that the imitation is similar to the original than it is to get the same kind of result through admiration. You must agree, however, that art reveals its full splendor when it tries to imitate the finest traits of Nature, to set before us a great soul in its brightest light, if it presents a hero who courageously stands upright under the weight of oppression, his head raised up to the skies, who undaunted hears the thunder crackling around his feet, and who pulls us close together with him in our anxiety for him. The way is hard, very hard, and only the great genius can hope to tread it with success. I grant it, but when has my Lessing worried about the roads on which ordinary souls ought to travel? . . .

Do not apologize for your expression, "Admiration may be relief from pity." Surely, the analysis of the virtues that adorn the hero, or, much more, the revelations of his character, can frequently fill out a secondary scene and provide a relief from pity. However, this is not admiration but esteem, a lesser degree of admiration, which sustains us a while; just as in comedy, so that we will not be laughing all the time, we introduce touching scenes. But where admiration is supposed to be the chief emotion, it must have something more than this kind of menial employment in a Cato, a Brutus,[7] a Grandison,[8] and—why should I not say it?—in a Theophanes.[9] It is in general the fate of all theatrical passions that they are scarcely recognizable any longer if they appear as attendants of other passions. Love, for instance, is a raging and terrible passion when it is given the major emphasis, as in *Hippolytus*. How childish and ridiculous

---

[7] Brutus was a common figure in neoclassical tragedy.

[8] The reference is to the chief character in Samuel Richardson's *Sir Charles Grandison*, a character considered by sentimentalists of the eighteenth century to be the example of perfect male virtue.

[9] A character in Lessing's *Der Freigeist* (1749).

it is, however, in a thousand French plays in which it fills up only a few secondary scenes. I will not pardon Polyeucte.[10] When you compare him with the fellow who is supposed to cast himself down from the tower, I think the jumper has lost the *tertium comparationis*. The hero must consider the moral good a distinctly greater treasure than the physical good, When pain, fetters, slavery, and death are opposed to a duty, he must not hesitate to hasten to meet all these evils in order to keep his innocence unspotted. This internal victory which his godlike soul wins over his body delights us and creates in us a feeling in which no sensuous delight accompanies the pleasure. The mere admiration of corporeal skill, which you allow to your wheelbarrow-pusher, is without emotion, is without that internal feeling and that warmth of the bowels (if I may so express myself) with which we admire the greatness of, for instance, an Orestes and Pylades. (In passing, I remember that these are probably the only characters of the Ancients who arouse a true admiration.) I am being silent about a certain situation in a Chinese tragedy which you used to admire. At the command of a tyrant an old man is terribly beaten by his friend—by that particular friend for whose benefit he will not reveal a certain secret. He looks back with half angry glances at that man who is carrying out the commands of the tyrant on his back. Now should he open his mouth and utter a single word he can free himself from the terrible pain. But no! He looks at his friend. He calls to mind his duty and the gruesome power which compels his friend to become his tormentor. His anger is converted to sadness. He groans and remains faithful to his duty. Here is magnanimity, here is constancy, here is inner struggle, and the most lordly victory ever won by mortals!

If Reason approves of the emulation that is created in us by means of admiration, you will attribute the effect not to the admiration but to the clear knowledge. I, however, have shown in the pages that accompany this that the intuitive perception must increase the quantity of the motive if the virtuous resolution is to achieve actuality, and in my opinion nothing increases this quantity so much as admiration.

If Herr Nicolai claims that poetry is not concerned with the improvement of morals, he is clearly wrong, and I show the opposite

[10] Polyeucte is the chief character, a Christian martyr, in Corneille's *Polyeucte* (1640).

in the pages that are enclosed. If he claims, however, that the improvement of morals cannot be the chief end of tragedy because the imitation can still be perfect, even if the underlying morality is not in full accord with Reason, then I think that the most zealous defender of poetry must agree with him. The aesthetic illusion really depends upon the temporary silencing of the higher mental powers, as I have made reasonably clear in my "Thoughts on Illusion." However, it is made clear from what I have said about moral sensibility that even the readiness to feel pity . . . does not in itself always have a good effect. Our moral sensibility without the assistance of judgment only renders our emotionality weaker and incites us to search for both true and apparent good with greater desire. Your ideas on physical dexterity and the admiration that it arouses please me uncommonly, and you shame me when you complain about your inability to express your thoughts correctly. How can I answer you here without paying you a return compliment.

Do not exalt admiration for physical dexterity at the expense of the soul! You are uncommonly mistaken if you believe that generosity in specific single cases excites in us merely a wish to act generously in similar cases. In my "Thoughts on the Control of the Affections" you may see how useful it may be to virtue if general abstract ideas were reduced to single cases. This reduction can take place through experience, through example, or even through fiction. Our symbolic understanding always becomes converted into a contemplative understanding; the force of the motive becomes animated, and its quantity becomes greater with the increase in quantity of the sensuous pleasure that opposes it. . . .

David Hume

1711-1776

Although it is an example of pure speculation and has little to do with actual dramatic criticism, Hume's "Of Tragedy" (1757) is an important document for an understanding of general dramatic theory of the period under review, particularly of that kind of speculation which Hume himself indicates in his essay: Du Bos and Fontenelle—to which group we should add Addison and, later, Burke and the Priestleys and Alisons of the end of the century. Hume's essay exhibits the empirical approach, the analysis of common experience, the collecting of illustrations and examples from instances of human behavior elsewhere in order to explain our reactions to drama.

Hume gives ample evidence in his letters and other writings that he was willing to be sentimentally responsive to a dramatic production. The encouragement and assistance that he gave to men of letters in his day is likely to be overshadowed by his reputation as one of England's greatest philosophers and its first modern historian.

"Of Tragedy" was first published in *Four Dissertations. 1. The Natural History of Religion. 2. Of the Passions. 3. Of Tragedy. 4. Of the Standard of Taste,* by David Hume, Esq., London, 1757. Hume had, however, been polishing these essays for several years before publication.

Of Tragedy

[1757]

It seems an unaccountable pleasure, which the spectators of a well-written tragedy receive from sorrow, terror, anxiety, and other passions, that are in themselves disagreeable and uneasy. The more they are touched and affected, the more are they delighted with the spectacle; and as soon as the uneasy passions cease to operate, the piece is at an end. One scene of full joy and contentment and security is the utmost that any composition of this kind can bear; and it is sure always to be the concluding one. If, in the texture of the piece, there be interwoven any scenes of satisfaction, they afford only faint gleams of pleasure, which are thrown in by way of variety, and in order to plunge the actors into deeper distress by means of that contrast and disappointment. The whole art of the poet is employed in rousing and supporting the compassion and indignation, the anxiety and resentment of his audience. They are pleased in proportion as they are afflicted and never are so happy as when they employ tears, sobs, and cries to give vent to their sorrow and relieve their heart, swollen with the tenderest sympathy and compassion.

The few critics who have had some tincture of philosophy have remarked this singular phenomenon and have endeavored to account for it.

L'Abbé Du Bos, in his reflections on poetry and painting, asserts that nothing is in general so disagreeable to the mind as the languid, listless state of indolence into which it falls upon the removal of all passion and occupation.[1] To get rid of this painful situation, it seeks every amusement and pursuit; business, gaming, shows, executions; whatever will rouse the passions and take its attention from itself. No matter what the passion is: let it be disagreeable, afflicting, melancholy, disordered; it is still better than that insipid languor which arises from perfect tranquillity and repose.

It is impossible not to admit this account as being, at least in part, satisfactory. You may observe, when there are several tables of gaming, that all the company run to those where the deepest play is, even though they find not there the best players. The view, or at least imagination, of high passions arising from great loss or gain affects the spectator by sympathy, gives him some touches of the same passions, and serves him for a momentary entertainment. It makes the time pass the easier with him and is some relief to that oppression under which men commonly labour when left entirely to their own thoughts and meditations.

We find that common liars always magnify, in their narrations, all kinds of danger, pain, distress, sickness, deaths, murders, and cruelties; as well as joy, beauty, mirth, and magnificence. It is an absurd secret which they have for pleasing their company, fixing their atten-

[1] See Du Bos, p. 253.

tion, and attaching them to such marvellous relations by the passions and emotions which they excite.

There is, however, a difficulty in applying to the present subject, in its full extent, this solution, however ingenious and satisfactory it may appear. It is certain that the same object of distress which pleases in a tragedy, were it really set before us, would give the most unfeigned uneasiness, though it be then the most effectual cure to languor and indolence. Monsieur Fontenelle seems to have been sensible of this difficulty and accordingly attempts another solution of the phenomenon, at least makes some addition to the theory above mentioned.*

"Pleasure and pain," says he, "which are two sentiments so different in themselves, differ not so much in their cause. From the instance of tickling, it appears that the movement of pleasure pushed a little too far becomes pain, and that the movement of pain a little moderated becomes pleasure. Hence it proceeds that there is such a thing as a sorrow soft and agreeable: it is a pain weakened and diminished. The heart likes naturally to be moved and affected. Melancholy objects suit it, and even disastrous and sorrowful, provided they are softened by some circumstance. It is certain that, on the theatre, the representation has almost the effect of reality; yet it has not altogether that effect. However we may be hurried away by the spectacle, whatever dominion the senses and imagination may usurp over the reason, there still lurks at the bottom a certain idea of falsehood in the whole of what we see. This idea, though weak and disguised, suffices to diminish the pain which we suffer from the misfortunes of those whom we love, and to reduce that affliction to such a pitch as converts it into a pleasure. We weep for the misfortune of a hero to whom we are attached. In the same instant we comfort ourselves by reflecting that it is nothing but a fiction. And it is precisely that mixture of sentiments, which composes an agreeable sorrow, and tears that delight us. But as that affliction which is caused by exterior and sensible objects is stronger than the consolation which arises from an internal reflection, they are the effects and symptoms of sorrow that ought to predominate in the composition."

This solution seems just and convincing, but perhaps it wants still

* *Refléxions sur la poétique,* [see p. 289].

some new addition in order to make it answer fully the phenomenon which we here examine. All the passions, excited by eloquence, are agreeable in the highest degree, as well as those which are moved by painting and the theatre. The epilogues of Cicero are, on this account chiefly, the delight of every reader of taste, and it is difficult to read some of them without the deepest sympathy and sorrow. His merit as an orator no doubt depends much on his success in this particular. When he had raised tears in his judges and all his audience, they were then the most highly delighted and expressed the greatest satisfaction with the pleader. The pathetic description of the butchery made by Verres of the Sicilian captains is a masterpiece of this kind. But I believe none will affirm that the being present at a melancholy scene of that nature would afford any entertainment. Neither is the sorrow here softened by fiction, for the audience were convinced of the reality of every circumstance. What is it then which in this case raises a pleasure from the bosom of uneasiness, so to speak, and a pleasure which still retains all the features and outward symptoms of distress and sorrow?

I answer: this extraordinary effect proceeds from that very eloquence with which the melancholy scene is represented. The genius required to paint objects in a lively manner, the art employed in collecting all the pathetic circumstances, the judgment displayed in disposing them: the exercise, I say, of these noble talents, together with the force of expression and beauty of oratorial numbers, diffuse the highest satisfaction on the audience and excite the most delightful movements. By this means, the uneasiness of the melancholy passions is not only overpowered and effaced by something stronger of an opposite kind, but the whole impulse of those passions is converted into pleasure and swells the delight which the eloquence raises in us. The same force of oratory, employed on an uninteresting subject, would not please half so much, or rather would appear altogether ridiculous; and the mind, being left in absolute calmness and indifference, would relish none of those beauties of imagination or expression which, if joined to passion, give it such exquisite entertainment. The impulse, or vehemence, arising from sorrow, compassion, indignation, receives a new direction from the sentiments of beauty. The latter, being the predominant emotion, seize the whole mind and convert the former into themselves, at least tincture them so strongly as totally to alter their nature. And the soul, being at the same time roused by passion and charmed by eloquence, feels on the whole a strong movement which is altogether delightful.

The same principle takes places in tragedy; with this addition, that tragedy is an imitation, and imitation is always of itself agreeable. This circumstance serves still further to smooth the motions of passion and convert the whole feeling into one uniform and strong enjoyment. Objects of the greatest terror and distress please in painting, and please more than most beautiful objects that appear calm and indifferent.*

The affection, rousing the mind, excites a large stock of spirit and vehemence, which is all transformed into pleasure by the force of the prevailing movement. It is thus the fiction of tragedy softens the passion, by an infusion of a new feeling, not merely by weakening or diminishing the sorrow. You may by degrees weaken a real sorrow till it totally disappears; yet in none of its gradations will it ever give pleasure, except, perhaps, by accident to a man sunk under lethargic indolence, whom it rouses from that languid state.

To confirm this theory, it will be sufficient to produce other instances where the subordinate movement is converted into the predominant and gives force to it, though of a different, and even sometimes though of a contrary nature. '

Novelty naturally rouses the mind and attracts our attention, and the movements which it causes are always converted into any passion belonging to the object and join their force to it. Whether an event excite joy or sorrow, pride or shame, anger or good-will, it is sure to produce a stronger affection when new or unusual. And though novelty of itself be agreeable, it fortifies the painful as well as agreeable passions.

Had you any intention to move a person extremely by the narration of any event, the best method of increasing its effect would be artfully to delay informing him of it and first to excite his curiosity and im-

---

* Painters make no scruple of representing distress and sorrow as well as any other passion, but they seem not to dwell so much on these melancholy affections as the poets, who, though they copy every emotion of the human breast, yet pass very quickly over the agreeable sentiments. A painter represents only one instant, and if that be passionate enough, it is sure to affect and delight the spectator. But nothing can furnish to the poet a variety of scenes and incidents and sentiments except distress, terror, or anxiety. Complete joy and satisfaction is attended with security and leaves no further room for action.

patience before you let him into the secret. This is the artifice practised by Iago in the famous scene of Shakespeare, and every spectator is sensible that Othello's jealousy acquires additional force from his preceding impatience and that the subordinate passion is here readily transformed into the predominant one.

Difficulties increase passions of every kind; and by rousing our attention and exciting our active powers, they produce an emotion which nourishes the prevailing affection.

Parents commonly love that child most whose sickly, infirm frame of body has occasioned them the greatest pains, trouble, and anxiety in rearing him. The agreeable sentiment of affection here acquires force from sentiments of uneasiness.

Nothing endears so much a friend as sorrow for his death. The pleasure of his company has not so powerful an influence.

Jealousy is a painful passion; yet without some share of it, the agreeable affection of love has difficulty to subsist in its full force and violence. Absence is also a great source of complaint among lovers and gives them the greatest uneasiness; yet nothing is more favorable to their mutual passion than short intervals of that kind. And if long intervals often prove fatal, it is only because through time men are accustomed to them and they cease to give uneasiness. Jealousy and absence in love compose the *dolce peccante* of the Italians, which they suppose so essential to all pleasure.

There is a fine observation of the elder Pliny which illustrates the principle here insisted on. "It is very remarkable," says he, "that the last works of celebrated artists, which they left imperfect, are always the most prized, such as the Iris of Aristides, the Tyndarides of Nicomachus, the Medea of Timomachus, and the Venus of Appelles. These are valued even above their finished productions. The broken lineaments of the piece and the half-formed idea of the painter are carefully studied; and our very grief for that curious hand, which had been stopped by death, is an additional increase to our pleasure." *

These instances (and many more might be collected) are sufficient to afford us some insight into the analogy of Nature and to show us that the pleasure which poets, orators, and musicians give us, by exciting grief, sorrow, indignation, compassion, is not so extraordinary or paradoxical as it may at first sight appear. The force of imagination,

* Book XXXV, Chap. 11.

the energy of expression, the power of numbers, the charms of imitation—all these are naturally, of themselves, delightful to the mind. And when the object presented lays hold also of some affection, the pleasure still rises upon us by the conversion of this subordinate movement into that which is predominant. The passion, though, perhaps, naturally, and when excited by the simple appearance of a real object, it may be painful, yet is so smoothed and softened and mollified when raised by the finer arts that it affords the highest entertainment.

To confirm this reasoning, we may observe that if the movements of the imagination be not predominant above those of the passion, a contrary effect follows, and the former, being now subordinate, is converted into the latter and still farther increases the pain and affliction of the sufferer.

Who could ever think of it as a good expedient for comforting an afflicted parent to exaggerate with all the force of elocution the irreparable loss which he has met with by the death of a favourite child? The more power of imagination and expression you here employ, the more you increase his despair and affliction.

The shame, confusion, and terror of Verres no doubt rose in proportion to the noble eloquence and vehemence of Cicero. So also did his pain and uneasiness. These former passions were too strong for the pleasure arising from the beauties of elocution and operated, though from the same principle, yet in a contrary manner to the sympathy, compassion, and indignation of the audience.

Lord Clarendon, when he approaches towards the catastrophe of the royal party,[2] supposes that his narration must then become infinitely disagreeable, and he hurries over the king's death without giving us one circumstance of it. He considers it as too horrid a scene to be contemplated with any satisfaction, or even without the utmost pain and aversion. He himself, as well as the readers of that age, were too deeply concerned in the events and felt a pain from subjects which an historian and a reader of another age would regard as the most pathetic and most interesting, and, by consequence, the most agreeable.

An action represented in tragedy may be too bloody and atrocious. It may excite such movements of horror as will not soften into pleas-

[2] Edward Hyde, first Earl of Clarendon (1609–74), *History of the Rebellion*, (1702–4). A well-known history of the Civil Wars in England.

ure, and the greatest energy of expression bestowed on descriptions of that nature serves only to augment our uneasiness. Such is that action represented in *The Ambitious Stepmother* where a venerable old man, raised to the height of fury and despair, rushes against a pillar, and striking his head upon it, besmears it all over with mingled brains and gore.[3] The English theatre abounds too much with such shocking images.

Even the common sentiments of compassion require to be softened by some agreeable affection in order to give a thorough satisfaction to the audience. The mere suffering of plaintive virtue under the triumphant tyranny and oppression of vice forms a disagreeable spectacle and is carefully avoided by all masters of the drama. In order to dismiss the audience with entire satisfaction and contentment, the virtue must either convert itself into a noble courageous despair, or the vice receive its proper punishment.

Most painters appear in this light to have been very unhappy in their subjects. As they wrought much for churches and convents, they have chiefly represented such horrible subjects as crucifixions and martyrdoms, where nothing appears but tortures, wounds, executions, and passive suffering, without any action or affection. When they turned their pencil from this ghastly mythology, they had commonly recourse to Ovid, whose fictions, though passionate and agreeable, are scarcely natural or probable enough for painting.

The same inversion of that principle which is here insisted on displays itself in common life as in the effects of oratory and poetry. Raise so the subordinate passion that it becomes the predominant, it swallows up that affection which it before nourished and increased. Too much jealousy extinguishes love. Too much difficulty renders us indifferent. Too much sickness and infirmity disgusts a selfish and unkind parent.

What so disagreeable as the dismal, gloomy, disastrous stories with which melancholy people entertain their companions? The uneasy passion being there raised alone, unaccompanied with any spirit, genius, or eloquence, conveys a pure uneasiness and is attended with nothing that can soften it into pleasure or satisfaction.

[3] Nicholas Rowe, *The Ambitious Stepmother* (published in 1700/1701).

Denis Diderot

1713-1784

DENIS DIDEROT was one of the first writers to pick up Lillo's argument for domestic tragedy and apply it to his own practice and serious critical thinking. He altered Lillo's fatal endings to happy ones, and urged the adoption of a middle form, halfway between comedy and tragedy, to be called "drama." He seems to have arrived at this form through Lillo rather than through imitation of Steele and the sentimentalists. It is through Diderot that the influence of Lillo can be felt on such men as Lessing and Hebbel. Diderot's position can perhaps best be summed up in a statement in the Third *Entretien*, in which he is conversing with Dorval, his hero of *Le Fils naturel* (1757):
"It [domestic tragedy] is very near to us. It is a picture of the misfortunes which surround us. What! You don't perceive the effect which would be produced upon you by a realistic scene, true customs, discourse proportioned to the action, simple action, dangers before which it is impossible that you have not trembled for your parents, for your friends, for yourself? A reversal of fortune, fear of ignominy, the consequences of misery, a passion which conducts a man to his ruin, from his ruin to despair, from despair to a violent death—these are not rare happenings; and you believe that they won't affect you more than the fabulous death of a tyrant, or the sacrifice of a child to one of the gods of Athens or Rome?"

The essay *On Dramatic Poetry* appeared as an appendix to Diderot's second "drama," *Le Père de famille* (1758). The present translation is by John Gaywood Linn.

On Dramatic Poetry

TO MY FRIEND M. GRIMM

[1758]

I. ON DRAMATIC FORMS

IF A PEOPLE have never had anything but one kind of play which is gay and pleasant, and another kind which is serious and moving is suggested to them, do you know, my friend, what they would think of it? I am very much mistaken if men of sense, after having considered the possibility, would not say, "Of what use is this kind of play? Does life not bring us enough real afflictions, without inventing imaginary ones? Why should we admit melancholy even into our amusements?" They would speak like aliens of the pleasure of being moved to pity and the shedding of tears.

Habit holds us captive. Has a man appeared with a spark of genius? produced some work? At first he astonishes and divides the wits; gradually he reunites them; soon he is followed by a crowd of imitators; the models multiply; observations are collected, rules created; the art springs up, and its limits are fixed; and it is declared that everything which is not included in the narrow limits that have been outlined is bizarre and bad: these are the columns of Hercules; to go outside them is to wander astray.

However, nothing prevails against truth. The inferior passes, despite the praise of imbecility, and the superior remains, in spite of the indecision of ignorance and the clamor of envy. The exasperating thing is that men obtain justice only when they are no more. It is only after men have been tormented in life that their tombs are adorned with a few odorless flowers. What is to be done, then? Rest inactive, or submit to a law to which better men than we have been submissive? Bad luck to him who labors, if his work is not the source of his sweetest moments, or if he does not know how to content himself with a little approbation. The number of good judges is limited. Oh, my friend, when I have published something, whether it be the rough outline of a drama, a philosophic idea, a bit of ethics or literature—because my mind diverts itself by variety—I shall come to see you. If my presence does not disturb you, if you meet me with a satisfied air, I shall await without impatience for time, and justice, which time always brings, to appreciate my work.

If one form exists, it is difficult to introduce another. If it is introduced, another prejudice arises: soon people imagine that the two adopted forms are neighbors and are connected.

Zeno denied the reality of movement. As a complete answer, his adversary began to walk, and if he had merely limped, he would still have answered.

I tried, in *Le Fils naturel*,[1] to give the idea of a drama which was between comedy and tragedy.

Le Père de famille,[2] which I now promise, and which continual distractions have delayed, is between the serious form of *Le Fils naturel* and comedy.

And if I ever have the leisure and the courage, I do not despair of writing a drama which comes between the serious form and tragedy.

Whether some merit is recognized in these works, or if none is admitted, they will nonetheless demonstrate that the gap which I have discovered between the two established forms was not illusory.

II. On Serious Comedy

HERE, THEN, is the system of drama in its whole extent: gay comedy, which has for its object ridicule and vice; serious comedy, which has for its object virtue and the duties of man; the kind of tragedy which would have for its object our domestic afflictions; and tragedy which has for its object public catastrophes and the afflictions of the great.

But who shall skillfully paint the duties of man for us? What would be the qualities of the poet who gave himself that aim? He should be philosophically minded, should have examined himself, have observed human nature, be profoundly instructed in the conditions of society, and know its workings and consequences, its drawbacks and advantages.

"But how to include, in the strict limits of a drama, everything connected with a man's fate? Where is the plot which can include this purpose? Plays of this kind are written, the kind we call dramas of the study: episodic scenes follow scenes which are episodic and disconnected, or at most held together by a little plot which meanders through them: but no more unity, little action, no interest. Each scene will bring together the two points so much recommended by Horace, but there will be no general effect, and the whole will be without consistency or force."

If the circumstances of men provide us with plays, such as Molière's *Les Fâcheux*,[3] that is already something; but I believe that we could

---

[1] *Le Fils naturel* (1757) published together with his famous analysis of the play in the *Dorval et moi* dialogues, in which he discusses, with particular reference to *Le Fils naturel* many of the points made here.

[2] *Le Père de famille* (1758).   [3] *Les Fâcheux* (1661).

get a better part. The obligations and difficulties of a nation are not all of the same importance. It seems to me that one could seize the principal things, make of them the basis of the work, and add the rest in the details. That is what I tried in *Le Père de famille,* where the establishment of the son and that of the daughter are my two central pivots. Chance, birth, education, the duties of fathers toward their children, and the children toward their parents, marriage, celibacy —everything that appertains to the condition of a father of a family is brought out by the dialogue. Let another begin this career, let him have the talent which I lack, and you will see what his drama will become.

The objections raised against this form prove only one thing: that it is difficult to handle, that it cannot be the work of a child, and that it presupposes more art, more ideas, more seriousness and mental force than those who devote themselves to the theatre usually have.

To judge a work well, one should not compare it to another work. It was in this way that one of our leading critics erred. He says, "The Ancients had no opera, therefore opera is a bad form." [4] With more circumspection or learning, he might perhaps have said, "The Ancients had nothing but opera, therefore our tragedy is not good." With better logic, he could not reasonably have said the one or the other. Whether or not there were existing models is of no importance. There is a rule behind everything, and the poetic reason was that there were not yet any poets; otherwise, how could one have judged the first poem? Was it good because it was pleasing, or was it pleasing because it was good?

The duty of man is as rich a basis for the dramatic poet as his follies and vices; and sincere serious plays will succeed everywhere, but more certainly among a depraved people than elsewhere. It is in going to the theatre that they will preserve themselves from the company of the wicked by whom they are surrounded; it is in the theatre that they will find those among whom they would like to live; it is there that they will see humanity as it is, and become reconciled with it. Good men are rare, but they do exist. He who thinks otherwise accuses himself, and shows how unfortunate he is in his wife, his

---

[4] Voltaire, "Preface to *Oedipe*" (1730). Diderot paraphrases, and Voltaire later reversed this stand.

relations, his friends, and acquaintances. Someone said to me one day, after reading an honest work which had kept him delightfully occupied, "It seems to me that I am left solitary." The work merited that praise, but his friends did not merit that satire.

Virtue and virtuous men must always be kept in mind when one writes. It is you, my friend, that I evoke when I take up my pen; it is you whom I have before my eyes when I work. It is Sophie whom I wish to please. If you have smiled at me, if she has let fall a tear, if you have both liked me better, I am repaid.

When I heard the peasant scenes in *Le Faux généreux*,[5] I said, "There is something which will please all the world, at all times; there is something which will make them melt in tears." Fact has confirmed my judgment. That episode is entirely in the sincere, serious form.

It will be said, "The example of a happy episode proves nothing. And if you do not break up the monotonous discussion of virtue, by the brawling of some ridiculous, and even slightly forced characters, as everyone else has done, I still believe that you will bring out nothing but cold, colorless scenes; boring and unhappy morality; and sorts of sermons in dialogue."

Let us run through the parts of a drama, and let us see. Is it by the subject that it must be judged? In the sincere, serious form, the subject is no less important than in gay comedy, and it is treated in a truer fashion. Is it by the characters? They may be as diverse and as original, and the poet is forced to portray them more strongly. Is it by the passions? They are shown with proportionately more energy, as the interest is greater. Is it by style? It will be more vigorous, graver, more elevated, more violent, more susceptible to what we call sentiment, the quality without which no style speaks to the heart. Is it by the absence of the ridiculous? As if the folly of actions and talk, when they are suggested by a misunderstood interest or the transports of passion, were not the truly ridiculous in men and life!

I call forth the beautiful passages of Terence, and I ask in what form his scenes of fathers and lovers are written.

If, in *Le Père de famille*, I did not know how to respond to the importance of my subject; if the progress of it is slow, the passions long-winded and didactic; if the characters of the father, his son, Sophie,

---

5 *L'Orpheline, ou, le faux généreux*, a comedy by Antoine Bret (1758).

the Commander, Germeuil and Cécile all lack comic vigor, is that the fault of the form, or is it mine?

Let someone try to put on the stage the circumstances of a Judge; let him plot his subject in a way that is suitable to him and which I understand; let the man be forced by the duties of his position either to lose the dignity and sanctity of his post, and to dishonor himself in the eyes of others, or sacrifice himself in his passions, his tastes, his fortune, birth, wife, and children—and then they may say, if they like, that sincere, serious drama is without warmth, color, and strength.

One way of making up my mind, which has often been successful for me, and to which I return every time that my judgment is made uncertain by habit or novelty—for either one produces this effect—is to seize the objects in thought, transport them from Nature onto canvas, and examine them at that distance, where they are neither too near me, nor too far away.

Let us apply this method. Take two comedies, one in the serious form, the other in the gay; make of them, scene by scene, two galleries of pictures, and see in which we will walk the longest and most willingly, where we will feel the strongest and most agreeable sensations, and where we will feel most impelled to return.

I repeat therefore: the sincere, the sincere. It touches us in a more intimate and sweeter way than that which excites our scorn and laughter. Poet, are you sensitive and fastidious? Strike that chord, and you will hear it answer or vibrate in every soul.

"Is human nature good, then?"

Yes, my friend, and very good. Water, air, earth, fire—everything is good in Nature: the hurricane, which rises at the end of autumn, shakes up the forests, and, hitting the trees against each other, breaks off and separates out the dead branches; and the storm, which strikes the waters of the sea and purifies them; and the volcano, which spills waves of glowing matter from its opened side, and gives cleansing vapors to the air.

It is miserable conventions which pervert man, and not Nature which we must accuse. In fact, what affects us like the recounting of a generous action? Where is the unhappy soul who can listen coldly to the plaint of a good man?

The audience of a comedy is the only place where the tears of the virtuous man and the wicked man are mingled. There, the evildoer is angry at the injustices he would have perpetrated, feels the wrongs he would have occasioned, and becomes indignant at a man of his own character. But the impression is made; it remains with us, in spite of ourselves; and the evildoer leaves the theatre less disposed to work evil than if he had been reproved by a severe, harsh orator.

The poet, the novelist, and the comedian strike at the heart in an oblique fashion, and in so doing, strike the soul the more surely and strongly, so that it lays itself out and offers itself to the blow. The troubles by which they soften me are imaginary, agreed; but they do soften me. Every line of *L'Homme de qualité retiré du monde,* of *Le Doyen de Killerine,* and of *Cléveland* [6] excites in me a stirring of interest in the misfortunes of virtue, and costs me tears. What art could be more deadly than one which would make me a party to vice? But also what art could be more precious than one which would imperceptibly involve me in the fate of a good man, which would take me out of the sweet and tranquil situation which I enjoy, to make me walk with him, plunge me into the caverns where he has taken refuge, and associate me with all the misfortunes with which it pleases the poet to try his steadfastness.

O, what good it would restore to man if all the imitative arts should attempt a common object, and unite one day with the laws, to make us love virtue and hate vice! It is up to the philosopher to invite them; it is up to him to speak to the poet, the painter, the musician, and forcefully to ask them, "Men of genius, why has heaven made you gifted?" If he were heard, soon pictures of debauchery would no longer cover the walls of our palaces, our voices would no longer be organs of crime, and taste and manners would gain in this. Does one actually believe that the action of a blind husband and wife who still seek each other at an advanced age, and who, with their eyelids damp with tears of tenderness, clasp hands and caress them, so to speak, at the edge of the grave, does not demand the same talent, and does not interest me more than the spectacle of the violent pleasures at which their inexperienced senses became drunk in adolescence?

III. On a Type of Moral Drama

I HAVE SOMETIMES thought that in the theatre one could discuss the most important moral points, and do it without standing in the

---

[6] Romances of l'Abbé Prévost, written in 1731, 1735, and 1701–39, respectively.

way of the violent and rapid development of the dramatic action.

Of what would it actually be a question? Of arranging the poem so that the things should be brought about, like the abdication of the empire in *Cinna*. It is thus that a poet would treat the question of suicide, honor, a duel, fortune, dignity, and a hundred others. Our poems would take on a gravity which they do not have. If a certain scene is necessary, if it is basic, if it is forecast and the spectator wishes to see it, he will give it all his attention, and he will be much more affected by it than by those farfetched little sentences with which our modern works are stitched together.

It is not words that I want to carry away from the theatre, but impressions. He who says of a drama, from which many detached thoughts are quoted, that it is a mediocre work is seldom mistaken. The excellent poet is the one whose effect stays long with me.

O, dramatic poets! The applause which you ought to aim for is not that clapping of hands which suddenly spreads after a brilliant line, but that profound sigh which escapes from the soul after the constraint of a long silence, and offers solace. It is a still more violent impression, which you will understand if you were born for your art, and if you present all the magic of it: it is to put people as if to the rack. Their minds will be troubled, uncertain, floating, lost, and your spectators will be like those who in an earthquake see the walls of their houses tremble, and feel the earth disappearing beneath their feet.

IV. On a Type of Philosophical Drama

There is a type of drama in which the moral is directly and successfully presented. Here is an example. Listen carefully to what our judges will say of it, and if they find it cold, believe that they have neither energy of soul, nor any idea of true eloquence, nor feelings, nor heart. As for me, I think that the man of genius who masters it will not leave time for eyes to dry, and that we will be indebted to him for the most touching spectacle, and one of the most instructive and delightful lessons that we could get. It is the death of Socrates.

The scene is a prison. We see the philosopher in chains and lying on straw. He is asleep. His friends have corrupted the guards, and they come, at day break, to announce his deliverance.

All Athens is rife with rumors, but the just man sleeps.

Of the innocence of life. How sweet it is to have lived well, when one is at the point of death! *Scene one.*

Socrates wakes; he sees his friends; he is surprised to see them so early.

The dream of Socrates.

They tell him what they have done; he examines with them what it is right for him to do.

Of the respect which one owes oneself, and the sanctity of the laws. *Scene two.*

The guards arrive; one takes off his chains.

The story of pain and pleasure.

The judges enter, and with them the accusers of Socrates and a crowd of the people. He is accused, and he defends himself.

The apology. *Scene three.*

Here custom must be submitted to: the accusations must be read; Socrates must question his judges, his accusers, and the people; he must urge them, interrogate them, answer them. The thing must be shown as it happened, and the spectacle will be only more true, more striking, and more beautiful.

The judges retire; the friends of Socrates remain; they have a presentiment of his condemnation. Socrates talks with them and consoles them.

Of the immortality of the soul. *Scene four.*

He is judged. His death is pronounced. He sees his wife and children. The hemlock is brought to him. He dies. *Scene five.*

It is only one act, but if it is done well, it will have almost the extent of an ordinary play. What eloquence it requires, what depth of philosophy, what reality, what truth! If you grasp the firm, simple, tranquil, serene, and elevated character of the philosopher, you will feel how difficult it is to paint. At each moment he must bring a smile to the corner of the lips, and tears to the eyes. I should die happy if I had completed that task as I conceive it. Once more, if the critics see nothing in it but a chain of cold, philosophical speeches, oh, the poor souls, how I pity them!

V. ON SIMPLE DRAMAS AND COMPLICATED DRAMAS

As FOR ME, I think more of a passion, of a character, which develops little by little, and ends by showing itself in all its strength, than I do of those combinations of incidents from which are formed the tissue of a play where the characters and the spectators are kept equally in suspense. It seems to me that good taste disdains them, and that great events are not suited to them. That, however, is what we call action. The Ancients had another idea of it. A simple behavior, an action taken nearest its conclusion, so that everything was at its extremity; a catastrophe unendingly imminent and always delayed by a simple, believable circumstance; energetic speeches; strong passions; tableaux; one or two forcefully drawn characters: there is all their material. Sophocles needed no more to astound the mind. He who has been displeased by reading the Ancients does not know how much our Racine owes to Homer.

Have you not noticed, as I have, that, however complicated a play may be, there is almost no one who cannot recount it after the first presentation? One easily remembers events, but not speeches, and when the events are once known, the complicated play has lost its effect.

If a dramatic work is to be presented only once, and never printed, I say to the poet, "Be as complicated as you like; you will excite yourself, you will certainly be occupied; but be simple, if you wish to be read, and to survive."

One good scene contains more ideas than a whole drama could offer in incidents; and it is to ideas that we return, to them that we listen without tiring, and by them that we are always affected. The scene of Roland in the cavern, where he vainly awaits the perfidious Angelique; the speech of Lusignan to his daughter; that of Clytemnestra to Agamemnon—these are always new to me.

When I allow as many complications as one wishes, it is in the same action. It is almost impossible to carry on two plots at once, without one's being interesting at the expense of the other. How many modern examples I could cite! But I do not wish to offend.

What is more adroit than the way Terence has interlaced the loves of Pamphilia and Charinus in the *Andria*? However, has he done it without awkwardness? Does not one believe, at the beginning of the second act, that a second play begins? And does the fifth end in a very interesting fashion?

He who tries to carry on two plots at once imposes on himself the necessity of completing them at the same moment. If the principal plot ends first, the remaining one does not hold up; if, on the contrary, the episodic plot leaves the main one, there is another difficulty: the characters either disappear suddenly, or reappear without reason, and the work is mutilated or goes slack.

What would the play Terence called the *Heautontimorumenos,* or *The Self-Tormentor,* have become if the poet had not known how, by an effort of genius, to take up the plot about Clinia, which ends in the third act, and to tie it up again with the plot about Clitiphon!

Terence brought over the plot of Menander's *Perikeiromené* to the same Greek poet's *Andria,* and of two simple plays he made one complicated one. I did the opposite in *Le Fils naturel.* Goldoni had mixed in a three-act farce the *Avare* [7] of Molière and the characters of the true friend. I separated these subjects, and wrote a five-act play; good or bad, it is certain that on this point I was right.

Terence felt that in having doubled the subject of the *Heautontimorumenos* he had a new play; and I agree in that. As for a better, that is something else.

If I dared flatter myself on some skill in the *Père de famille,* it would be with having given Germeuil and Cécile a passion which they could not admit in the first acts, and having so subordinated it in the whole play to that of Saint-Albin for Sophie, that even after a declaration, Germeuil and Cécile could not talk of their passion, although they found themselves together at every moment.

There is no middle ground; one always loses on one side what one gains on the other. If you gain interest and speed by multiplication of incidents, you will have no more conversation; your characters will hardly have time to speak; they become excited instead of developing. I speak of this from experience.

[7] *L'Avare* (1668).

Edmund Burke

1729-1797

EDMUND BURKE, known in history primarily as a statesman and political writer, was a young man of twenty-seven when his *Philosophical Inquiry into the Origin of Our Ideas of the Sublime and Beautiful,* his first major publication, appeared in 1756. This treatise, one of a long series of empirical investigations in the eighteenth century into our psychological reactions to works of art, took its impetus, as did the rest, from the revived interest in Longinus that began about 1674 with the translation by Rapin of the famous treatise *On the Sublime.* Burke's immediate point of departure was Addison's series of essays in the *Spectator* on the "Pleasures of Imagination." Upon the body of aesthetic ideas to be found in Addison, Burke grafted the sentimental doctrines of the Shaftesbury-Hutcheson school, especially in his treatment of our reactions to tragedy, for like that school he based our enjoyment of tragedy upon a God-implanted "moral sense," the exercise of which is accompanied by pleasure and leads us to right action without the use of reason. Although this explanation belongs to pure aesthetic speculation, the presence of the theory certainly had much to do with encouraging playwrights of the eighteenth century to strive for sentimentalism in effects. The prologue of many tragedies of the period contains references to this type of theorizing.

Burke, who was born, reared, and educated in Ireland, had left Trinity College in Dublin in 1748 and was not to achieve political prominence until the 1760s. The *Philosophical Inquiry* had considerable influence upon Lessing and Moses Mendelssohn in Germany, in addition to its influence upon the writers on aesthetics and upon playwrights during the decades following its publication.

A Philosophical Inquiry into the Origin of Our Ideas of the Sublime and the Beautiful

[1756; excerpts]

PART I

SECTION XIII

IT IS BY . . . [sympathy] that we enter into the concerns of others; that we are moved as they are moved, and are never suffered to be indifferent spectators of almost anything which men can do or suffer. For sympathy must be considered as a sort of substitution, by which we are put into the place of another man, and affected in many respects as he is affected; so that this passion may either partake of the nature of those that regard self-preservation, and turning upon pain may be a source of the sublime, or it may turn upon ideas of pleasure; and then whatever has been said of the social affections, whether they regard society in general, or only some particular modes of it, may be applicable here. It is by this principle chiefly that poetry, painting, and other affecting arts, transfuse their passions from one breast to another, and are often capable of grafting a delight on wretchedness, misery, and death itself. It is a common observation, that objects which in the reality would shock, are in tragical, and such like representations, the source of a very high species of pleasure. This, taken as a fact, has been the cause of much reasoning. The satisfaction has been commonly attributed, first, to the comfort we receive in considering that so melancholy a story is no more than a fiction; and, next, from the contemplation of our own freedom from the evils which we see represented. I am afraid it is a practice much too common in inquiries of this nature, to attribute the cause of feelings which merely arise from the mechanical structure of our bodies, or from the natural frame and constitution of our minds, to certain conclusions of the reasoning faculty on the objects presented to us; for I should imagine that the influence of reason in producing our passions is nothing near so extensive as it is commonly believed.

To EXAMINE this point concerning the effect of tragedy in a proper manner, we must previously consider how we are affected by the feelings of our fellow-creatures in circumstances of real distress. I am convinced we have a degree of delight, and that no small one, in the real misfortunes and pains of others; for let the affection be what it will in appearance, if it does not make us shun such objects, if on the contrary it induces us to approach them, if it makes us dwell upon them, in this case I conceive we must have a delight or pleasure of some species or other in contemplating objects of this kind. Do we not read the authentic histories of scenes of this nature with as much pleasure as romances or poems, where the incidents are fictitious? The prosperity of no empire, nor the grandeur of no king, can so agreeably affect in the reading, as the ruin of the state of Macedon, and the distress of its unhappy prince. Such a catastrophe touches us in history as much as the destruction of Troy does in fable. Our delight, in cases of this kind, is very greatly heightened, if the sufferer be some excellent person who sinks under an unworthy fortune. Scipio and Cato are both virtuous characters; but we are more deeply affected by the violent death of the one, and the ruin of the great cause he adhered to, than with the deserved triumphs and uninterrupted prosperity of the other; for terror is a passion which always produces delight when it does not press too closely; and pity is a passion accompanied with pleasure, because it arises from love and social affection. Whenever we are formed by nature to any active purpose, the passion which animates us to it is attended with delight, or a pleasure of some kind, let the subject matter be what it will; and as our Creator has designed that we should be united by the bond of sympathy, He has strengthened that bond by a proportionable delight; and there most where our sympathy is most wanted—in the distresses of others. If this passion was simply painful, we would shun with the greatest care all persons and places that could excite such a passion; as some, who are so far gone in indolence as not to endure any strong impression, actually do. But the case is widely different with the greater part of mankind; there is no spectacle we so eagerly pursue as that of some uncommon and grievous calamity; so that whether the misfortune is before our eyes, or whether they are turned back to it in history, it always touches with delight. This is not an unmixed delight, but blended with no small uneasiness. The delight we have in such things hinders us from shunning scenes of misery; and the pain we feel prompts us to relieve ourselves in relieving those who suffer; and all this antecedent to any reasoning, by an instinct that works us to its own purposes without our concurrence.

SECTION XV

IT IS THUS in real calamities. In imitated distresses the only difference is the pleasure resulting from the effects of imitation; for it is never so perfect but we can perceive it is imitation, and on that principle are somewhat pleased with it. And indeed in some cases we derive as much or more pleasure from that source than from the thing itself. But then I imagine we shall be much mistaken if we attribute any considerable part of our satisfaction in tragedy to the consideration that tragedy is a deceit, and its representations no realities. The nearer it approaches the reality, and the farther it removes us from all idea of fiction, the more perfect is its power. But be its power of what kind it will, it never approaches to what it represents. Choose a day on which to represent the most sublime and affecting tragedy we have; appoint the most favorite actors; spare no costs upon the scenes and decorations; unite the greatest efforts of poetry, painting, and music; and when you have collected your audience, just at the moments when their minds are erect with expectation, let it be reported that a state criminal of high rank is on the point of being executed in an adjoining square; in a moment the emptiness of the theatre would demonstrate the comparative weakness of the imitative arts, and proclaim the triumph of the real sympathy. I believe that this notion of our having a simple pain in the reality, yet a delight in the representation, arises from hence, that we do not sufficiently distinguish what we would by no means choose to do, from what we should be eager enough to see if it was once done. We delight in seeing things, which, so far from doing, our heartiest wishes would be to see redressed. This noble capital, the pride of England and of Europe, I believe no man is so strangely wicked as to desire to see destroyed by a conflagration or an earthquake, though he should be removed himself to the greatest distance from the danger. But suppose such a fatal accident to have happened, what numbers from all parts would crowd to behold the ruins, and amongst many who would have been content never to have seen London in its glory! Nor is it, either in real or fictitious distresses, our immunity from them which produces our delight; in my own mind I can discover nothing like it. I apprehend that this mistake is owing to a sort of sophism, by which we are frequently imposed upon; it arises from our not distinguishing between what is indeed a necessary condition to our doing or suffering anything in general, and what is the *cause* of some particular act. If a man kills me with a sword, it is a necessary condition to this that we should have been both of us alive before the fact; and yet it would be absurd to say that our being both living creatures was the cause of his crime and of my death. So it is certain that it is absolutely necessary my life should be out of any imminent hazard, before I can take a delight in the suffering of others, real or imaginary, or indeed in anything else from any cause whatsoever. But then it is a sophism to argue from thence, that this immunity is the cause of my delight either on these or on any occasions. No one can distinguish such a cause of satisfaction in his own mind, I believe; nay, when we do not suffer any very acute pain, nor are exposed to any imminent danger of our lives, we can feel for others, whilst we suffer ourselves; and often then most when we are softened by affliction; we see with pity even distresses which we would accept in the place of our own.

Beaumarchais

1732-1799

PIERRE-AUGUSTUS CARON took the name Beaumarchais in 1757 and used it
from that time on. His literary activity was fairly extensive, although he
had in addition a career as a kind of secret agent for the King of France.
Beaumarchais is best known for his plays, *Le Barbier de Seville* (1772) and
Le Mariage de Figaro (1784). His first published work was the play
Eugénie (1767), prefaced by the essay printed here.

Beaumarchais came, at this stage in his life, under the influence of
Diderot's arguments for some middle kind of drama between comedy
and tragedy, which would be serious, moral, and moving, but which would
usually end happily. He experimented with this serious comedy in *Eugénie*
and in *Les Deux amis* (1770), but the coldness of the reception of both
plays turned him to pure comedy. In his dedicatory letter to *Le Barbier
de Seville* he renounced the whole position he so carefully builds up here,
saying,
". . . I had the weakness once, monsieur, to present to you at different
times, two sad dramas; monstrous productions, as everyone knows! because
no one fails to recognize that there is no middle ground between comedy
and tragedy; that point is decided. The master has said it, and the school
retains it, and I am so completely convinced, that if today I wanted to
put into the theatre a distressed mother, a betrayed wife, a distracted
sister, a disinherited son, I should, in order to present them decently to
the public, begin by supposing for them a fine kingdom where they would
have reigned wisely—in some far archipelago or some such corner of the
world; certain after that, that the improbability of the fable, the enormity
of the deeds, the bombast of the characters, the exaggerated ideas and the
buffoonery of the language, far from imputing reproach to me, would in-
sure my success.

"Present men of middle condition dejected and in sorrow? Fie upon it!
That is worthy only of being laughed at. Ridiculous citizens and unhappy
kings—there is your existing and possible theatre, and I content myself
with saying, it is done, and I don't want to quarrel with anyone."

Essay on the Genre of Serious Drama

[1767; excerpts]

I LACK the talent to be a critic; I have had neither the time nor the ability to become one; but for about eight years, I have amused myself by writing down some ideas about serious drama, which stands between heroic tragedy and pleasant comedy. Of the several types of literature on which I might have tried my ability, this one was perhaps the least important. And for this reason, I gave it preference. I have always been too occupied with serious matters to hunt anything but honest relaxation in literature—*"Neque semper arcum tendit Apollo."* The subject pleased me, it carried me away, but I was not slow in feeling that I was wrong in desiring to prove by reason the merits of a type which requires only persuasion by feeling. Therefore I desired passionately to be able to substitute example for precept: an infallible method of producing proselytes if one succeeds, but which exposes the unfortunate failure to the double grief of missing his point and being ridiculed for overestimating his ability.

Being too enthusiastic to be capable of this last thought, I wrote the drama which I offer today. *Miss Fanny, Miss Jenny, Miss Polly,*[1] etc., charming proclamations! *Eugénie* would have gained, no doubt, through having you as a model, but she existed before you had your existence, without which one cannot model for anyone. I refer your authors to the new little Spaniard of the Court at Belflor, in *Le Diable boiteux.*[2] She was the source from which I got my idea. The feeble character that I have drawn will leave them few regrets that they could not have been of any use to me.

The making of the plan, this rapid work, which only throws together masses, indicates situations, sketches the characters, moving with heat, did not slow my courage, but when it became necessary to cut the subject or to sketch it, to put it in work form, my head, cooled by the details of execution, discovered the difficulty, became frightened of the work, abandoned the drama and dissertation, and, just as a child thwarted in his efforts to pick fruit on too high a branch,

---

[1] *Miss Fanny, Miss Jenny,* and *Miss Polly:* the first refers to a play, *Fanny,* by d'Arnaud (1764), the second to *Jenny* by Mme Riccoboni (1769); the third may refer to l'Abbé Prévost's translation of Richardson's *Pamela* (1742).

[2] *Le Diable boiteux,* by Floret Carton, Sieur Dancourt; not published until 1782.

sulks and ends by consoling himself in picking flowers at the foot of the same tree, a song or some verses to Thémire made me forget the useless trouble I had taken.

A little while later, M. Diderot produced his *Père de famille*.[3] The genius of this poet, his strong style, the virile and vigorous tone of his work, should have torn the brush from my hand, but the route which he had just marked had such charms for me that I consulted my inclination more than my weakness. I took up my drama with new enthusiasm. I put on the finishing touches, and I have since given it to the actors. Thus a child whom a man's success renders headstrong, sometimes reaches the fruits he desired. He is happy in tasting them if he does not find them bitter. There is the story of the play.

Now that it has been played, I am going to examine all the praise and censure which it has occasioned, but I will only bring up those directly concerned with the type in which I was pleased to work because it is the only point which can interest the public today. I will be silent on personalities. *"Iam dolor in morem venit meus"* (Ovid). In the same way, I will leave without answer all that has been said against the work, being persuaded that the greatest honor one could pay an author, except being entertained at the theatre, was not to judge him unworthy of criticism.

And do not think that I am using false modesty here. My *sang froid* to the rigorous censure of the opening night did not come from indifference or conceit; it was the result of this reasoning which appeared to me clear without reply. If the critic is just, the work could not have avoided it; it is not in point for me to complain but either to correct it to the satisfaction of the critics, or to abandon it completely. If some secret animosity heats their spirits, I, for one, have two reasons for peace of mind. Would I have wished to do less well to have avoided envy? And could I flatter myself that I will disarm it when I do better?

I have seen people really angry to see that serious drama had found its partisans. "An equivocal type!" they said; "We don't know what it is! What is a play in which there is not one word to laugh at? Where five mortal acts of dragging prose without comic salt, without maxims, without characters, hold us suspended on the thread of a romanesque event which often has no more probability than reality? Is it not

[3] Diderot's *Père de famille* (1758).

opening the door to licence and favoring laziness to endure such works? The facility of the prose will disgust our young people with the laborious work of verse writing, and our theatre will soon fall again into the barbarity from which poets have had such pains in extracting it. It is not that certain of these pieces have not appealed to me—I don't know how—but it would be dreadful if a similar type took hold; besides which, it does not suit our nation at all; everyone knows what celebrated authors have thought where opinion makes authority. They have banished it as a type equally disinherited of Melpomone and Thalia. Would it be necessary to create a new muse to preside over this trivial buskin, this comic *echassé?* Tragi-comedy, bourgeois tragedy, *comédie larmoyante,*—one does not know what name to give these monstrous productions! And may a puny author not come to preen himself before the momentary suffrance of the public, the just reward of the work and talent of the comedians! . . . The public? What, again, is the public? When this collective being dissolves, the individuals disperse; what remains for forming general opinions, if not the opinions of each individual, of which the most enlightened have a natural influence over the others, which brings them back, sooner or later, to their opinion? From which one sees that it is to the judgment of a small number, and not that of the multitude that one must refer."

That is enough: we dare answer this torrent of objections, which I have not weakened or glossed over in reporting. Let us begin by making our judge favorable in defending our rights. Just as the censurers say, the assembled public is nonetheless the only judge of works destined to amuse them. All are equally submitted to them, and to wish to stop the efforts of genius in the creation of a new type of spectacle, in the extensions of those they already know, is an attack against their rights, an enterprise contrary to their pleasures. I agree that a difficult truth will be met sooner, grasped better, judged more sanely by a smaller group of enlightened people than by the multitude through rumor; for if this were not so, this truth would not be called difficult; but the objects of taste, of sentiment, of pure effect, in a word, of spectacle never being admitted except in the sudden and powerful sensations which they produce in all the spectators, should they be judged by these same rules? When it is less a question of discussing and investigating than of feeling and being amused or touched, is it not as hazardous to maintain that the emotional judgment of the public is false and misplaced as it would be to pretend that a type of spectacle which had a lively and generally pleasing effect on a whole nation would not have a degree of suitability to this nation? What weight would the satires on serious drama issued from the pens of some authors have against the public taste, particularly when their pleasantries insult charming works of this type? Besides it is necessary to be consistent; the light weapon and the switch of sarcasm have never decided matters; it is only right to use them and even more permissible against these lazy, good for nothing adversaries who, withdrawn behind piles of authorities, refuse to try their strength with reasoners in open country. It suits our handsome wits of society to do nothing but skim the surface of what they judge and they are like the light-armed troops or lost children of literature. But here by an unusual reversal, the serious authors joke and the people of the world argue. I hear big words mentioned everywhere, and arrayed against the serious type, Aristotle, the Ancients, the *Poetics,* the usage of the theatre, the Rules, and above all, the Rules—that eternal common ground of critics, that bugbear of ordinary intellects. In what type has one seen Rules produce masterpieces? On the contrary, is it not the great examples which have always served as the basis and foundation of these Rules with which one makes a trap for genius and a reversal of the order of things? Would men ever have advanced in arts and sciences if they had servilely respected the false boundaries their predecessors had prescribed? The new world would still be in the process of birth for us if the hardy navigator from Genoa had not trampled underfoot this *ne plus ultra* of the colonies of Alcide. . . . The curious genius, impatient always with the narrow circle of acquired knowledge, suspects something more than is known; moved by the sentiment which impresses him, he torments himself, undertakes, extends himself; and, finally breaking the barriers of precedent, he throws himself beyond known boundaries. He strays sometimes, but it is he alone who carries the torch toward which others crowd far into the night of the possible. He has taken a giant step and the art is extended. . . . Let us stop. There is no point in arguing heatedly, but rather let us discuss it coolly. Let us, therefore, reduce to simple terms the question which has never yet been asked. To carry it to the tribunal of reason, here is how I would express it.

Is it permitted to try to interest the people in the theatre, and to try to make their tears flow concerning an event which if it were true and happened under their eyes among our citizens, would never fail to produce this effect on them? For such is the object of the honest and serious type. If anyone is barbarous enough, classic enough to dare to uphold the negative, we must ask him if what he understands by the word "drama," or "theatrical piece" is not a faithful picture of men's actions? We must read him Richardson's novels, which are true dramas, just as the drama is the conclusion and the most interesting moment of any romance; we must teach him, if he does not know it, that several scenes of *L'Enfant prodigue*,[4] all of *Nanine*,[5] *Mélanide*,[6] *Cénie*,[7] *Le Père de famille*, *L'Écossaise*,[8] *Le Philosophe sans le savoir* [9] have already made us know to what beauty the serious type [of play] is susceptible, and have accustomed us to please ourselves with the touching painting of a domestic misfortune, the more powerful in our hearts the closer it appears to menace us, an effect that one can never hope for in the same degree from the great pictures of heroic tragedy.

Before going further, I warn that what I have left to say is irrelevant to our famous tragedians. They would have shone equally in another pursuit; genius born of itself owes nothing to subjects and applies itself to everything. I talk about the essence of things in regarding the merit of authors; I compare the types and do not discuss the talents at all. Here, therefore, is my comparison.

It is the essence of the serious genre to offer a more pressing interest, a morality more direct than that of heroic tragedy, and deeper than that of pleasant comedy, other things being equal.

I hear already a thousand voices lifting themselves, and crying, "Impious!" But I ask for all grace that they listen to me before pronouncing anathema. These ideas are too new not to need to be developed.

In the tragedy of the Ancients, an involuntary indignation against their cruel gods is the feeling which seizes me at the sight of the evils

[4] *L'Enfant prodigue*, by Voltaire (1736).
[5] *Nanine*, by Voltaire (1749), based on *Pamela*, but the scene is transferred to France.
[6] *Mélanide*, a sentimental comedy, by N. de la Chaussée (1733).
[7] *Cénie*, a sentimental comedy by Mme de Graffigny (1750).
[8] *L'Ecossaise*, a sentimental comedy by Voltaire (1760), the source of Colman's *The English Merchant* (1767).   [9] *Le Philosophe sans le savoir*, by M. J. Sédaine (1765).

with which they allow an innocent victim to be crushed. *Oedipus*,[10] *Jocasta*,[11] *Phaedria*,[12] *Aradiane*,[13] *Phyloctetes*,[14] *Orestes*,[15] and many others inspire me less with interest than with terror. Devout and passive beings, blind instruments of the fancy of these gods—I am much more affrighted by, than sympathetic for, their lot. Everything is enormous in these dramas: the passions always unrestrained, the crimes always atrocious, as far from Nature as unprecedented in our customs; we walk only among ruins, across seas of blood, on piles of corpses, and only arrive at the catastrophe by poisoning, assassination, incest, or parricide. The occasional tears we shed are painful, rare, burning; they burn the forehead long before flowing. It takes incredible effort to drag them from us, and all the genius of the sublime author barely suffices.

Moreover, the inevitable blows of destiny offer no moral judgment to the intelligence. When we can only tremble and be silent, is it not dreadful to reflect? If we drew a moral from a like kind of spectacle, it would be terrible and would incite so many souls to crime who would use fate as an excuse that it would discourage us from following the path of virtue, to which all the stress of this system guarantees nothing. If there are no virtues without sacrifices, there are no sacrifices without the hope of reward. All belief in fate degrades man in taking away liberty, without which there is no morality in his actions.

On the other hand, let us examine, in heroic tragedy, what kind of interest the heroes and the kings, properly called, excite in us, and we will recognize, perhaps, that the great events, the pompous characters which it presents to us are only traps extended to our self-esteem, to which the heart rarely bends. It is our vanity which finds its reward in being initiated into these secrets of a proud heart, in entering into a plan which is going to change the face of a state, to penetrate as far as the cabinet of a queen, where we would hardly be permitted to look.

We love to believe ourselves in the confidence of an unhappy

10 *Oedipus* by Sophocles.
11 *Jocasta:* No surviving ancient tragedy bears this name, but perhaps Seneca's *Oedipus* is meant, for Jocasta plays a prominent role in this play. However, the subject was common in France.
12 *Phaedria* by Seneca.
13 *Aradiane*—Ariadne. No ancient play exists on this story. She was the sister of Phaedria and, falling in love with Theseus, helped him to find his way out of the labyrinth.
14 *Phyloctetes* by Sophocles.   15 *Orestes,* by Euripides.

prince, because his griefs, his tears, his weaknesses, appear to approach the condition of our own, which consoles us for his lofty position; we fail to perceive that each of us tries to increase the size of his own sphere, and our ego nourishes itself in the pleasure of judging in the theatre these masters of the world, who anywhere else can trample us underfoot. Men are greater gulls themselves than they believe. The best of them is often moved by motives which would make him blush if he understood them better. But if emotions enter into the interest which we take in the characters of tragedy, it is less because they are heroes or kings than because they are men and unhappy. Is it the Queen of Messina who touches me in *Mérope?* [16] It is the mother of Aegisthus; nature alone has rights on our hearts.

If the theatre is the faithful picture of what passes in the world, the interest which it excites in us has, therefore, a necessary bearing on our way of looking at real objects. But I have observed that often a great prince, at the peak of his good fortune, covered with glory and all shining with success, wins from us only sterile admiration, which is a stranger to our hearts. Perhaps we never feel how dear he is until he falls into some disgrace; this touching enthusiasm of the people, who reward and recompense good kings, seizes them only at the moment that they see him unhappy or when they fear to lose him. Then, the compassion for a suffering man is such a true feeling, so profound, that one would say that it can compensate the king for his lost happiness. The true interest of the heart, its true relation, is therefore always of man to man, and not of man to a king. Also, far from the fame of rank augmenting the interest I take in the personages of tragedy, it puts it, on the contrary, in the shade. The more the condition of a suffering man approaches my own, the more his misfortune moves me. "Would it not be desirable," says M. Rousseau, "that our sublime authors should deign to descend a little from their everlasting elevation, and bring our attention sometimes to suffering humanity; for fear of having pity only for unfortunate heroes, we never have it for anyone."

What do the revolutions of Athens and Rome matter to me, a peaceful subject of a monarchic state of the eighteenth century? What real interest can I take in the death of a Peloponnesian tyrant or the sacrifice of a young princess at Aulis? I cannot see anything note-

16 *Mérope* by Voltaire (1741).

worthy in all those, no moral which fits my needs. For, what is morality? It is the fruitful result, and the personal application of reflections,
which an event forces from us. What is interest? It is the involuntary
feeling by which we adapt that event for ourselves, a feeling which
places us in the place of the suffering man, in the middle of his situation. A comparison taken at hazard from Nature will make my idea
clear to the whole world.

Why does the account of the earthquake which engulfed Lima
and smote people, three thousand leagues away, trouble me, when
that of the judicial murder of Charles I, committed in London, causes
me only indignation? It is because if a volcano erupts in Peru, one
might explode in Paris, to bury me under its ruins, and perhaps threat-
ens me now; on the other hand, I cannot conceive of a fate like that
unheard of misfortune of the King of England happening to me. This
feeling is in the hearts of all mankind; it serves as the basis of a certain
principle of art, that there is no moral, no interest in the theatre, without a secret rapport of the dramatic subject with us. It is certain,
then, that heroic tragedy can touch us only at that point where it
comes close to the serious genre in depicting for us men, and not
kings; and that the subjects which it places in action are so far from
our customs, and the personnages so strange to our ways as private
citizens, that the interest in it is less pressing than that of a serious
drama, and the moral less direct, more arid, often null and void for
us, at least unless it consoles us for our mediocrity in showing us
that the great crimes and the great griefs are the ordinary lot of those
who entangle themselves with governing the world.

After what has gone before I do not believe there is need to prove
that a person will have more interest in a serious drama than in a
comic play. The whole world knows that touching subjects affect us
more than pleasant ones of equal degree of merit. It will suffice only
to develop the causes of this effect, as natural as it is constant, and to
examine the moral aim in the comparison of the two genres.

Light gaiety distracts us; in some fashion it draws our soul out of
itself and makes it glow about us. A person laughs well only in company. But if the gay picture of ridicule amuses the wit for a moment at
the spectacle, experience teaches us that the laughter which it excites
in us dies absolutely on reaching its victim, without ever reaching our
hearts. Self-esteem, carefully avoiding the application, saves itself by

means of the uproar of the crowd, and profits by the general tumult to scatter all that can fit us in the epigram. That far the evil is not great, provided that one has not been exposed to public laughter, as a pedant, a fop, a coquette, a coxcomb, a fool, a rake—in a word, all the false wits of society. But is the mockery which punishes them the weapon by which vice may be attacked? Is it by joking that it expects to destroy? Not only does it miss its goal, but it accomplishes precisely the opposite from what it intends. We see that happening in most comedies; to the shame of the moral, the spectator catches himself very often being interested in the knave instead of the honest man, because the latter is often the less pleasing of the two. But if the gaiety of the scenes has entranced me a moment, soon, humiliated at having been trapped by witticisms or a good bit of theatre, I leave discontented with the author, with the work, and with myself. The morality of the pleasant type is then either scarcely profound or nothing at all, or even the opposite of that which ought to be in the theatre.

The drama which appeals to our emotions, concerns our daily lives, is different. If loud laughter is the enemy of reflection, compassion, on the contrary, brings silence. It harbors us, it isolates us from everything. He who weeps at a spectacle is alone; and the more he is moved, the more he weeps with delight, and especially in honest serious drama, which moves the heart by such natural and such true means. Often in the middle of an agreeable scene, a charming emotion causes abandoned and easy tears to fall, which mingling with the indulgence of a smile, paint compassion and joy on the face. Is not such a touching conflict the finest triumph of art, the sweetest feeling experienced by a person?

Compassion has this further moral advantage over laughter, because it does not attach itself to any object without working a powerful reaction in us at the same time.

The picture of the unhappiness of an honest man stirs the heart, in moving us works sweetly, and soon forces reflection. When I see virtue persecuted, the victim of wickedness, but always beautiful, always glorious, and even in the gulf of unhappiness preferable to everything, the effect of the drama is unequivocal; it is in this unfortunate being, alone, that I am interested, and then if I am not happy myself, if base envy attempts to make me degrade myself, if it attacks me in my person, my honor, or my fortune, how much does this genre of drama please me! And what a fine moral I can draw from it! The subject carries me along naturally; I do not interest myself solely in the unfortunate man who suffers unjustly but I also ponder over the results of lightness of character, lack of discretion, overweening ambition, or unfortunate circumstance; thus I am drawn from my own haunting shame, and my conclusion is surely to learn to correct myself; and I leave the performance better than I came, simply because I have been moved.

If the injury that has been done to me is unjust, and the fault is more that of others than my own, the affecting morality of the drama will be much sweeter to me. I will look into my heart with pleasure; and there, if I have fulfilled my obligations to society, if I have been a good parent, a fair master, a gracious friend, a just man, and a useful citizen, the inner feeling will console me for the outer injury; I will cherish the play which has recalled to me that I draw from the practice of virtue the greatest pleasure to which a wise man can pretend, that of being content with himself, and I will return to weep with pleasure at the picture of persecuted innocence or virtue.

Is my situation happy when, as happens rarely, the drama cannot offer me any personal application? Then the morality turning completely to the profit of my sensibility, I would wish to think myself capable of feeling moved about the evils which cannot menace me nor overtake me—that would prove to me that my soul is good, and that it does not differ from the reactions of charitable virtue. I would leave satisfied, moved, and as contented with the theatre as with myself.

Although these reflections are evident truths, I do not address them indiscriminately to everyone. The man who fears to weep, the one who refuses to be moved, has vice in heart, or for strong reasons does not dare to come to terms with himself—it is not to him that I speak; he is a stranger to all that I have said. I speak to a man of sensibility, who often must take his leave immediately after a moving play. I address myself to those who prefer the useful and pleasing emotion into which the performance has plunged them to the diversions and pleasantries of the after-play, which, when the curtain has fallen, leaves nothing in the heart.

For my own part, when a tragic subject has affected me deeply, my soul occupies itself deliciously during the interval between the two plays, and for a long time, I feel myself ready to regret the second. It seems to me then that my heart shuts itself up again by degrees, as a flower, open at the first sunshine of spring, shuts itself in the evening as the cold of the night succeeds the warmth of the day.

Some have claimed that the serious type would have more success in the provinces than in Paris, because, they say, people are better there than here, and the more a person is corrupted, the less he is pleased at being moved. It is clear that a man who would have his father killed, who puts his son in captivity, who puts away his wife, who disdains his bastard family, who loves no one, and who, in a word, makes public profession of his evil heart, can only see in this kind of play bitter censure of his conduct, a public reproach for his hardness; he must either flee or correct himself, and the first is more suited to him. His face will betray him; his bearing will accuse him to his conscience: *Heu, quam difficile est crimen non prodere vultu!* says Ovid. And one cannot help admitting that these disorders are more felt in the capital than elsewhere. But this reflection is too distressing to be pushed any further; I would rather turn his own argument against my objecter, and the success of *Eugénie* will serve my turn somewhat better. That play, poorly written, gives perhaps less honor to the wit than to the heart of its author. Then it is in favor of the sentiment and of the honesty of the moral that people have received kindly the defects of the work, and it must be conceded that Paris does not yield anything in sensibility to the provinces of the kingdom; and for myself, I believe that if the vices which impress my censurer seem more common here, it is only by reason of the great number of persons which this city brings together, and the elevation of the theatre in which they are placed.

The noble and serious genre is reproached for lacking vigor, warmth, power, or comic wit. Because the *vis comica* of the Latins includes all these things, let us see if this reproach is justified. Every object too new to contain in itself the positive rules of discussion is judged by analogy with better-known objects of the same nature. Let us apply this method to the present question. Serious and moving drama holds the mean between heroic tragedy and pleasant comedy. If I examine that part of it which has contact with tragedy, I ask myself: Do the warmth and power of a character stem from the worldly position or origin of that character? A glance at the models which Nature has furnished to the imitator, art, teaches me that the vigor of character does not appertain any more to a prince than to anyone else. Three men were nurtured in Rome and divided the empire of the world. The first is mean-spirited and cowardly; the second, valiant, presumptuous, and ferocious; and the third, an adroit villain, who despoils the other two. But Lepidus, Antony, and Octavius embarked upon the triumvirate with characters which alone decided the differences of their fates in the enjoyment of the common usurpation. And the softness of one, the violence of another, and the cunning of the third all could have had effect equally were these men concerned only with the establishment of their private succession. Every man is himself because of his character; his station in life is indicated by destiny, which station his character can influence greatly; from which it follows that serious drama, which represents to me men much moved by situations, is more susceptible of strength, power, and elevation than is heroic tragedy, which also shows me men who are much moved, but who exist only in exalted stations. If I observe the noble and serious drama at the point where it touches on the comic, I cannot deny that the *vis comica* is a necessary ingredient to good comedy. But then I wonder why a defect of warmth has been imputed to serious drama, which defect, if it exists, could only proceed from the clumsiness of the author. Since this genre takes its characters from everyday life, as does gay comedy, must these characters which it presents have less vigor, stand out with any less force in grief or rage at an event which concerns honor and life than when these characters are engaged in working out interests less pressing, in simple difficulties, or in purely comic subjects? Even if all these dramas which I have just cited lack comic force—and I am inclined to doubt it—even if *Eugénie,* of which I scarcely dare to speak after all these models, were even weaker, the question revolves around the varying capacity of the authors, and not about a genre which in its nature is less turgid, but contains the best fiber of any, the same as it would be imprudent to say anything bad of the epic if the *Iliad* and *Henriad* [17] did not exist and the only examples we had to cite of this type were *Clovis* [18] or *La Pucelle* (I mean that of Chapelain).[19]

This raises another question, on which I will state my feelings

---

[17] *Henriade,* an epic by Voltaire (1730).

[18] *Clovis,* an epic by Jean Desmarets de Saint-Sorlin (1657).

[19] *La Pucelle,* an epic by Chapelain, (12 cantos published in 1656, the remainder not published until 1882). The other mentioned is by Voltaire (1755).

with the more freedom since it does not form an objection against the genre I am defending. Should serious drama or domestic tragedy be written in prose or in verse? As I ask this question, I know already that, far from being unimportant whether we write in one or the other manner, it matters considerably. But there are no means of applying methods of analogy by precedent. Here all reasons of preference are lacking, outside of those which we can draw from the nature of things. Let us establish them then with care. The example of M. de la Motte, although he is a little foreign to the question, will serve nonetheless to bring the matter out into broad daylight. The unfortunate essay which he wrote on prose in his *Oedipe* [20] transported the wits and carried them to decide in favor of verse. On the other side, M. Diderot, in his estimable work on dramatic art, decides for prose, but only by feeling, and without entering into the reasons which made him prefer it. The partisans of verse, in the case of M. de la Motte, have likewise judged by feeling; both sides are equally correct, because they are fundamentally in accord. It is only for lack of an explanation that they seem divided, and that apparent opposition is precisely what decides the question.

Since M. de la Motte wishes his language to approach that of Nature, he must not choose the tragic subjects of his dramas in the families of Cadmus, Tantalus, or Atrides. Those heroic and fabulous times, full of extensive action, are mixed throughout with gods and heroes, enlarge in our imaginations the objects which they present to us, and carry with them a marvel for which the pompous rhythm and cadence of verse seems to have been invented, and with which it amalgamates perfectly. Thus the heroes of Homer, which appear only grand and superb in epic poetry, would become grotesquely great in a prose story.

The language of prose, too true, and too near us, is like the workshop of a sculptor, where everything in it is colossal. Poetry is the true pedestal which places these enormous groups at the point of perspective favorable to the eye; and this is as true in heroic tragedy as in epic poetry. There we have the reason for blaming M. de la Motte for having treated the heroic subject of Oedipus in familiar language. Perhaps he would have made no less of an offense against truth, probability, and good taste, if he had treated in magnificent verse an unfortunate happening taking place among the citizens. Because, fol-

[20] *Oedipe* by Houdar de la Motte (1730). See pp. 247–50.

lowing that rule of Aristotle, *Comoedia enim deteriores, tragoedia meliores quam nunc sunt, imitari conantur.* If tragedy should represent men greater and comedy less than they really are, the imitation of one and the other type cannot be an exact truth, their language has no need to reproduce exactly the Rules of Nature. We must make the human spirit so much the greater as to be worth marvelous verse, from which we can make it exceed the limitatlons of Nature; the subjects having then only a poetic or conventional truth, they easily accommodate themselves to everything. That is why tragedy is written successfully in verse and comedy as well one way as the other. But the serious drama, which holds the middle ground between the other two, must show us men absolutely as they are, and cannot permit the slightest liberty toward the language, customs, or costumes of those it portrays on the stage. "But," you will say, "the language of tragedy is very different from that of epic—more regular, less charged with metaphors, and comes closer to Nature—what is to prevent its successful use in the serious genre?" That is well said. But take one step more, and conclude with me that the more language approaches life, the better it suits the serious genre, and that fact restores the preference for prose, and that is what M. Diderot implies. So, if the art of the comedian consists in making me forget the labor the author was put to in writing his work in verse, it is much better if he does not take any trouble where the entire merit lies in the vanquished difficulty; the kind of beauty he achieves is perhaps an honor to his talent, but does not convince anyone of the importance of his work. Let us not forget, however, that it is in relation to serious drama that I reason thus. If I should treat a comic drama, perhaps I would join the charm of poetry to the gaiety of the subject. True, its coloring, more brilliant than that of prose, gives the work a rich and agreeable air in the eyes of the audience. . . .

The serious drama then admits only a simple style, without flowers or garlands; it must draw all its beauties from the depth, the texture, the interest, and the progress of its subject. As it is also true as Nature herself, the sentences and the plumes of tragedy, the points and rosettes of comedy are absolutely forbidden to it; no maxims, unless they be set in the action. Its characters must always appear there under such circumstances that they scarcely need to speak to interest us. Its true eloquence is that of situations; and the sole coloring which is permitted to it is lively language, urgent, clipped, tumultuous, and true in passion, so far from the compass of the caesura and the affectations of rhyme, that all the care of the poet could not prevent its being perceived that the drama was in verse. So that the serious genre should have all the truth it has a right to have, the first object of the author must be to transport me so far from the wings, and to make the business of the actors, the theatrical appearance, disappear from before my eyes that their memory cannot come to me once during the entire course of his drama. Now is not the first effect of rhymed conversation, which has only a truth of convention, to draw me back to the theatre, and to destroy all the illusions that has been made for me? . . . I think then, as M. Diderot, that the serious genre must always be written in prose. I think that this prose must not be charged with ornaments, and that elegance must always be sacrificed to energy when a choice must be made between them.

My work will be very well advanced if I have convinced my readers that the serious genre exists, that it is good, that it offers a lively interest, a direct and profound moral, and can have only language which is that of Nature; that besides the advantages in common with other types, it has a great beauty all its own; that it is a new kind of play, in which a genius may rise to new heights, since it embraces all the estates of life and all the situations of each estate, where the dramatist can again employ the great figures of comedy who have nearly exhausted their own situations, and finally that he can draw out of this kind of play an abundant source of pleasures and of lessons for society. . . .

[Beaumarchais then proceeds to analyze his own play, *Eugénie,* in terms of the principles he has stated.]

Oliver Goldsmith

1728? -1774

It is often stated that Oliver Goldsmith attacked the sentimental position in the essay printed here. This view can be challenged, however, for Goldsmith was far too good-natured a person to attack the basic idea of sentimentalism, that human nature is fundamentally good. Upon examination, the position Goldsmith takes in this essay is that comedy should have laughter in it, and that laughter is not necessarily "low." The laughter he is looking for is as far as possible removed from the cynical wit of a Congreve. His humor is of gross incongruity, of situation, and not the intellectual wit of the Restoration. There is no scorn in Goldsmith's plays, and it is clear that his fifty-years' delayed reaction to Steele's "crying comedy" is a healthy objection to the method, but not to a basic premise of the sentimentalists that mankind is fundamentally good.

The Essay on the Theatre; or, A Comparison between Sentimental and Laughing Comedy first appeared in the *Westminster Magazine,* January, 1773.

An Essay on the Theatre; or, A Comparison between Laughing and Sentimental Comedy

[1773]

The theatre, like all other amusements, has its fashions and its prejudices; and, when satiated with its excellence, mankind begin to mistake change for improvement. For some years tragedy was the reigning entertainment, but of late it has entirely given way to comedy, and our best efforts are now exerted in these lighter kinds of composition. The pompous train, the swelling phrase, and the unnatural rant are displaced for that natural portrait of human folly and frailty, of which all are judges, because all have sat for the picture.

But as in describing Nature it is presented with a double face, either of mirth or sadness, our modern writers find themselves at a loss which chiefly to copy from; and it is now debated, whether the exhibition of human distress is likely to afford the mind more entertainment than that of human absurdity?

└Comedy is defined by Aristotle to be a picture of the frailties of the lower part of mankind, to distinguish it from tragedy, which is an exhibition of the misfortunes of the great. When comedy, therefore, ascends to produce the characters of princes or generals upon the stage, it is out of its walk, since low life and middle life are entirely its object. The principal question, therefore, is, whether, in describing low or middle life, an exhibition of its follies be not preferable to a detail of its calamities? Or, in other words, which deserves the preference—the weeping sentimental comedy so much in fashion at present, or the laughing, and even low comedy, which seems to have been last exhibited by Vanbrugh and Cibber?

If we apply to authorities, all the great masters in the dramatic art have but one opinion. Their rule is, that as tragedy displays the calamities of the great, so comedy should excite our laughter by ridiculously exhibiting the follies of the lower part of mankind. Boileau, one of the best modern critics, asserts that comedy will not admit of tragic distress:—

> *Le comique, ennemi des soupirs et des pleurs,*
> *N'admet point dans ses vers de tragiques douleurs.*

Nor is this rule without the strongest foundation in Nature, as the distresses of the mean by no means affect us so strongly as the calamities of the great. When tragedy exhibits to us some great man fallen from his height and struggling with want and adversity, we feel his situation in the same manner as we suppose he himself must feel, and our pity is increased in proportion to the height from which he fell. On the contrary, we do not so strongly sympathize with one born in humbler circumstances, and encountering accidental distress: so that while we melt for Belisarius,[1] we scarcely give halfpence to the beggar who accosts us in the street. The one has our pity, the other our contempt. Distress, therefore, is the proper object of tragedy, since the great excite our pity by their fall; but not equally so of comedy, since the actors employed in it are originally so mean that they sink but little by their fall.

---

[1] Belisarius was a great general under Justinian, Emperor of Constantinople. His successes aroused the Emperor's jealousy, and he was disgraced and sent to prison. Later he was restored to favor, but died soon after.

Since the first origin of the stage, tragedy and comedy have run in distinct channels, and never till of late encroached upon the provinces of each other. Terence, who seems to have made the nearest approaches, always judiciously stops short before he comes to the downright pathetic; and yet he is even reproached by Caesar for wanting the *vis comica*. All the other comic writers of antiquity aim only at rendering folly or vice ridiculous, but never exalt their characters into buskined pomp, or make what Voltaire humorously calls *a tradesmen's tragedy*.

Yet notwithstanding this weight of authority, and the universal practice of former ages, a new species of dramatic composition has been introduced, under the name of *sentimental* comedy, in which the virtues of private life are exhibited, rather than the vices exposed; and the distresses rather than the faults of mankind make our interest in the piece. These comedies have had of late great success, perhaps from their novelty, and also from their flattering every man in his favorite foible. In these plays almost all the characters are good, and exceedingly generous; they are lavish enough of their *tin* money on the stage: and though they want humor, have abundance of sentiment and feeling. If they happen to have faults or foibles, the spectator is taught not only to pardon but to applaud them, in consideration of the goodness of their hearts; so that folly, instead of being ridiculed, is commended, and the comedy aims at touching our passions without the power of being truly pathetic. In this manner we are likely to lose one great source of entertainment on the stage; for while the comic poet is invading the province of the tragic muse, he leaves her lovely sister quite neglected. Of this, however, he is no way solicitous, as he measures his fame by his profits.

But it will be said that the theatre is formed to amuse mankind, and that it matters little, if this end be answered, by what means it is obtained. If mankind find delight in weeping at comedy, it would be cruel to abridge them in that or any other innocent pleasure. If those pieces are denied the name of comedies, yet call them by any other name, and if they are delightful, they are good. Their success, it will be said, is a mark of their merit, and it is only abridging our happiness to deny us an inlet to amusement.

These objections, however, are rather specious than solid. It is true that amusement is a great object of the theatre, and it will be allowed that these sentimental pieces do often amuse us, but the question is whether the true comedy would not amuse us more? The question is whether a character supported throughout a piece, with its ridicule still attending would not give us more delight than this species of bastard tragedy, which only is applauded because it is new?

A friend of mine, who was sitting unmoved at one of these sentimental pieces, was asked how he could be so indifferent? "Why, truly," says he, "as the hero is but a tradesman, it is indifferent to me whether he be turned out of his counting-house on Fish Street Hill, since he will still have enough left to open shop in St. Giles's."

The other objection is as ill-grounded; for though we should give those pieces another name, it will not mend their efficacy. It will continue a kind of *mulish* production, with all the defects of its opposite parents, and marked with sterility. If we are permitted to make comedy weep, we have an equal right to make tragedy laugh and to set down in blank verse the jests and repartees of all the attendants in a funeral procession.

But there is one argument in favor of sentimental comedy, which will keep it on the stage in spite of all that can be said against it. It is, of all others, the most easily written. Those abilities that can hammer out a novel are fully sufficient for the production of a sentimental comedy. It is only sufficient to raise the characters a little; to deck out the hero with a riband, or give the heroine a title; then to put an insipid dialogue, without character or humor, into their mouths, give them mighty good hearts, very fine clothes, furnish a new set of scenes, make a pathetic scene or two, with a sprinkling of tender melancholy conversation through the whole, and there is no doubt but all the ladies will cry and all the gentlemen applaud.

Humor at present seems to be departing from the stage, and it will soon happen that our comic players will have nothing left for it but a fine coat and a song. It depends upon the audience whether they will actually drive those poor merry creatures from the stage, or sit at a play as gloomy as at the Tabernacle. It is not easy to recover an art when once lost; and it will be but a just punishment, that when, by our being too fastidious, we have banished humor from the stage, we should ourselves be deprived of the art of laughing.

Sebastien Mercier

1740-1814

WITH MERCIER we are on the eve of the French Revolution. The voices of sentimentalism have swelled, have taken on new meanings, have become a crusade for a new order. The tones are confident. Nothing solid resists, only the shadow of outworn conventions and an archaic social structure. The dawn is coming. Universal benevolence will soon prevail. The generous weeping for the woes of others will soon be rewarded with a new social order.

Mercier's long treatise *Du théâtre* (1773) is fertile ground for the student of sentimentalism in eighteenth-century drama. The system is complete, fully developed. However shabby and inadequate some of these doctrines may be, we do the sentimentalists of the eighteenth century an injustice if we fail to recognize that sentimental dramatic theory cannot be separated from life as a whole, that it is all part of an optimistic philosophy with historical significance, and that the ideas were maintained by many minds for which it is necessary to have high respect.

The Theatre; or, New Essay on Dramatic Art

[1773]

INTRODUCTION [EXCERPTS]

THE STAGE is a lie; its aim is to bring the lie close to the greatest truth. The stage is a picture; its aim is to make the picture useful, that is, to bring it to the threshold of the greatest number of people so that the image it presents will serve to bind men together by means of the all-conquering sentiments of pity and compassion. It is thus not sufficient that the mind of the spectator be occupied—not even that it be moved; it is necessary that it be impelled toward the good; it is necessary that the moral purpose, without being either hidden or too open, should lay hold on the heart and establish itself there as ruler.

To be a writer is in itself a great thing, but to be a useful writer, to have influence on the behavior of one's fellow citizens, to purify them in the flame of morality, is to avail oneself of the highest privilege open to human nature.

Dramatic poetry introduces man to man, teaches us to deal with our fellows, accelerates the march of our ideas, improves our reason and our sensibility, makes us blush, and aids us in correcting our faults. By means of this picture we can cure ourselves of the meanness and the withdrawals of self-love, and this kind censor speaks so secretly that we can correct our faults without another's eye being visibly struck by the change.

I feel a real joy in seeing dramatic poetry, which is the most seductive and ingenious of the arts of imitation, universally diffused and universally esteemed. It is the most precious heritage transmitted to us by the Ancients. It needs now only to be perfected. I shall explain what I mean when I say "perfected"; if it is stupid not to admire our best works, only a rigidly circumscribed mind will not have some feeling that the art still lacks a possible new degree of vitality and interest. This art is so extensive that not even the genius of our greatest poets can encompass all of it; even they have been unable to give it full development. Perhaps the first form and direction given to stage plays were not the best possible. Perhaps a new genre can be created that would surpass the present forms of comedy and tragedy, even the most admired of the current forms. The dramatic art, whatever is said of it, is perhaps not at its highest point so long as all ranks of citizens do not equally enjoy it; it is not at its high point when stage illusion fails in some respects; it is, finally, not at its high point when it has not produced all the effects that can be expected from it.

A theatre is with us the only gathering place where men can be brought together and can raise their voices in concert. There it is that one can experience the triumph of the intimate sensibility that penetrates the mind and—to use the phrase of a disciple of Pythagoras—that gives witness of its divinity. On account of that triumph, dramatic art becomes more important, more valuable, more interesting; thus the theatre can be called the masterpiece of society.*

* It is not good for man to be alone, says the Scripture. Indeed, compassion can come to being and can force deep roots only in those societies where men can communicate their

Chapter I, Of the End Which Dramatic Art Should Propose for Itself

WHAT IS the dramatic art? It is the art that especially exercises all our sensibility, converts into action all the rich faculties that we receive from Nature, opens the treasuries of the human heart, generates its pity and its compassion, and teaches us to be upright and virtuous —for virtue is something that has to be learned, even with some effort. If we allow these precious faculties of man to sleep, they will perhaps vanish. By inertia or by habit man will become hardhearted. Arouse them and man will be tender, feeling, compassionate. In a similar way, vocal cords that are exercised acquire suppleness, sweetness, force, and range.

Many men sin because their souls are stunted and commonplace; it is for lack of having been expanded by the warmth of emotion that they remain cold and numb. If they once come to feel the warmth of that sympathy that binds one being to another, if tears have once melted the ice of their hearts, they will, once softened, choose the path of virtue.

J. J. Rousseau has said that only the man who has never done wrong to his fellow man can consider himself virtuous. If there is a proper place for engraving this maxim in the hearts of mankind, that place is the theatre: it is there that the voice of the poet responds to the interior voice that warns man to respect all beings who have feeling. It is there that the virtue which derives from sensibility obtains the suffrage of the assembled men. It is there that the proudest prejudices fall and that mankind, hauled before the tribunal of Nature, often led astray by that ingenious sophist Reason, discovers the truth in the electric shock of sentiment.

How noble a benefactor is an excellent poet! if he really loves men, if he is infused with that divine fire that still more ennobles genius, if he does not degrade it by bending his knee before the powers of the earth, if, instead, he uses it to harvest the sighs of the unfortunate, to carry them to the exalted ears of those who have caused

---

feelings with one another and can learn each other's needs and weaknesses. Isolated or absorbed people know only their own kind of existence; in order to get them outside of themselves and to share the sufferings of others, they must of necessity learn the language of misfortune. The theatre develops this instinct, this natural bond with our fellow men that all of us feel.

them—ah, with what thankfulness we should reward his labors! He it is who teaches us what is good and upright; he fixes our unstable opinions; he reigns by means of sentiment—sentiment—that invincible and mighty force that demands the submission even of the most rebellious of men. By the exquisite and repeated sensations with which it attacks the human heart, it relieves the vicious of their prey, despots of their clubs, and the wicked of the ability of being deaf to their remorse.

Multiply then before the eyes of the wicked the image of the woes that they have caused, so that the image will pursue them everywhere and so that, like Bessus, they will hear in the song of the swallow a reproach for parricide, until they could wish to put a stop to the singing of all birds.

But will the poet who knows the nature of men choose to offer them heroic actions that demand an absolute sacrifice and have their origin in an extravagant and astonishing trait of mind? If he is a philosopher, perhaps he will demand less in order to obtain more; he will no doubt feel that the devotions of a Kodrus,[1] a Curtius,[2] or a Scaevola [3] are uncommon. He will say instead, "Look around you; everything nearby speaks with an energetic language. How many unfortunates there are to succor, to console! Surrounded by sufferers to whose sorrows you can give solace, will you go abroad to seek ancient and imaginary misfortunes? Lower your sights. There is imposed on you only the satisfying pleasure of coming to know your fellow men."

The effect of the theatre comes from impressions, not from teachings. Retire, cold moralist, and take your heavy book with you. What signifies the spinning out of your dry maxims when it is compared with the eloquent painting that shows the scene in full color? You will not find in the painting any metaphysical shadows, any subtle scholastic distinctions. Approach, O man; see, touch, feel. . . . Do you weep? Yes, surely. Is your control of your mind so firm that it can resist this irresistible, sympathetic force that invades it entirely? Your

1 Kodrus was the last king of Athens. He killed himself to prevent the capture of Athens by the Lacedaemonians.

2 In B.C. 362, M. Curtius committed suicide by leaping into a chasm which had opened up in the Roman Forum. This act was in propitiation for the crimes of Rome. (Cf. Livy, VII, vi, 4.)

3 Roman Mucius Scaevola, captured in an unsuccessful attempt in B.C. 509 to kill besieging King Porsenna, thrust his hand into a fire prepared for sacrifice and held it there without flinching. For this act of bravery, Porsenna ordered him released.

mind will rise to the level of the great and splendid action; it will yearn to imitate it; it will become one with the feelings of the man who groans; it will suffer perhaps even more than he and, by clinging to his misfortunes, it will cling also to the desire of relieving them.

The mind of man cannot be too much softened by repeated impressions of pity and commiseration. Since both of these are virtues, they cannot assume too great prominence in his heart. A child will clutch a bird as he would a stone because he does not yet understand the law that brings all sentient beings under the sway of sensibility, but let him once feel the prick of sorrow and reflect upon the forces of oppression, and he will understand the cry of the distressed and will respect all sufferers.

Thus it is that the dramatic writer insensibly softens us and saddens us only for our own interest and our own pleasure. He compels us to tears, but to those delightful tears which are the gentlest attribute and the natural expression of our sensibility: *nostri pars optima sensus* (Juv. Sat. XV).

How often have we not had opportunity to wonder at the influence on men near at hand of cries, groans, and sobs. These are the sovereign decrees of Nature. If the poet joins his voice to them, what force will it not have? His voice will then teach this important truth, that whoever does evil, sows only to reap and wounds himself in wounding others.

Our precious sensibility is like the sacred fire. We must watch never to let it be extinguished. It constitutes the moral life. The minds of all men can be judged by the degree of emotion they manifest in the theatre. If the face of a man remains unmoved and if his eye is not wet when the father of the family says to his son,[4] "Where are you going, unhappy one?" and if the fires of indignation do not burn in his heart when Narcisse tries to corrupt Neron,[5] that is certainly a wicked man; only by avowing his imbecility can he rid himself of that epithet.

Some moralists, who believe that severity is virtue and that ennui is meritorious, have so badly reasoned, in the cold solitude of their cloisters or their cabinets, that they come to say that when the heart is made more sensitive it is made at the same time more susceptible to violent passions. These are the hackneyed arguments of our ancient

---

[4] Diderot, *Père de famille* (1758). [5] Characters in Racine's *Britannicus* (1669).

and modern visionaries. Riccoboni repeats this prolix thesis to the point of disgust in his book on the reformation of the theatre.* Ah, not at all, masters of the syllogism! All of the dangerous passions are born from hardness of heart; such are hate, envy, avarice, and pride —passions cold and solitary; an unbridled self-love gives them their being. I believe that love, friendship, gratitude, and the desire for glory—all active and generous passions—warm the soul with a fire that is more alive and exalt it to the height where it strives toward the most heroic virtues.

Is it really true that the wise man should be so indifferent that his more than peaceful mind is moved neither by the sight of a beautiful countryside nor by the recital of a magnanimous action, one who watches time roll before him like the water of a river, one who has never known the danger of the passions because he has never felt their sting, who has nothing to combat because he has nothing to repress, who, without hate and without love, has never seen beauties in men of marked differences and in Nature that are truly real? Oh thou, sweet and gracious emotions that are felt in the theatre and that serve to develop and perfect the moral and internal sense that we all share although we stifle it sometimes by disdaining it; thou, agreeable sentiments, O noble and sweet passions, swarm about this passionless man, soften his mind, and do for it what the dew does to a dry and hardened earth.

But how should the poet speak to the multitude? What effects must he choose to make himself understood by his fellow citizens? The theatre is created, I think, to make up for youth's lack of experience, to rectify the ideas of those who have misunderstood, to give aid to

* Is it necessary to repeat here what has been proved a thousand times: that passions are necessary to man, that they are by nature good, that it is the feeling of pleasure that acts most powerfully on our being, and that it is a great wrong not to enjoy oneself when one can do it without giving offense either to others or to himself. Ah! if he tries to combat that invincible force, can he succeed in destroying it? Loaded down with all the chains which barbarism and imbecility have been able to conceive, it still undergoes metamorphosis; it is reborn in the prison of the solitary; it braves austerities and haircloth; it breaks through the most sacred barriers; it lives with us because it composes our essence. It is as a result of trying to restrain the passions that they become terrible and wild, just as the bit excites horses more than the most exciting race. Agreeable sensations form the mind to gentleness, generosity, and benevolence. I do not believe that a heart delightfully stirred by emotions is capable of nourishing the cruelties of intolerance and the harsh faults of savage pride. In a purified theatre the impressions are conducive to all the virtues that honor humanity; they can enfeeble only the weak minds that are at the mercy of all other kinds of force.

the intelligence of mediocre minds, to teach men who are sometimes uncertain in their ideas what they ought to hate, love, or hold in esteem.

Employed in this glorious task, will the poet follow the road constructed by his predecessors? Will he try to stir up the ashes of old kings? Will he see nothing in the world to portray except heads that wear diadems? Or, among his fellows, will he confine himself, like the poets of high society, to the elegant noblemen who replace kings in our comedy and who pretend to give to society the tone that it ought to follow? Will the poet act as if there are only these two kinds of men on earth? I believe that he would do better to work for the interest of all men. As he extends his stage with his thought, it will become as wide as the stage of the universe; his characters will be as varied as the people he sees; his meditations will be those of a writer of sensibility, of a faithful painter, of a philosopher, and, believing himself in the eighteenth century, he will let the monarchs sleep in their old tombs. With a glance he will embrace his beloved contemporaries, and finding more useful lessons to give them in the portrayal of present manners, instead of composing a tragedy, he will perhaps create what is called a *drame*.

At the mention of this word (for words are at all times the cause of serious quarrels), I can see some excited journalists who consider themselves the defenders of literature banish it—this word which, according to them, is an outrage to "taste," another rallying word which is pleasing to all those who have a need of writing a great number of words daily.

I dare however to say (let all their anathemas fall on my head) that if at first the poets had not been limited to these names of tragedy and comedy, which have often led them into error by forcing them to show each face in its extreme and to employ only glaring colors whereas it is blended and mixed colors that ought to result in true portrayal of character: I dare, say I, that the art would today without doubt have reached the degree of perfection that we look for and desire. It is not genius that our poets lack but the art of knowing how to give poetry a striking effect and a generally recognizable utility. But without quarrelling here about words, let us see if we cannot enrich ourselves with a genre that is truer and more instructive even than tragedy and comedy. For if the new dramatic genre, that is so much reviled by the people who pass judgments only on habit, can bring together both the interest of tragedy through its pathetic scenes and the simple charm of comedy through the painting of manners, if it did not have, like tragedy, the disadvantage of deifying great crimes, and, like comedy, the disadvantage of immolating a ridiculous thing with fierceness, if from the mixture of these clumsily separated genres would result a new genre, more sound, more touching, and more useful, where all rises naturally from the situations, perhaps the *drame* would be incomparably preferable both in its end and in its effects. . . .

CHAPTER V [EXCERPTS]

JUST AS tears are not always a proof of unhappiness, laughter is not always a signal of joy. In great sorrows there is no weeping; the eye is dry, the face immobile. An immoderate laugh indicates only the unbalance of a mind that is pushed beyond the bounds of reason. One teardrop that comes from the heart causes more pleasure than tears shed abundantly. The mechanical sort of laughter speaks not to the soul like that soft smile that applauds whatever is respectable, noble, and touching. Since all emotions are compounded in this way, it is absurd to want them to be absolute and extreme. Mixed sensations are the most pleasant of all; they bring to the mind a new and very delicious sensation. . . .

•   •   •

Only a maker of farces can fail to see that laughter and tears, as two emotions of the mind, have at bottom the same origin, that they are contiguous, that they are intermingled, that they are neither the absolute sign of joy nor the absolute sign of sadness, that twenty persons will be variously affected by one object, and that there is a bitter and painful kind of laughter as well as delightful tears. Consequently, let us stop saying, "I am going to make the audience laugh in this play; I am going to make them weep in that one." Instead, let us give portrayals that are exact, vigorous, and faithful, and leave to the spectator the task of creating his own sensation. . . .

•   •   •

It is the business of comedy to make scenes, not portraits. It is not so much the individual that one should try to depict as the species.

The playwright should create several figures, group them, put them in motion, and give them speech and life, all equally. A too detached character will soon seem isolated. What I want is not a statue on a pedestal; what I want is a group picture with various characters. I wish to see great masses, opposed tastes, mixed humors, and especially the consequences of contemporary manners. Let the poet open before me the scene of the world and not the sanctuary of a single man. Whoever has reflected on the flairs, the temperaments, the behavior, or the characters of the various men in his experience will not depict them detached but in action. What alone gives vitality to drama and weight to morality is the simultaneous and reciprocal action of all characters. In all the so-called "character" plays, the principal character has always a colossal stature and dominates the action so much that the other characters act only as shadows to him.

CHAPTER VIII [EXCERPTS]

IN THE INFANCY of our theatre there was to be found tragi-comedy. This was a genre that was bad not in itself but from the manner in which it was treated, because the mixture was extreme and absurd, because the passages were rapid and revolting, because high-born characters contrasted with low-born, because the low and not the familiar choked out the serious, because there was not in it the unity which is not so much a rule of Aristotle as of common sense. This genre, which by nature was good and by practice detestable, was killed off by a mass of productions which inevitably discredited it. It was easier for Corneille to push it entirely aside than to mix and marry his colors, as did, in their counties, Calderon, Shakespeare, Lope de Vega, and Goldoni. His soft and serious genius, which strengthened itself in the cabinet and visited the world little, was more suited to discover in Livy, in Tacitus, and in Lucan the great traits that characterized the Romans than to study the manners of his contemporaries. . . .

If there should remain for posterity only the tragedies of Corneille, of Racine, and of Voltaire, or even the comedies of Molière, could one recognize at all the manners, the character, the genius of our nation and of our century, the details of our private life? Could one know what virtues have been the most highly esteemed at this time, what were the respectable vices? Would one have a just idea of the form of our legislation, of the temper of our minds, of the range of our imaginations, of the way finally in which we conceive the throne and the court, and the lively and transient fads that emanate from it? Could one discover the picture of our present ways of living, the interior of our houses, that interior which is to an empire what entrails are to the human body? That is what I want to know and what demands a positive answer.

Index

398   Index

Index